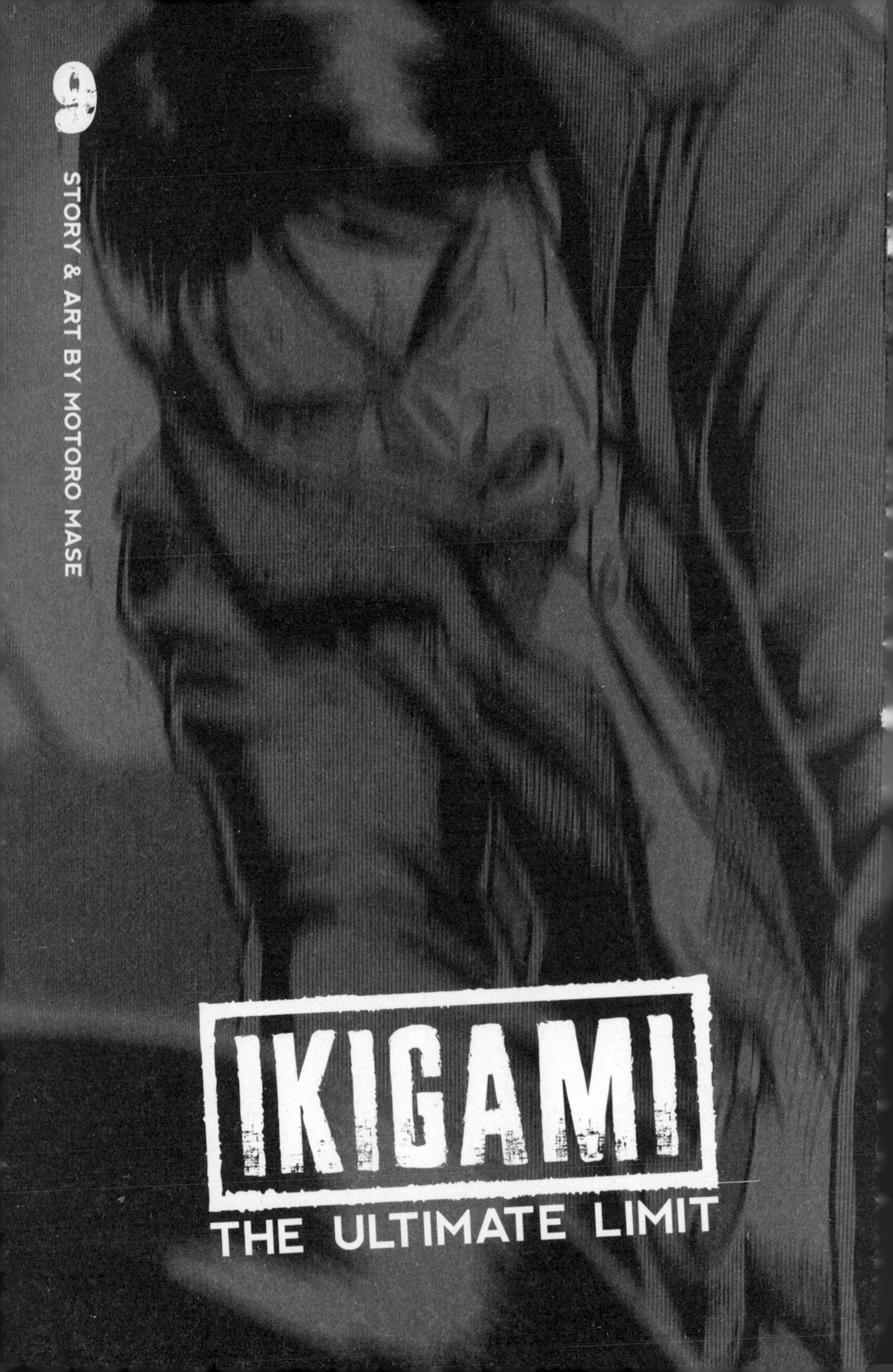
9
STORY & ART BY MOTORO MASE
IKIGAMI
THE ULTIMATE LIMIT

IKIGAMI: THE ULTIMATE LIMIT
Volume 9
VIZ Signature Edition

Story and Art by **MOTORO MASE**

IKIGAMI Vol. 9
by Motoro MASE
© 2005 Motoro MASE
All rights reserved.
Original Japanese edition published
by SHOGAKUKAN.
English translation rights in the United States
of America, Canada, the United Kingdom
and Ireland arranged with SHOGAKUKAN.

Translation/John Werry
English Adaptation/Kristina Blachere
Touch-up Art & Lettering/Freeman Wong
Design/Amy Martin
Editor/Erica Yee

Printed in the U.S.A.

Published by VIZ Media, LLC
P.O. Box 77010
San Francisco, CA 94107

10 9 8 7 6 5 4 3 2 1
First printing, August 2013

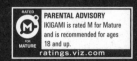

PARENTAL ADVISORY
IKIGAMI is rated M for Mature
and is recommended for ages
18 and up.
ratings.viz.com

www.viz.com

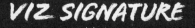

VIZ SIGNATURE
www.vizsignature.com

IKIGAMI

THE ULTIMATE LIMIT

VOL. 9 STORY & ART BY MOTORO MASE

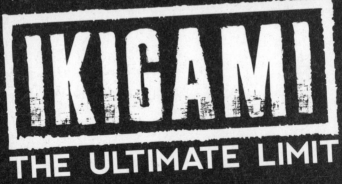

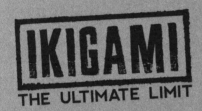

THE ULTIMATE LIMIT

CONTENTS

Episode 17 National Welfare Immunization Act1

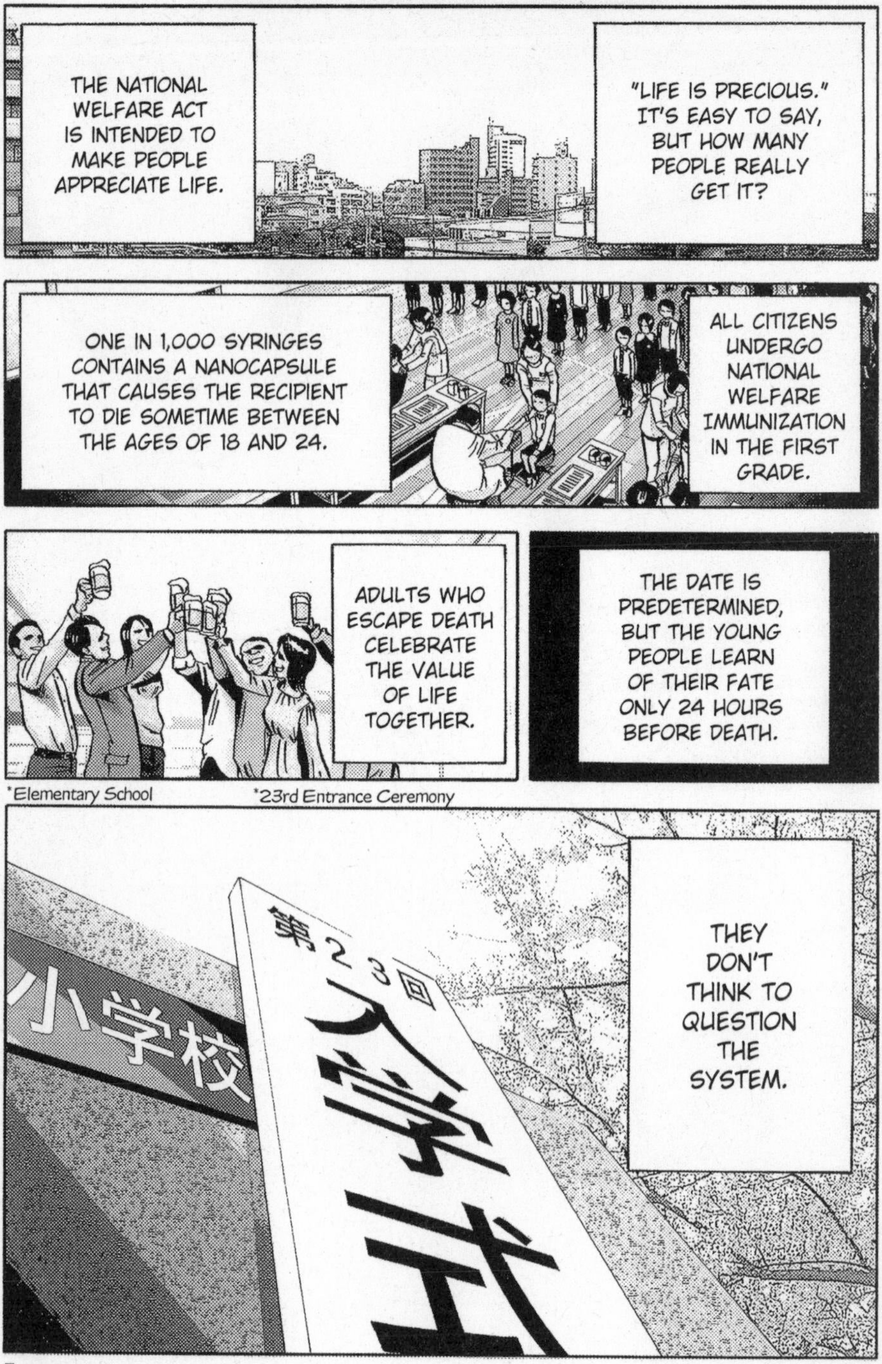
"LIFE IS PRECIOUS." IT'S EASY TO SAY, BUT HOW MANY PEOPLE REALLY GET IT?
THE NATIONAL WELFARE ACT IS INTENDED TO MAKE PEOPLE APPRECIATE LIFE.
ALL CITIZENS UNDERGO NATIONAL WELFARE IMMUNIZATION IN THE FIRST GRADE.
ONE IN 1,000 SYRINGES CONTAINS A NANOCAPSULE THAT CAUSES THE RECIPIENT TO DIE SOMETIME BETWEEN THE AGES OF 18 AND 24.
THE DATE IS PREDETERMINED, BUT THE YOUNG PEOPLE LEARN OF THEIR FATE ONLY 24 HOURS BEFORE DEATH.
ADULTS WHO ESCAPE DEATH CELEBRATE THE VALUE OF LIFE TOGETHER.
*Elementary School
*23rd Entrance Ceremony
THEY DON'T THINK TO QUESTION THE SYSTEM.
第23回
入学式
小学校

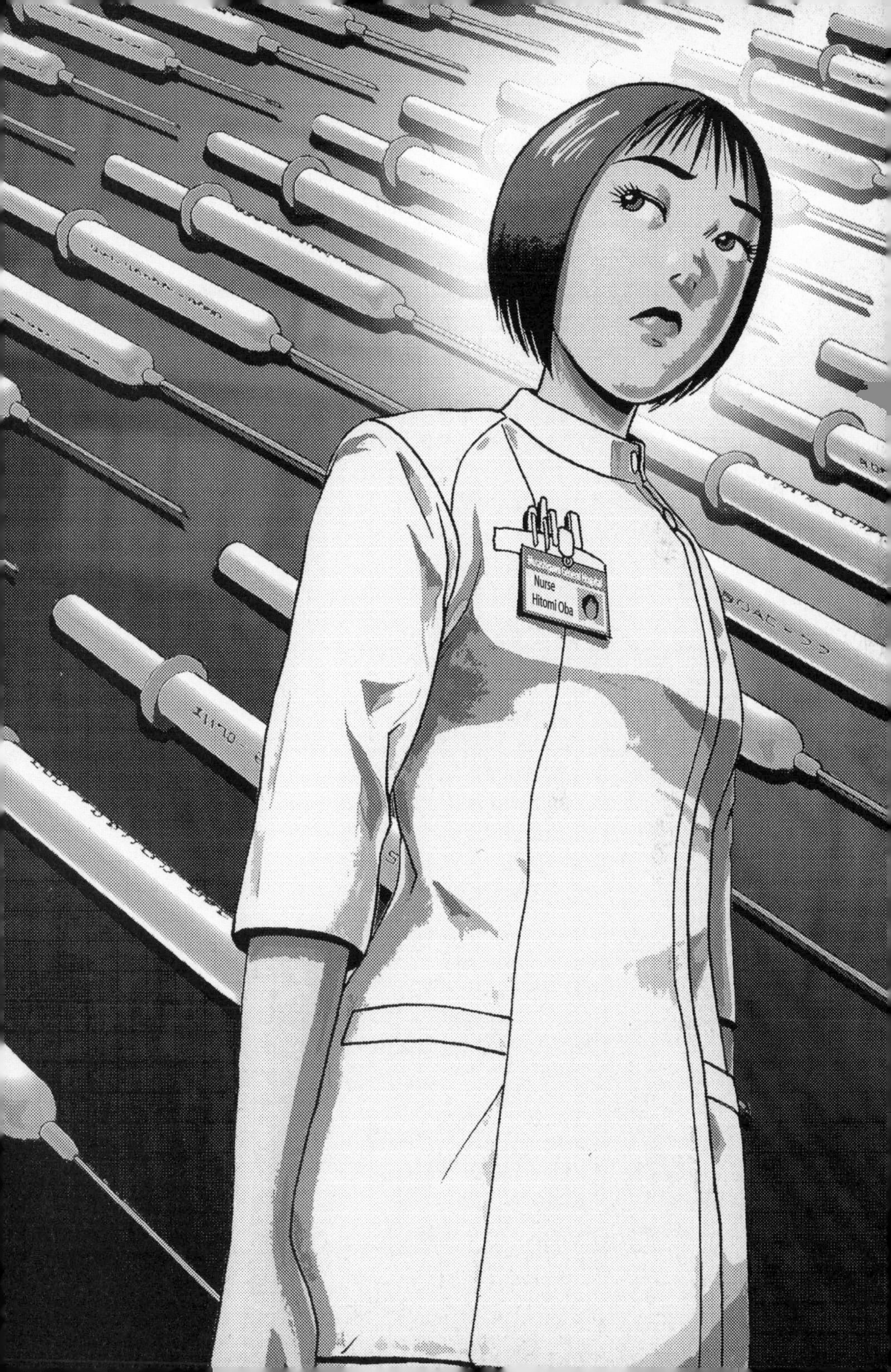
Nurse
Hitomi Oba

Episode 17 National Welfare Immunization Act 1

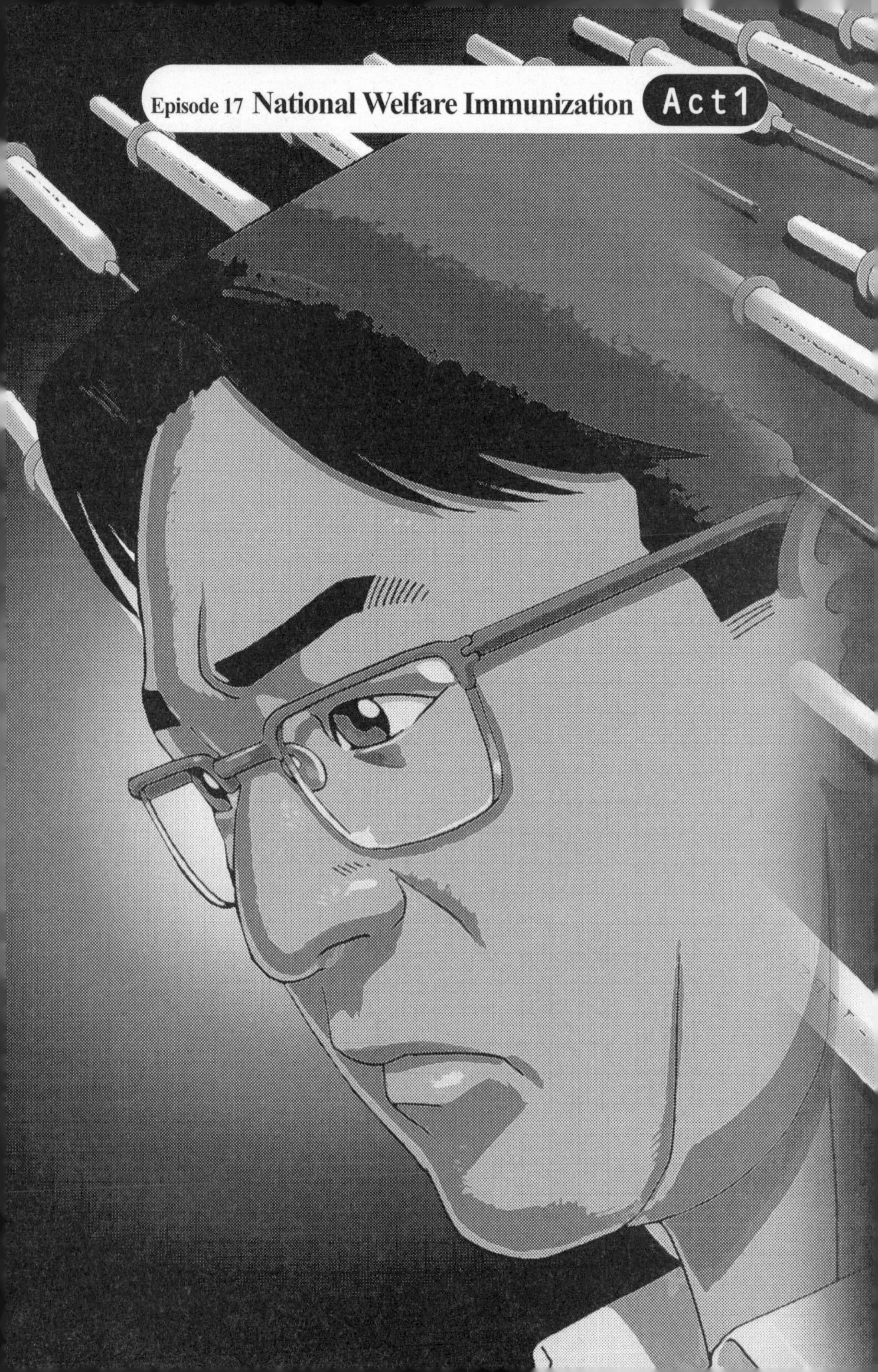

*Musashigawa General Hospital

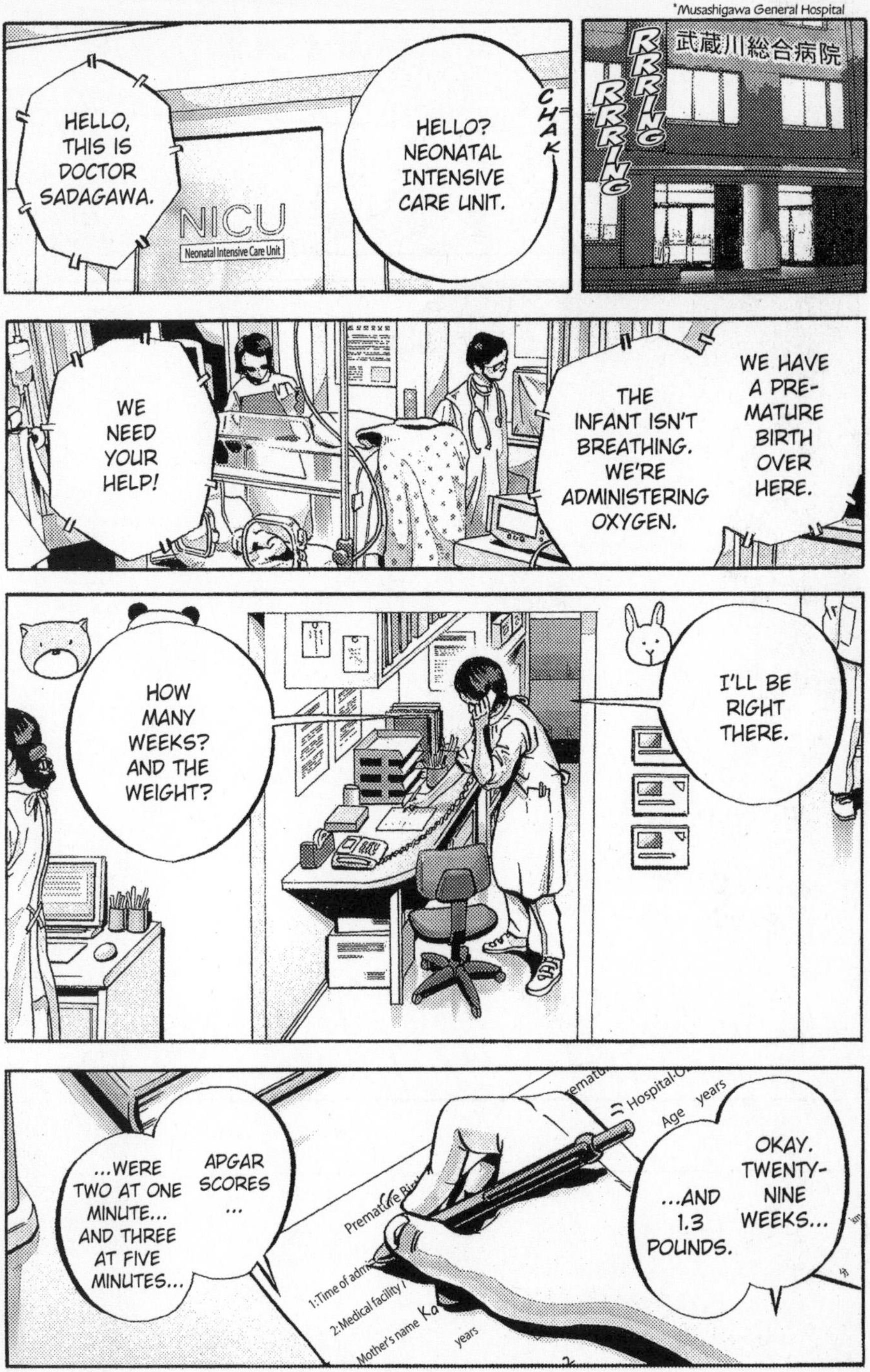
RRRING
RRRING
武蔵川総合病院
HELLO? NEONATAL INTENSIVE CARE UNIT.
CHAK
HELLO, THIS IS DOCTOR SADAGAWA.
NICU
Neonatal Intensive Care Unit
WE HAVE A PRE-MATURE BIRTH OVER HERE.
THE INFANT ISN'T BREATHING. WE'RE ADMINISTERING OXYGEN.
WE NEED YOUR HELP!
I'LL BE RIGHT THERE.
HOW MANY WEEKS? AND THE WEIGHT?
OKAY. TWENTY-NINE WEEKS...
...AND 1.3 POUNDS.
APGAR SCORES ...
...WERE TWO AT ONE MINUTE... AND THREE AT FIVE MINUTES...
Age years
Mother's name
years

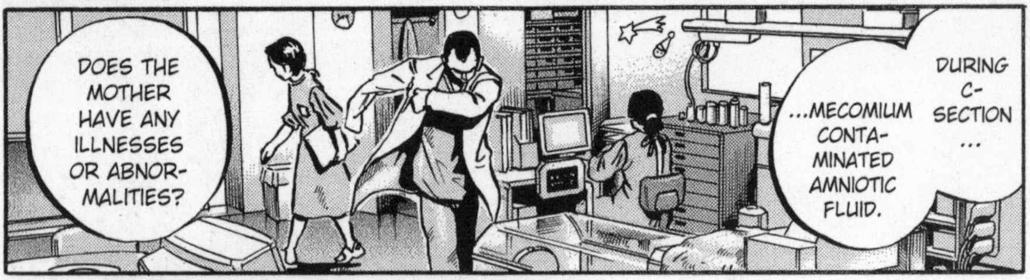
DURING C-SECTION...
...MECOMIUM CONTAMINATED AMNIOTIC FLUID.
DOES THE MOTHER HAVE ANY ILLNESSES OR ABNORMALITIES?

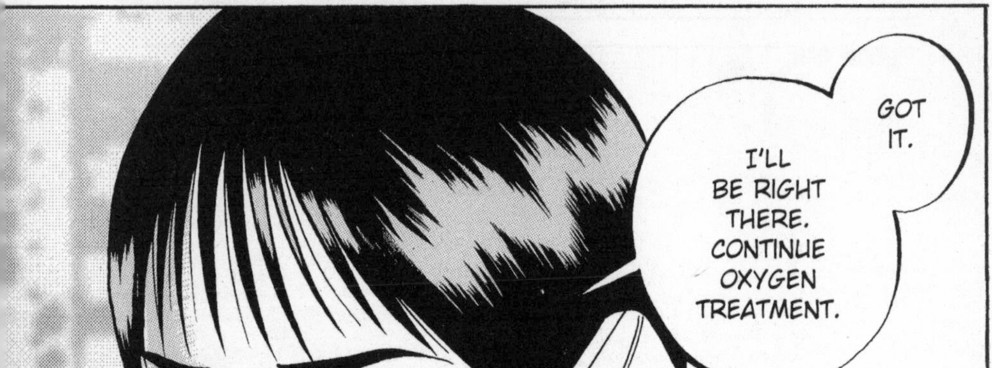
GOT IT.
I'LL BE RIGHT THERE. CONTINUE OXYGEN TREATMENT.

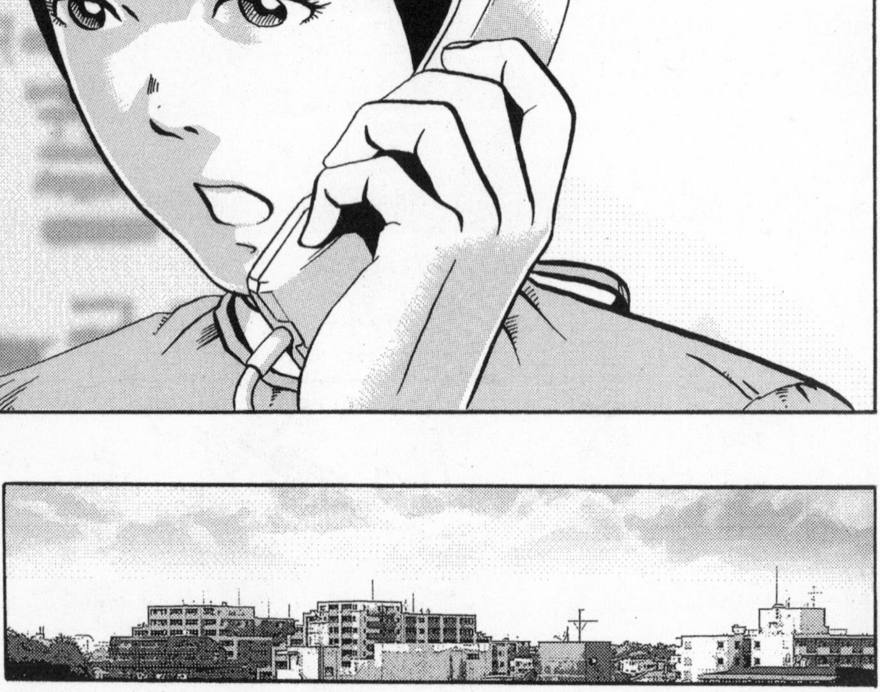

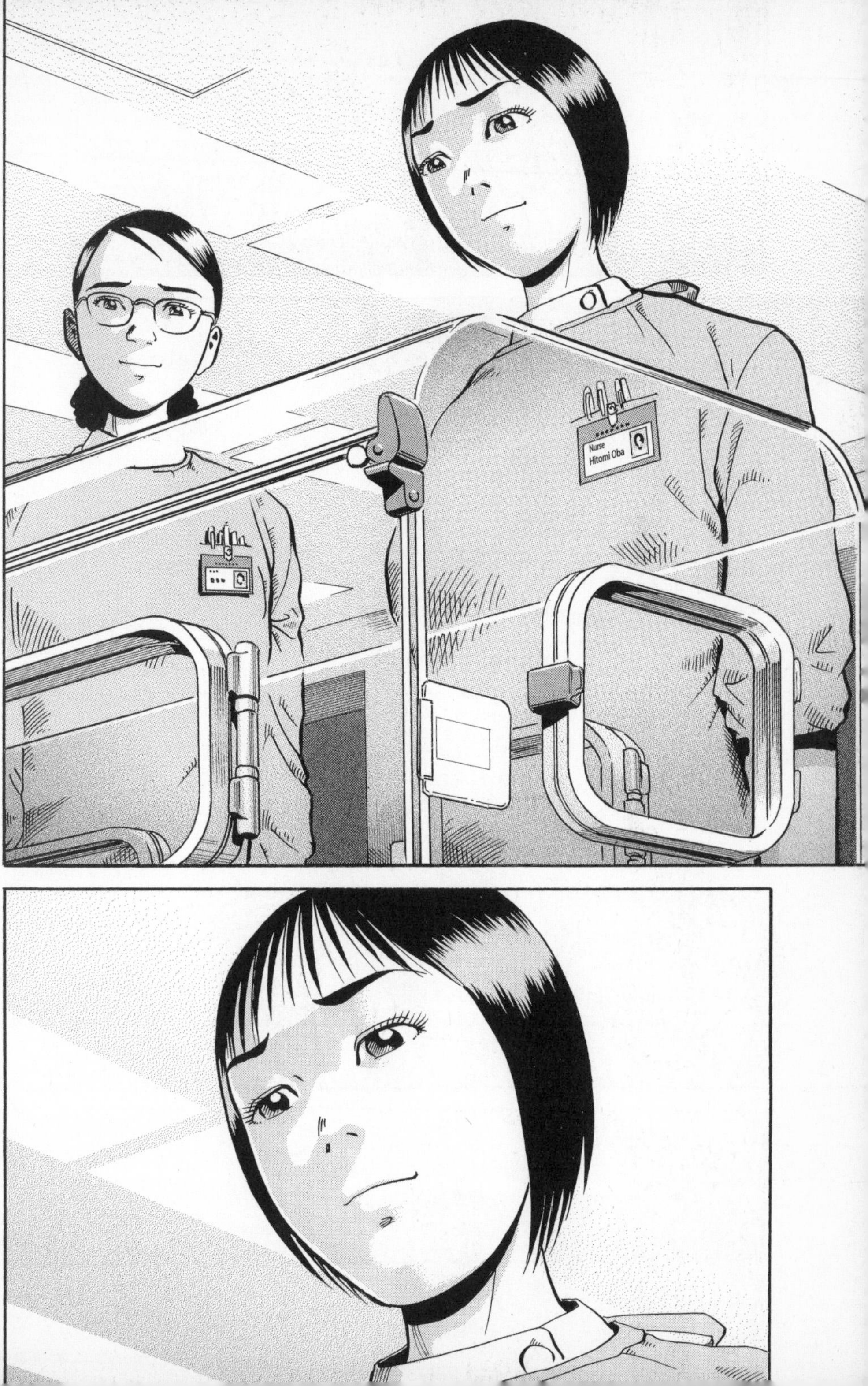
Nurse
Hitomi Oba

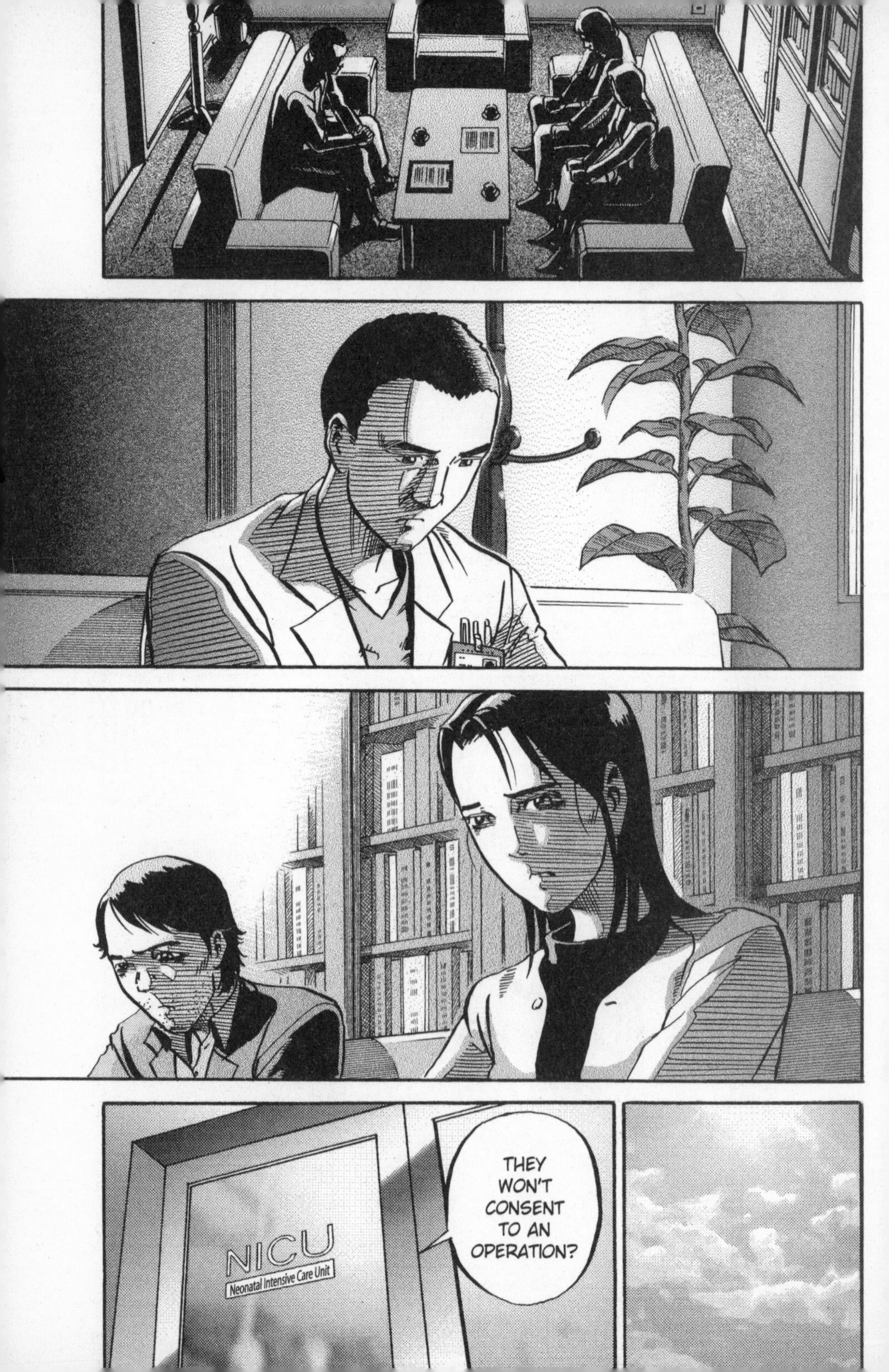
NICU
Neonatal Intensive Care Unit
THEY WON'T CONSENT TO AN OPERATION?

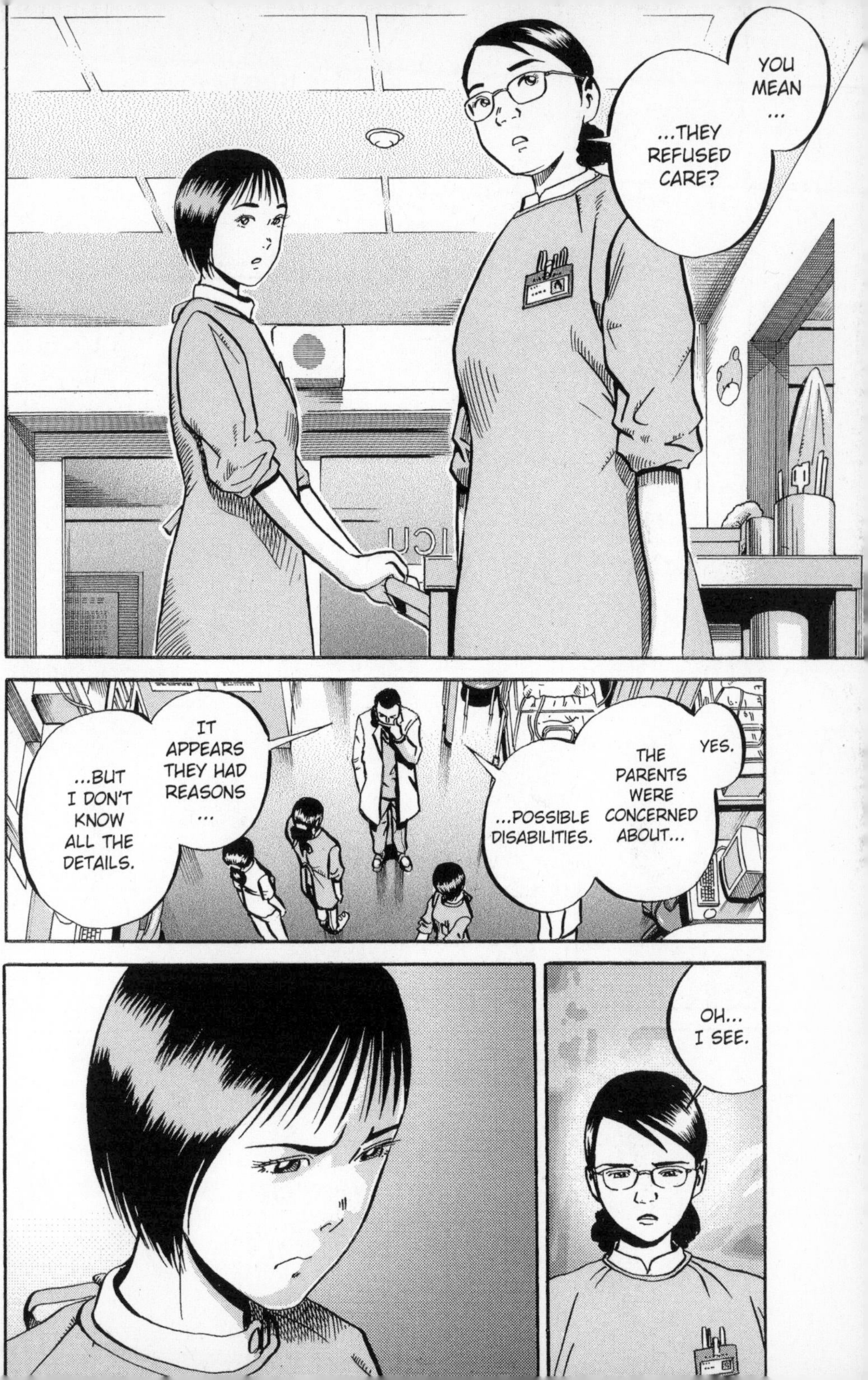
YOU MEAN ...
...THEY REFUSED CARE?
YES.
THE PARENTS WERE CONCERNED ABOUT...
...POSSIBLE DISABILITIES.
IT APPEARS THEY HAD REASONS ...
...BUT I DON'T KNOW ALL THE DETAILS.
OH... I SEE.

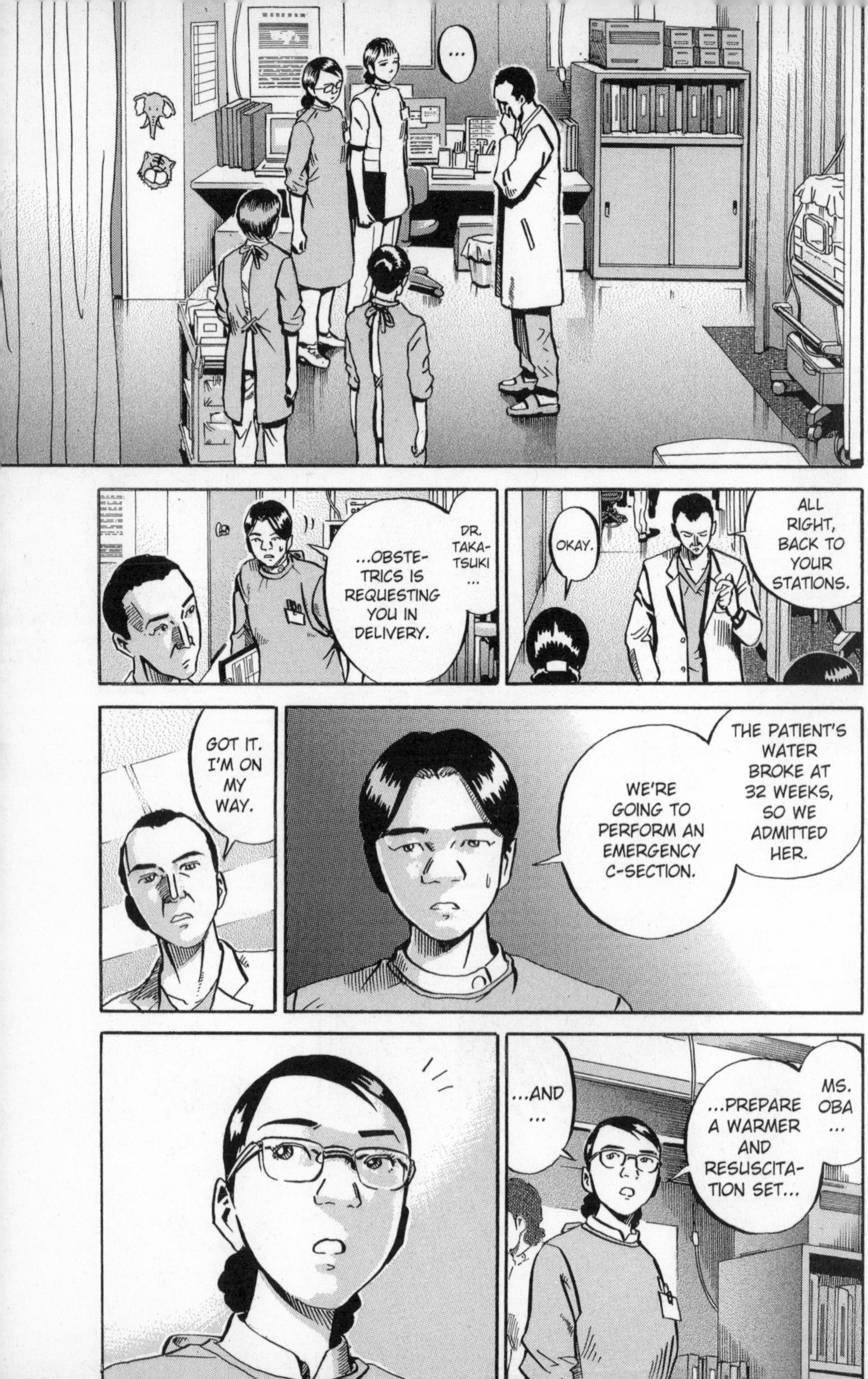
…
ALL RIGHT, BACK TO YOUR STATIONS.
OKAY.
DR. TAKATSUKI…
…OBSTETRICS IS REQUESTING YOU IN DELIVERY.
THE PATIENT'S WATER BROKE AT 32 WEEKS, SO WE ADMITTED HER.
WE'RE GOING TO PERFORM AN EMERGENCY C-SECTION.
GOT IT. I'M ON MY WAY.
MS. OBA…
…PREPARE A WARMER AND RESUSCITATION SET…
…AND…

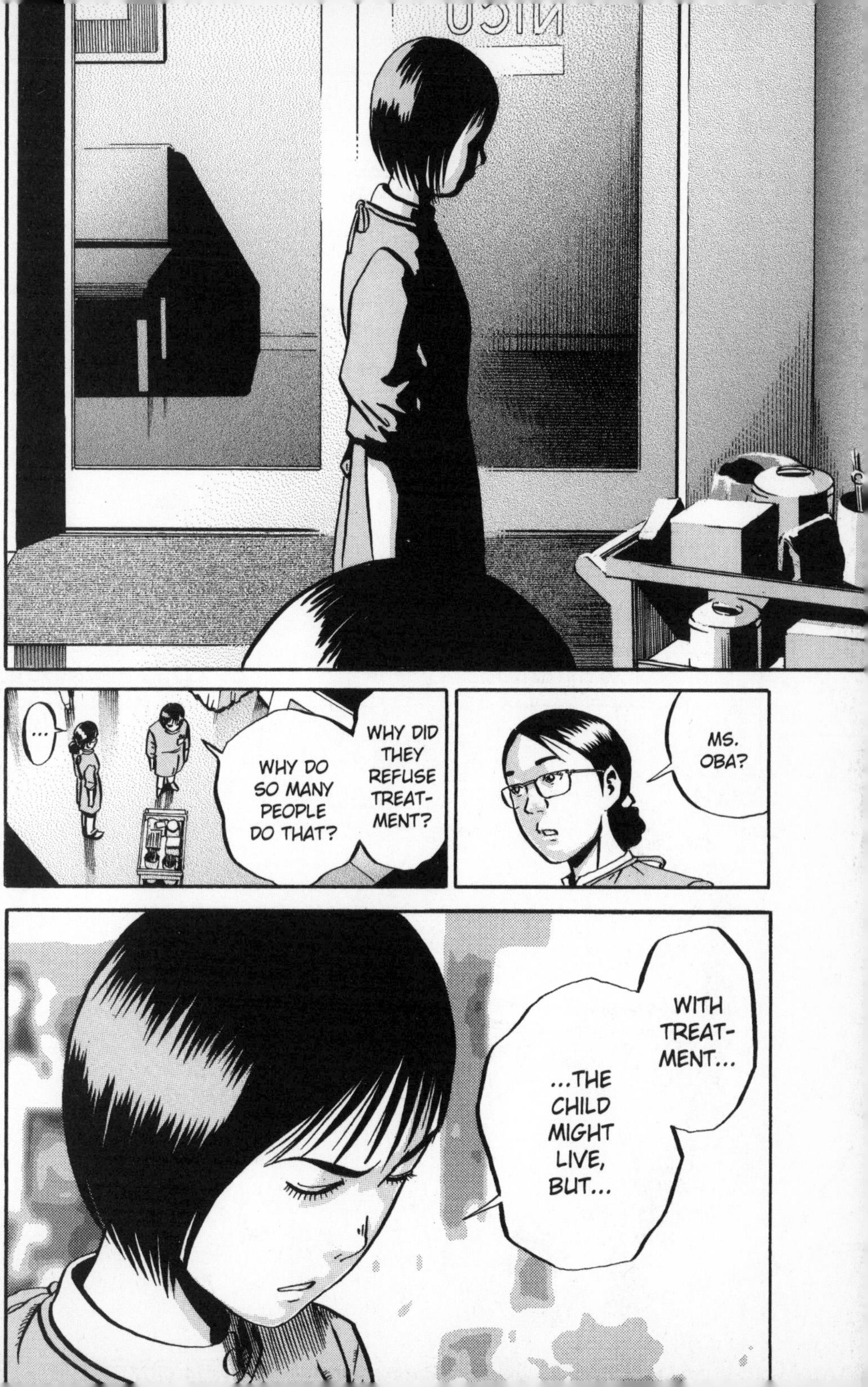
MS. OBA?
WHY DID THEY REFUSE TREATMENT?
WHY DO SO MANY PEOPLE DO THAT?
...
WITH TREATMENT...
...THE CHILD MIGHT LIVE, BUT...

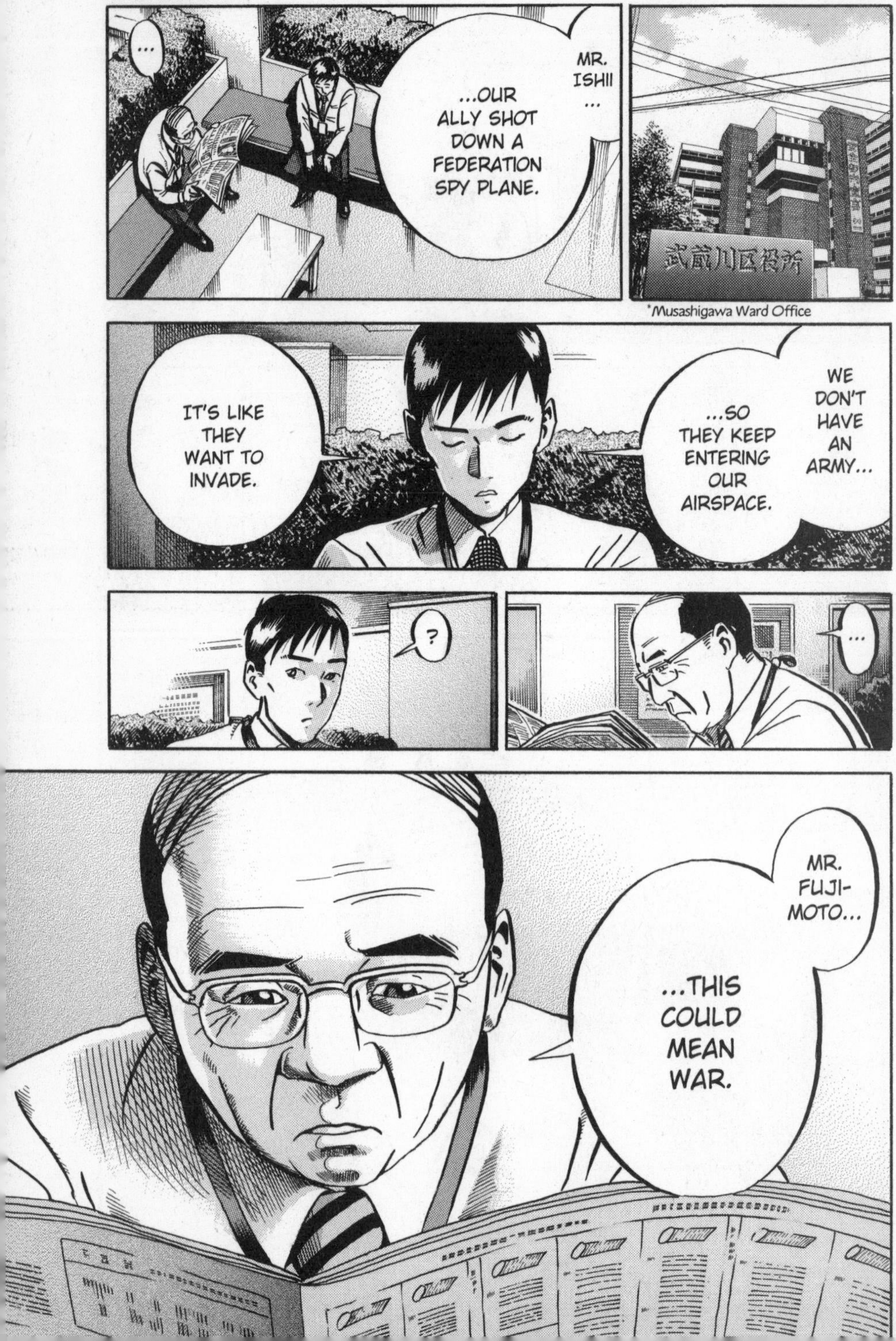
武蔵川区役所
*Musashigawa Ward Office
MR. ISHII ...
...OUR ALLY SHOT DOWN A FEDERATION SPY PLANE.
...
WE DON'T HAVE AN ARMY...
...SO THEY KEEP ENTERING OUR AIRSPACE.
IT'S LIKE THEY WANT TO INVADE.
...
?
MR. FUJIMOTO...
...THIS COULD MEAN WAR.

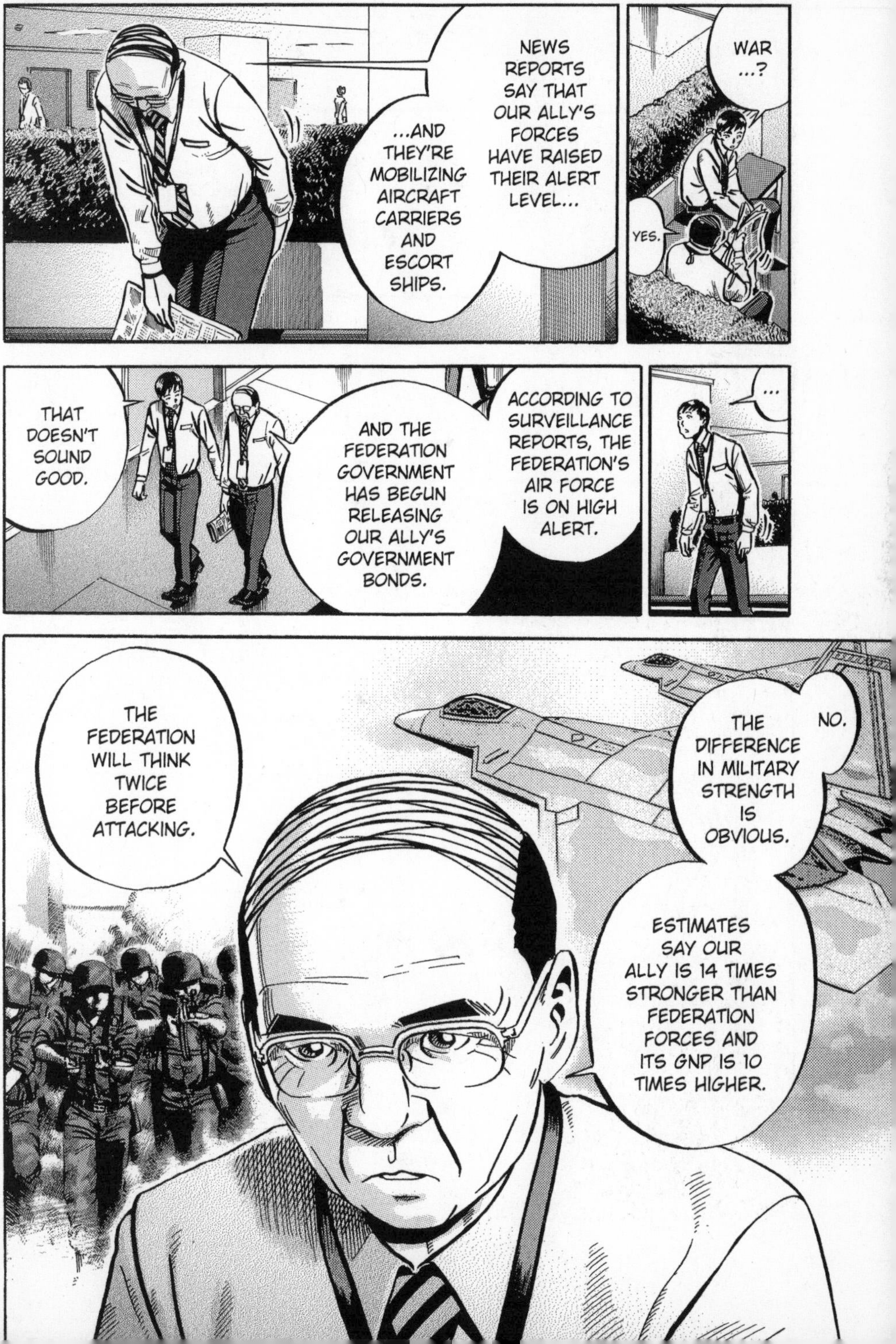
WAR ...?
YES.
NEWS REPORTS SAY THAT OUR ALLY'S FORCES HAVE RAISED THEIR ALERT LEVEL...
...AND THEY'RE MOBILIZING AIRCRAFT CARRIERS AND ESCORT SHIPS.
...
ACCORDING TO SURVEILLANCE REPORTS, THE FEDERATION'S AIR FORCE IS ON HIGH ALERT.
AND THE FEDERATION GOVERNMENT HAS BEGUN RELEASING OUR ALLY'S GOVERNMENT BONDS.
THAT DOESN'T SOUND GOOD.
NO.
THE DIFFERENCE IN MILITARY STRENGTH IS OBVIOUS.
ESTIMATES SAY OUR ALLY IS 14 TIMES STRONGER THAN FEDERATION FORCES AND ITS GNP IS 10 TIMES HIGHER.
THE FEDERATION WILL THINK TWICE BEFORE ATTACKING.

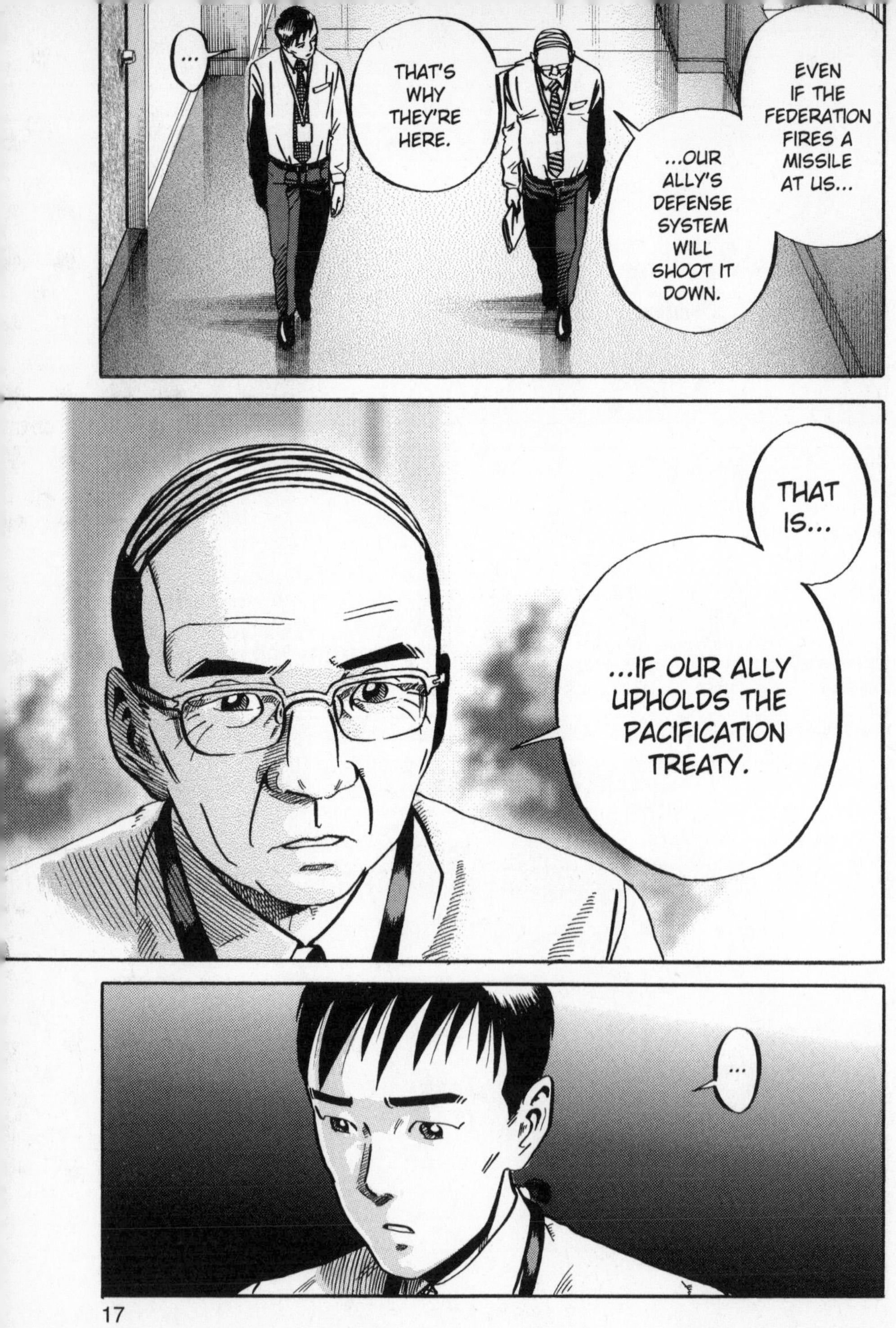
EVEN IF THE FEDERATION FIRES A MISSILE AT US...
...OUR ALLY'S DEFENSE SYSTEM WILL SHOOT IT DOWN.
THAT'S WHY THEY'RE HERE.
...
THAT IS...
...IF OUR ALLY UPHOLDS THE PACIFICATION TREATY.
...

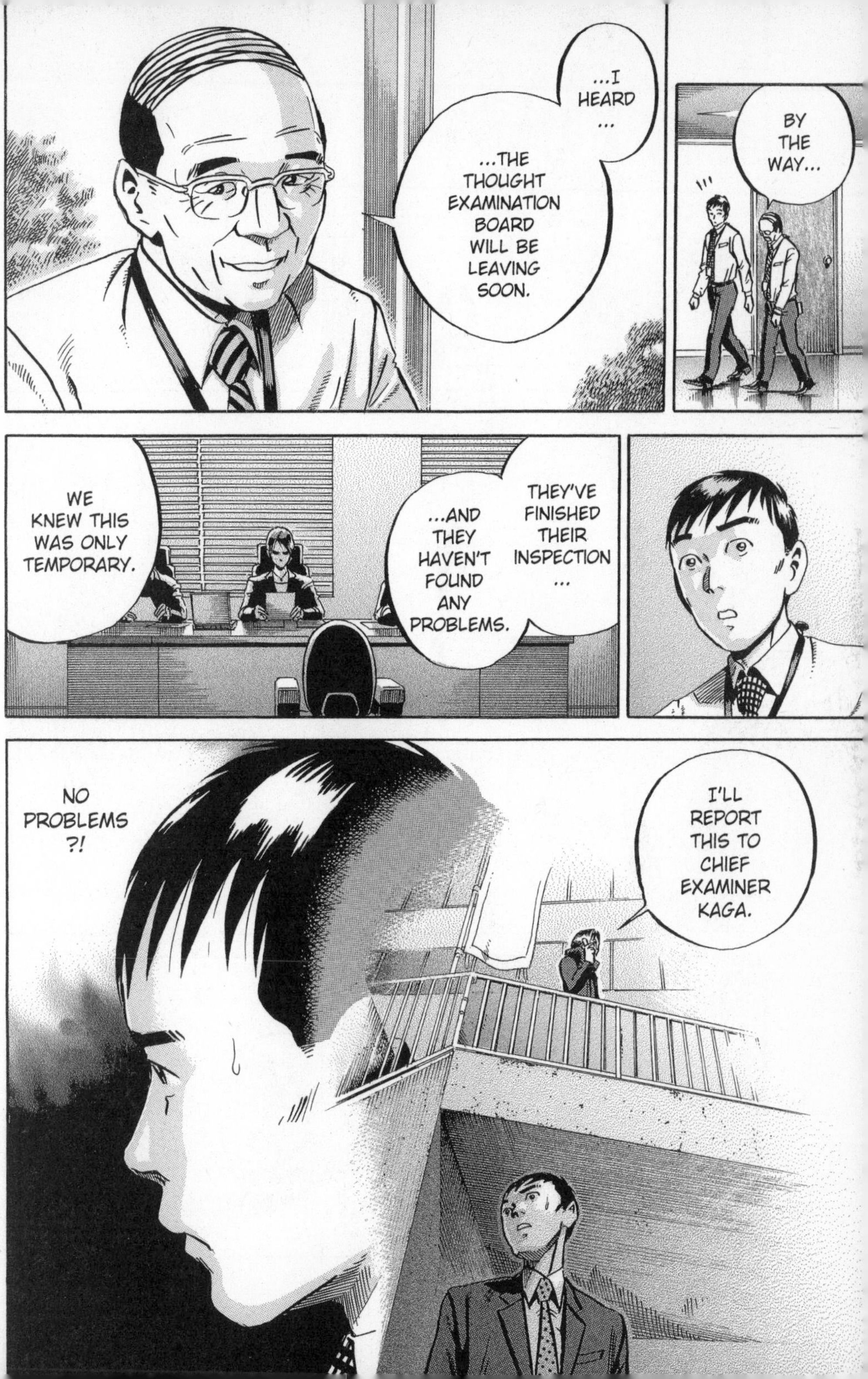
BY THE WAY...
...I HEARD...
...THE THOUGHT EXAMINATION BOARD WILL BE LEAVING SOON.
THEY'VE FINISHED THEIR INSPECTION...
...AND THEY HAVEN'T FOUND ANY PROBLEMS.
WE KNEW THIS WAS ONLY TEMPORARY.
I'LL REPORT THIS TO CHIEF EXAMINER KAGA.
NO PROBLEMS?!

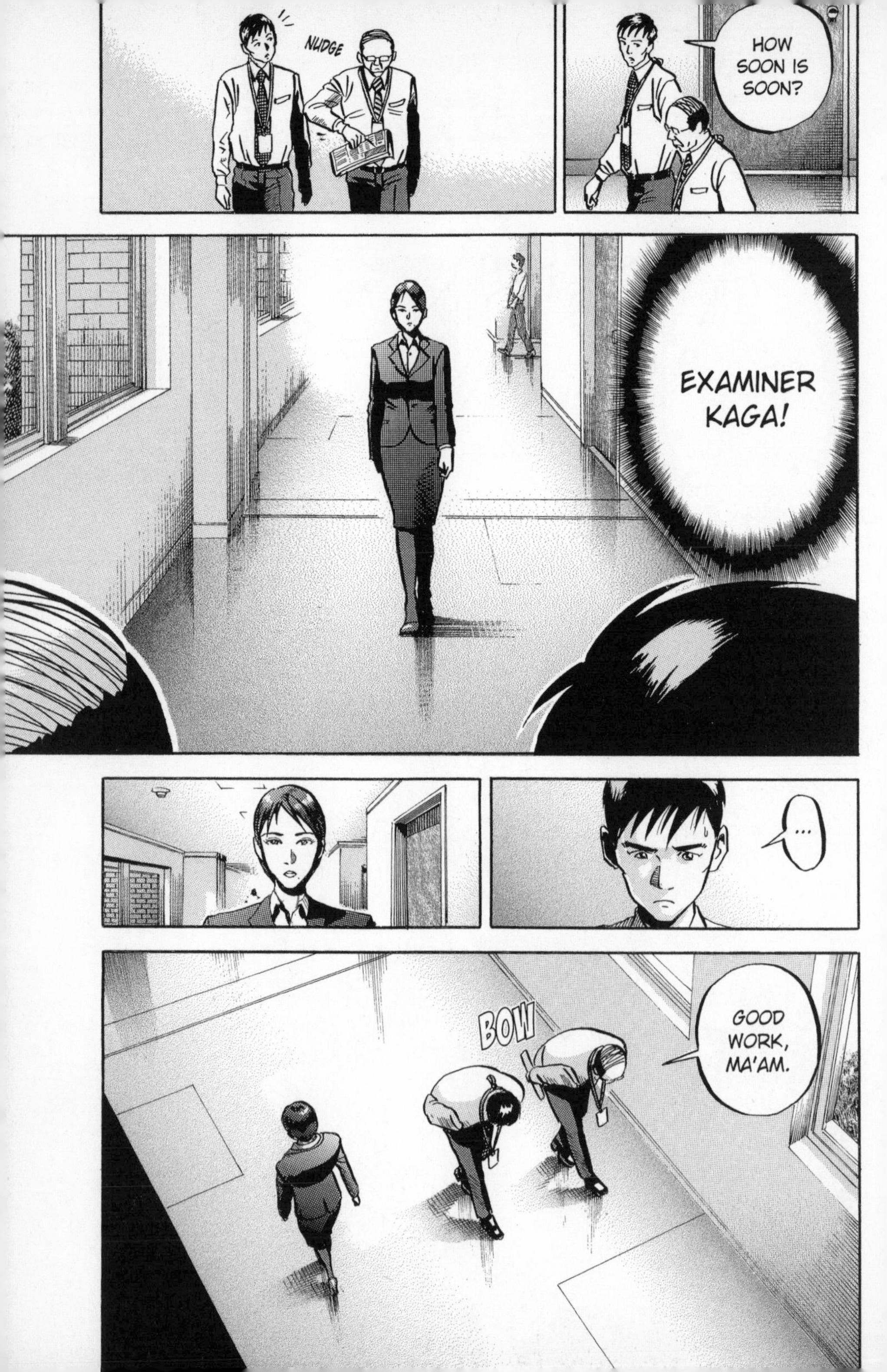
HOW SOON IS SOON?
NUDGE
EXAMINER KAGA!
...
GOOD WORK, MA'AM.
BOW

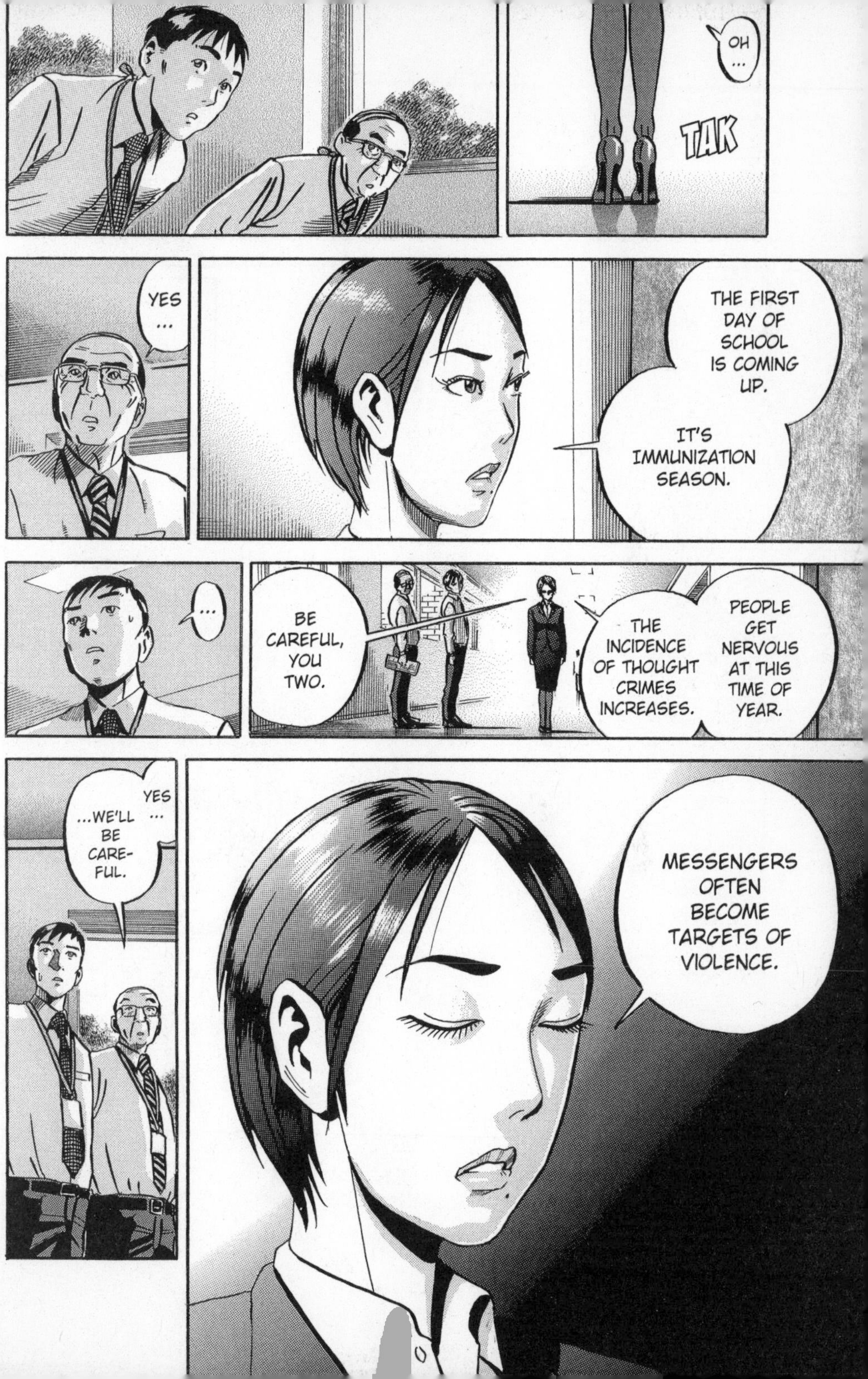
OH ...
TAK
THE FIRST DAY OF SCHOOL IS COMING UP.
IT'S IMMUNIZATION SEASON.
YES ...
PEOPLE GET NERVOUS AT THIS TIME OF YEAR.
THE INCIDENCE OF THOUGHT CRIMES INCREASES.
BE CAREFUL, YOU TWO.
...
MESSENGERS OFTEN BECOME TARGETS OF VIOLENCE.
YES ...
...WE'LL BE CARE-FUL.

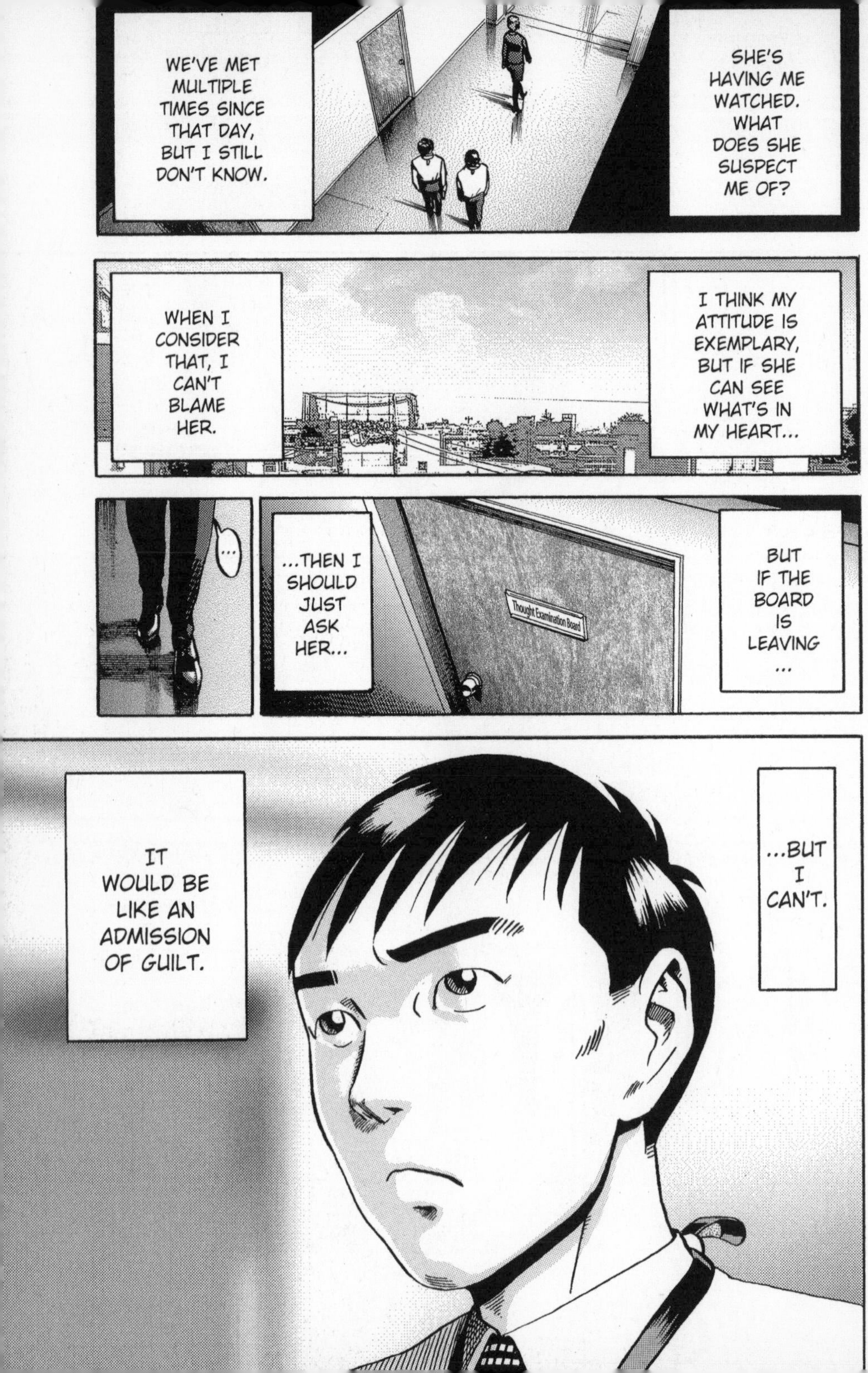
SHE'S HAVING ME WATCHED. WHAT DOES SHE SUSPECT ME OF?
WE'VE MET MULTIPLE TIMES SINCE THAT DAY, BUT I STILL DON'T KNOW.
I THINK MY ATTITUDE IS EXEMPLARY, BUT IF SHE CAN SEE WHAT'S IN MY HEART...
WHEN I CONSIDER THAT, I CAN'T BLAME HER.
BUT IF THE BOARD IS LEAVING ...
Thought Examination Board
...THEN I SHOULD JUST ASK HER...
...
...BUT I CAN'T.
IT WOULD BE LIKE AN ADMISSION OF GUILT.

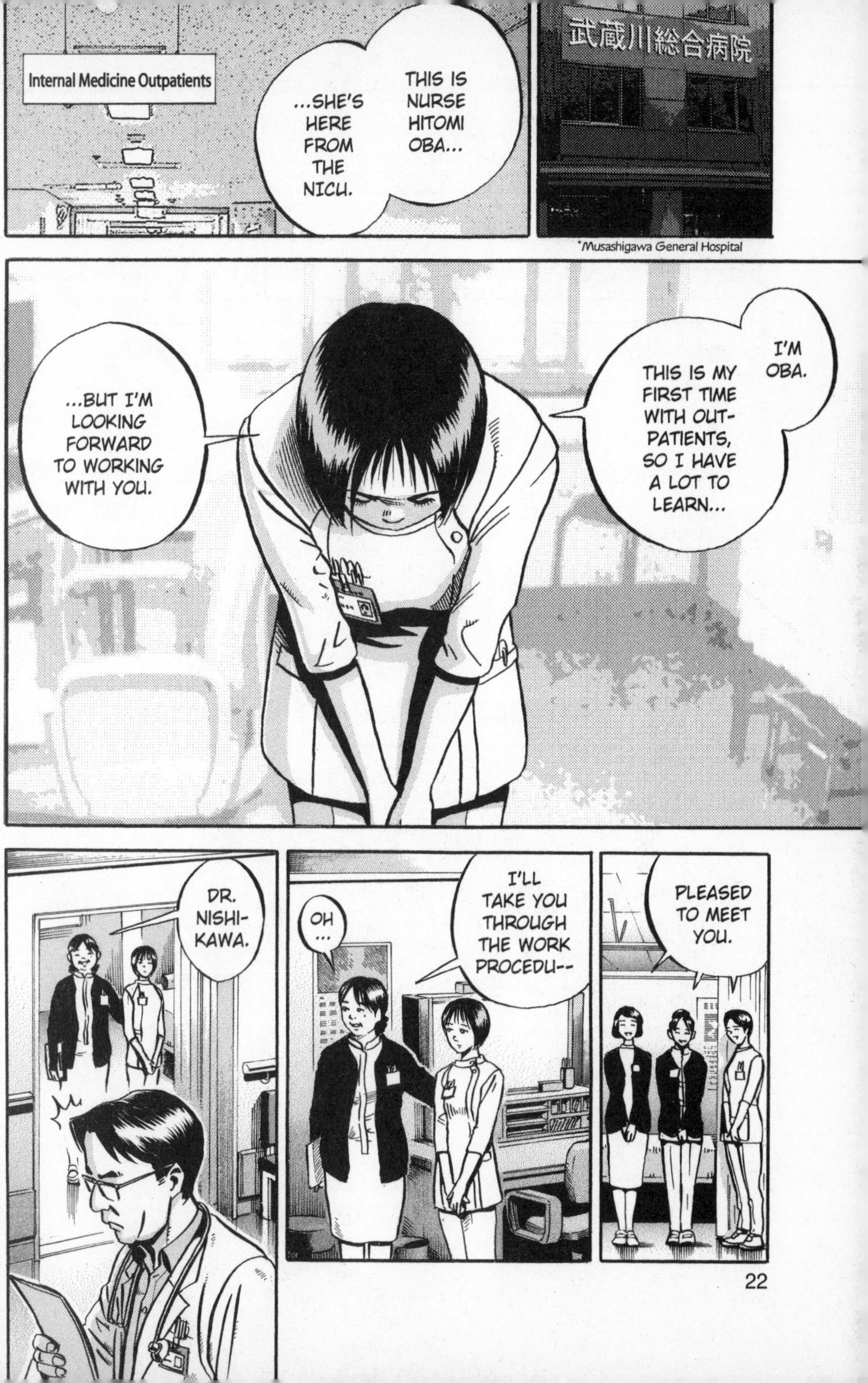
武蔵川総合病院
*Musashigawa General Hospital
Internal Medicine Outpatients
THIS IS NURSE HITOMI OBA...
...SHE'S HERE FROM THE NICU.
I'M OBA.
THIS IS MY FIRST TIME WITH OUT-PATIENTS, SO I HAVE A LOT TO LEARN...
...BUT I'M LOOKING FORWARD TO WORKING WITH YOU.
PLEASED TO MEET YOU.
I'LL TAKE YOU THROUGH THE WORK PROCEDU--
OH ...
DR. NISHI-KAWA.

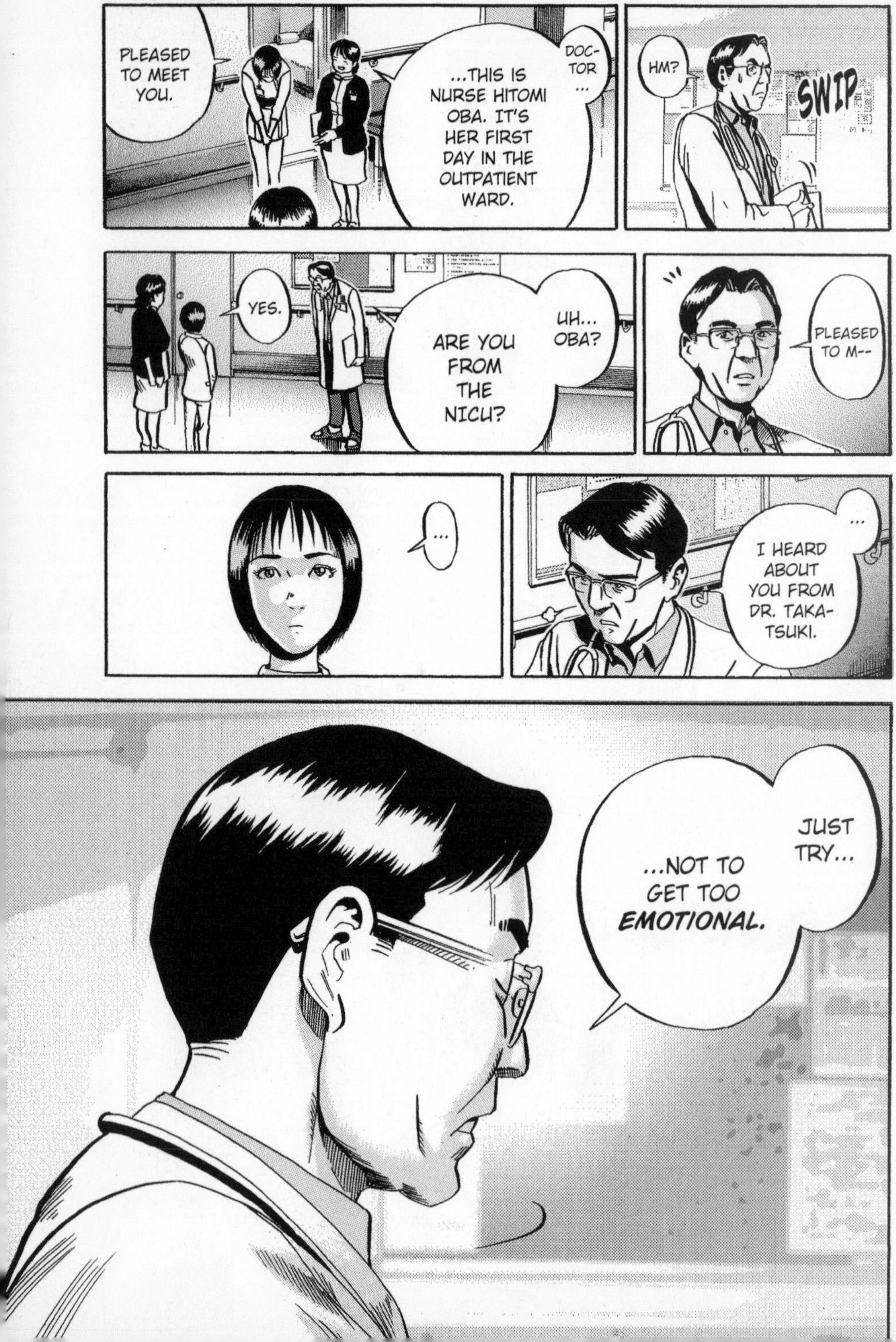
HM?
SWIP
DOC-TOR ...
...THIS IS NURSE HITOMI OBA. IT'S HER FIRST DAY IN THE OUTPATIENT WARD.
PLEASED TO MEET YOU.
PLEASED TO M--
UH... OBA?
ARE YOU FROM THE NICU?
YES.
...
I HEARD ABOUT YOU FROM DR. TAKA-TSUKI.
...
JUST TRY...
...NOT TO GET TOO **EMOTIONAL.**

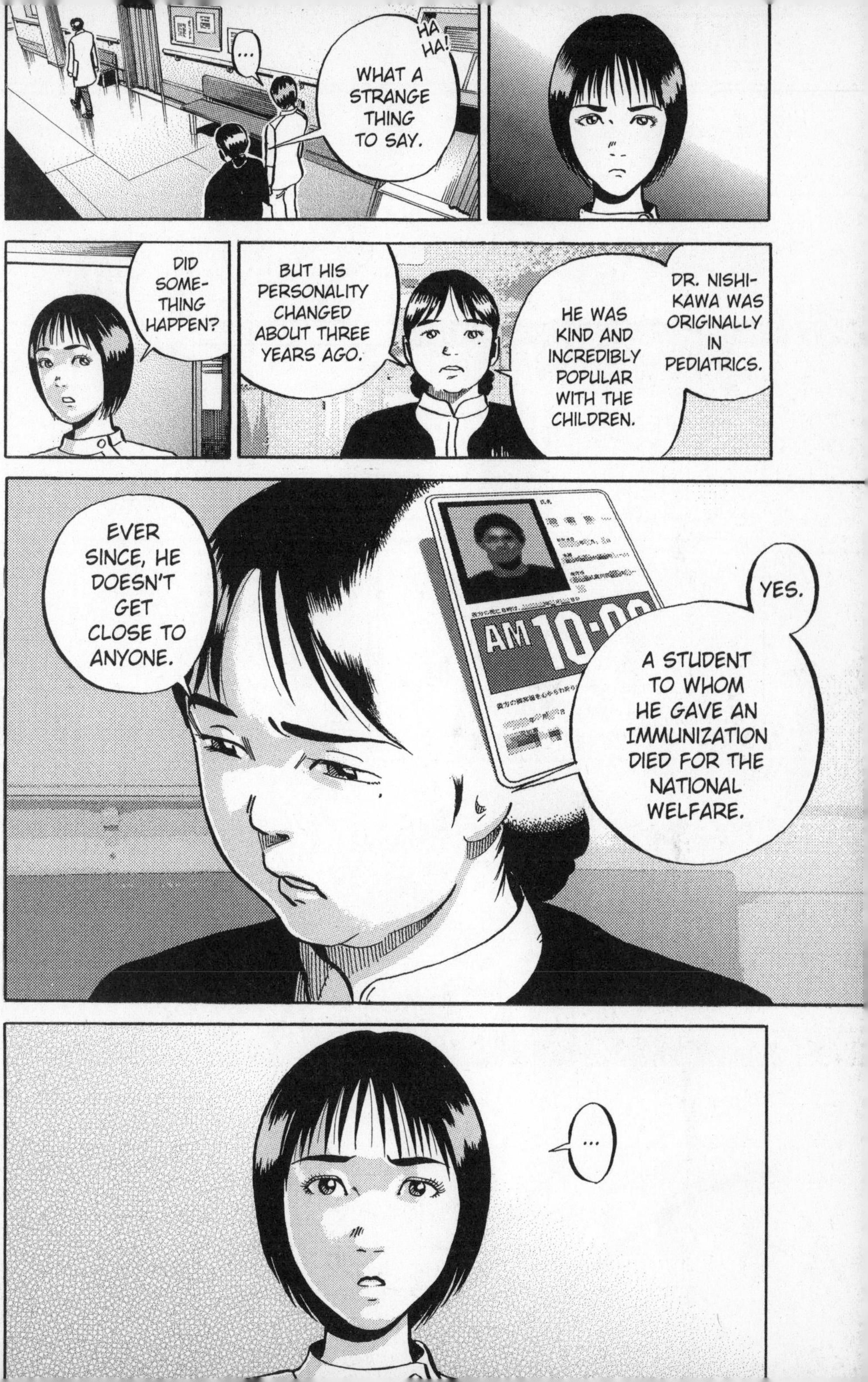
HA HA! WHAT A STRANGE THING TO SAY.
...
DR. NISHIKAWA WAS ORIGINALLY IN PEDIATRICS.
HE WAS KIND AND INCREDIBLY POPULAR WITH THE CHILDREN.
BUT HIS PERSONALITY CHANGED ABOUT THREE YEARS AGO.
DID SOMETHING HAPPEN?
YES.
A STUDENT TO WHOM HE GAVE AN IMMUNIZATION DIED FOR THE NATIONAL WELFARE.
EVER SINCE, HE DOESN'T GET CLOSE TO ANYONE.
...

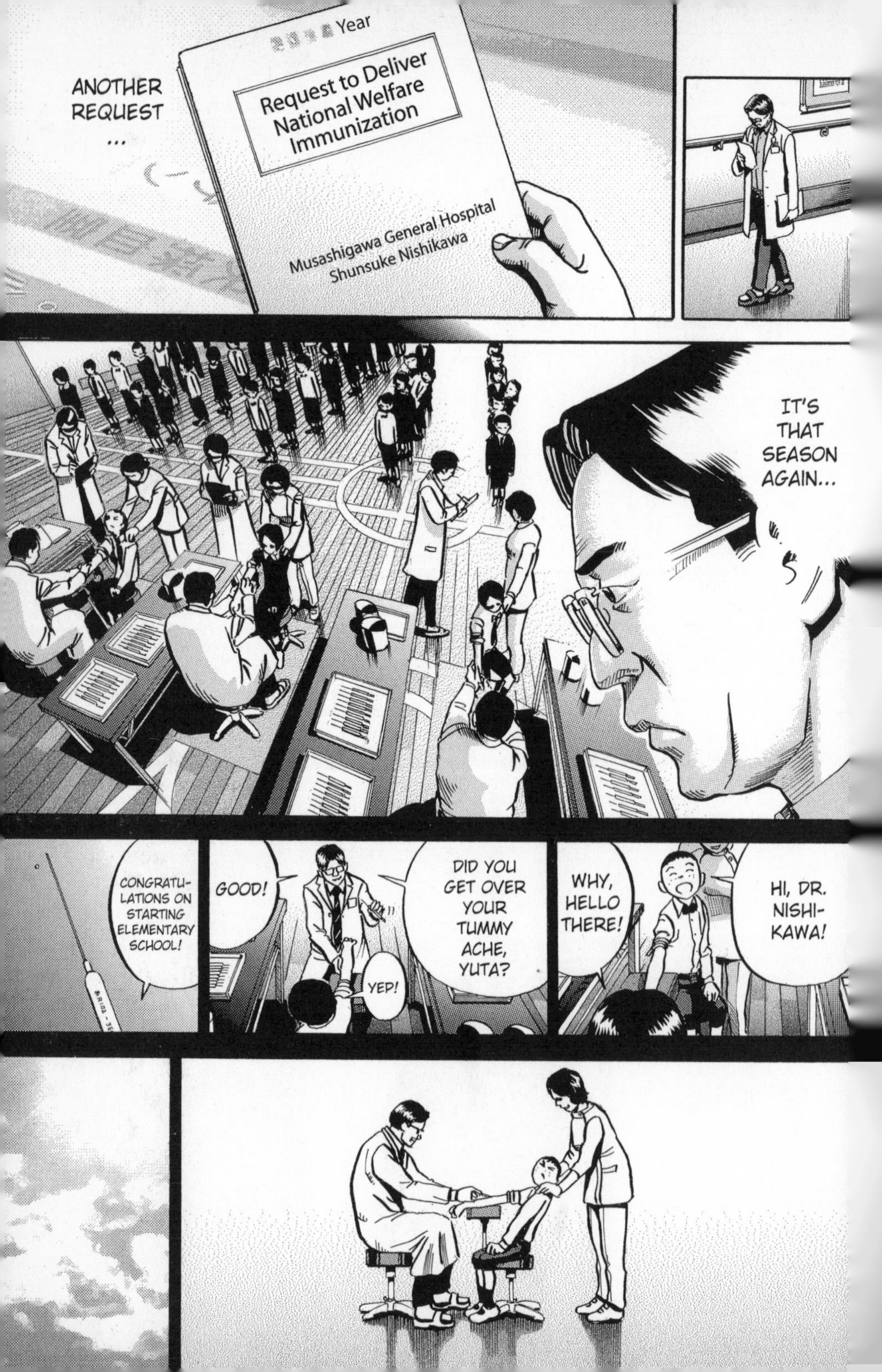
Year
Request to Deliver National Welfare Immunization
Musashigawa General Hospital
Shunsuke Nishikawa
ANOTHER REQUEST ...
IT'S THAT SEASON AGAIN...
HI, DR. NISHI-KAWA!
WHY, HELLO THERE!
DID YOU GET OVER YOUR TUMMY ACHE, YUTA?
YEP!
GOOD!
CONGRATU-LATIONS ON STARTING ELEMENTARY SCHOOL!

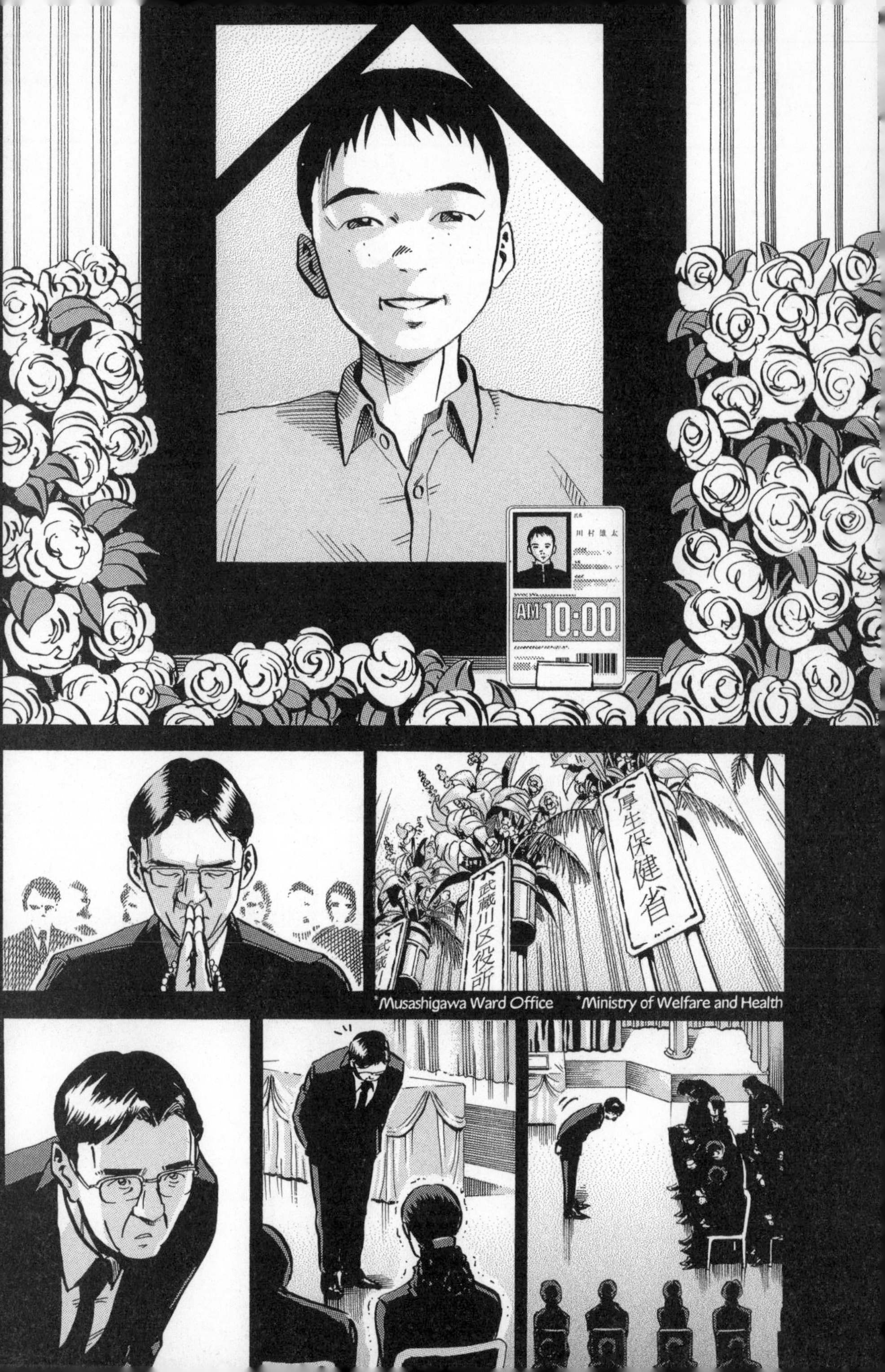
AM 10:00
厚生保健省
武蔵川区役所
*Musashigawa Ward Office
*Ministry of Welfare and Health

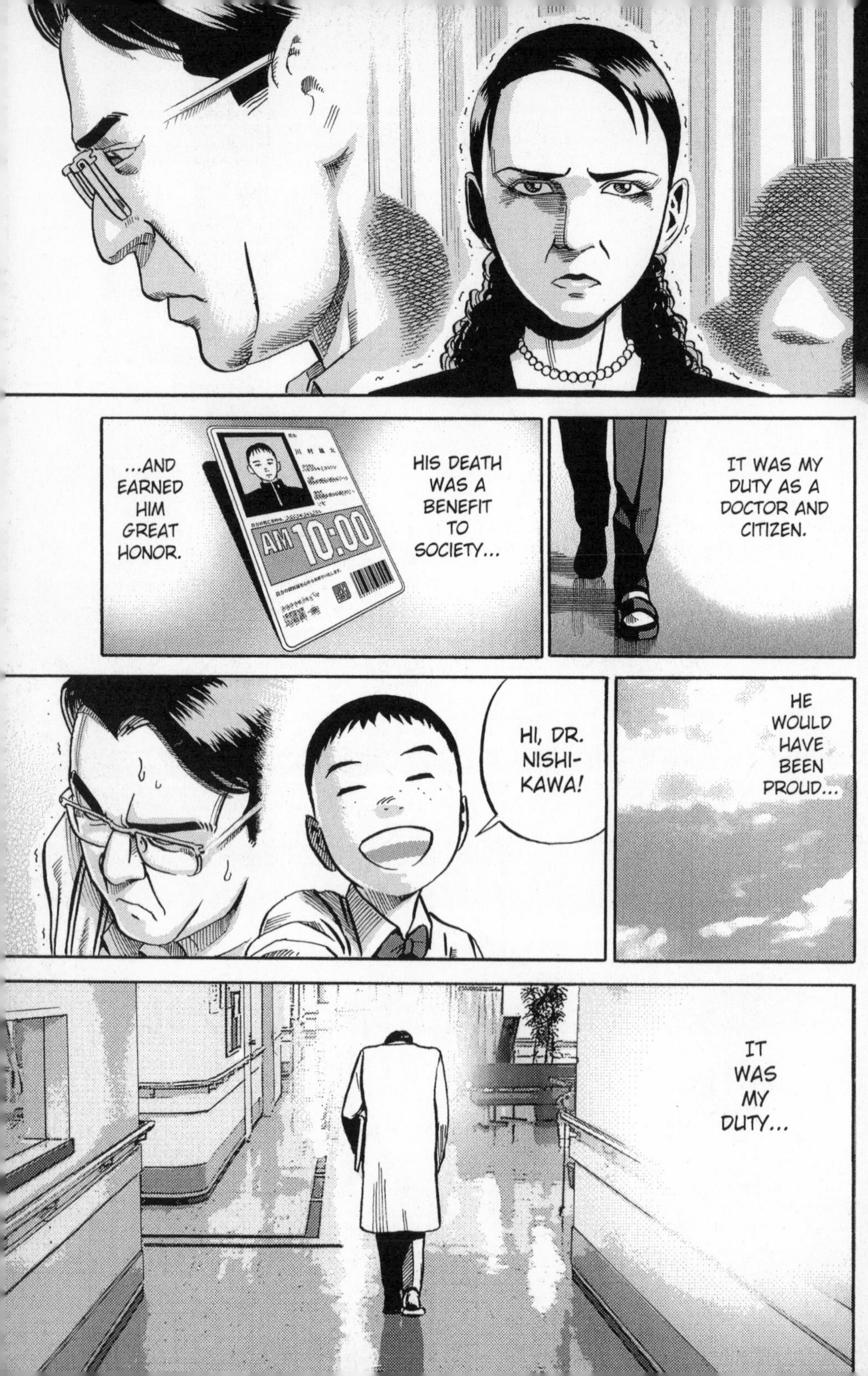
IT WAS MY DUTY AS A DOCTOR AND CITIZEN.
HIS DEATH WAS A BENEFIT TO SOCIETY...
AM 10:00
...AND EARNED HIM GREAT HONOR.
HE WOULD HAVE BEEN PROUD...
HI, DR. NISHI-KAWA!
IT WAS MY DUTY...

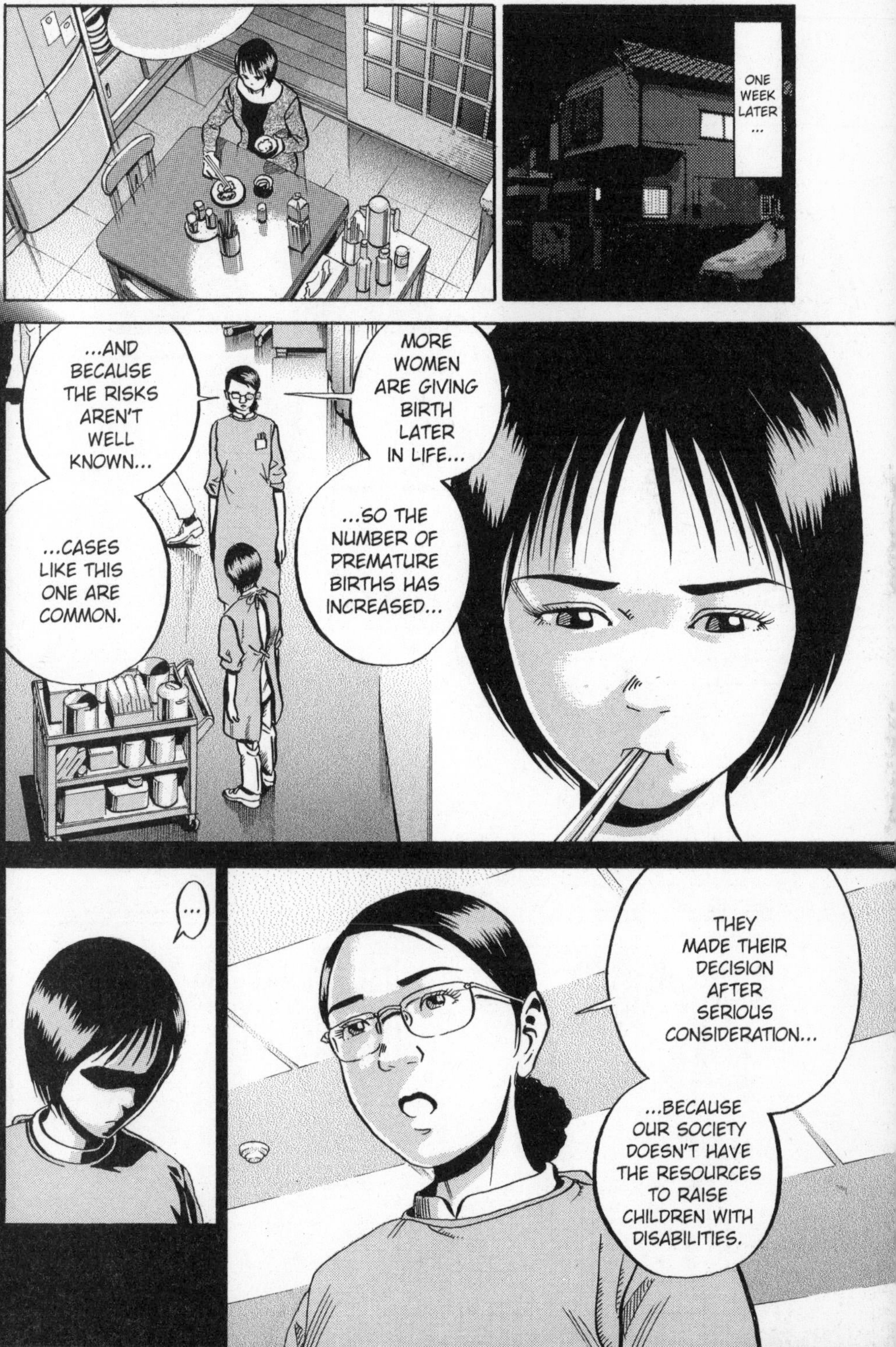
ONE WEEK LATER ...
MORE WOMEN ARE GIVING BIRTH LATER IN LIFE...
...SO THE NUMBER OF PREMATURE BIRTHS HAS INCREASED...
...AND BECAUSE THE RISKS AREN'T WELL KNOWN...
...CASES LIKE THIS ONE ARE COMMON.
THEY MADE THEIR DECISION AFTER SERIOUS CONSIDERATION...
...BECAUSE OUR SOCIETY DOESN'T HAVE THE RESOURCES TO RAISE CHILDREN WITH DISABILITIES.
...

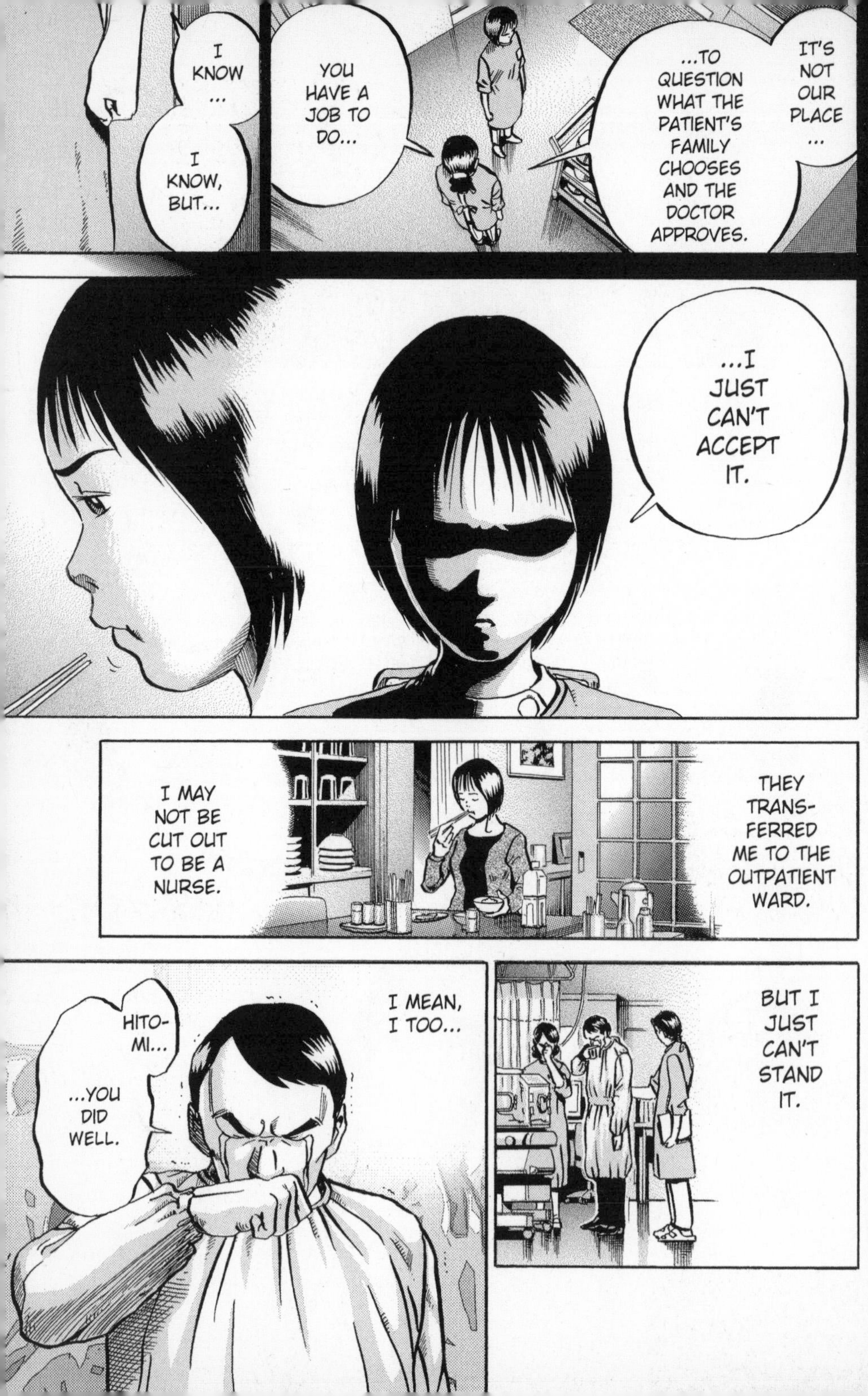
IT'S NOT OUR PLACE ...
...TO QUESTION WHAT THE PATIENT'S FAMILY CHOOSES AND THE DOCTOR APPROVES.
YOU HAVE A JOB TO DO...
I KNOW ...
I KNOW, BUT...
...I JUST CAN'T ACCEPT IT.
THEY TRANS-FERRED ME TO THE OUTPATIENT WARD.
I MAY NOT BE CUT OUT TO BE A NURSE.
BUT I JUST CAN'T STAND IT.
I MEAN, I TOO...
HITO-MI...
...YOU DID WELL.

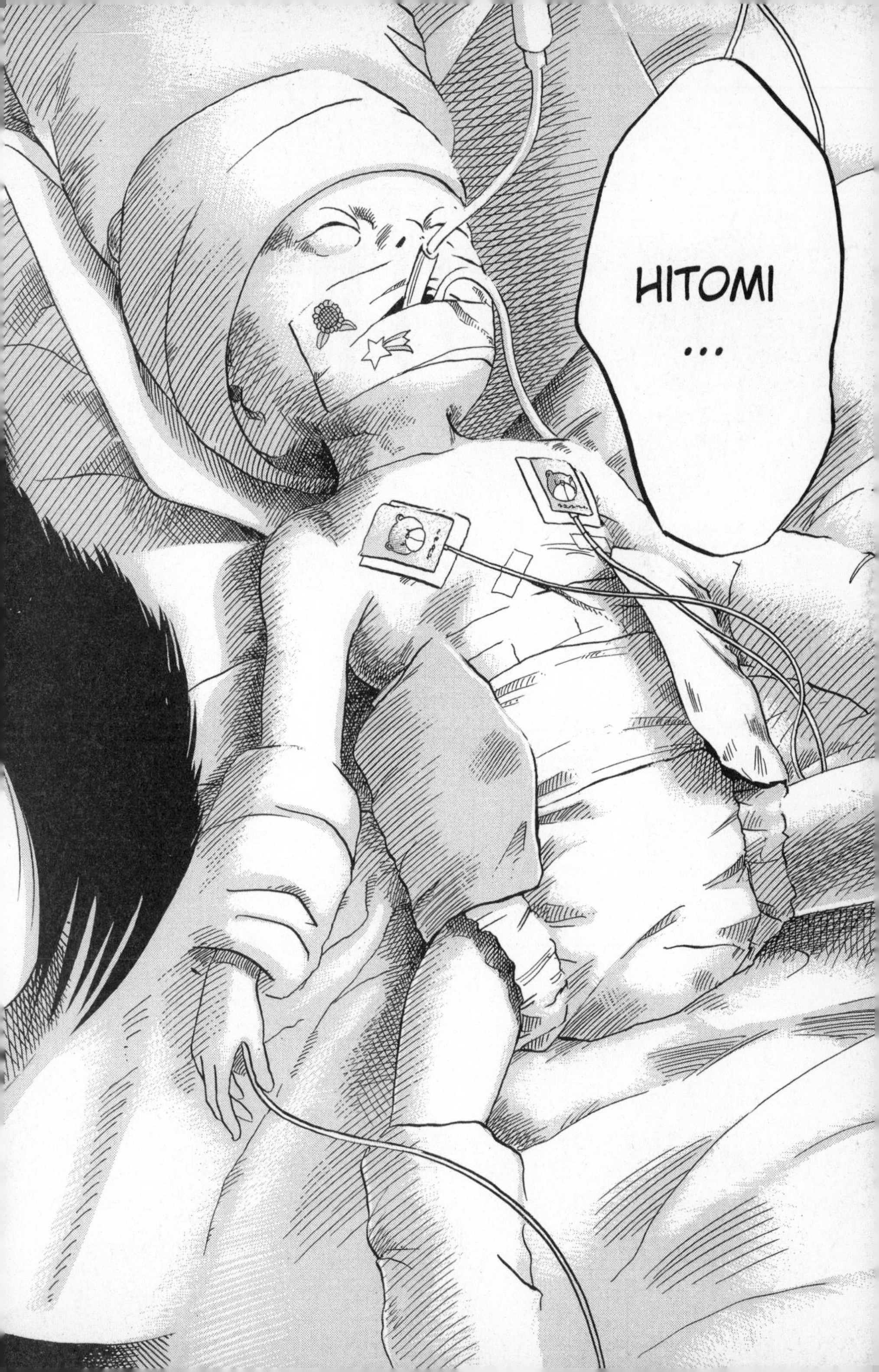
HITOMI
...

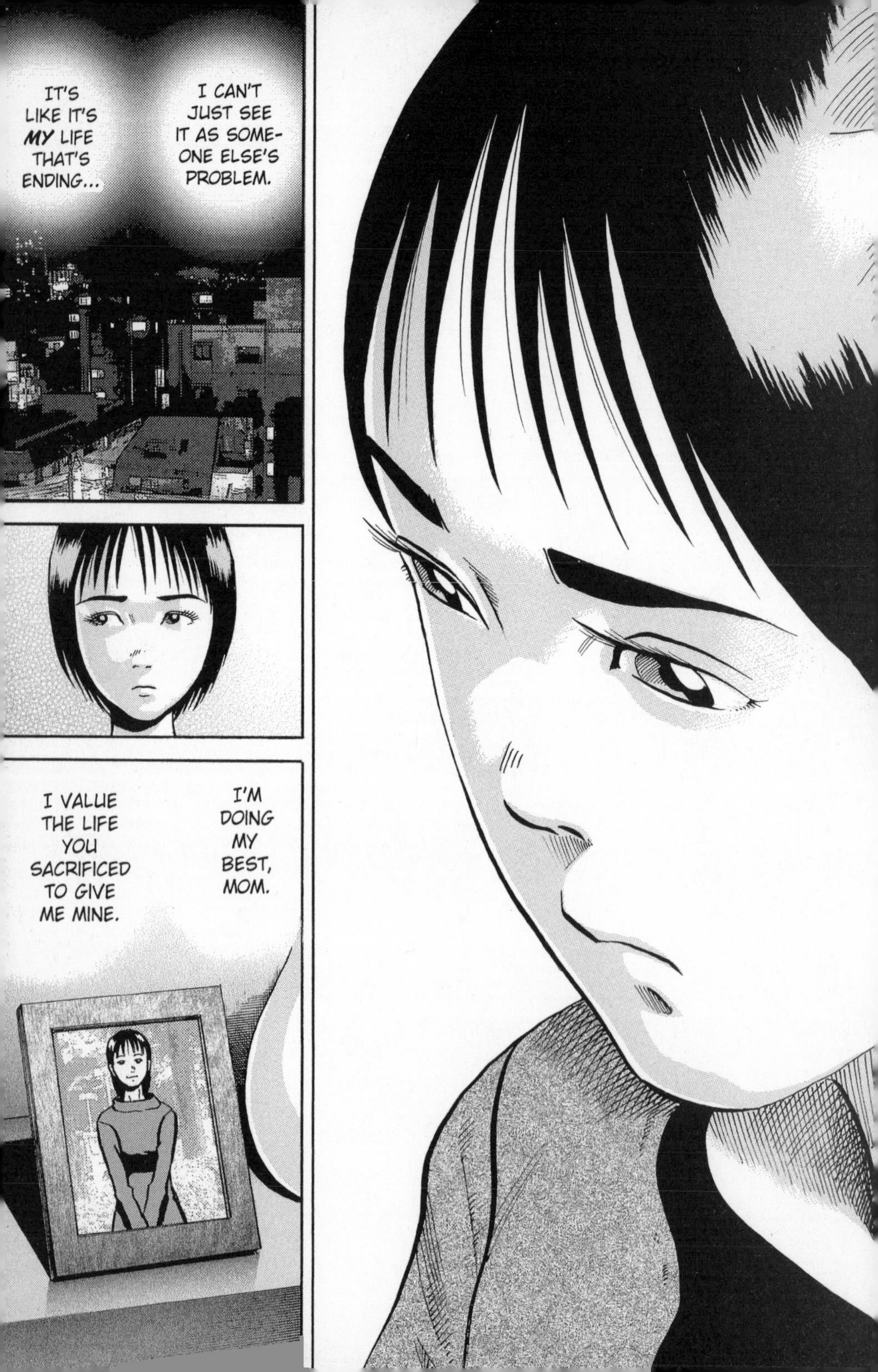
I CAN'T JUST SEE IT AS SOME-ONE ELSE'S PROBLEM.
IT'S LIKE IT'S ***MY*** LIFE THAT'S ENDING...
I'M DOING MY BEST, MOM.
I VALUE THE LIFE YOU SACRIFICED TO GIVE ME MINE.

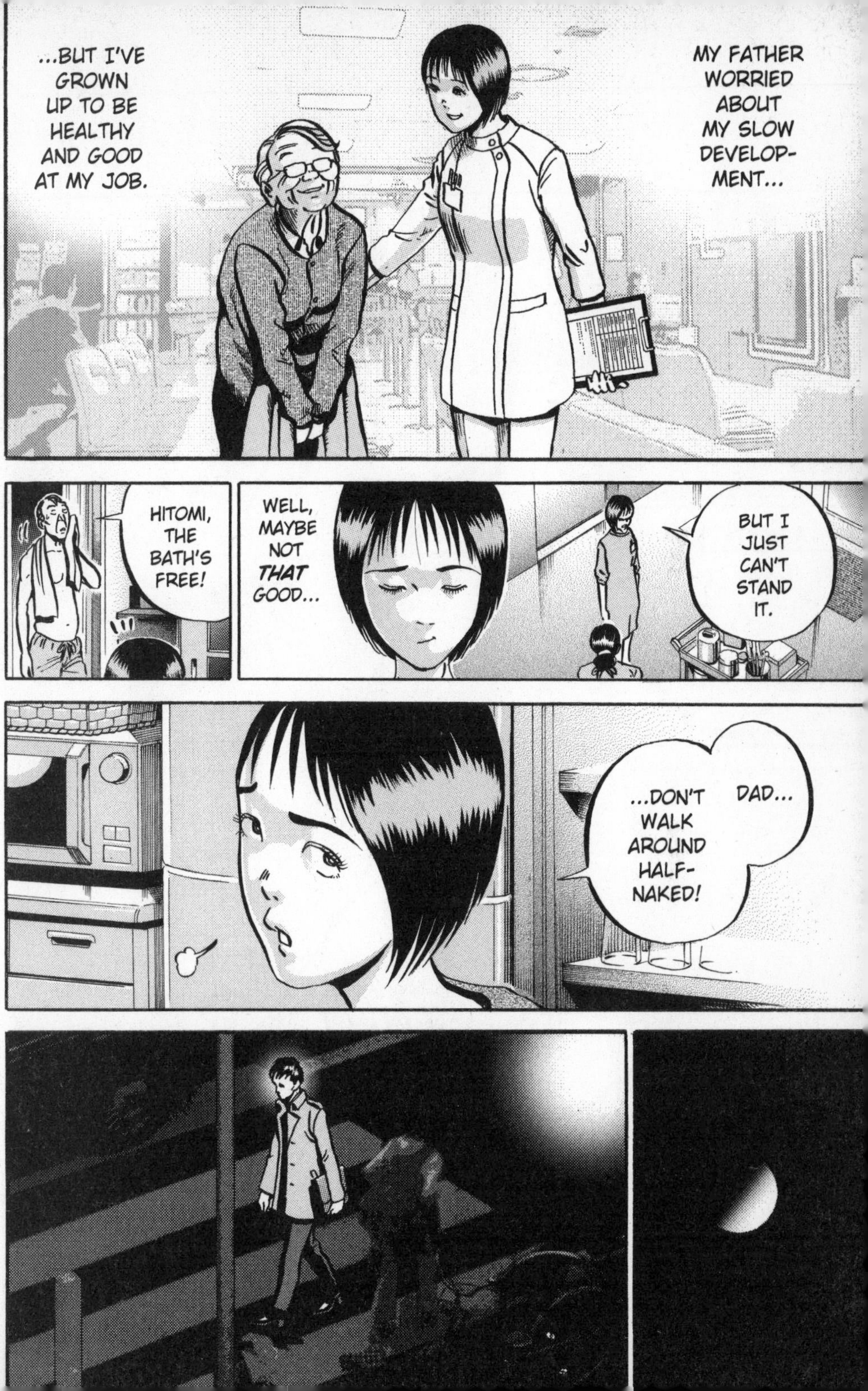
MY FATHER WORRIED ABOUT MY SLOW DEVELOPMENT...
...BUT I'VE GROWN UP TO BE HEALTHY AND GOOD AT MY JOB.
WELL, MAYBE NOT *THAT* GOOD...
BUT I JUST CAN'T STAND IT.
HITOMI, THE BATH'S FREE!
DAD...
...DON'T WALK AROUND HALF-NAKED!

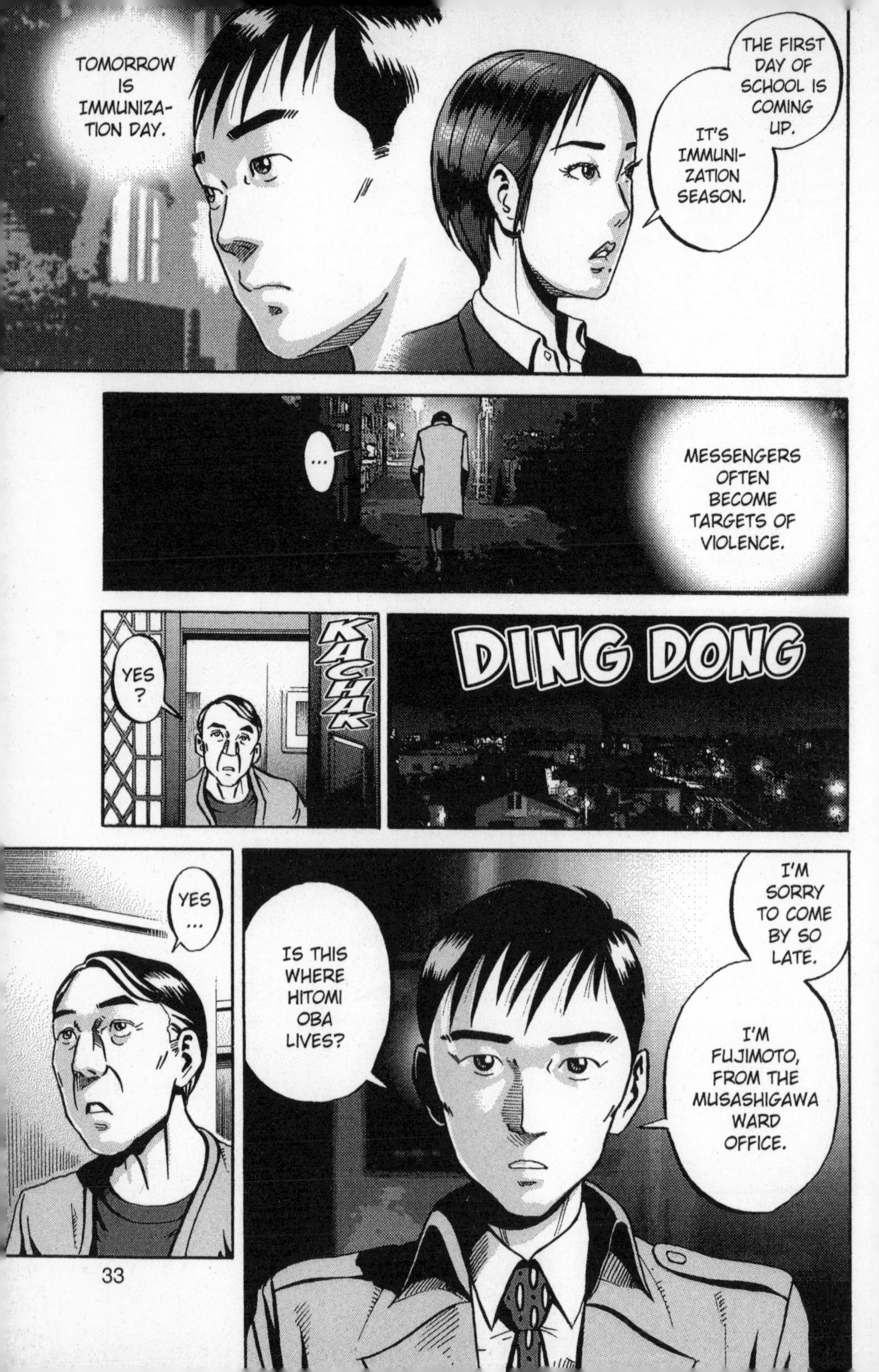
THE FIRST DAY OF SCHOOL IS COMING UP.
IT'S IMMUNIZATION SEASON.
TOMORROW IS IMMUNIZATION DAY.
MESSENGERS OFTEN BECOME TARGETS OF VIOLENCE.
...
DING DONG
KACHAK
YES?
I'M SORRY TO COME BY SO LATE.
I'M FUJIMOTO, FROM THE MUSASHIGAWA WARD OFFICE.
IS THIS WHERE HITOMI OBA LIVES?
YES...

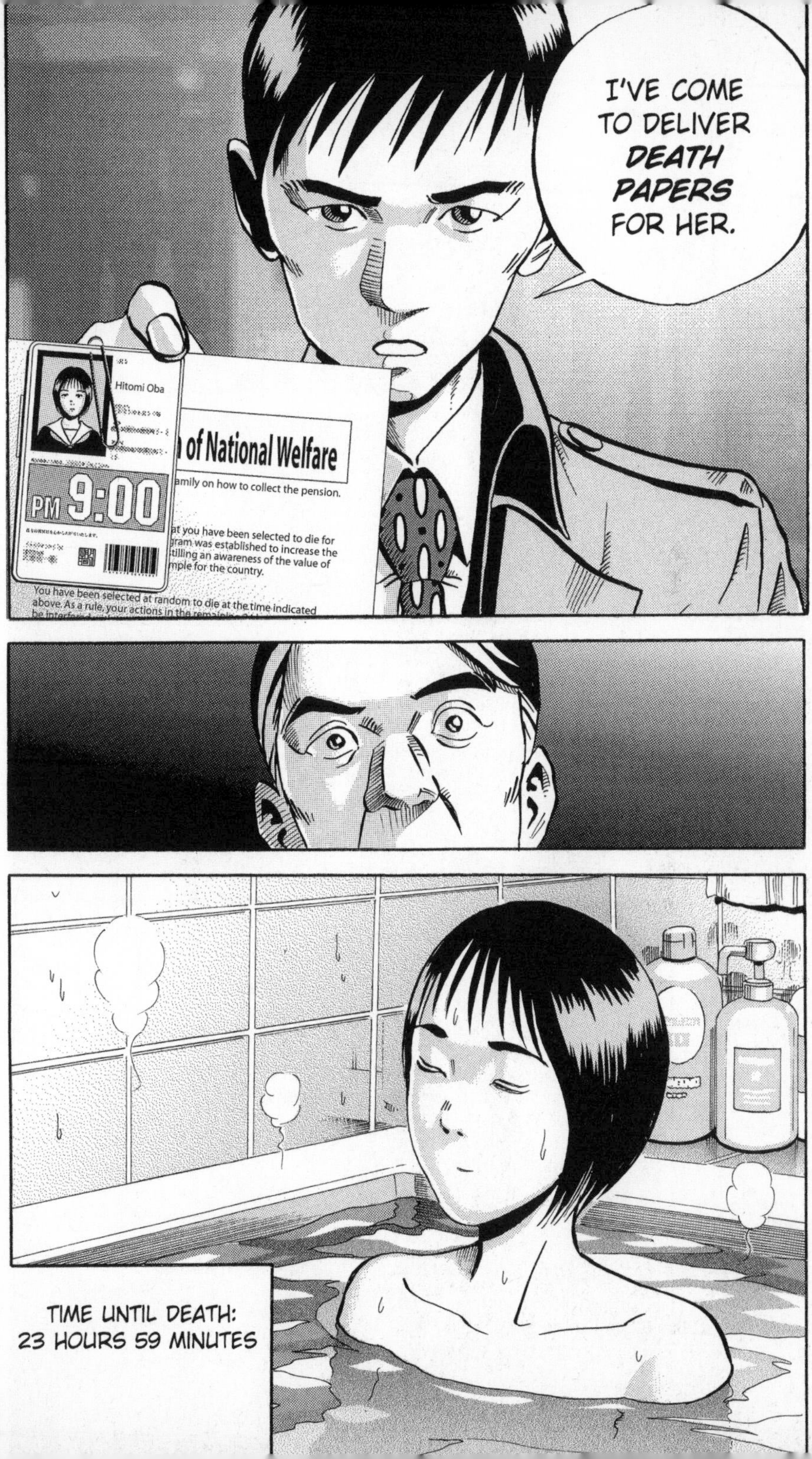
I'VE COME TO DELIVER DEATH PAPERS FOR HER.
Hitomi Oba
PM 9:00
of National Welfare
amily on how to collect the pension.
at you have been selected to die for
gram was established to increase the
tilling an awareness of the value of
mple for the country.
You have been selected at random to die at the time indicated
above. As a rule, your actions in the remaining
TIME UNTIL DEATH: 23 HOURS 59 MINUTES

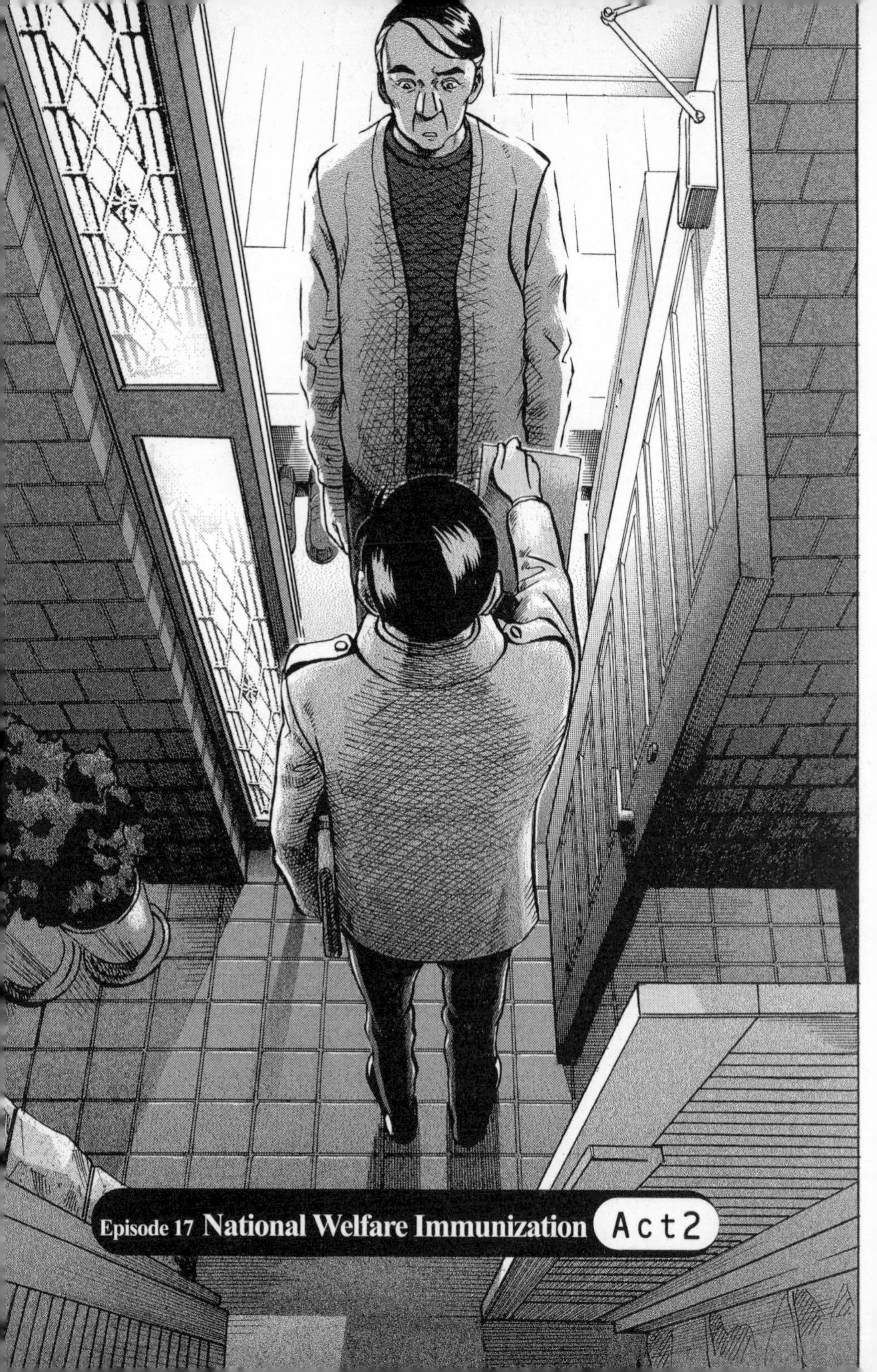
Episode 17 National Welfare Immunization Act2

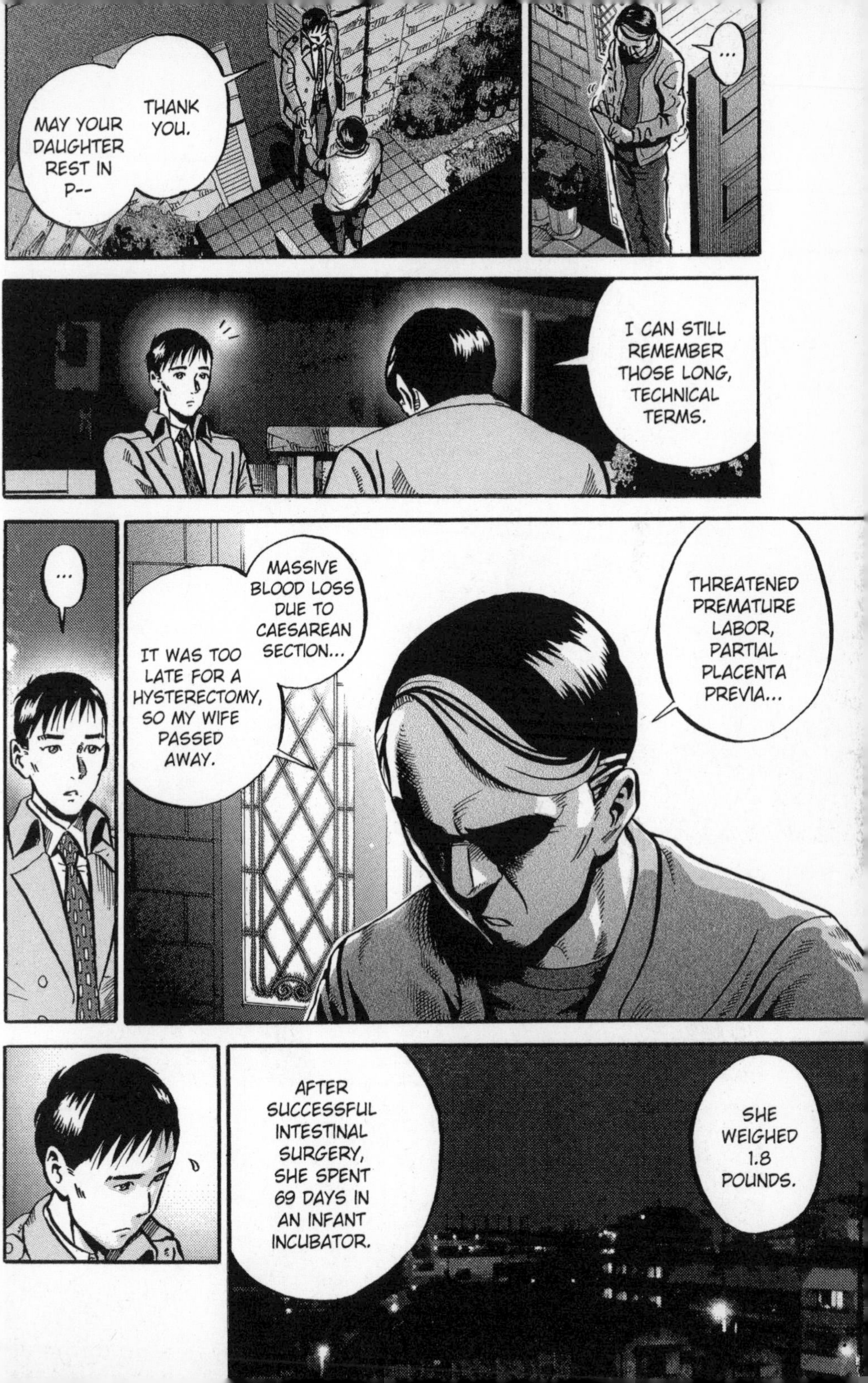
...
THANK YOU.
MAY YOUR DAUGHTER REST IN P--
I CAN STILL REMEMBER THOSE LONG, TECHNICAL TERMS.
THREATENED PREMATURE LABOR, PARTIAL PLACENTA PREVIA...
MASSIVE BLOOD LOSS DUE TO CAESAREAN SECTION...
IT WAS TOO LATE FOR A HYSTERECTOMY, SO MY WIFE PASSED AWAY.
...
SHE WEIGHED 1.8 POUNDS.
AFTER SUCCESSFUL INTESTINAL SURGERY, SHE SPENT 69 DAYS IN AN INFANT INCUBATOR.

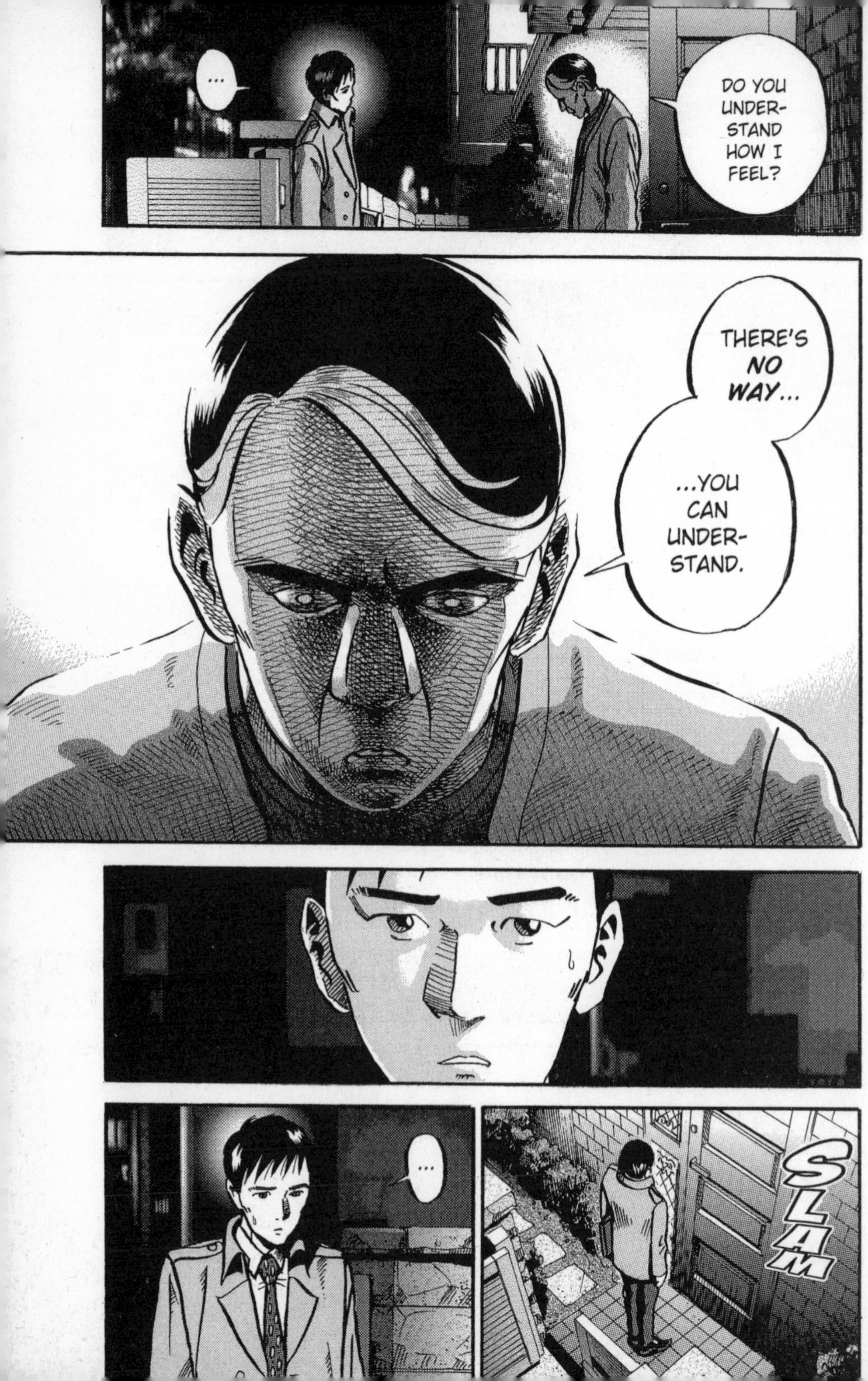
DO YOU UNDER-STAND HOW I FEEL?
...
THERE'S NO WAY...
...YOU CAN UNDER-STAND.
SLAM
...

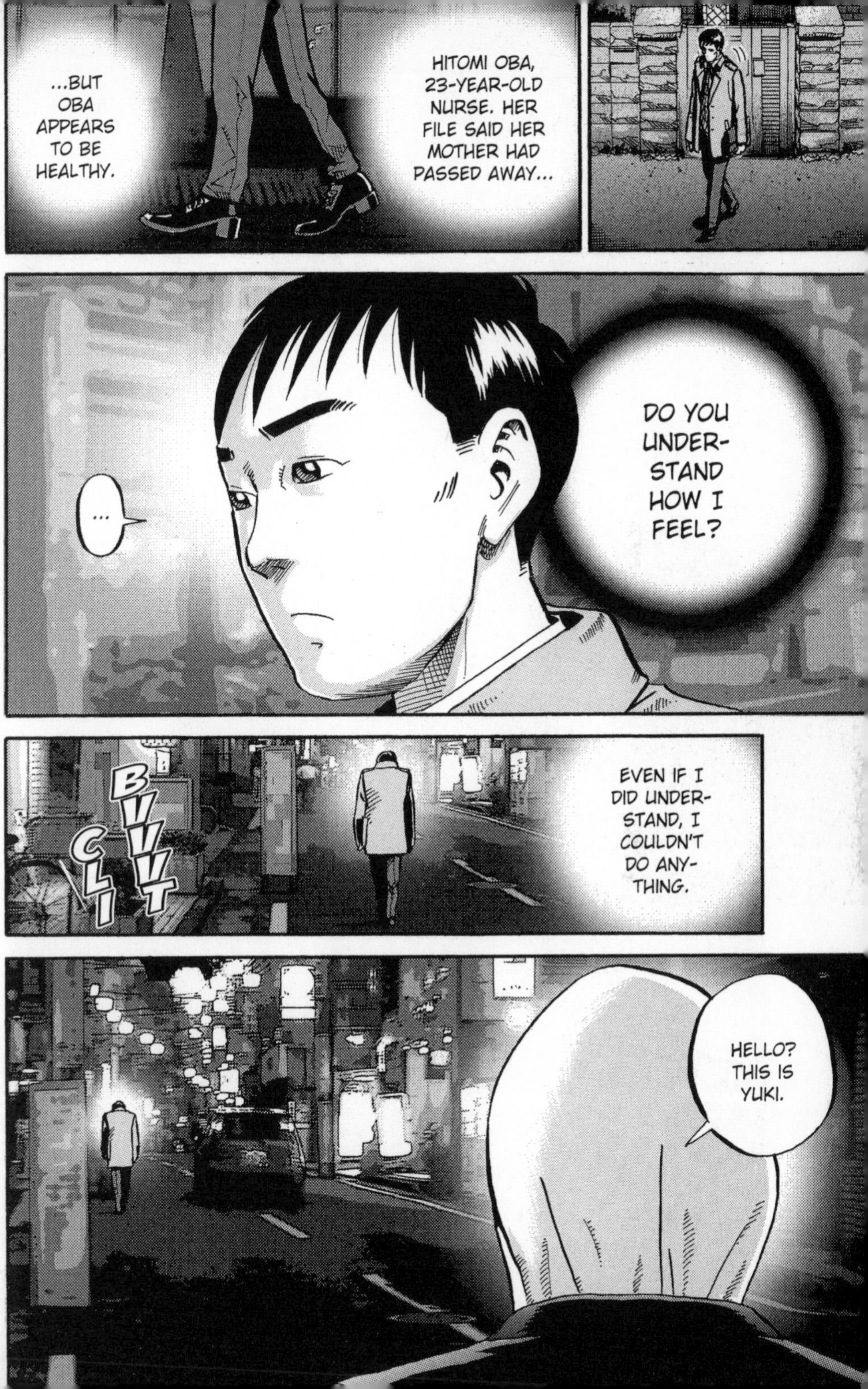
HITOMI OBA, 23-YEAR-OLD NURSE. HER FILE SAID HER MOTHER HAD PASSED AWAY...
...BUT OBA APPEARS TO BE HEALTHY.
DO YOU UNDER-STAND HOW I FEEL?
...
EVEN IF I DID UNDER-STAND, I COULDN'T DO ANY-THING.
BVVVT
CLI
HELLO? THIS IS YUKI.

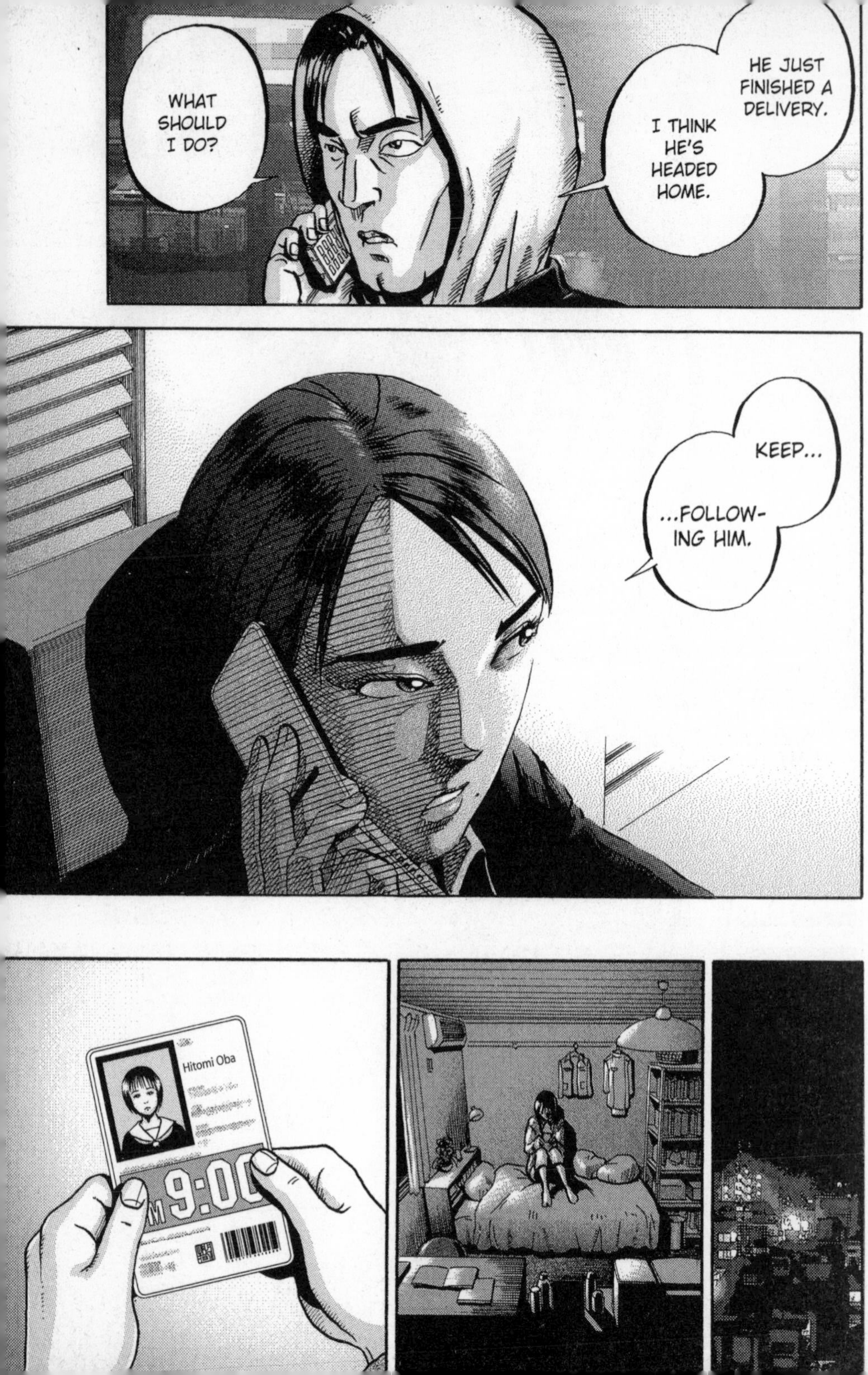
HE JUST FINISHED A DELIVERY.
I THINK HE'S HEADED HOME.
WHAT SHOULD I DO?
KEEP...
...FOLLOWING HIM.
Hitomi Oba
9:00

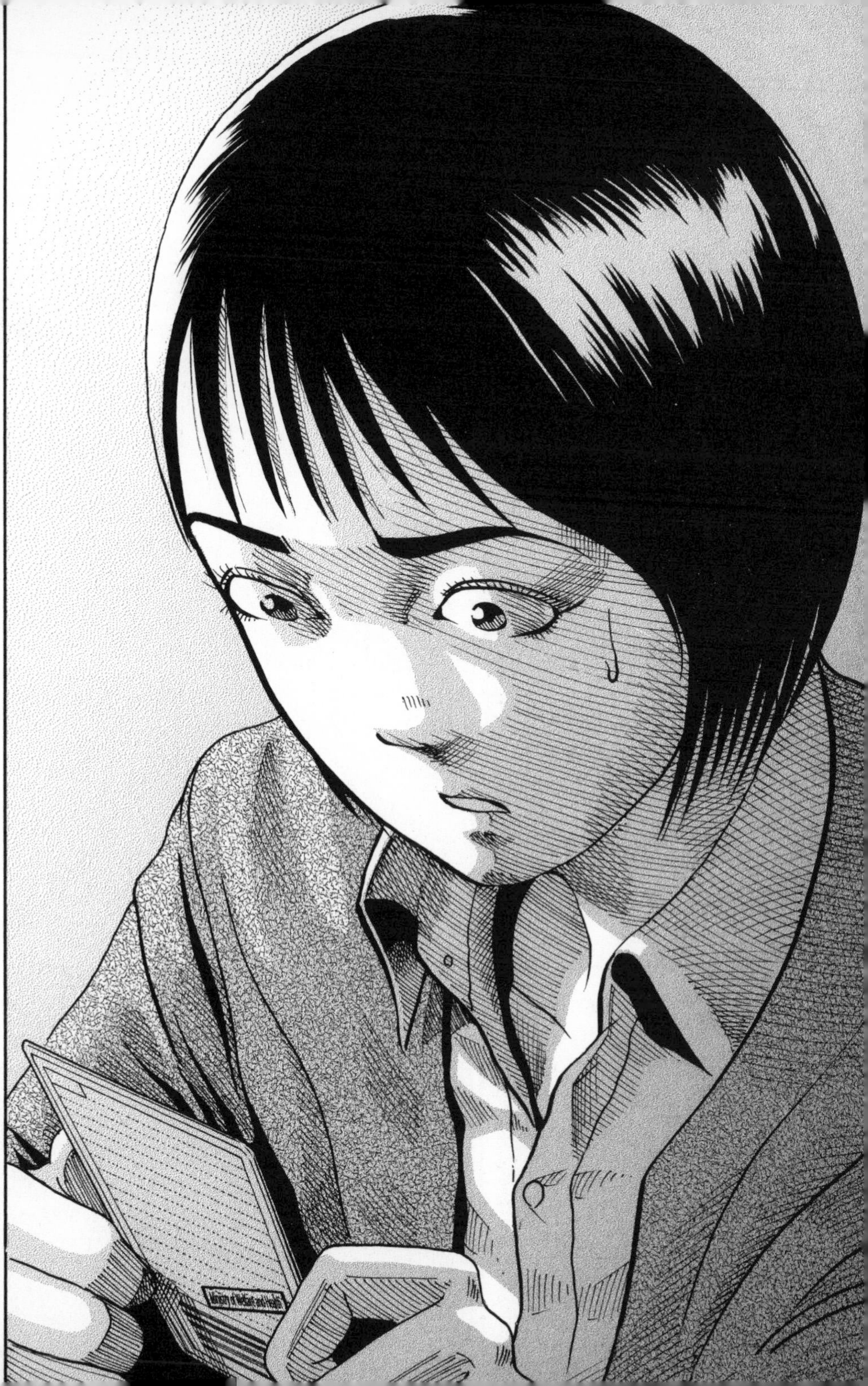
Ministry of Welfare and Health

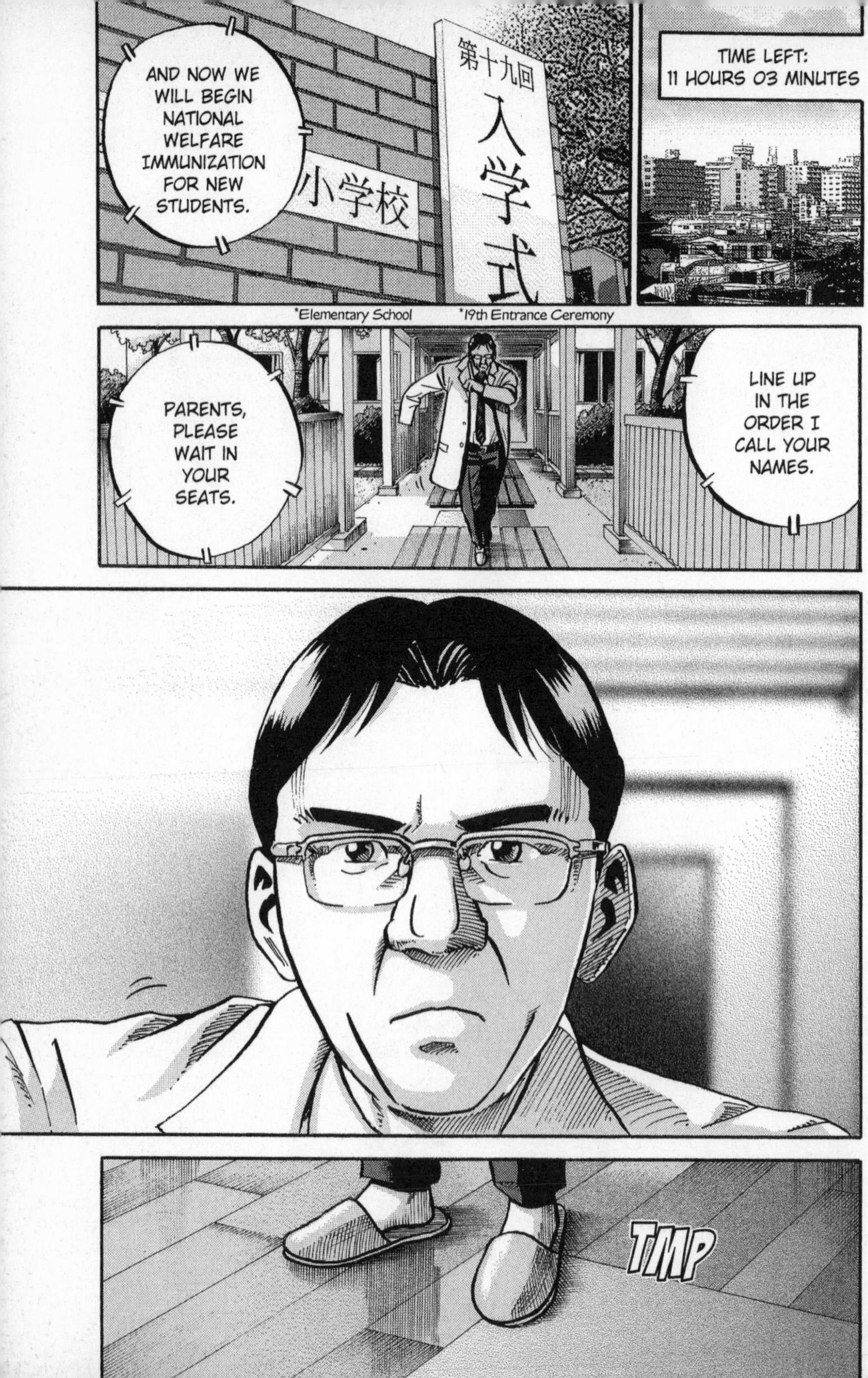
TIME LEFT: 11 HOURS 03 MINUTES
第十九回 入学式
小学校
AND NOW WE WILL BEGIN NATIONAL WELFARE IMMUNIZATION FOR NEW STUDENTS.
*Elementary School
*19th Entrance Ceremony
LINE UP IN THE ORDER I CALL YOUR NAMES.
PARENTS, PLEASE WAIT IN YOUR SEATS.
TMP

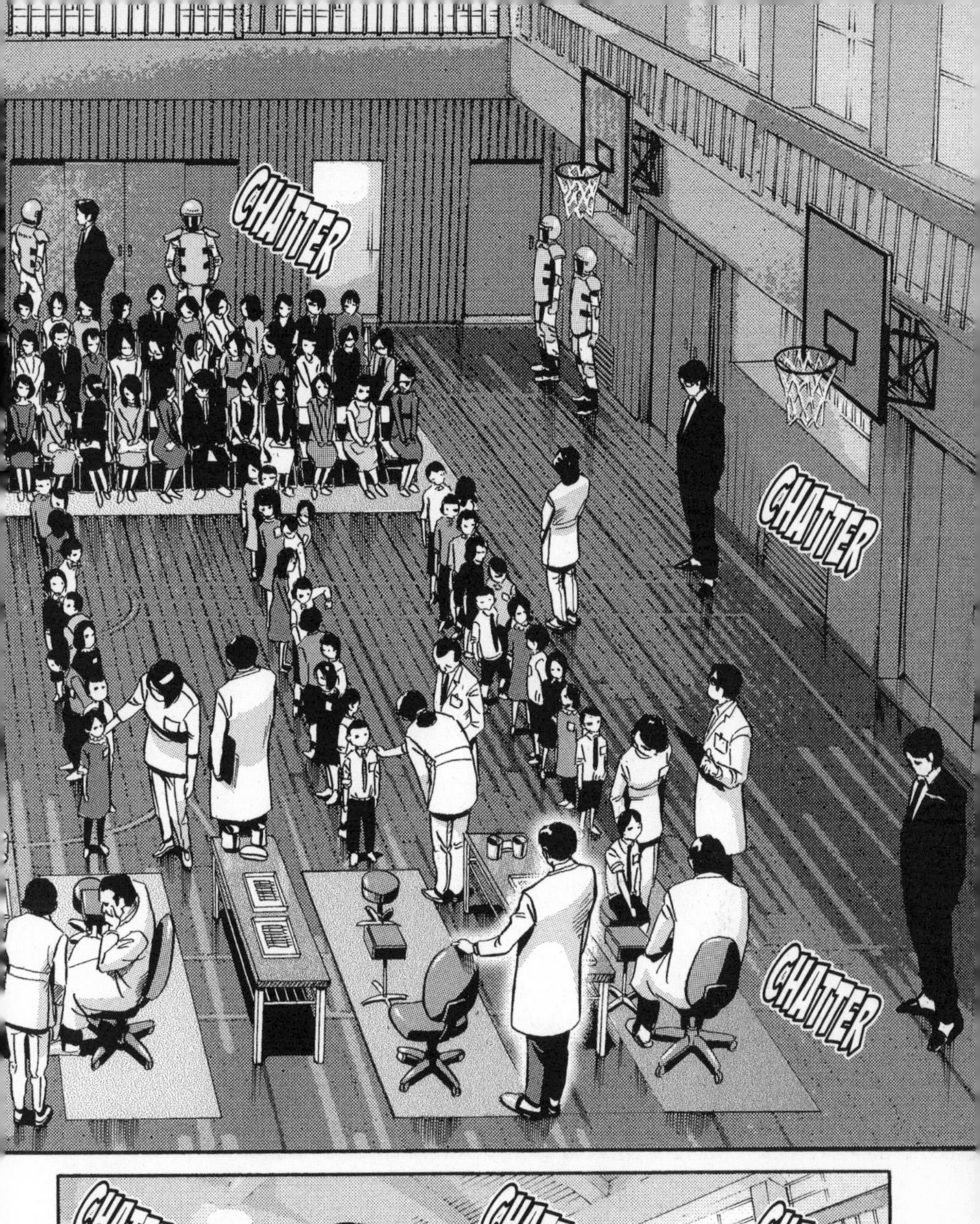
CHATTER
CHATTER
CHATTER

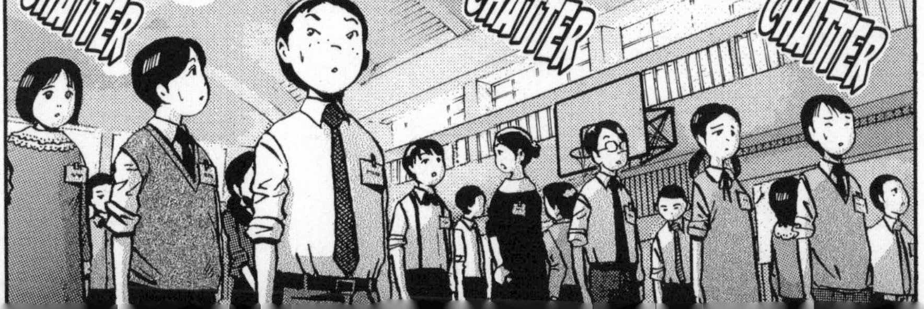
CHATTER
CHATTER
CHATTER

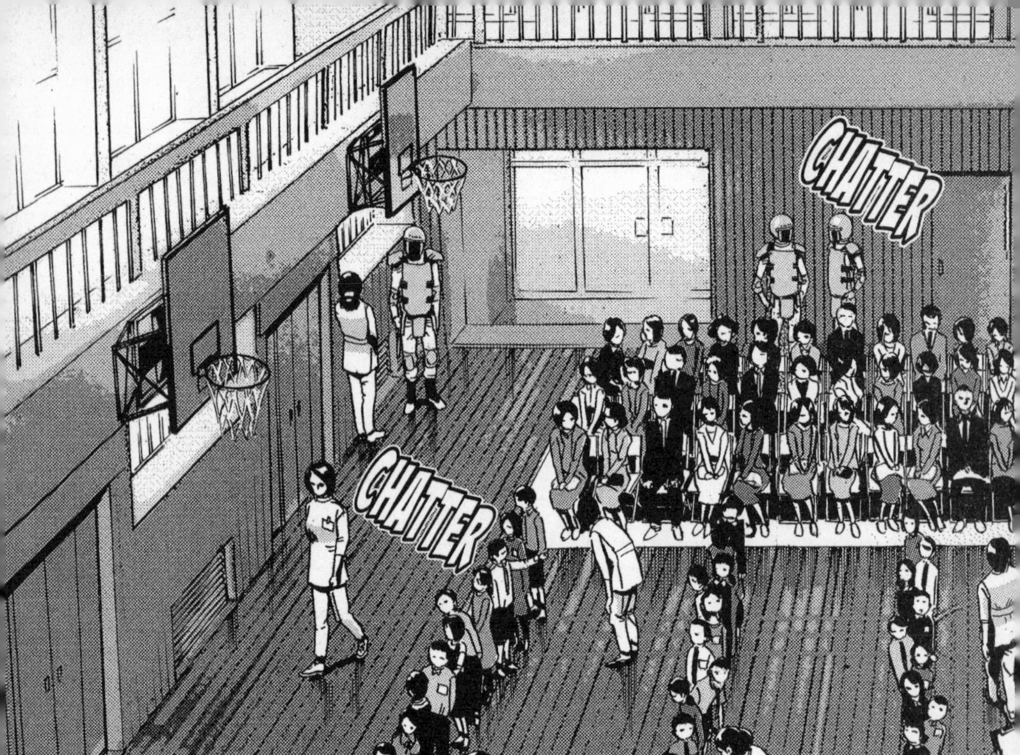
CHATTER
CHATTER
CHATTER

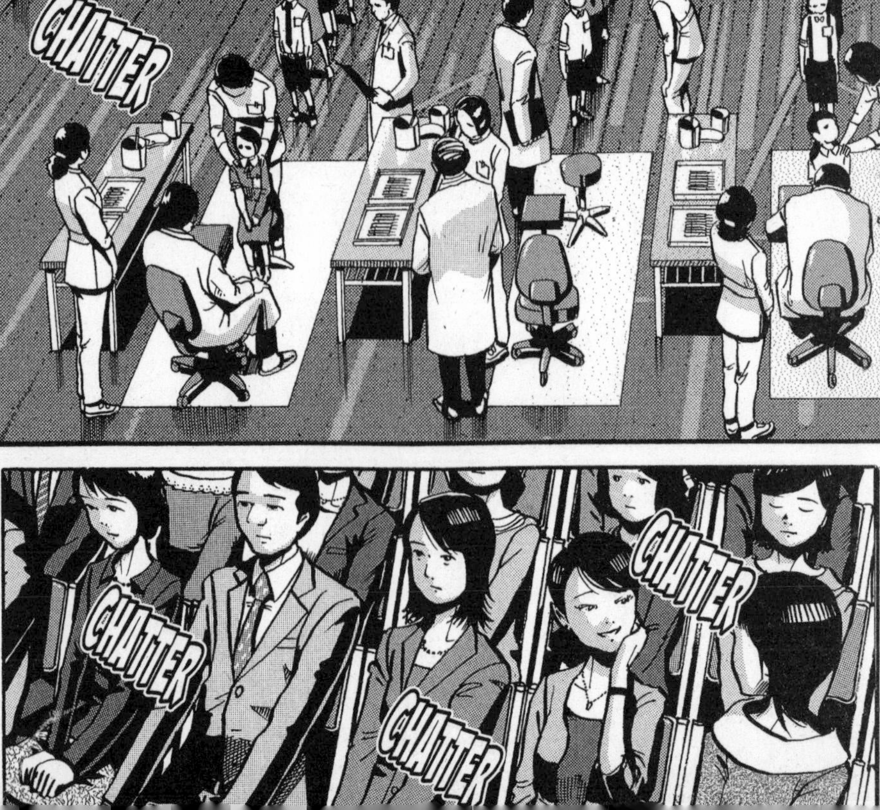
CHATTER
CHATTER
CHATTER

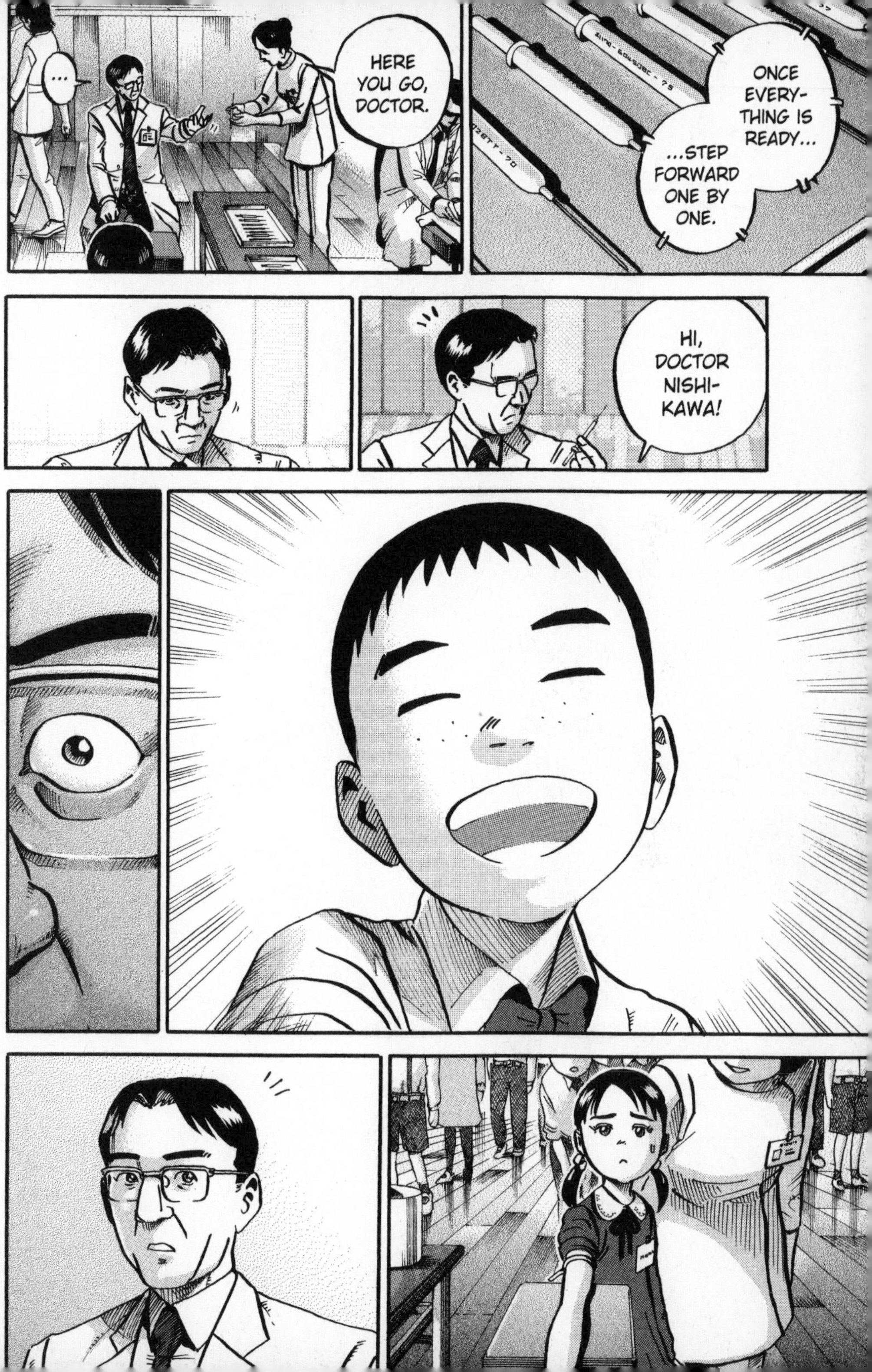
ONCE EVERY-THING IS READY...
...STEP FORWARD ONE BY ONE.
HERE YOU GO, DOCTOR.
...
HI, DOCTOR NISHI-KAWA!

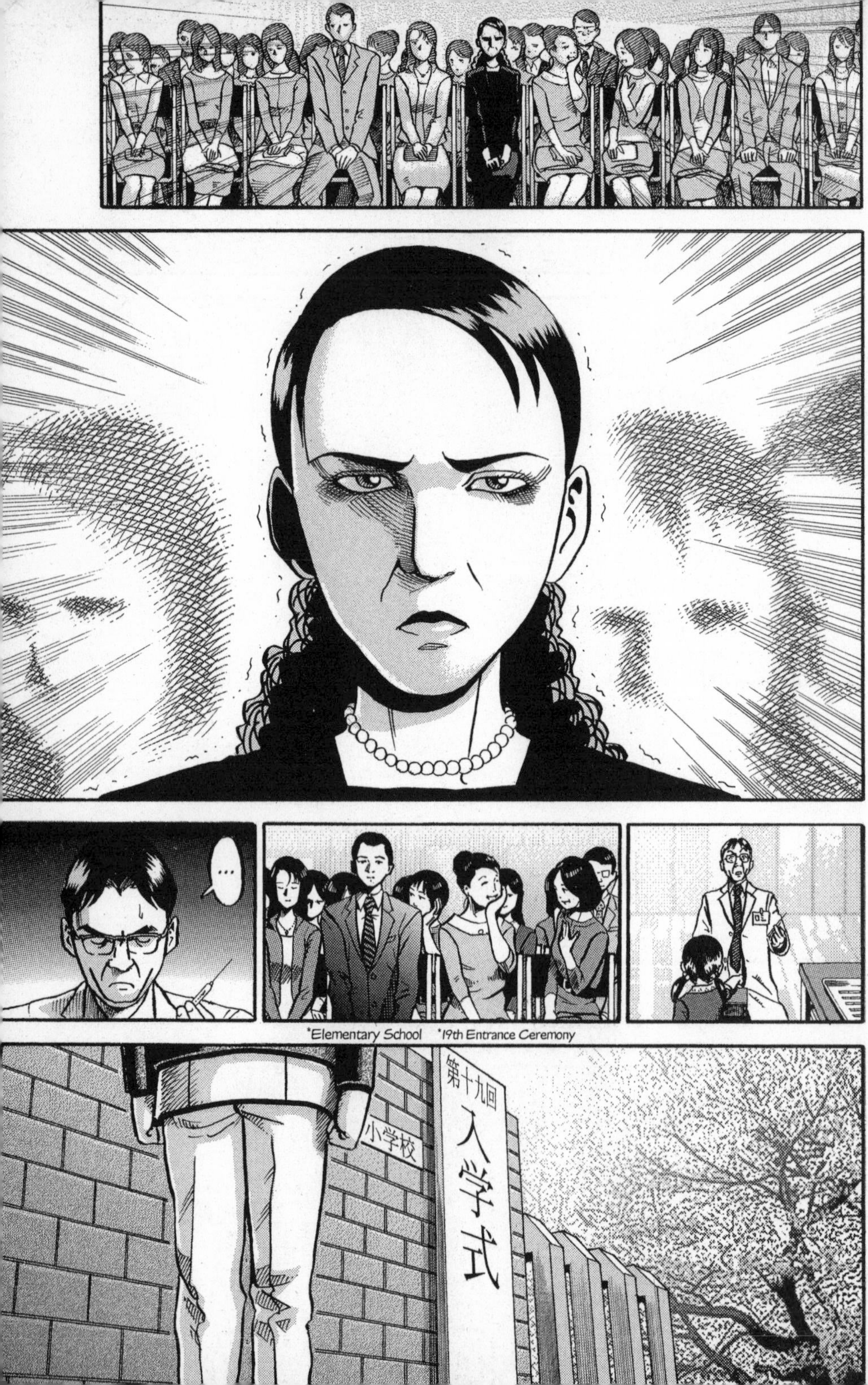
...
*Elementary School *19th Entrance Ceremony
第十九回
入学式
小学校

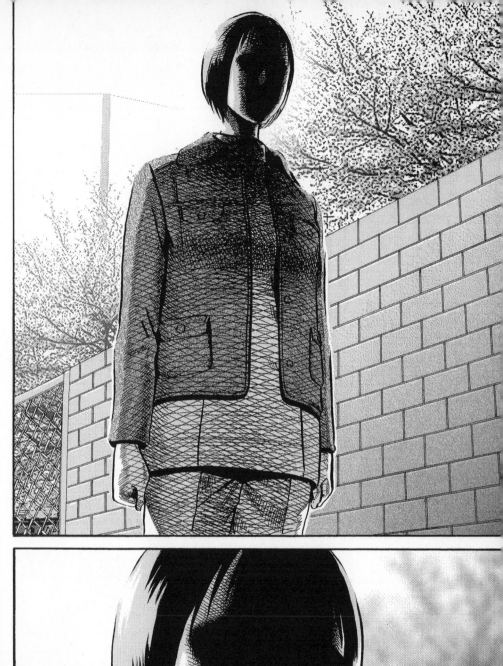
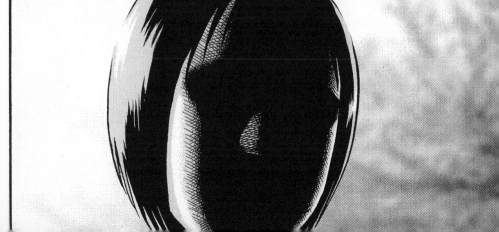

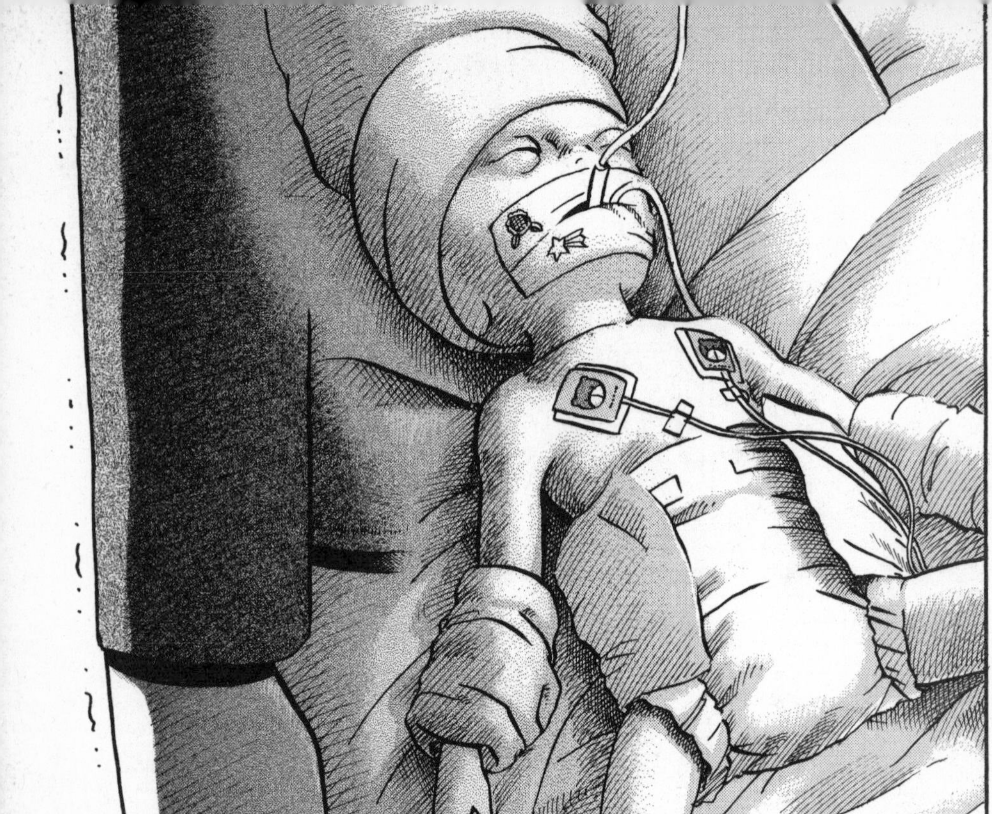

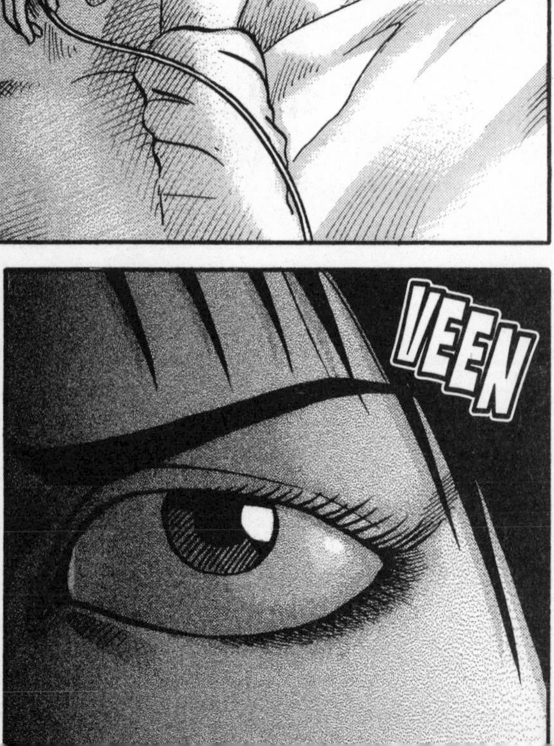
VEEN

*Elementary School *19th Entrance Ceremony

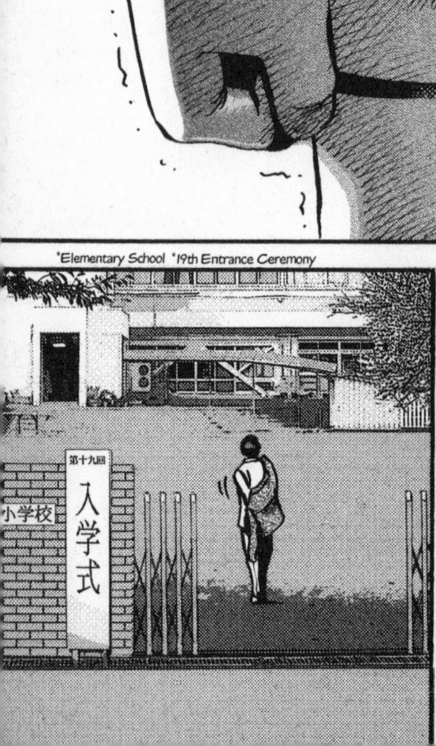
第十九回
入学式
小学校

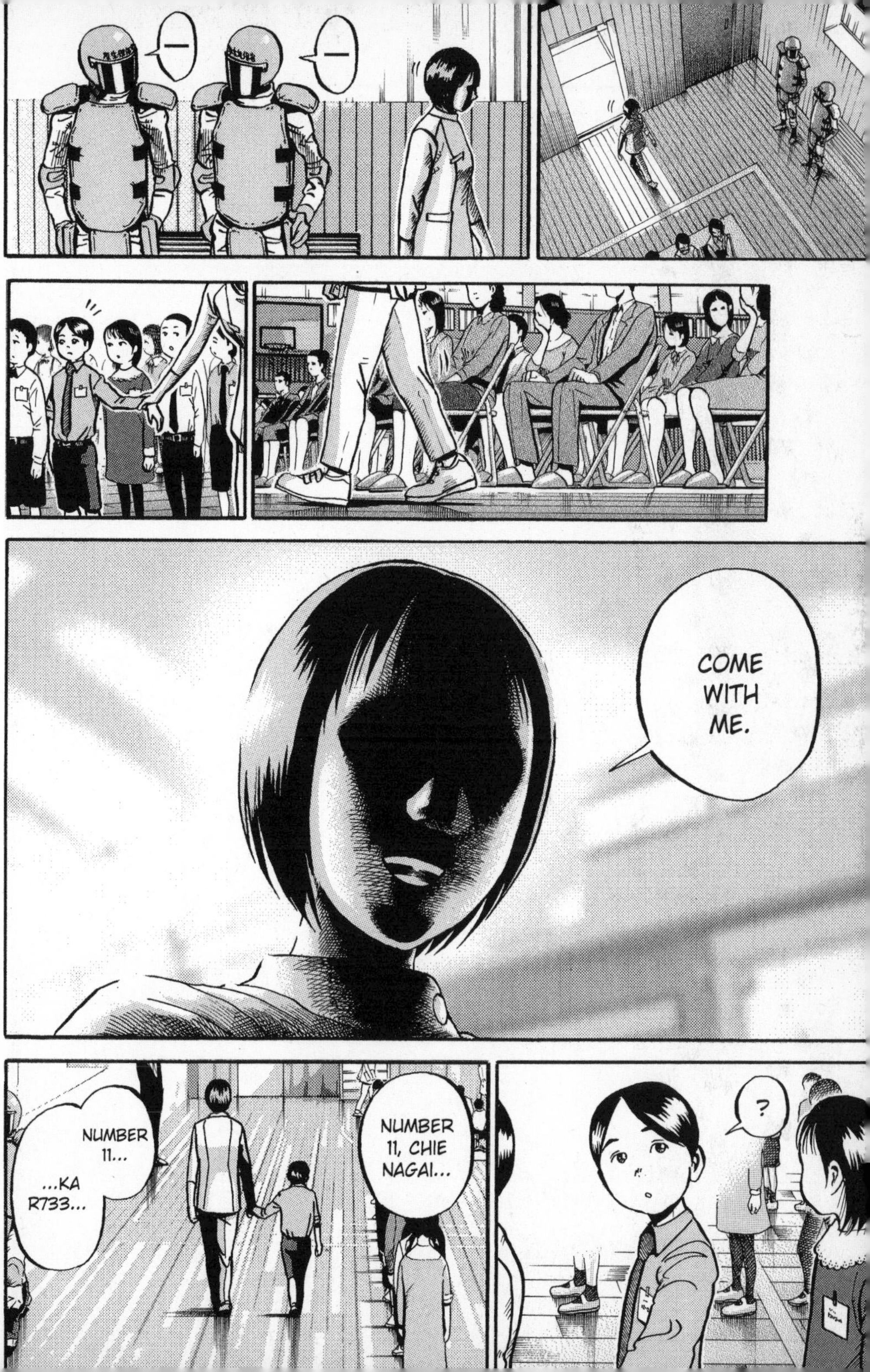
—
—
COME WITH ME.
?
NUMBER 11, CHIE NAGAI...
NUMBER 11...
...KA R733...

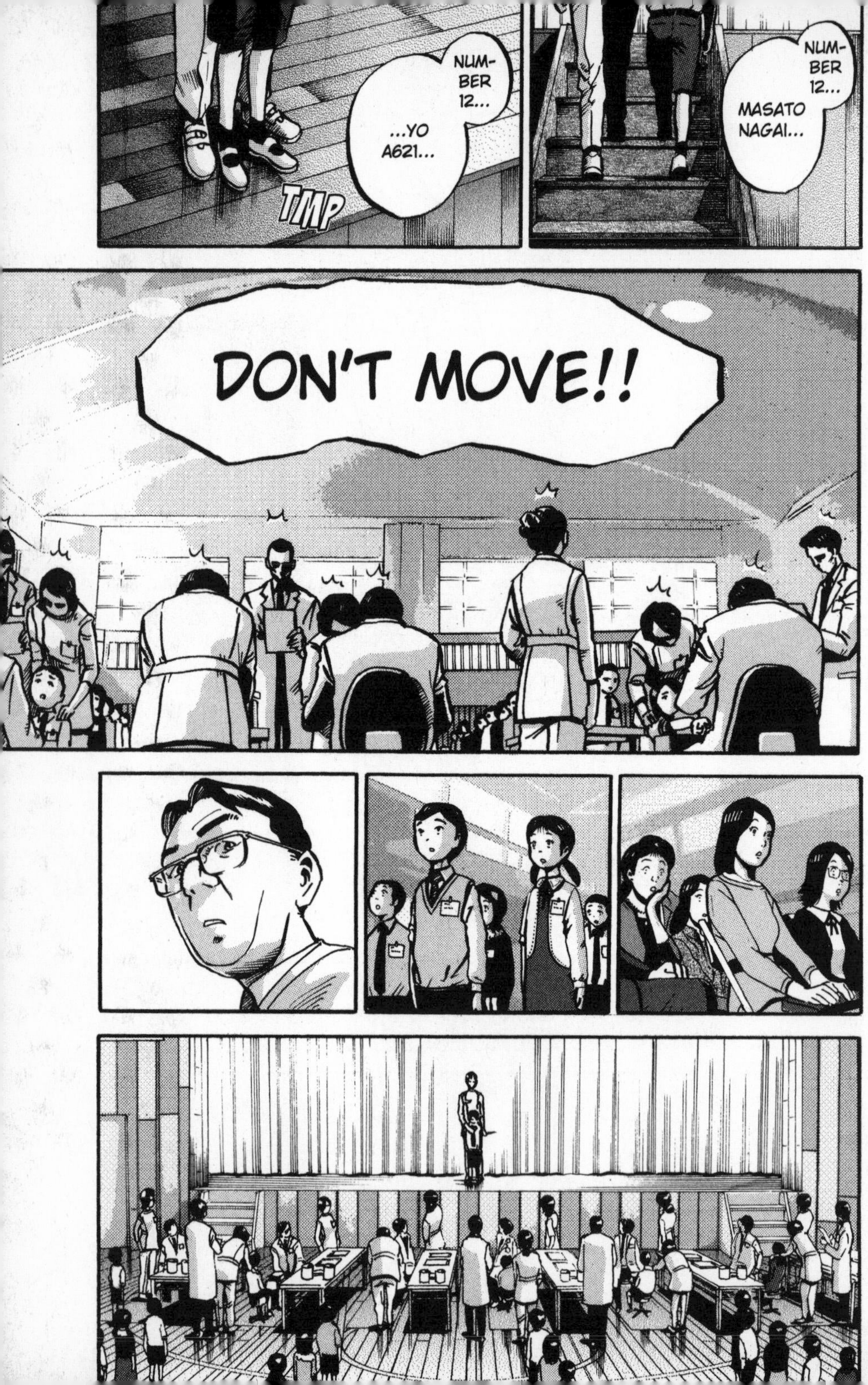
NUMBER 12... MASATO NAGAI...
NUMBER 12... ...YO A621...
TMP
DON'T MOVE!!

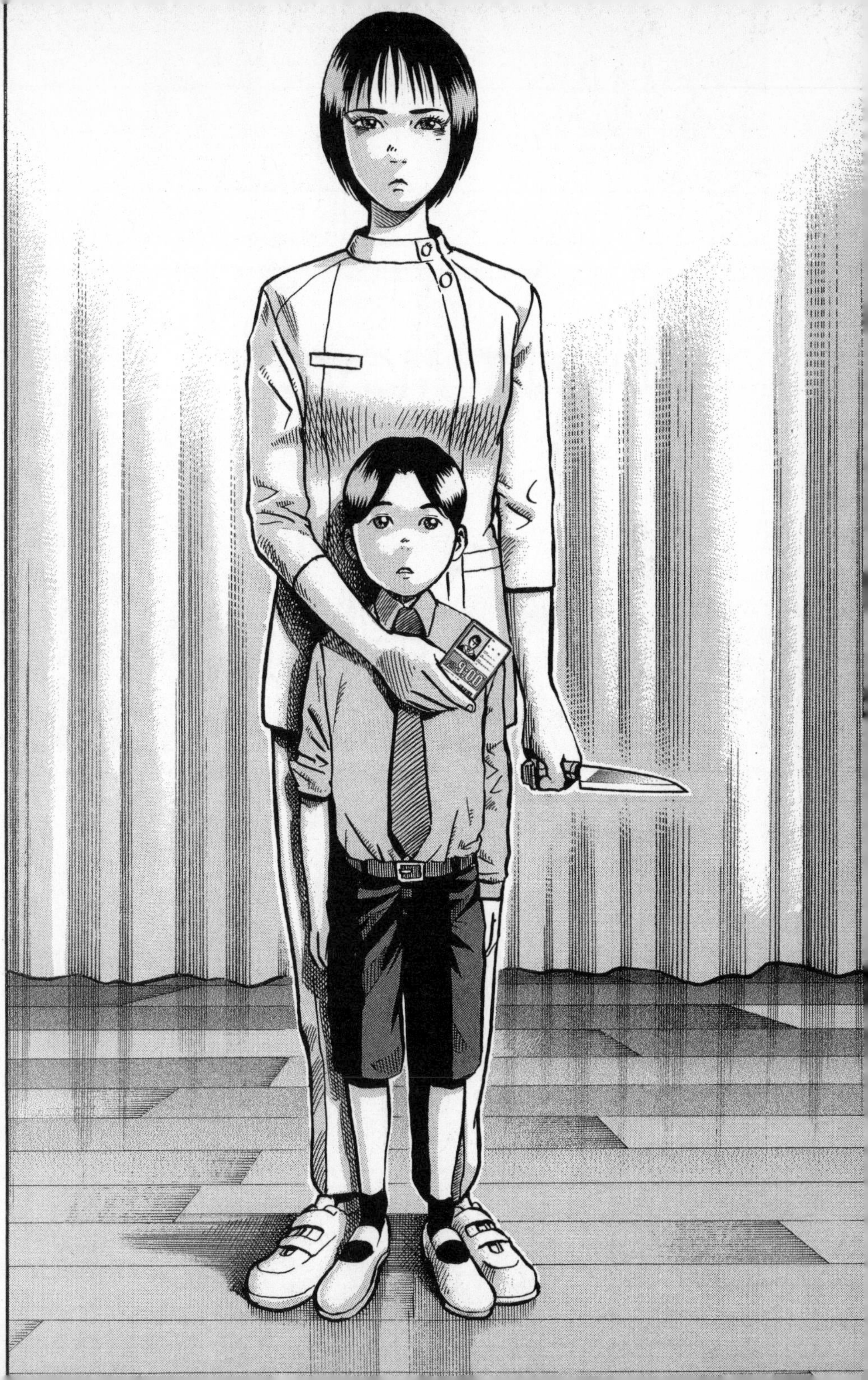

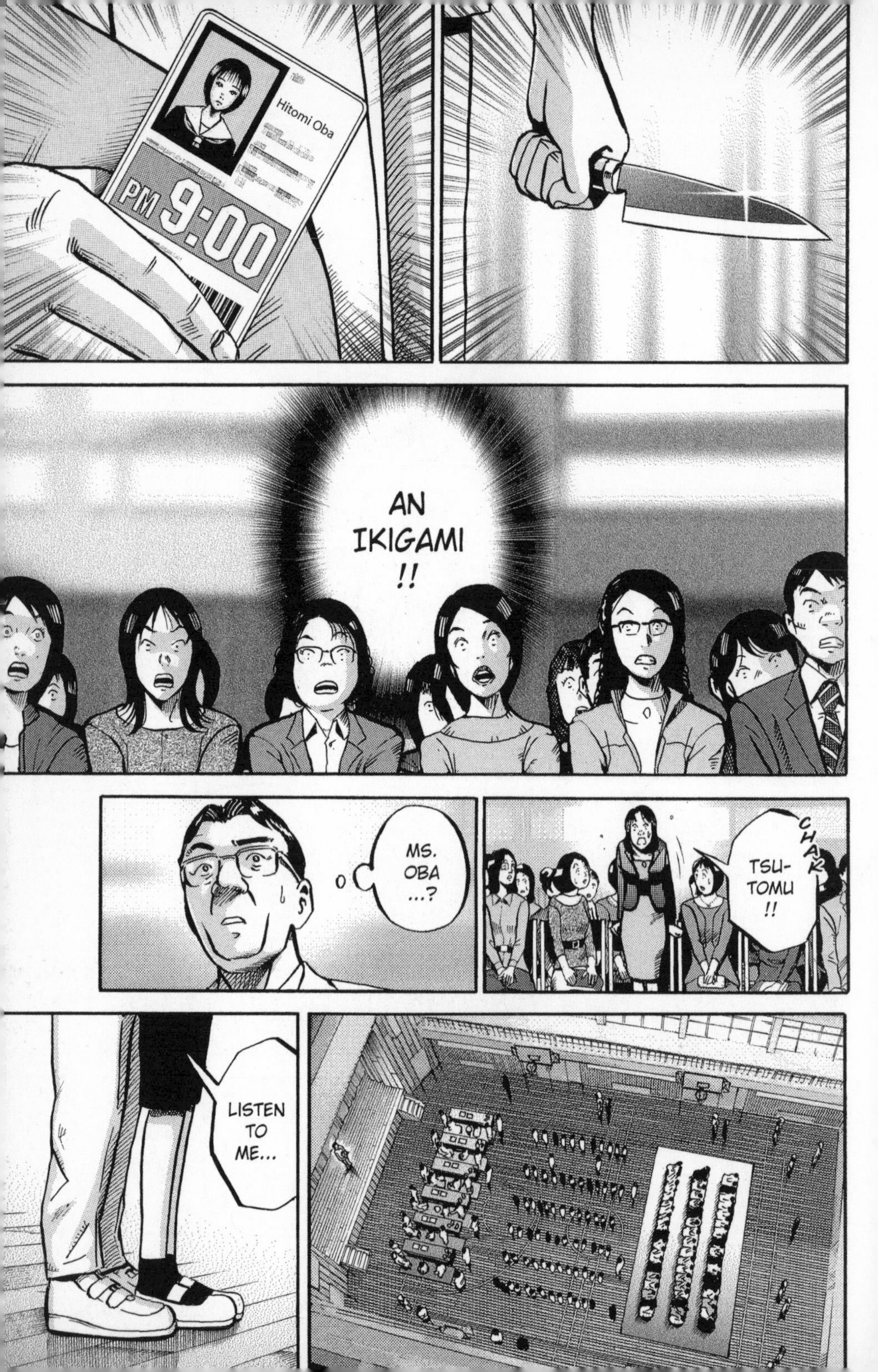
Hitomi Oba
PM 9:00
AN IKIGAMI !!
CHAK
TSU-TOMU !!
MS. OBA ...?
LISTEN TO ME...

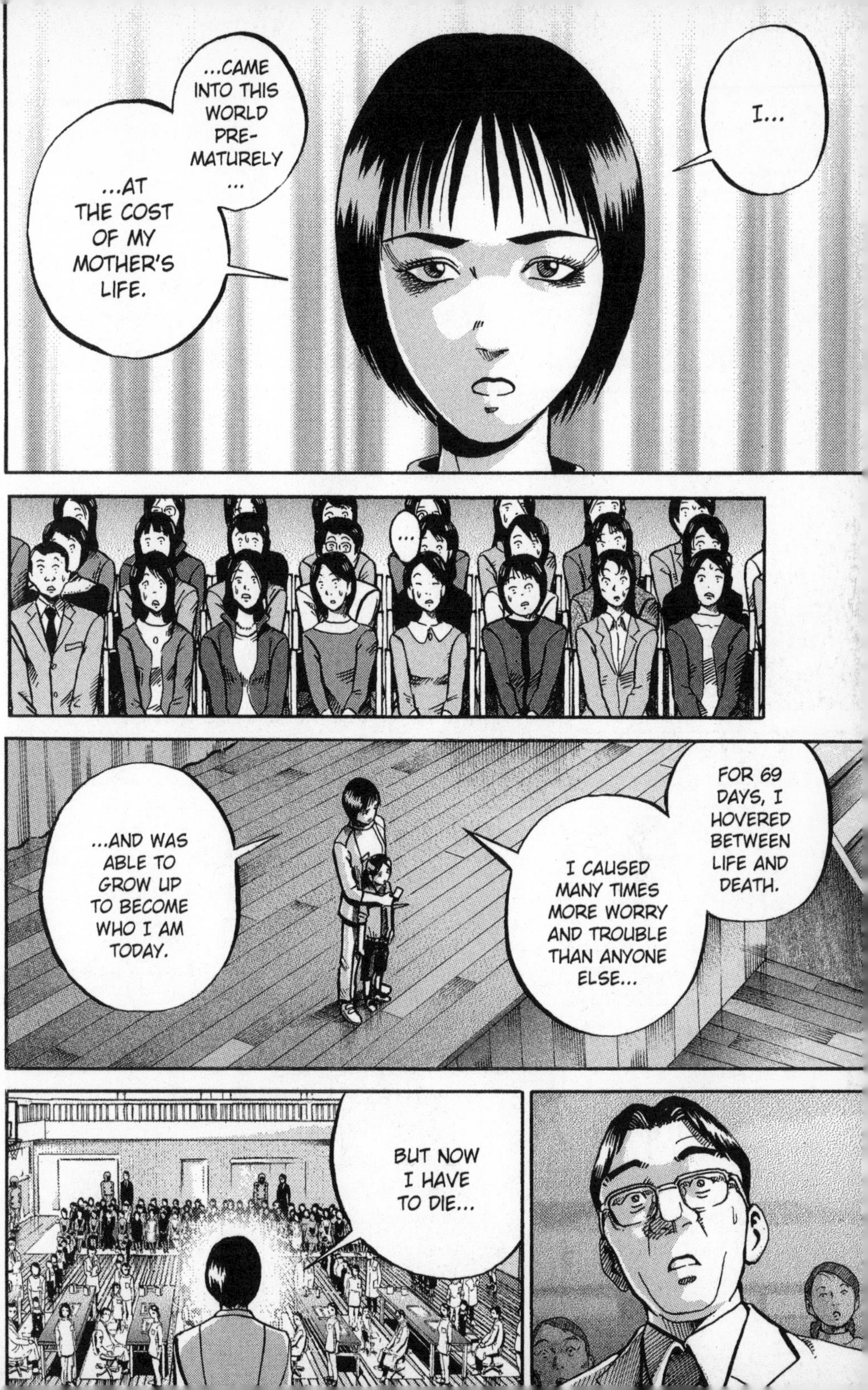
I...
...CAME INTO THIS WORLD PRE-MATURELY ...
...AT THE COST OF MY MOTHER'S LIFE.
...
FOR 69 DAYS, I HOVERED BETWEEN LIFE AND DEATH.
I CAUSED MANY TIMES MORE WORRY AND TROUBLE THAN ANYONE ELSE...
...AND WAS ABLE TO GROW UP TO BECOME WHO I AM TODAY.
BUT NOW I HAVE TO DIE...

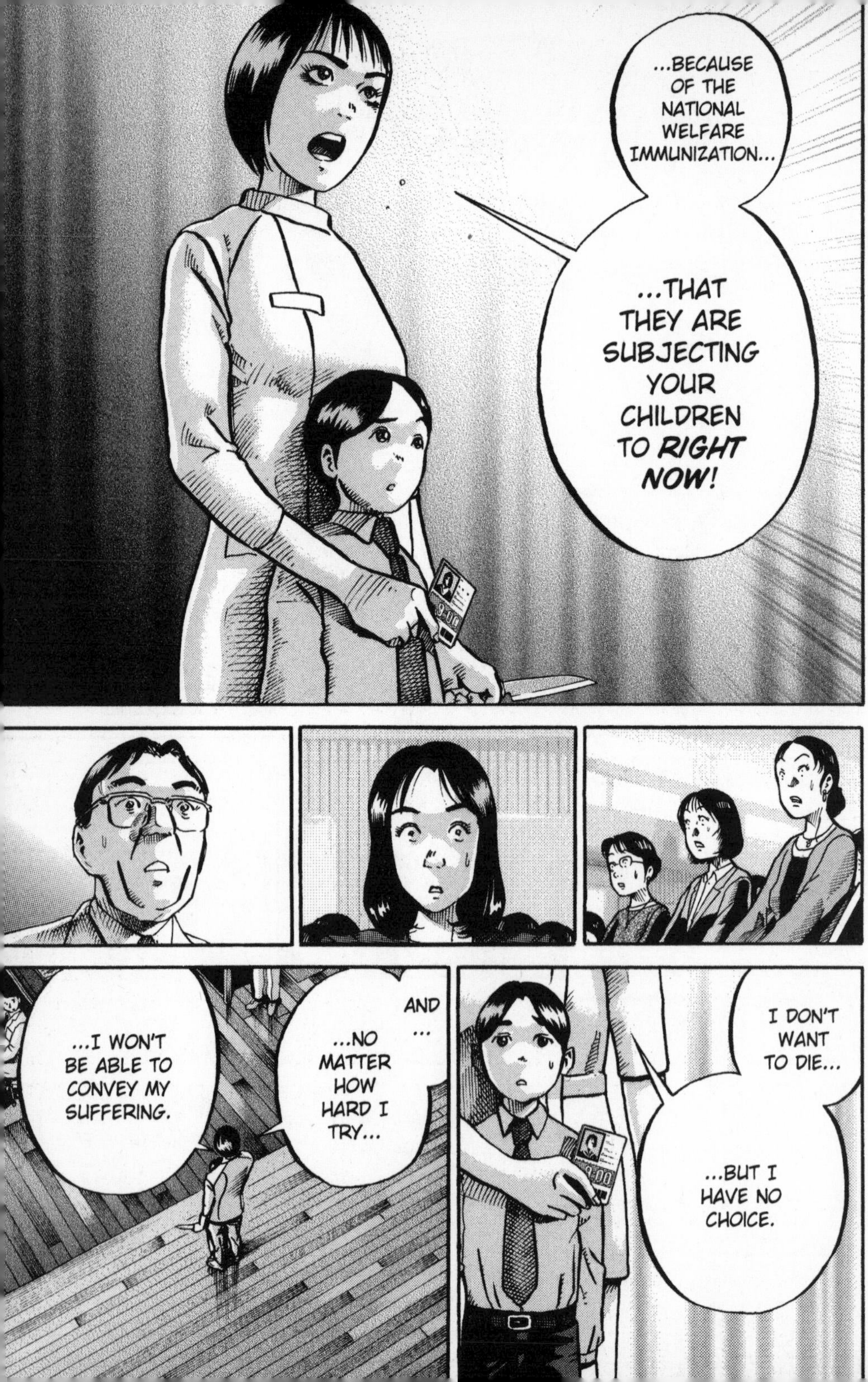
...BECAUSE OF THE NATIONAL WELFARE IMMUNIZATION...
...THAT THEY ARE SUBJECTING YOUR CHILDREN TO *RIGHT NOW*!
I DON'T WANT TO DIE...
...BUT I HAVE NO CHOICE.
AND ...
...NO MATTER HOW HARD I TRY...
...I WON'T BE ABLE TO CONVEY MY SUFFERING.

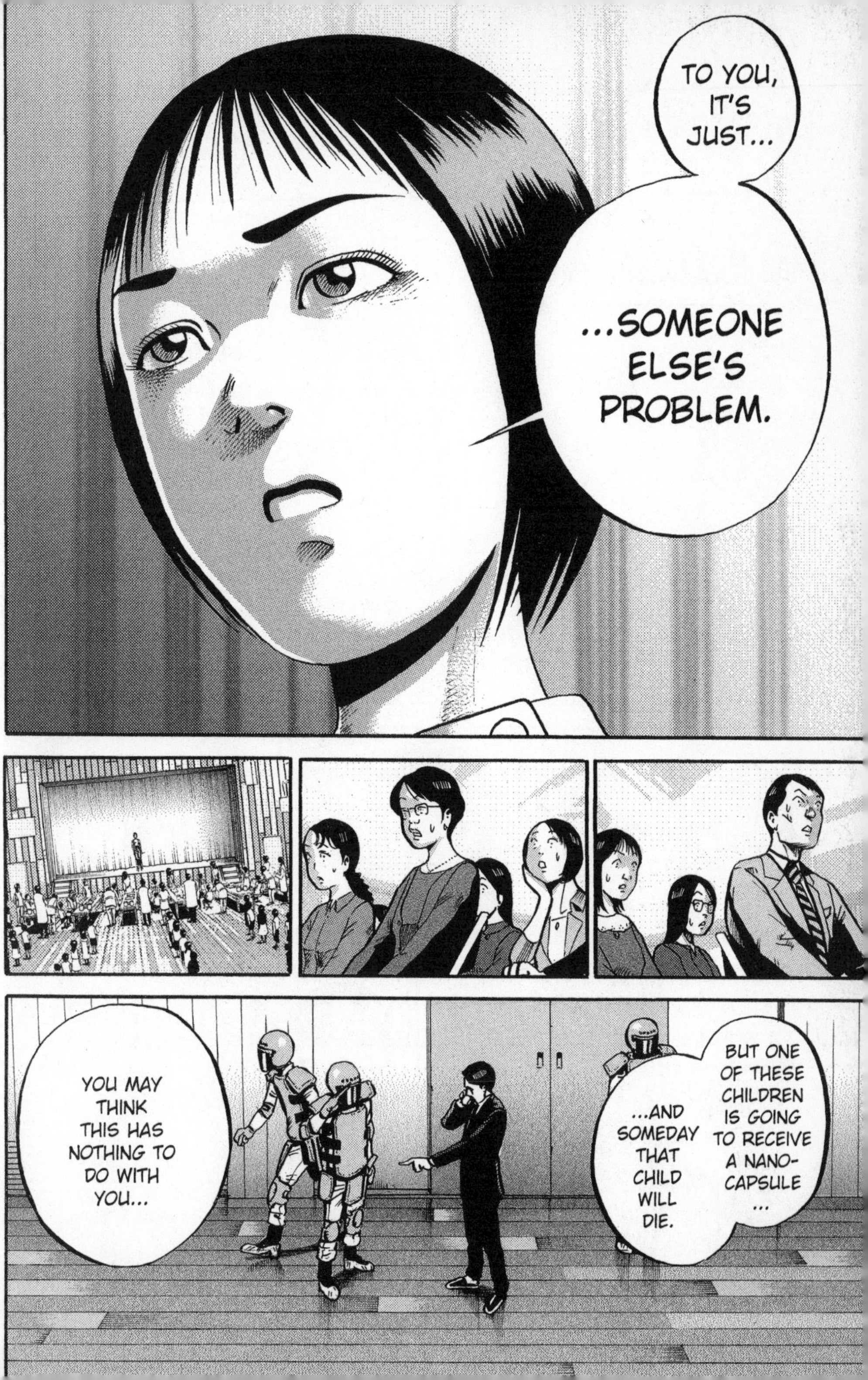
TO YOU, IT'S JUST...
...SOMEONE ELSE'S PROBLEM.
BUT ONE OF THESE CHILDREN IS GOING TO RECEIVE A NANO-CAPSULE ...
...AND SOMEDAY THAT CHILD WILL DIE.
YOU MAY THINK THIS HAS NOTHING TO DO WITH YOU...

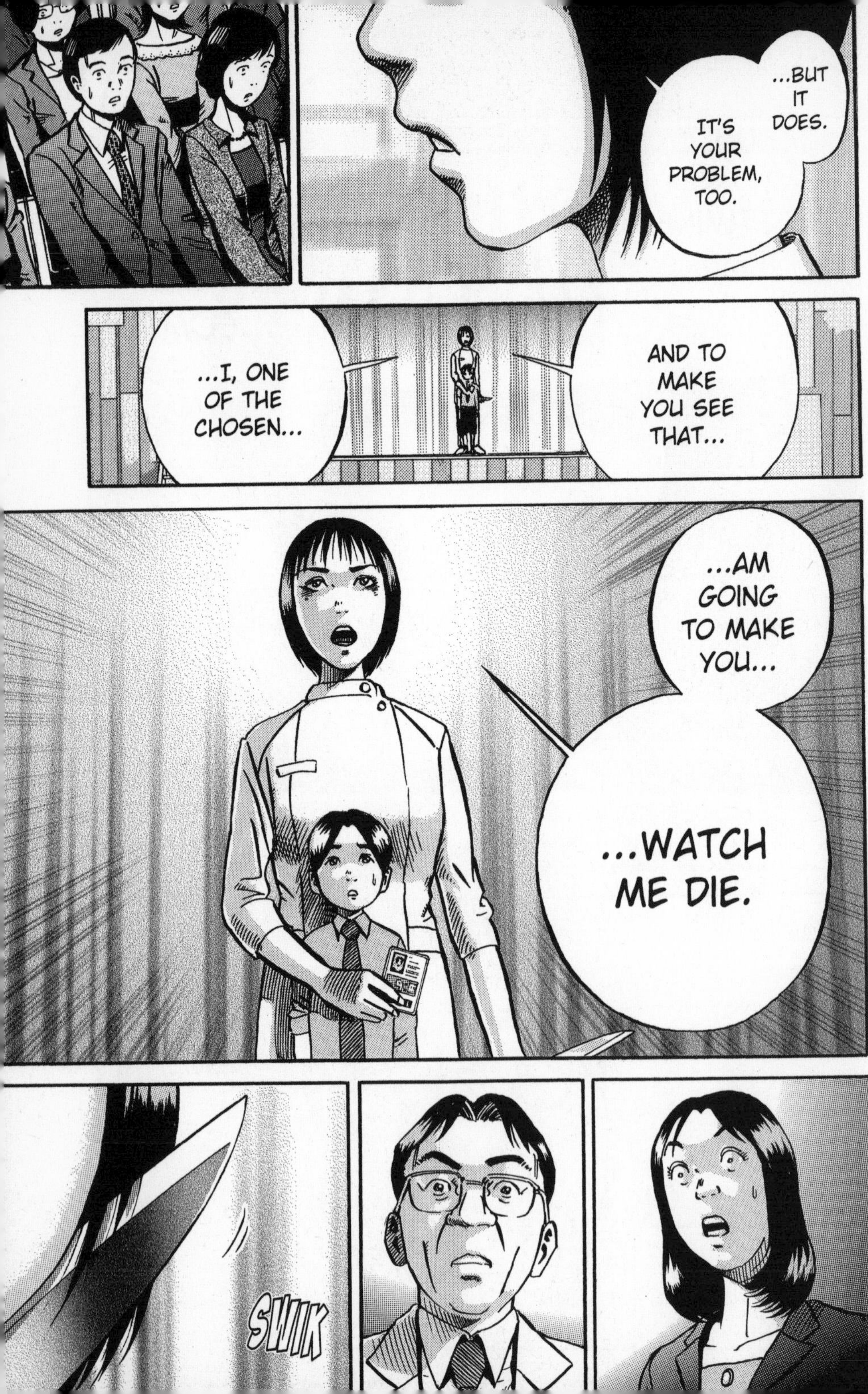
...BUT IT DOES.
IT'S YOUR PROBLEM, TOO.
AND TO MAKE YOU SEE THAT...
...I, ONE OF THE CHOSEN...
...AM GOING TO MAKE YOU...
...WATCH ME DIE.
SWIK

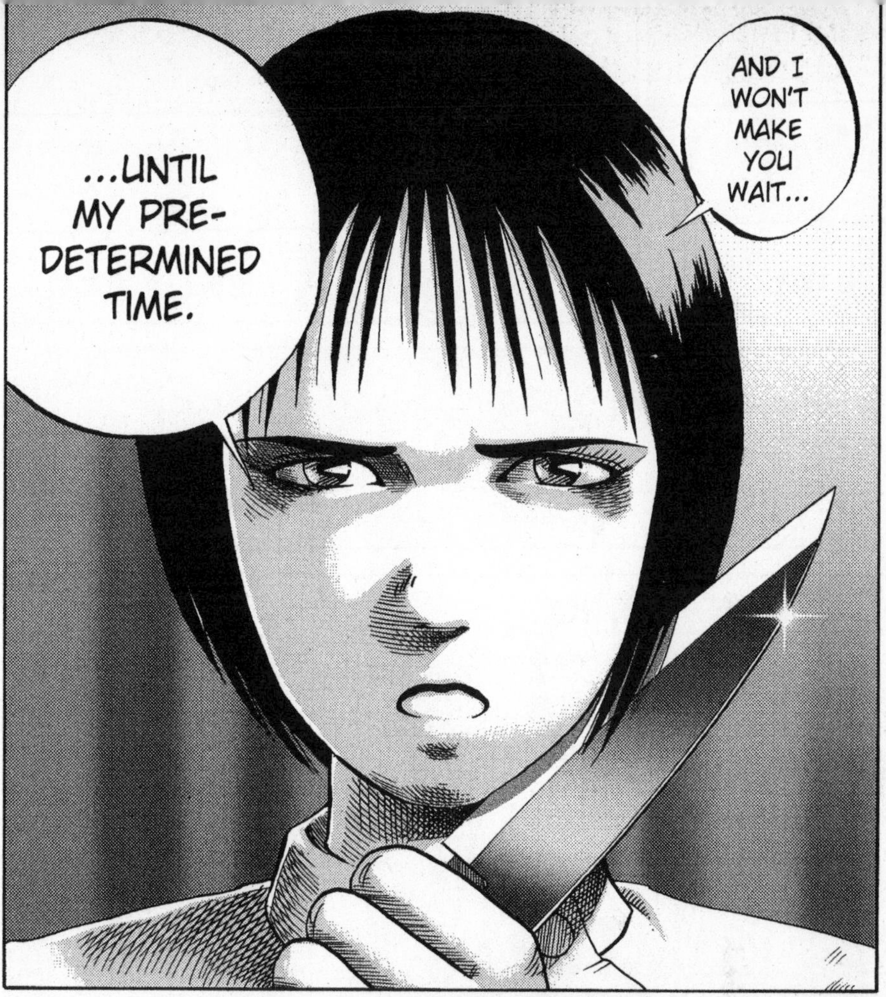
AND I WON'T MAKE YOU WAIT...
...UNTIL MY PRE-DETERMINED TIME.
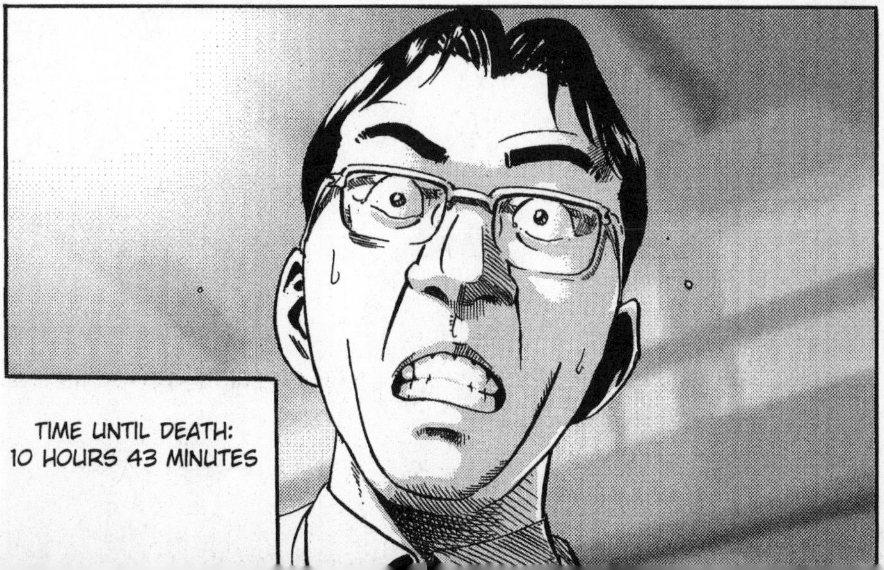
TIME UNTIL DEATH:
10 HOURS 43 MINUTES

Episode 17 National Welfare Immunization Act3

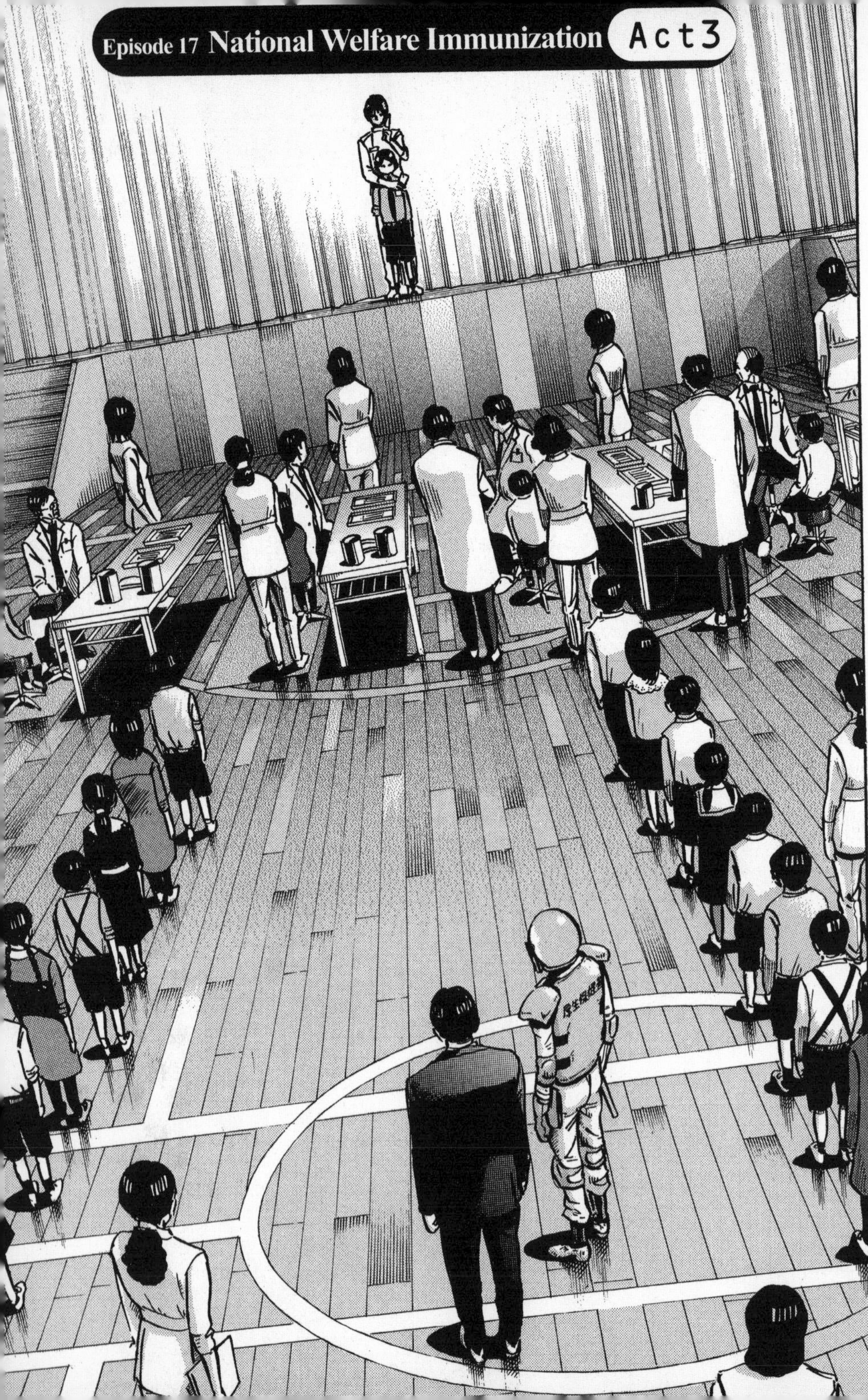

Vests: Ministry of Welfare and Health

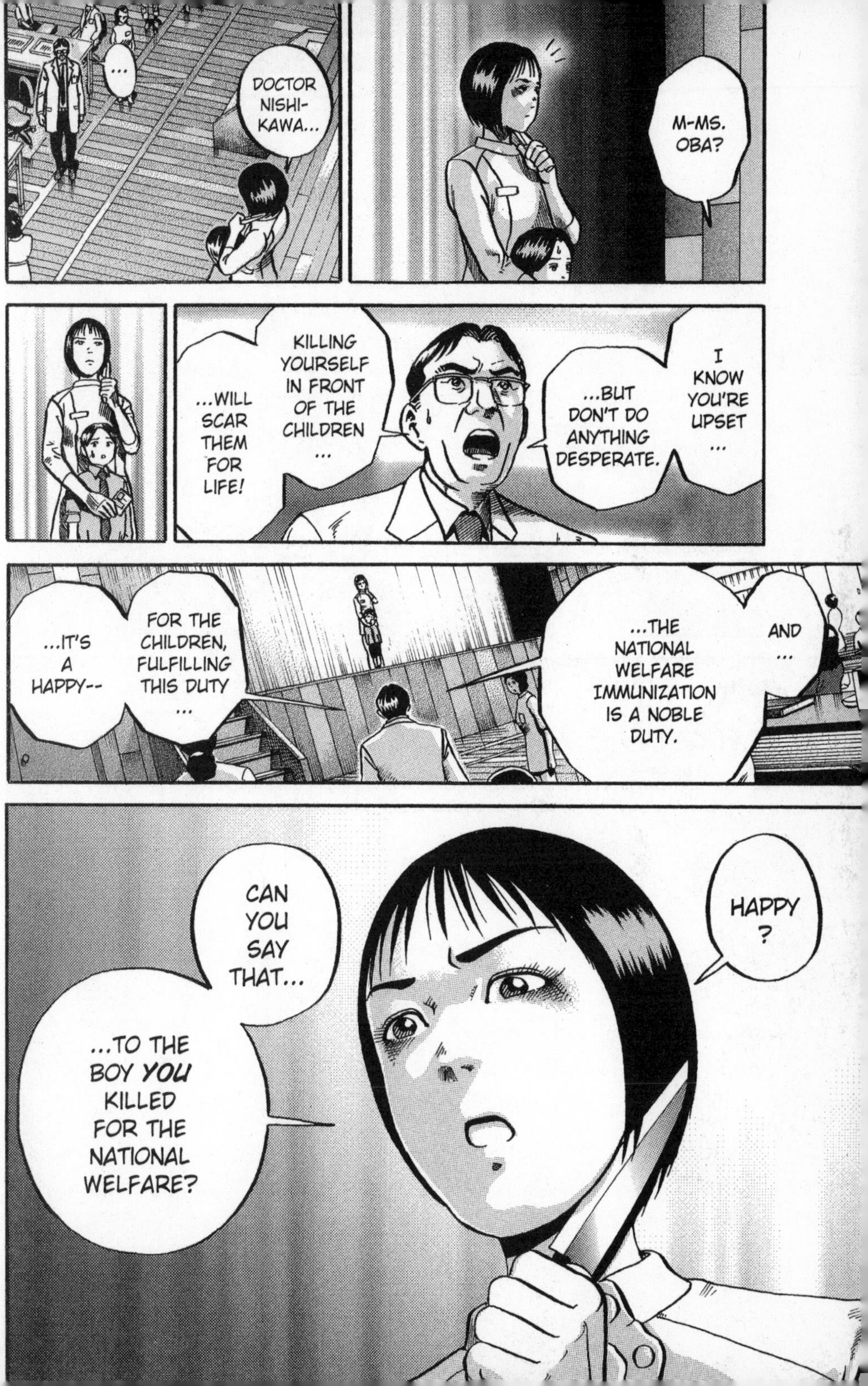
M-MS. OBA?
DOCTOR NISHI-KAWA...
...
I KNOW YOU'RE UPSET ...
...BUT DON'T DO ANYTHING DESPERATE.
KILLING YOURSELF IN FRONT OF THE CHILDREN ...
...WILL SCAR THEM FOR LIFE!
AND ...
...THE NATIONAL WELFARE IMMUNIZATION IS A NOBLE DUTY.
FOR THE CHILDREN, FULFILLING THIS DUTY ...
...IT'S A HAPPY--
HAPPY ?
CAN YOU SAY THAT...
...TO THE BOY *YOU* KILLED FOR THE NATIONAL WELFARE?

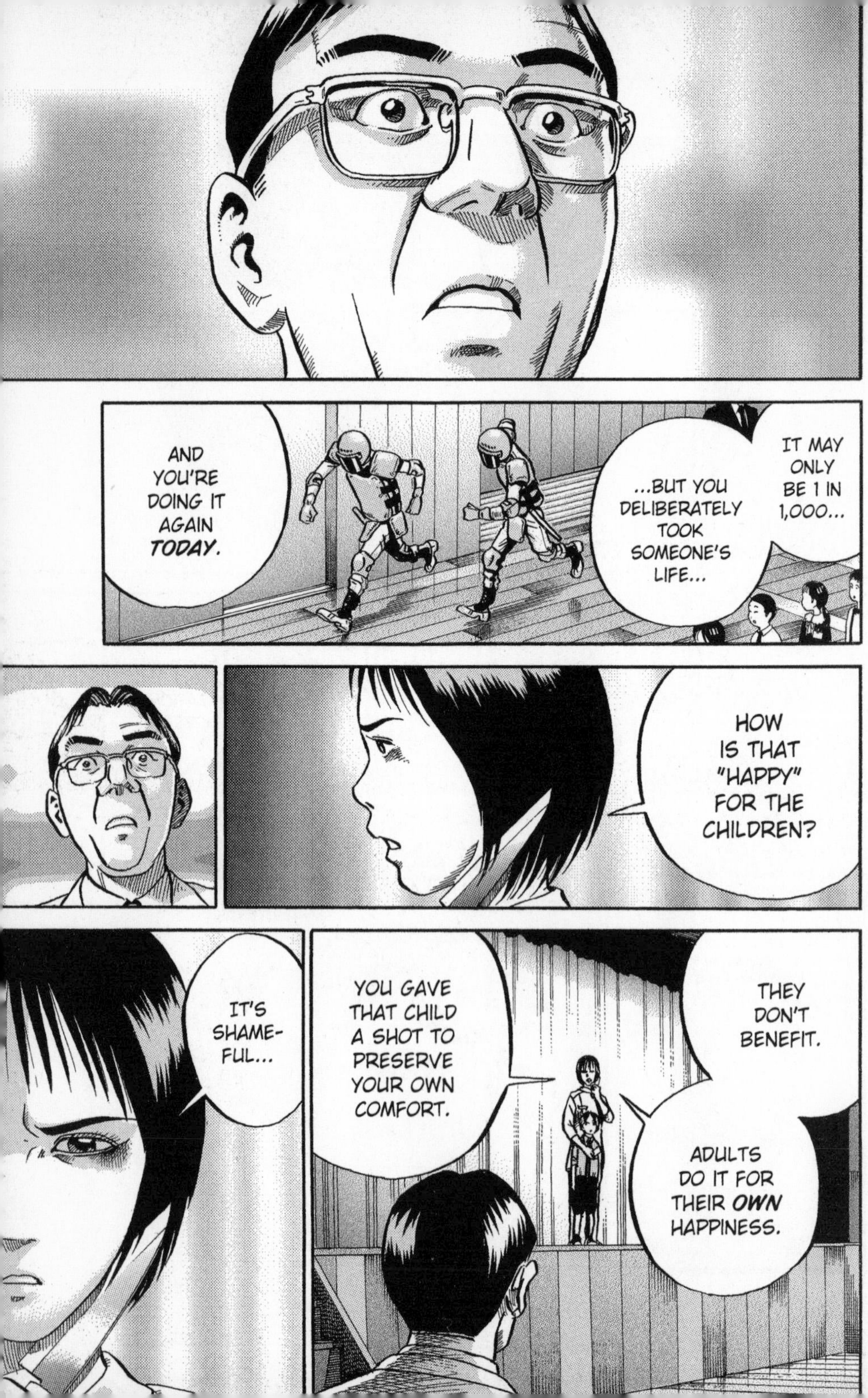
IT MAY ONLY BE 1 IN 1,000...
...BUT YOU DELIBERATELY TOOK SOMEONE'S LIFE...
AND YOU'RE DOING IT AGAIN *TODAY*.
HOW IS THAT "HAPPY" FOR THE CHILDREN?
THEY DON'T BENEFIT.
ADULTS DO IT FOR THEIR *OWN* HAPPINESS.
YOU GAVE THAT CHILD A SHOT TO PRESERVE YOUR OWN COMFORT.
IT'S SHAME-FUL...

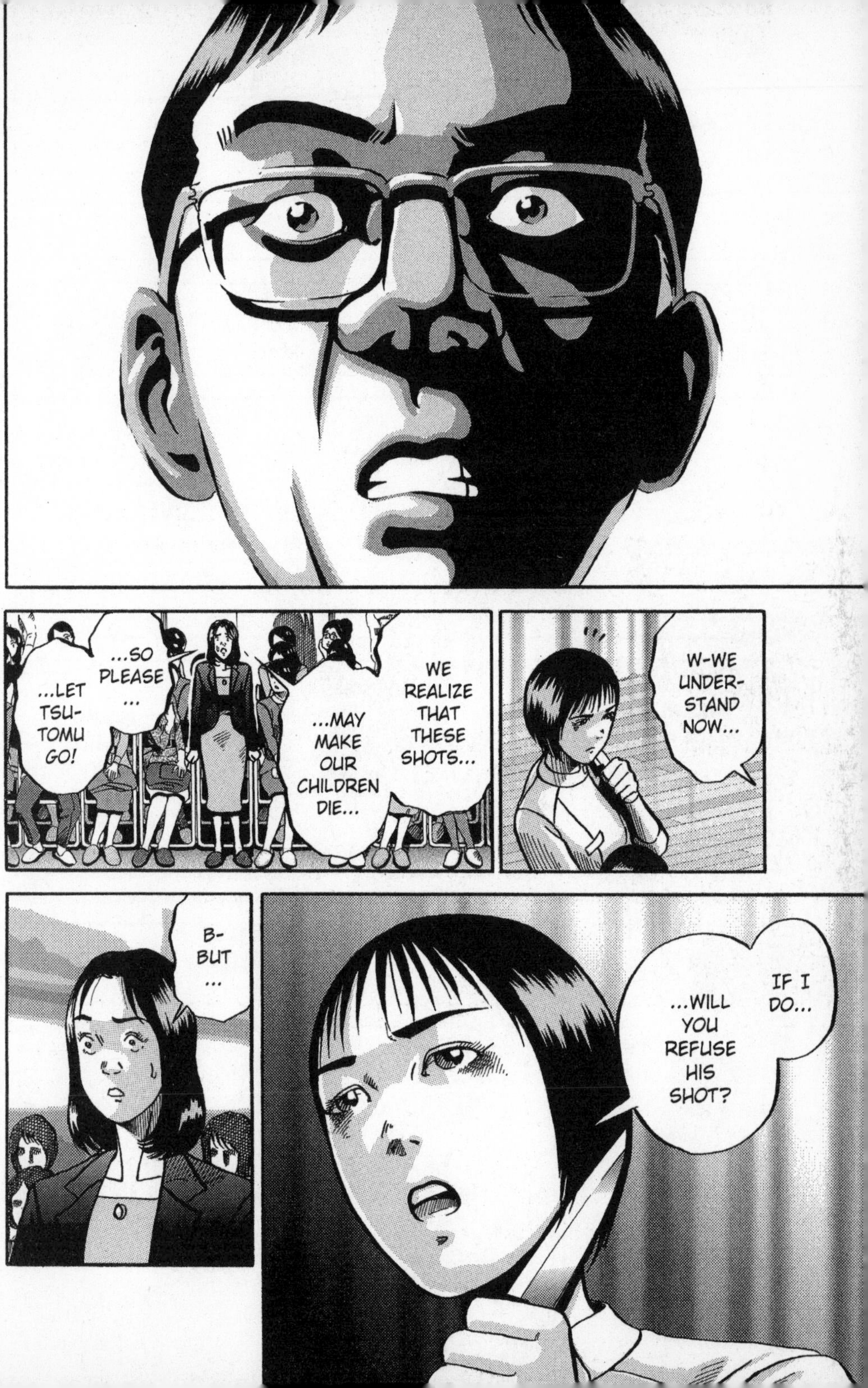
W-WE UNDER-STAND NOW...
WE REALIZE THAT THESE SHOTS...
...MAY MAKE OUR CHILDREN DIE...
...SO PLEASE...
...LET TSU-TOMU GO!
IF I DO...
...WILL YOU REFUSE HIS SHOT?
B-BUT...

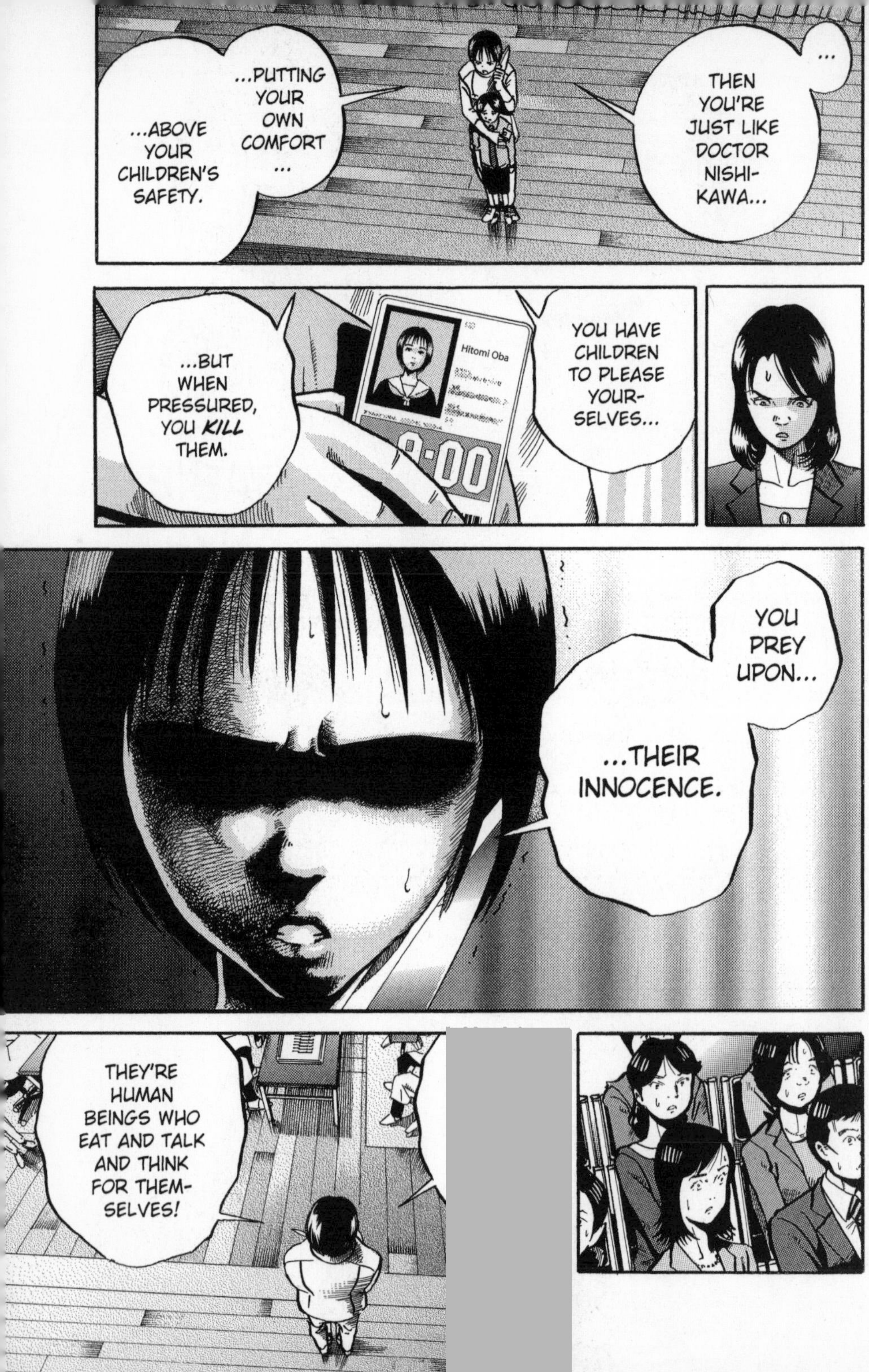
...
THEN YOU'RE JUST LIKE DOCTOR NISHI-KAWA...
...PUTTING YOUR OWN COMFORT...
...ABOVE YOUR CHILDREN'S SAFETY.
YOU HAVE CHILDREN TO PLEASE YOUR-SELVES...
Hitomi Oba
...BUT WHEN PRESSURED, YOU *KILL* THEM.
YOU PREY UPON...
...THEIR INNOCENCE.
THEY'RE HUMAN BEINGS WHO EAT AND TALK AND THINK FOR THEM-SELVES!

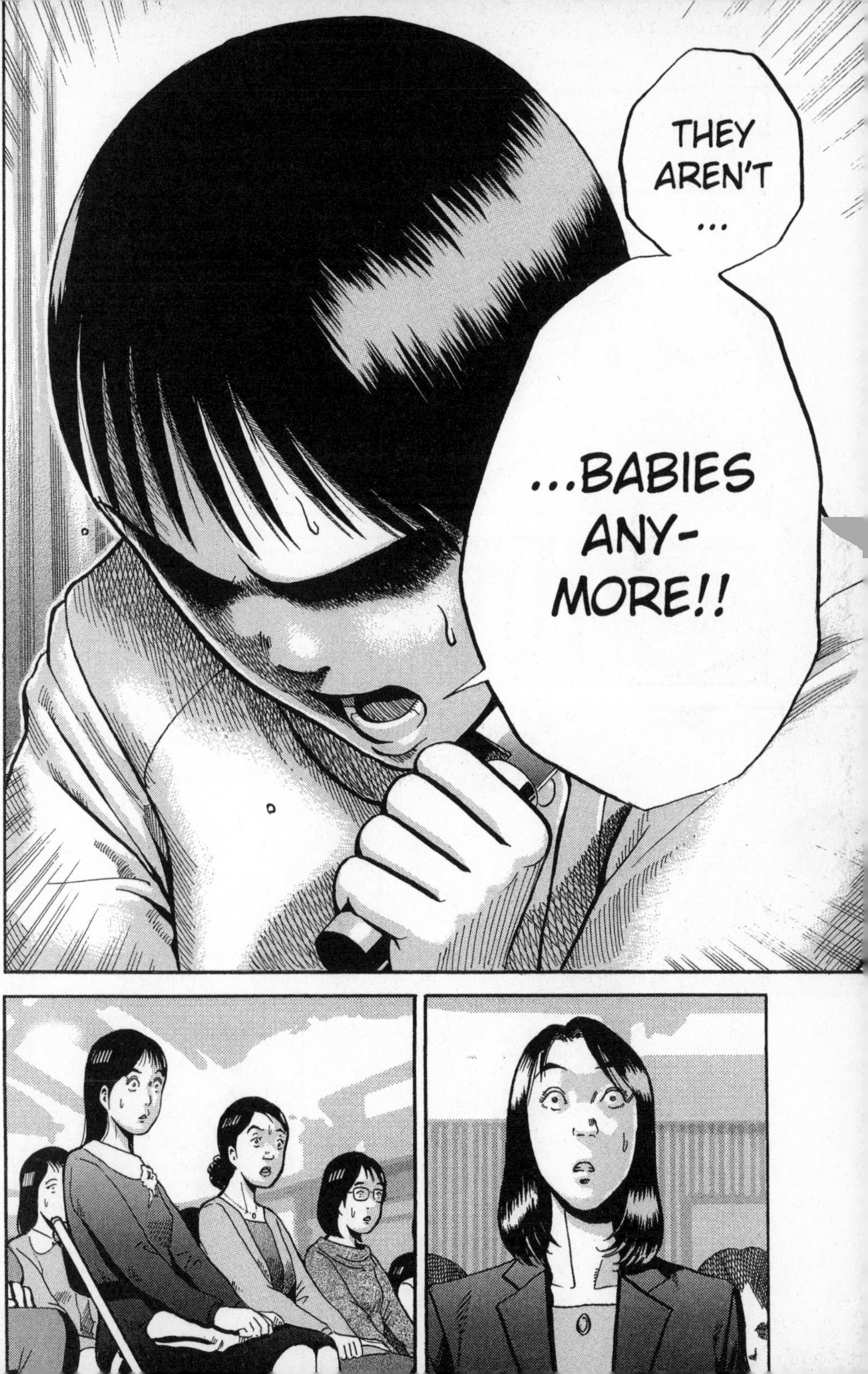
THEY AREN'T ...
...BABIES ANY-MORE!!

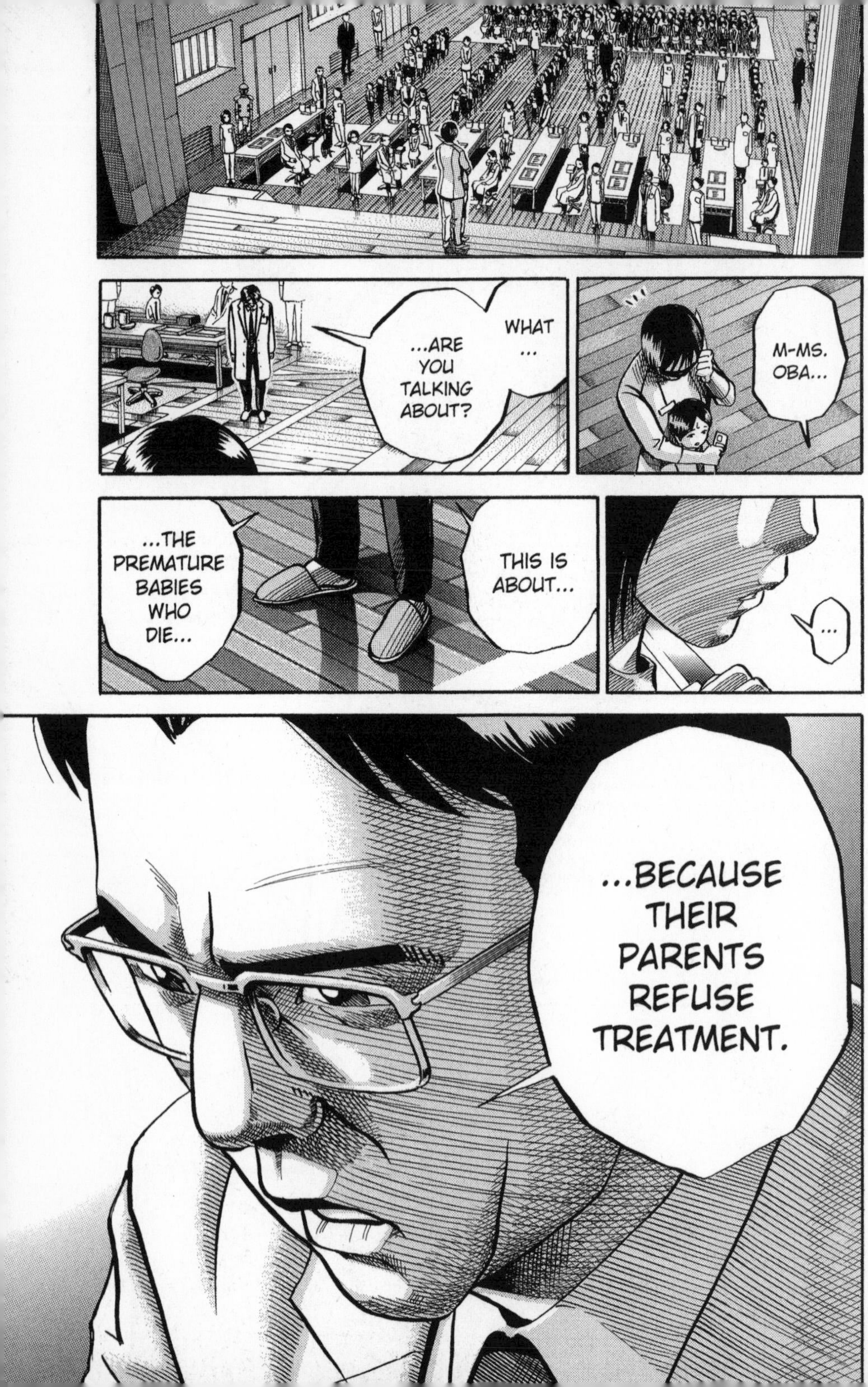
M-MS. OBA...
WHAT... ...ARE YOU TALKING ABOUT?
...
THIS IS ABOUT...
...THE PREMATURE BABIES WHO DIE...
...BECAUSE THEIR PARENTS REFUSE TREATMENT.

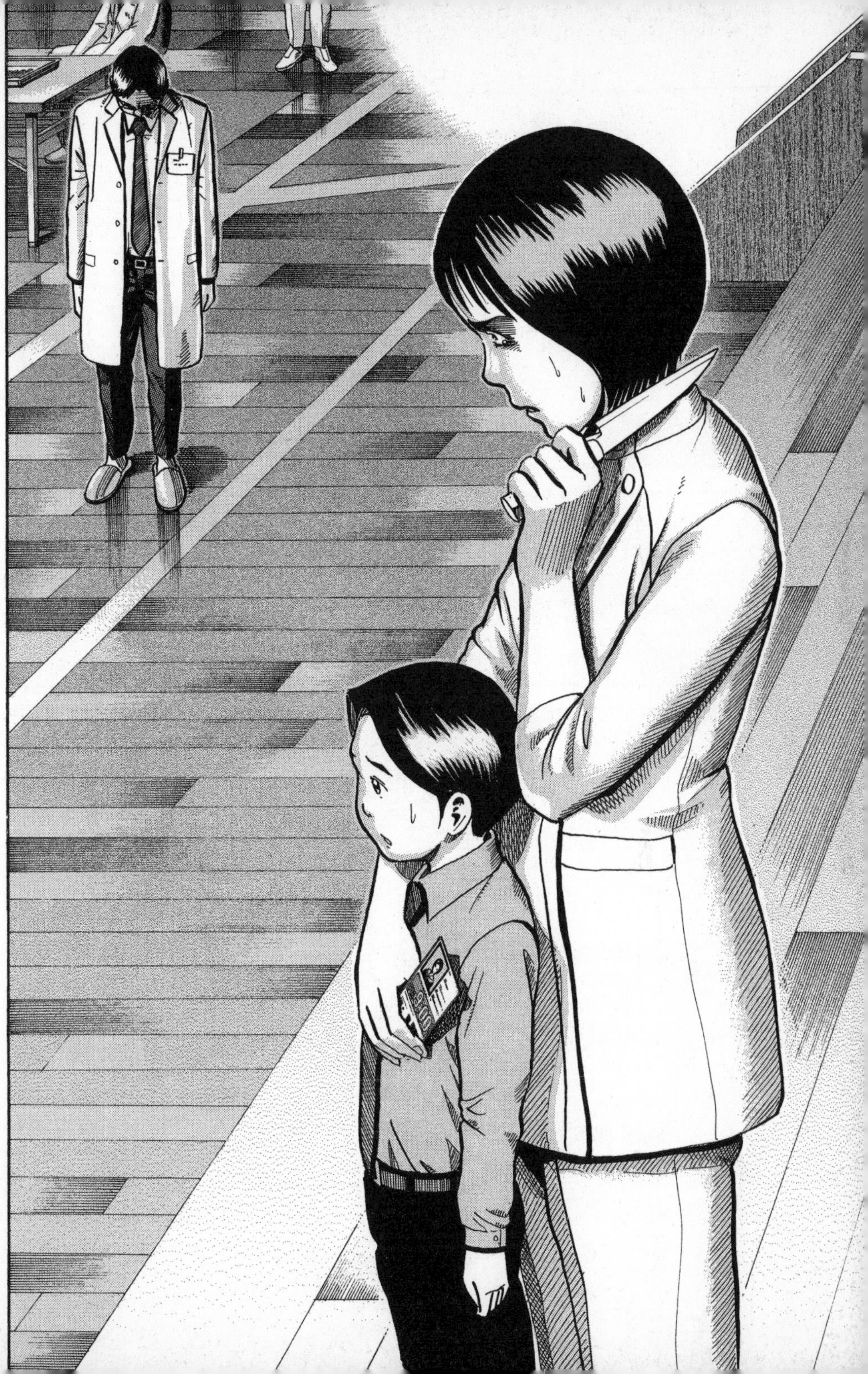

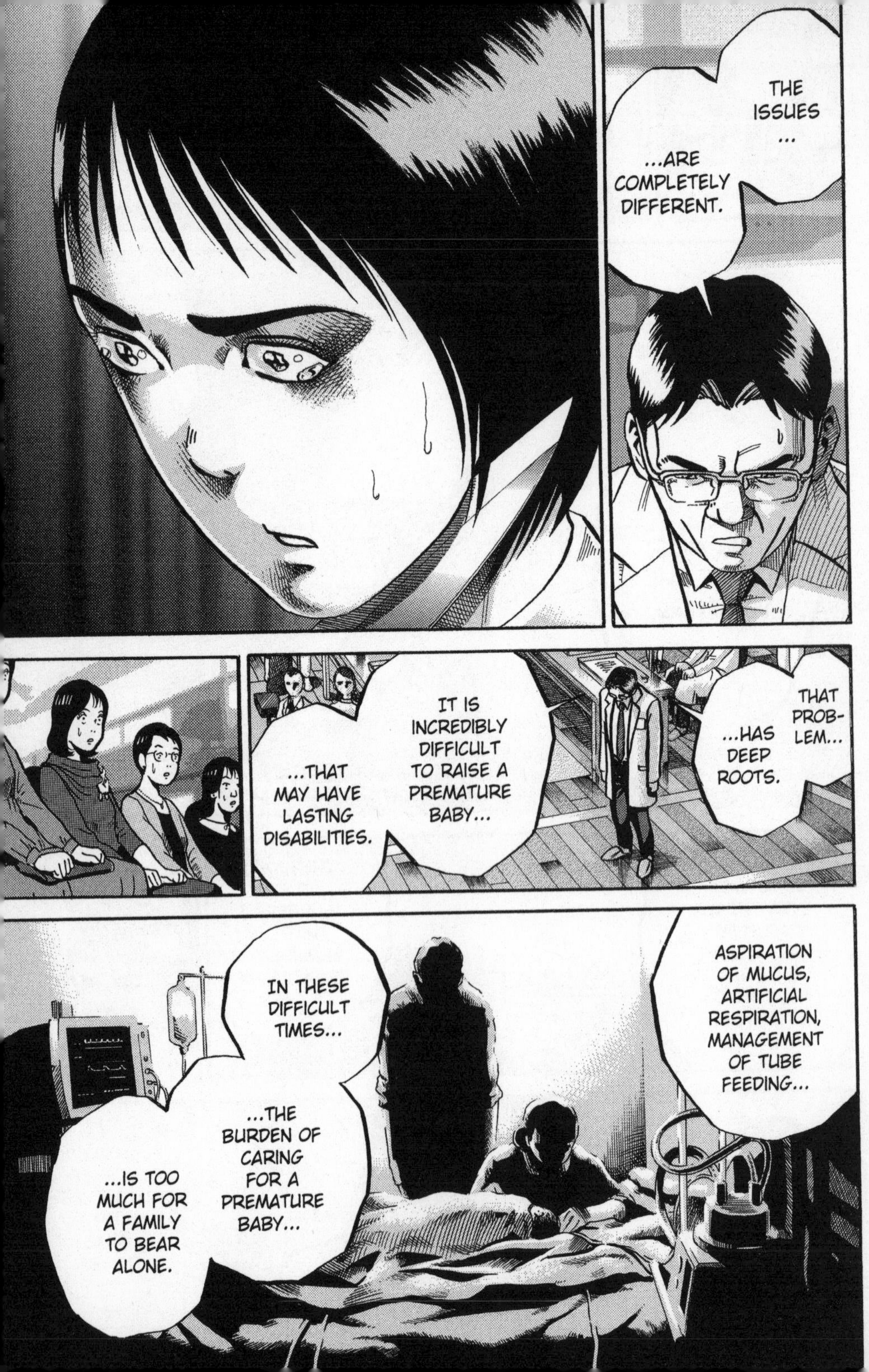
THE ISSUES...
...ARE COMPLETELY DIFFERENT.
THAT PROB-LEM...
...HAS DEEP ROOTS.
IT IS INCREDIBLY DIFFICULT TO RAISE A PREMATURE BABY...
...THAT MAY HAVE LASTING DISABILITIES.
ASPIRATION OF MUCUS, ARTIFICIAL RESPIRATION, MANAGEMENT OF TUBE FEEDING...
IN THESE DIFFICULT TIMES...
...THE BURDEN OF CARING FOR A PREMATURE BABY...
...IS TOO MUCH FOR A FAMILY TO BEAR ALONE.

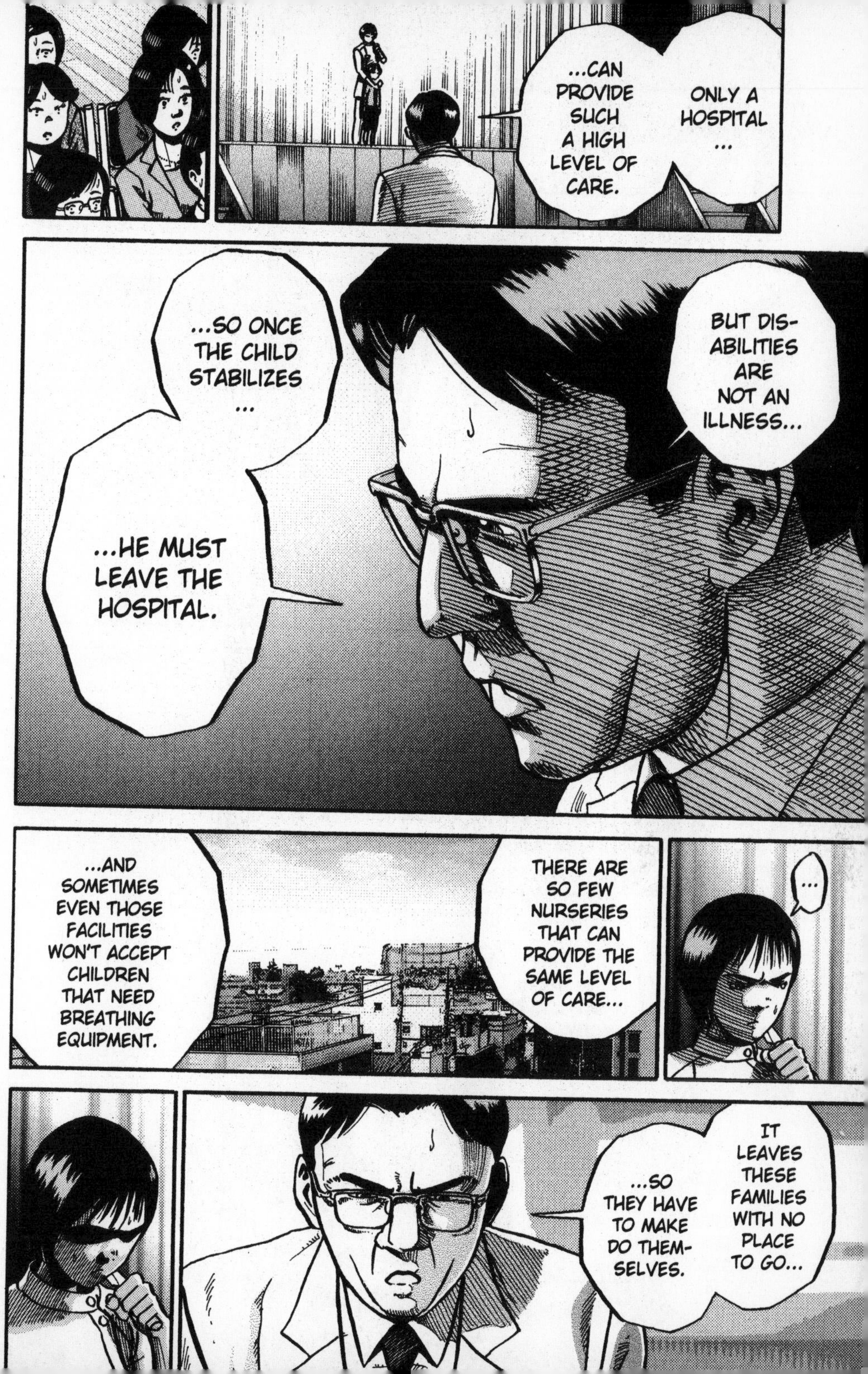
ONLY A HOSPITAL ...
...CAN PROVIDE SUCH A HIGH LEVEL OF CARE.
BUT DIS-ABILITIES ARE NOT AN ILLNESS...
...SO ONCE THE CHILD STABILIZES ...
...HE MUST LEAVE THE HOSPITAL.
...
THERE ARE SO FEW NURSERIES THAT CAN PROVIDE THE SAME LEVEL OF CARE...
...AND SOMETIMES EVEN THOSE FACILITIES WON'T ACCEPT CHILDREN THAT NEED BREATHING EQUIPMENT.
IT LEAVES THESE FAMILIES WITH NO PLACE TO GO...
...SO THEY HAVE TO MAKE DO THEM-SELVES.

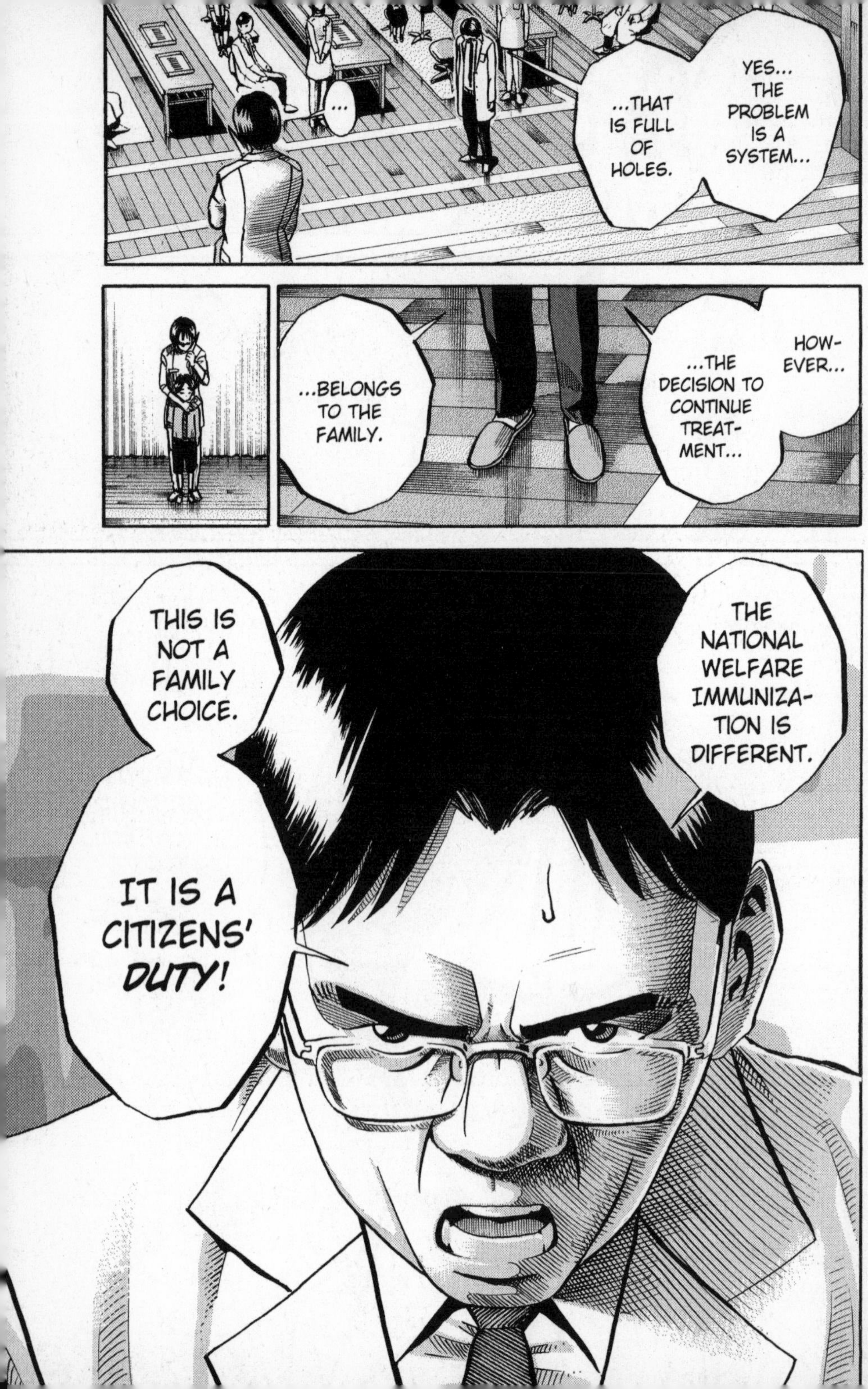
YES... THE PROBLEM IS A SYSTEM...
...THAT IS FULL OF HOLES.
...
HOW-EVER...
...THE DECISION TO CONTINUE TREAT-MENT...
...BELONGS TO THE FAMILY.
THE NATIONAL WELFARE IMMUNIZA-TION IS DIFFERENT.
THIS IS NOT A FAMILY CHOICE.
IT IS A CITIZENS' *DUTY*!

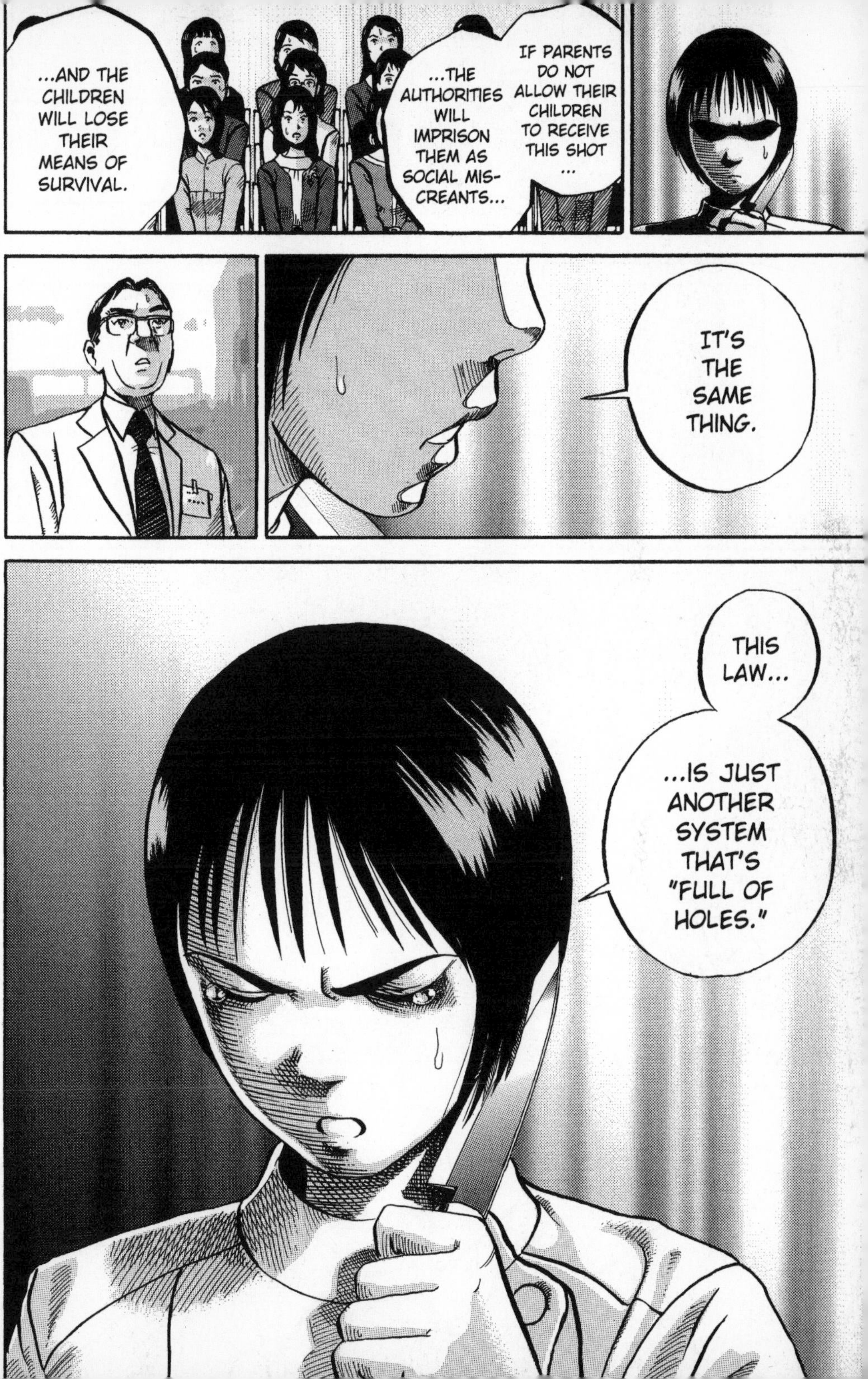
IF PARENTS DO NOT ALLOW THEIR CHILDREN TO RECEIVE THIS SHOT ...
...THE AUTHORITIES WILL IMPRISON THEM AS SOCIAL MIS-CREANTS...
...AND THE CHILDREN WILL LOSE THEIR MEANS OF SURVIVAL.
IT'S THE SAME THING.
THIS LAW...
...IS JUST ANOTHER SYSTEM THAT'S "FULL OF HOLES."

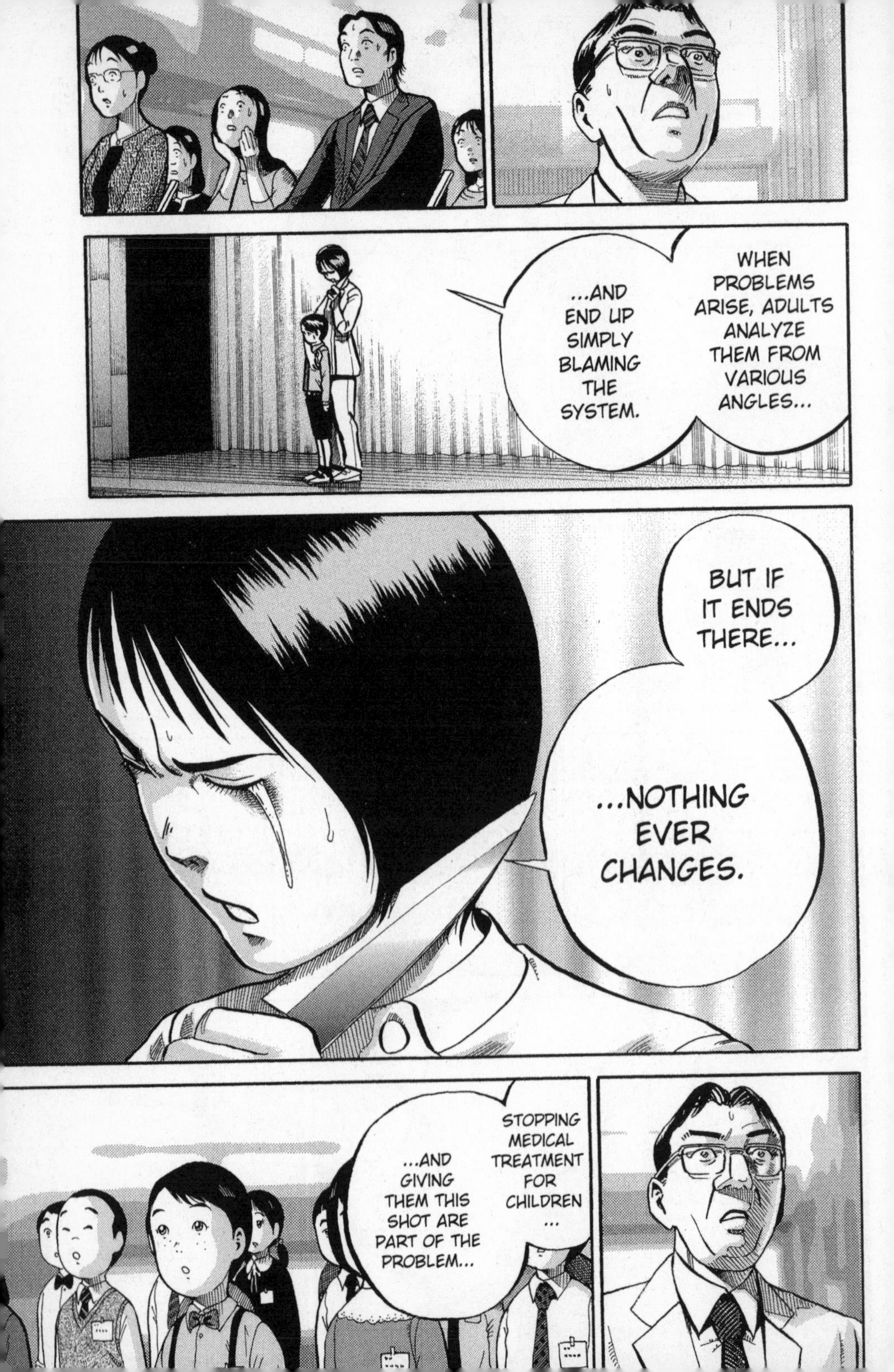
WHEN PROBLEMS ARISE, ADULTS ANALYZE THEM FROM VARIOUS ANGLES...
...AND END UP SIMPLY BLAMING THE SYSTEM.
BUT IF IT ENDS THERE...
...NOTHING EVER CHANGES.
STOPPING MEDICAL TREATMENT FOR CHILDREN ...
...AND GIVING THEM THIS SHOT ARE PART OF THE PROBLEM...

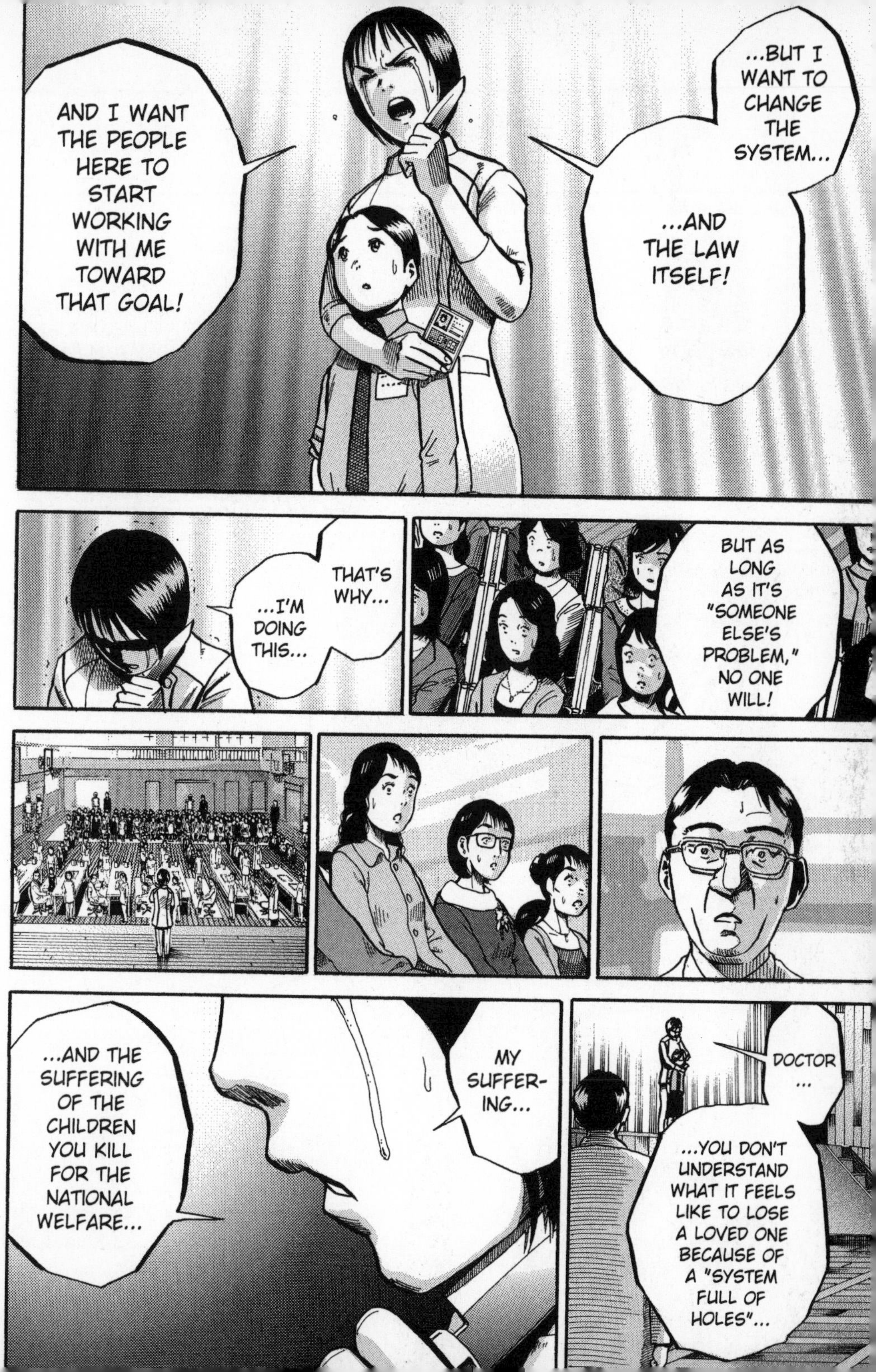
...BUT I WANT TO CHANGE THE SYSTEM...
...AND THE LAW ITSELF!
AND I WANT THE PEOPLE HERE TO START WORKING WITH ME TOWARD THAT GOAL!
BUT AS LONG AS IT'S "SOMEONE ELSE'S PROBLEM," NO ONE WILL!
THAT'S WHY...
...I'M DOING THIS...
DOCTOR...
...YOU DON'T UNDERSTAND WHAT IT FEELS LIKE TO LOSE A LOVED ONE BECAUSE OF A "SYSTEM FULL OF HOLES"...
MY SUFFER-ING...
...AND THE SUFFERING OF THE CHILDREN YOU KILL FOR THE NATIONAL WELFARE...

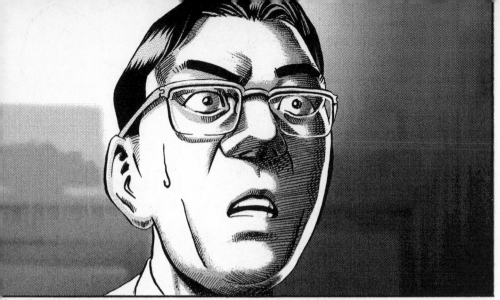

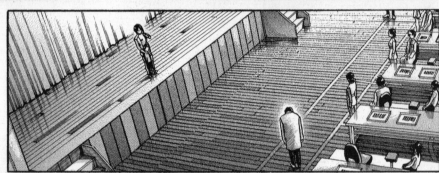

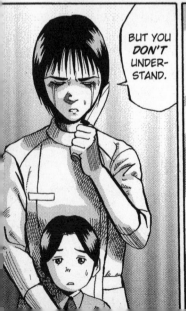

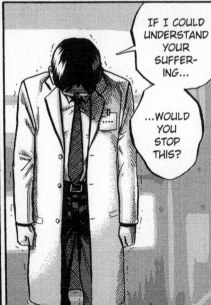

!
IF I COULD UNDERSTAND YOUR SUFFER-ING...
...WOULD YOU STOP THIS?
BUT YOU *DON'T* UNDER-STAND.

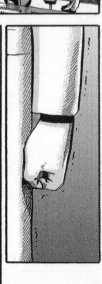

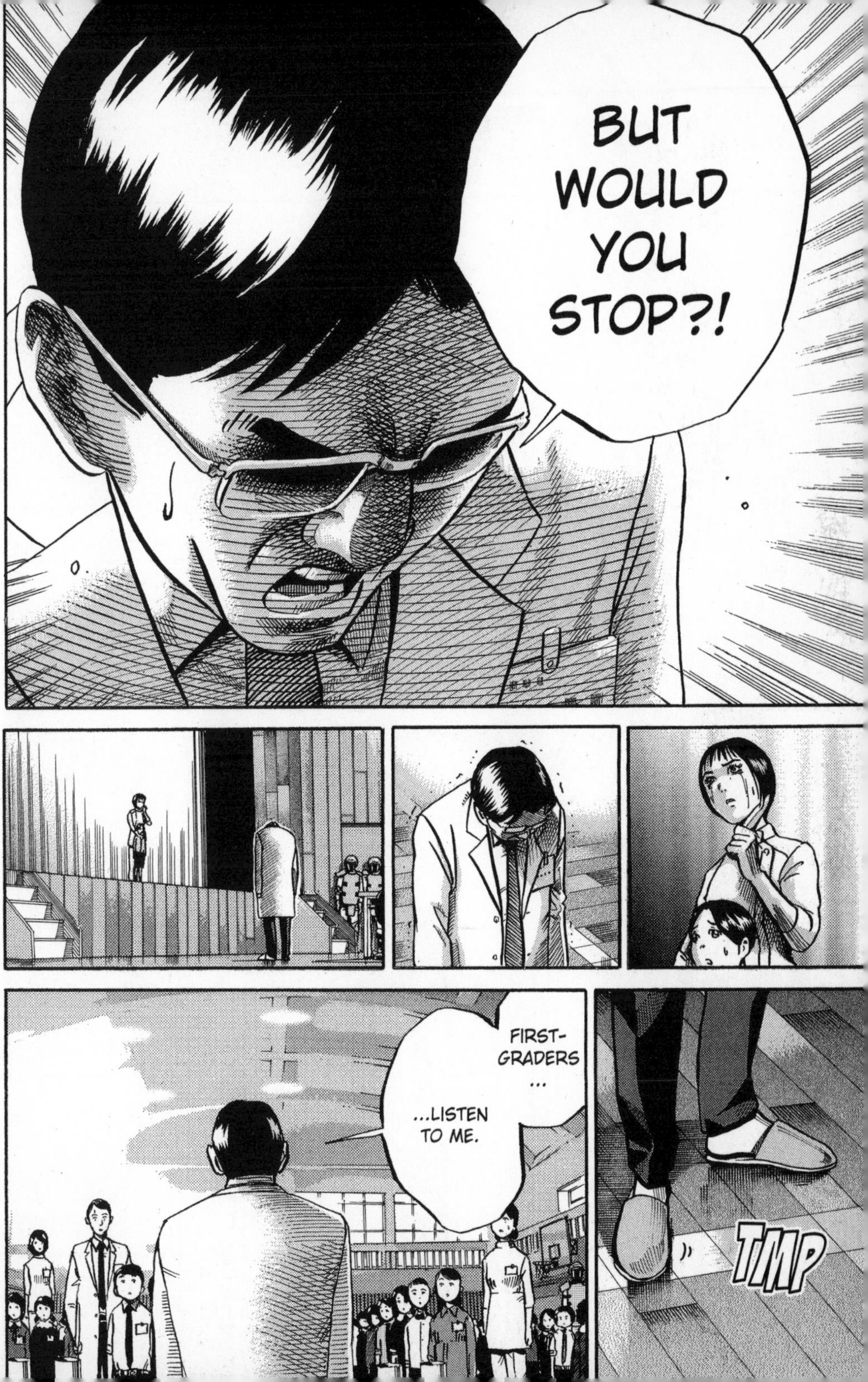
BUT WOULD YOU STOP?!
TMP
FIRST-GRADERS ...
...LISTEN TO ME.

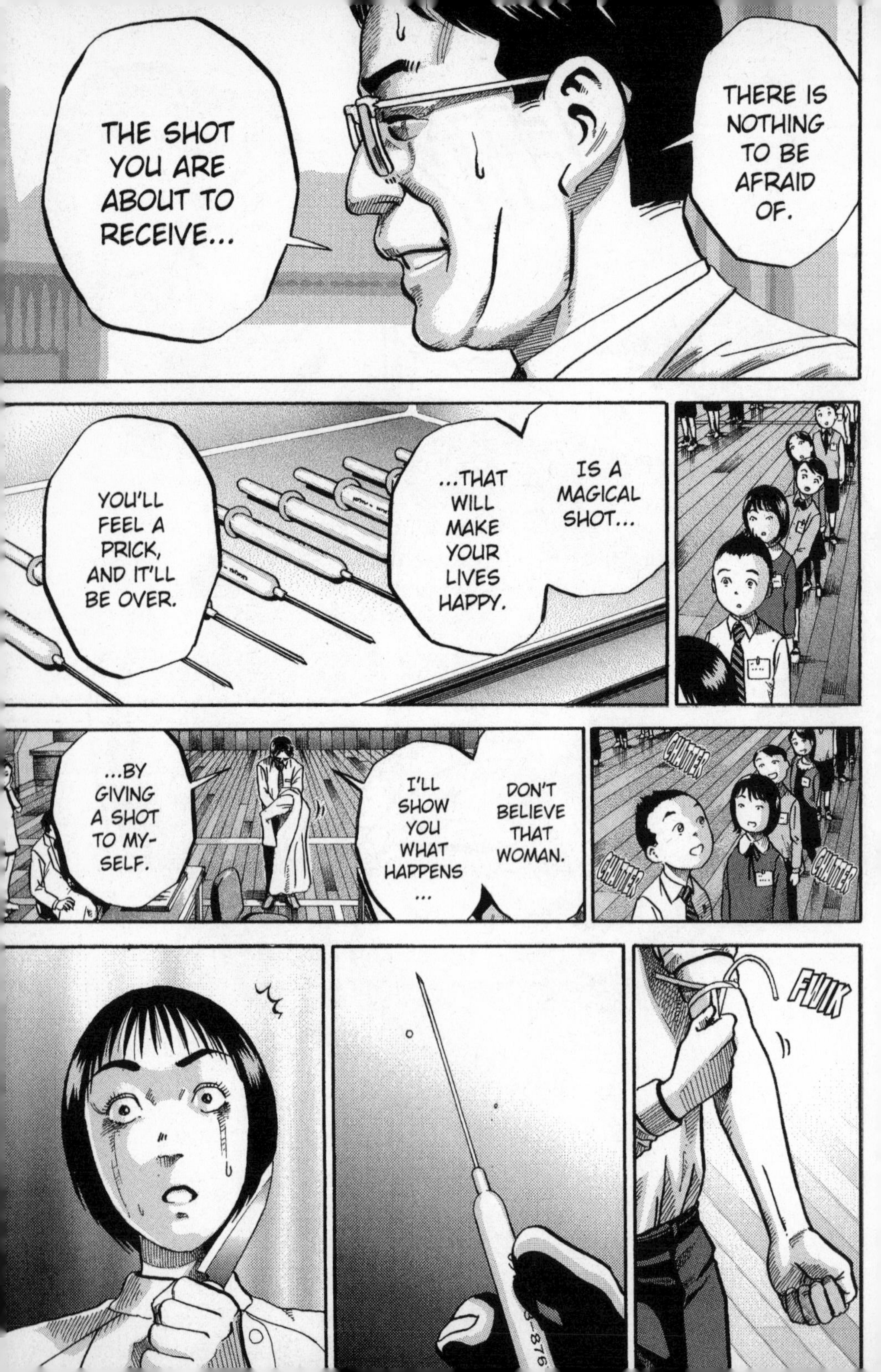
THERE IS NOTHING TO BE AFRAID OF.
THE SHOT YOU ARE ABOUT TO RECEIVE...
IS A MAGICAL SHOT...
...THAT WILL MAKE YOUR LIVES HAPPY.
YOU'LL FEEL A PRICK, AND IT'LL BE OVER.
CHATTER
CHATTER
CHATTER
DON'T BELIEVE THAT WOMAN.
I'LL SHOW YOU WHAT HAPPENS...
...BY GIVING A SHOT TO MY-SELF.
FWIK

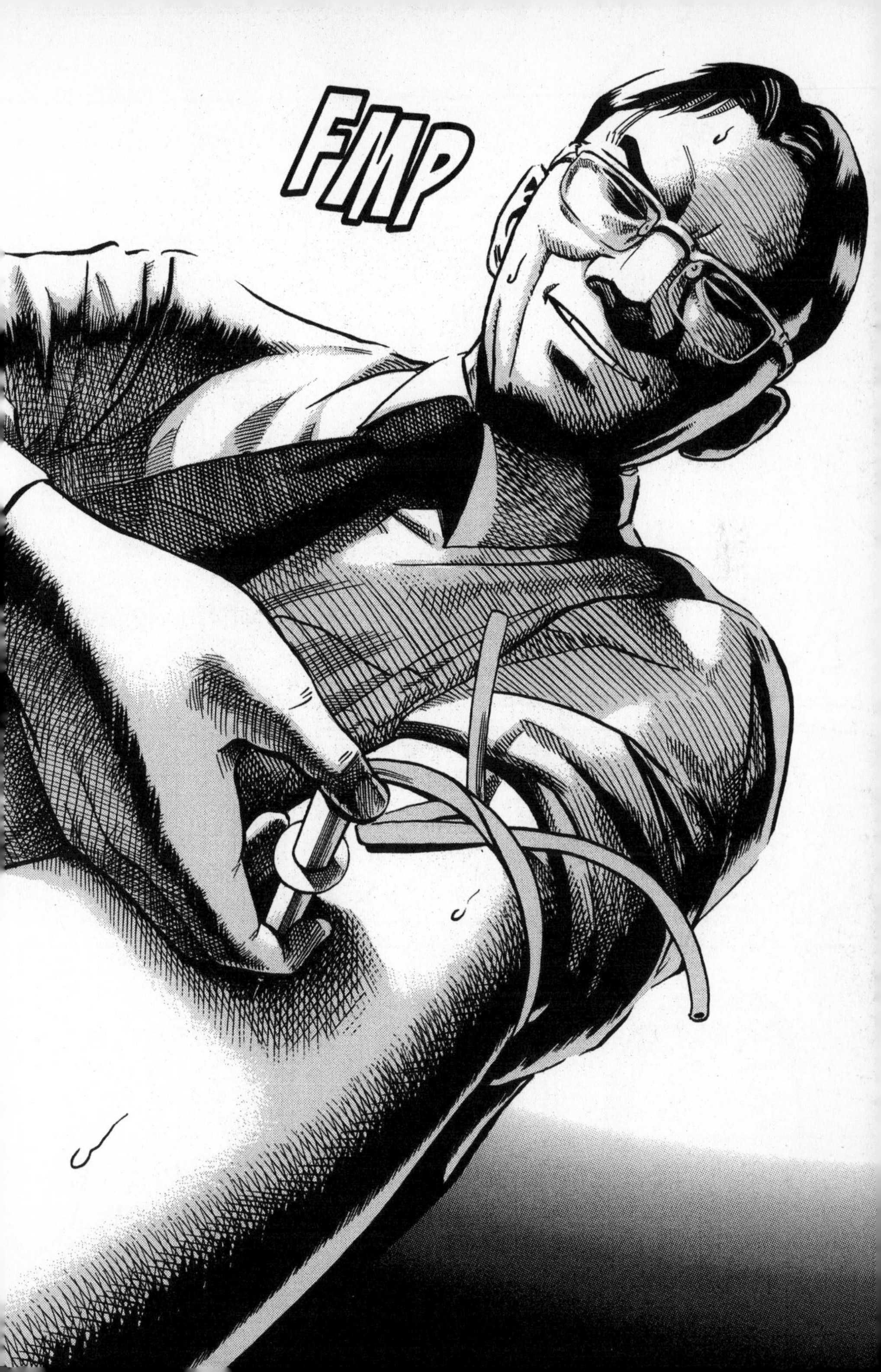
FMP

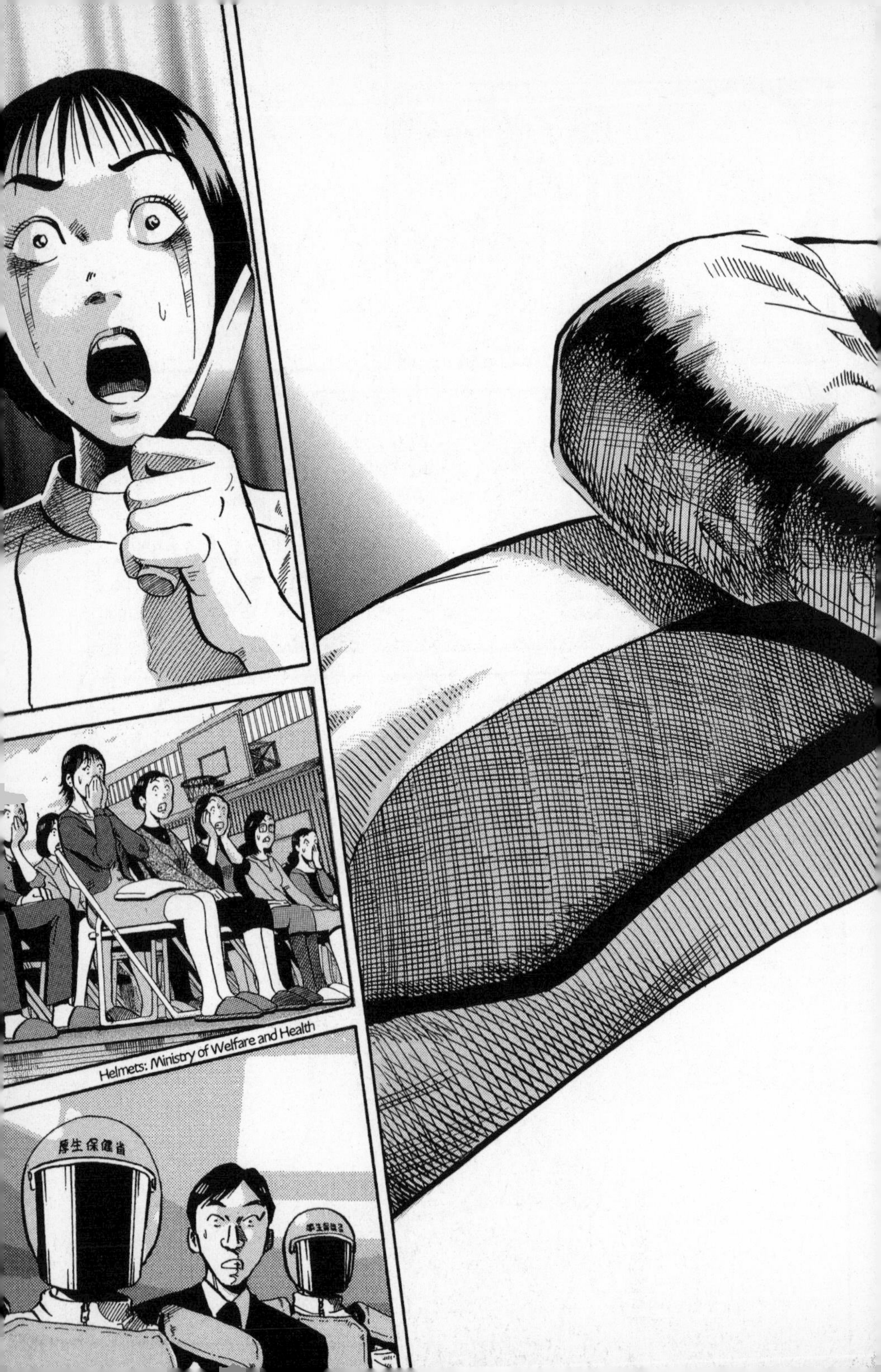
Helmets: Ministry of Welfare and Health
厚生保健省

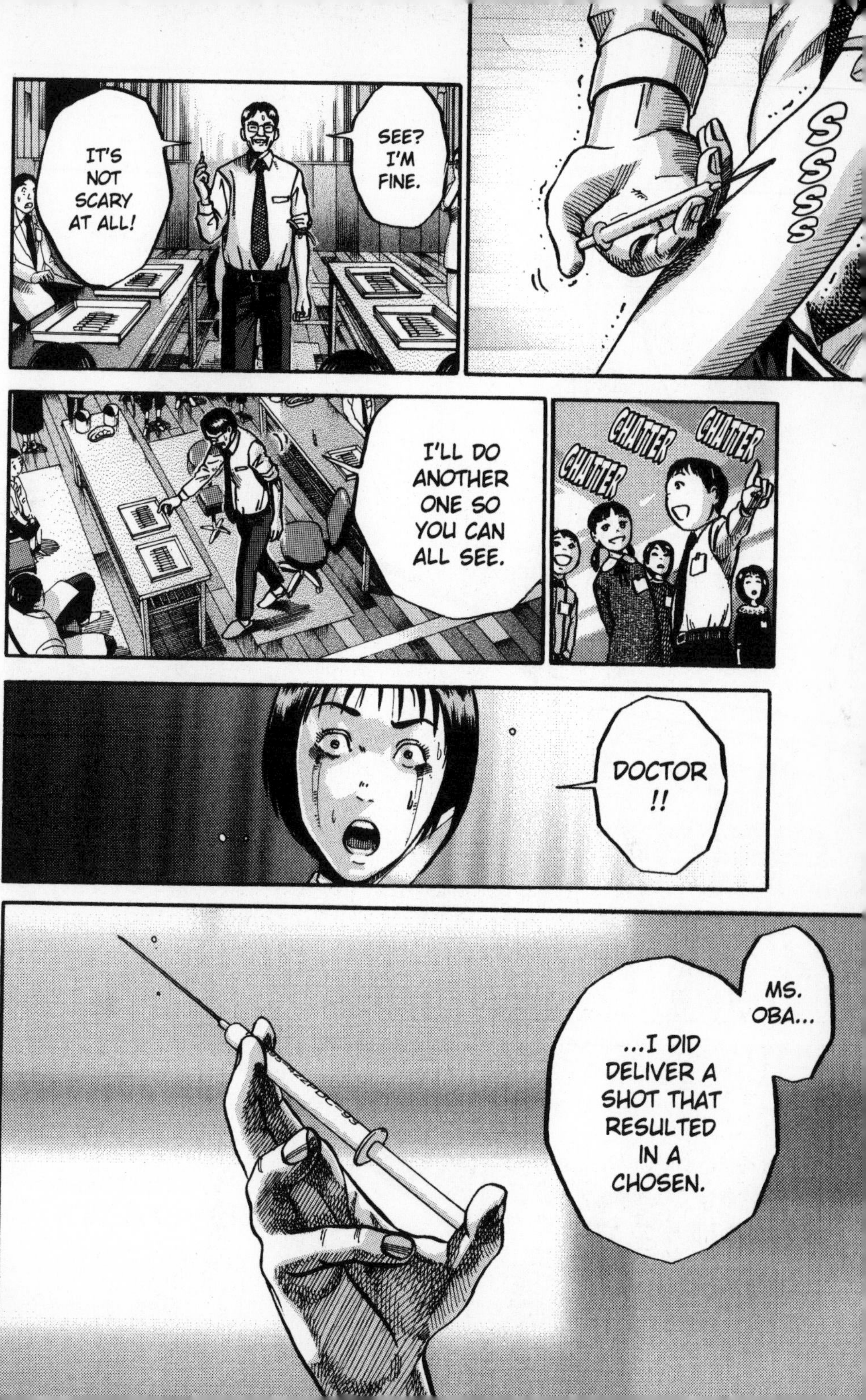
SSSS
SEE? I'M FINE.
IT'S NOT SCARY AT ALL!
CHATTER CHATTER CHATTER
I'LL DO ANOTHER ONE SO YOU CAN ALL SEE.
DOCTOR !!
MS. OBA...
...I DID DELIVER A SHOT THAT RESULTED IN A CHOSEN.

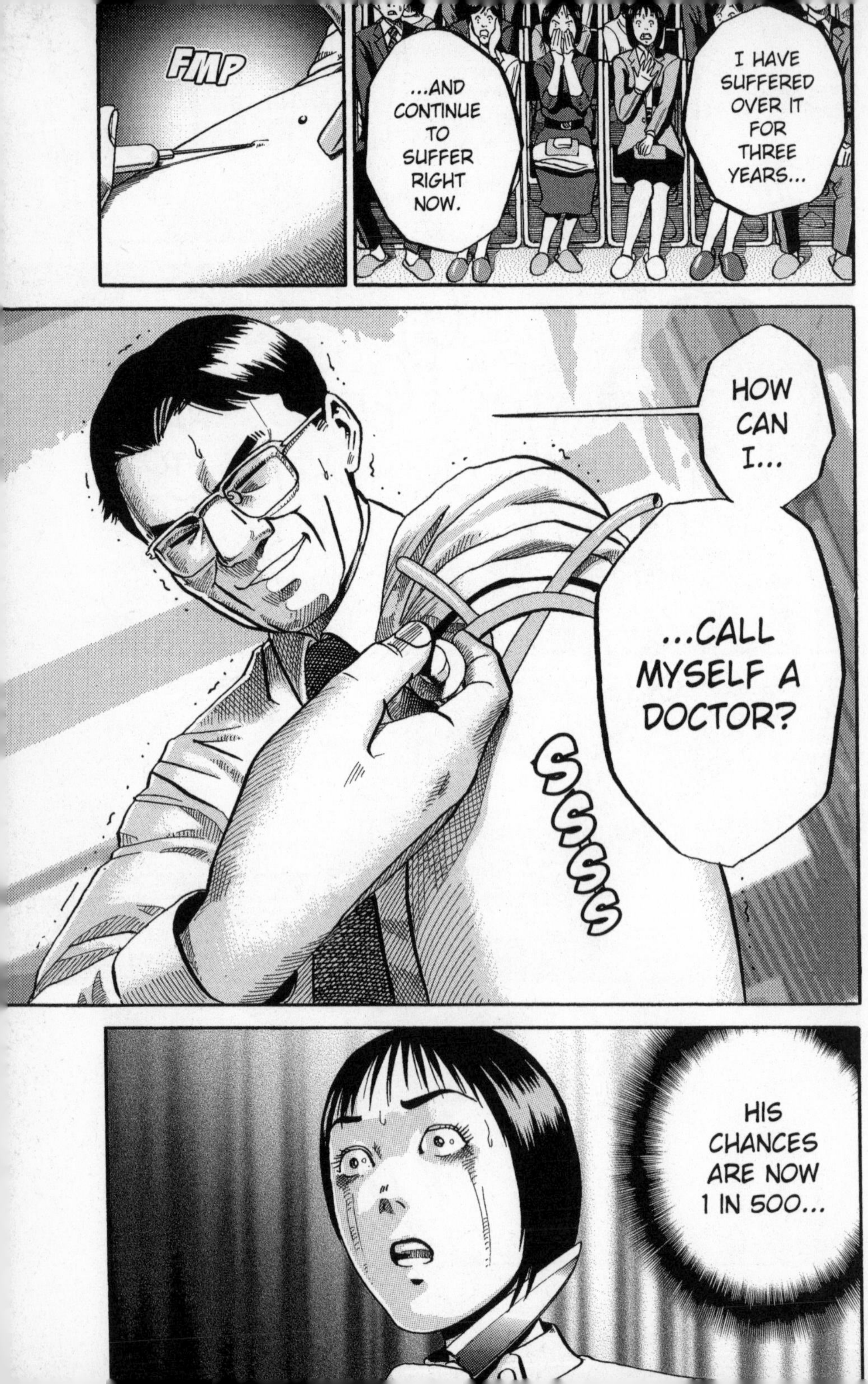
I HAVE SUFFERED OVER IT FOR THREE YEARS...
...AND CONTINUE TO SUFFER RIGHT NOW.
FMP
HOW CAN I...
...CALL MYSELF A DOCTOR?
SSSS
HIS CHANCES ARE NOW 1 IN 500...

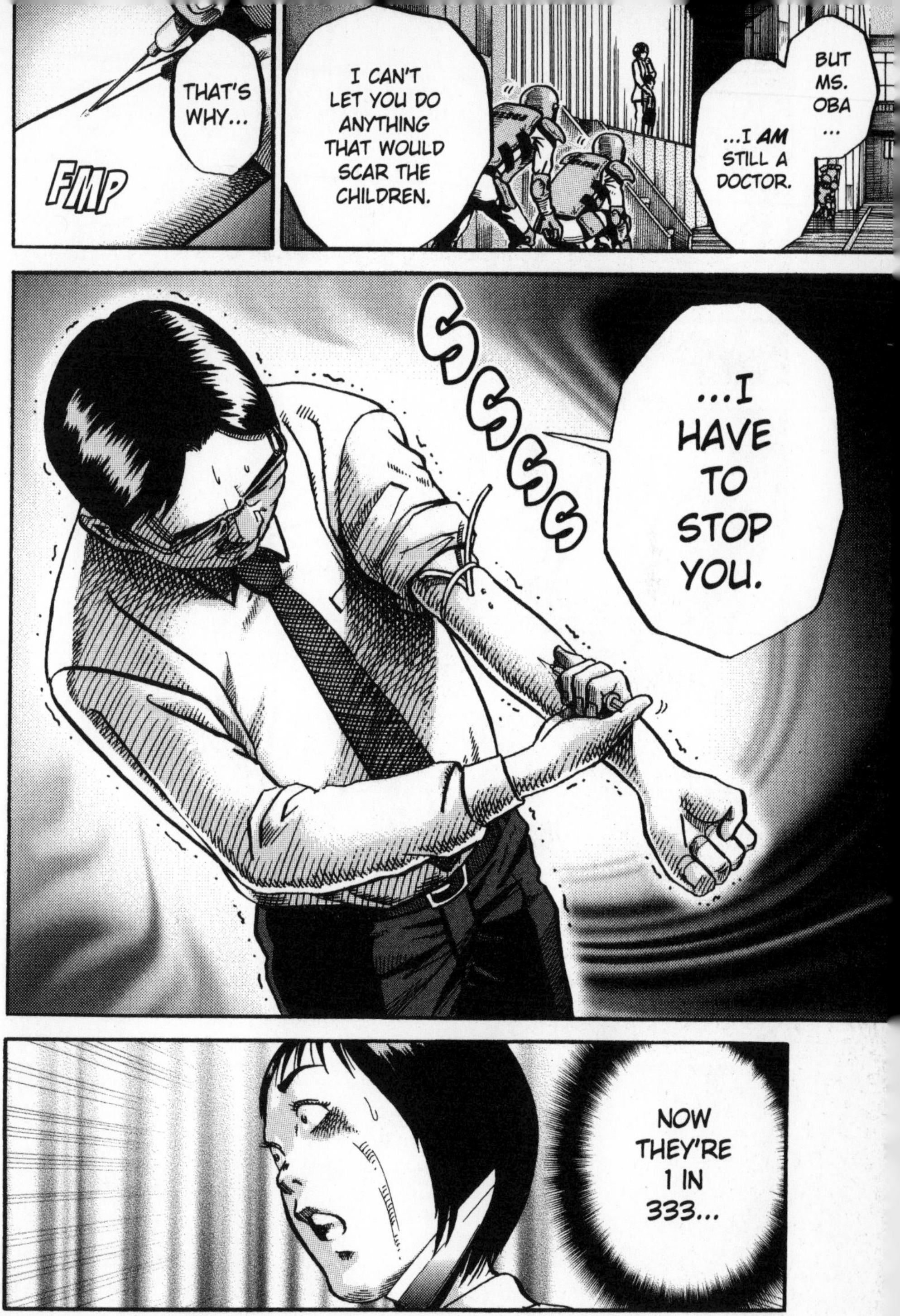

BUT MS. OBA ...
...I *AM* STILL A DOCTOR.
I CAN'T LET YOU DO ANYTHING THAT WOULD SCAR THE CHILDREN.
THAT'S WHY...
FMP
...I HAVE TO STOP YOU.
SSSSS
NOW THEY'RE 1 IN 333...

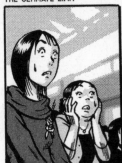

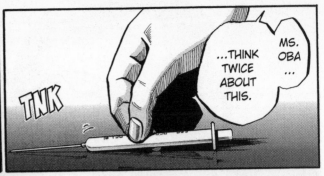

...THINK TWICE ABOUT THIS.

MS. OBA...

Helmets: Ministry of Welfare and Health

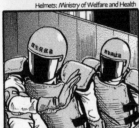

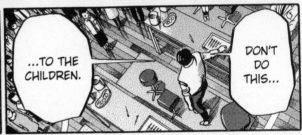

...TO THE CHILDREN.

DON'T DO THIS...

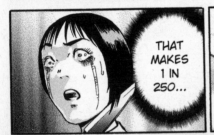

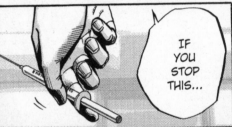

THAT MAKES 1 IN 250...

IF YOU STOP THIS...

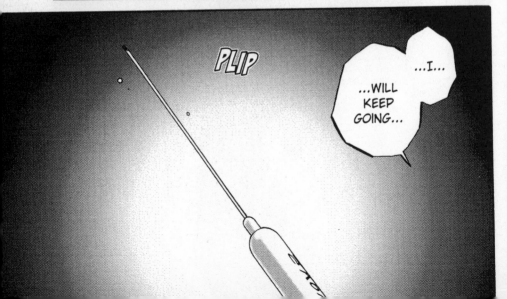

PLIP

...I...

...WILL KEEP GOING...

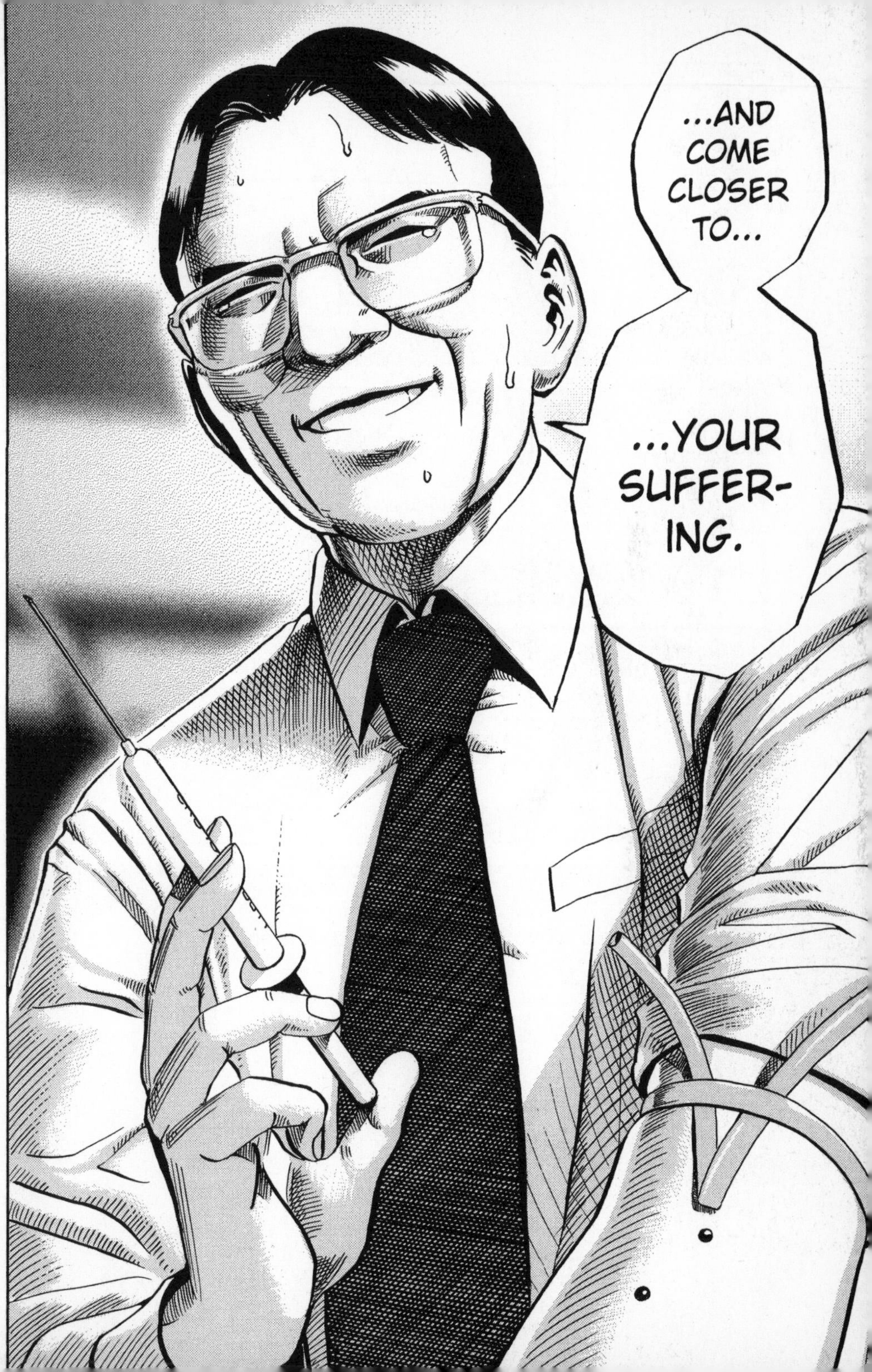
...AND COME CLOSER TO...
...YOUR SUFFER-ING.

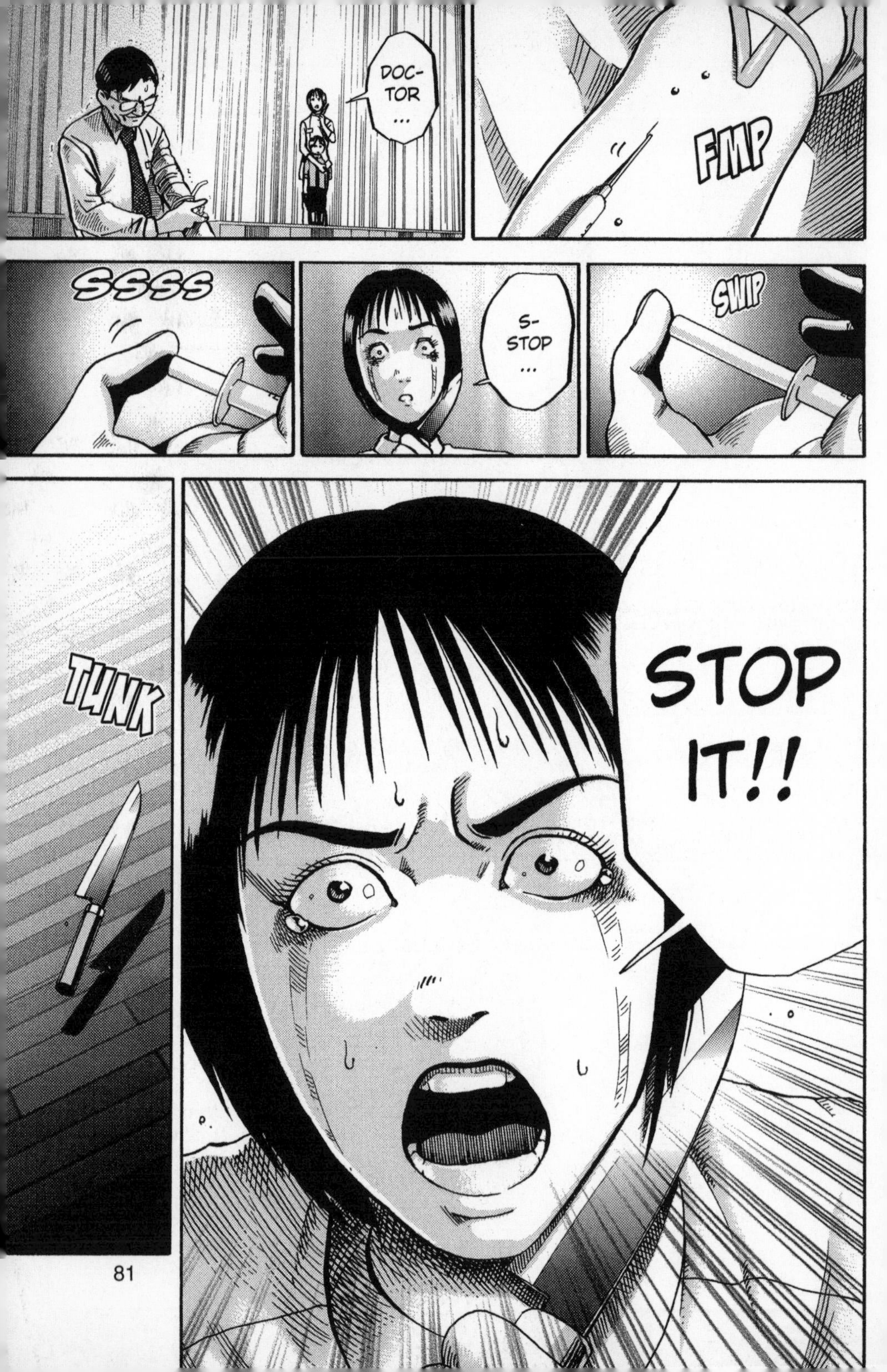
FMP
DOC-
TOR
...
SWIP
S-
STOP
...
SSSS
STOP
IT!!
TUNK

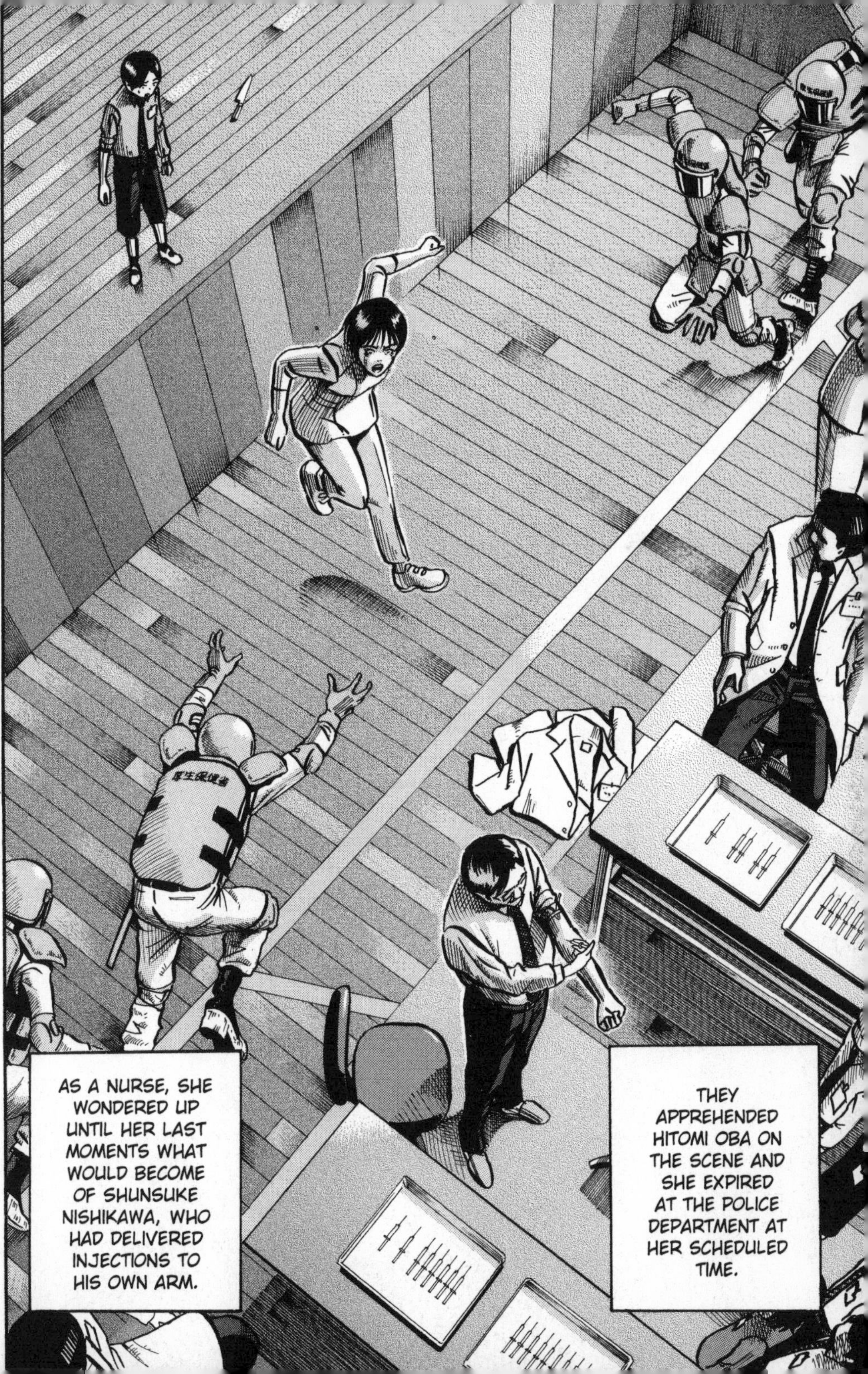
THEY APPREHENDED HITOMI OBA ON THE SCENE AND SHE EXPIRED AT THE POLICE DEPARTMENT AT HER SCHEDULED TIME.
AS A NURSE, SHE WONDERED UP UNTIL HER LAST MOMENTS WHAT WOULD BECOME OF SHUNSUKE NISHIKAWA, WHO HAD DELIVERED INJECTIONS TO HIS OWN ARM.
Armor: Ministry of Welfare and Health

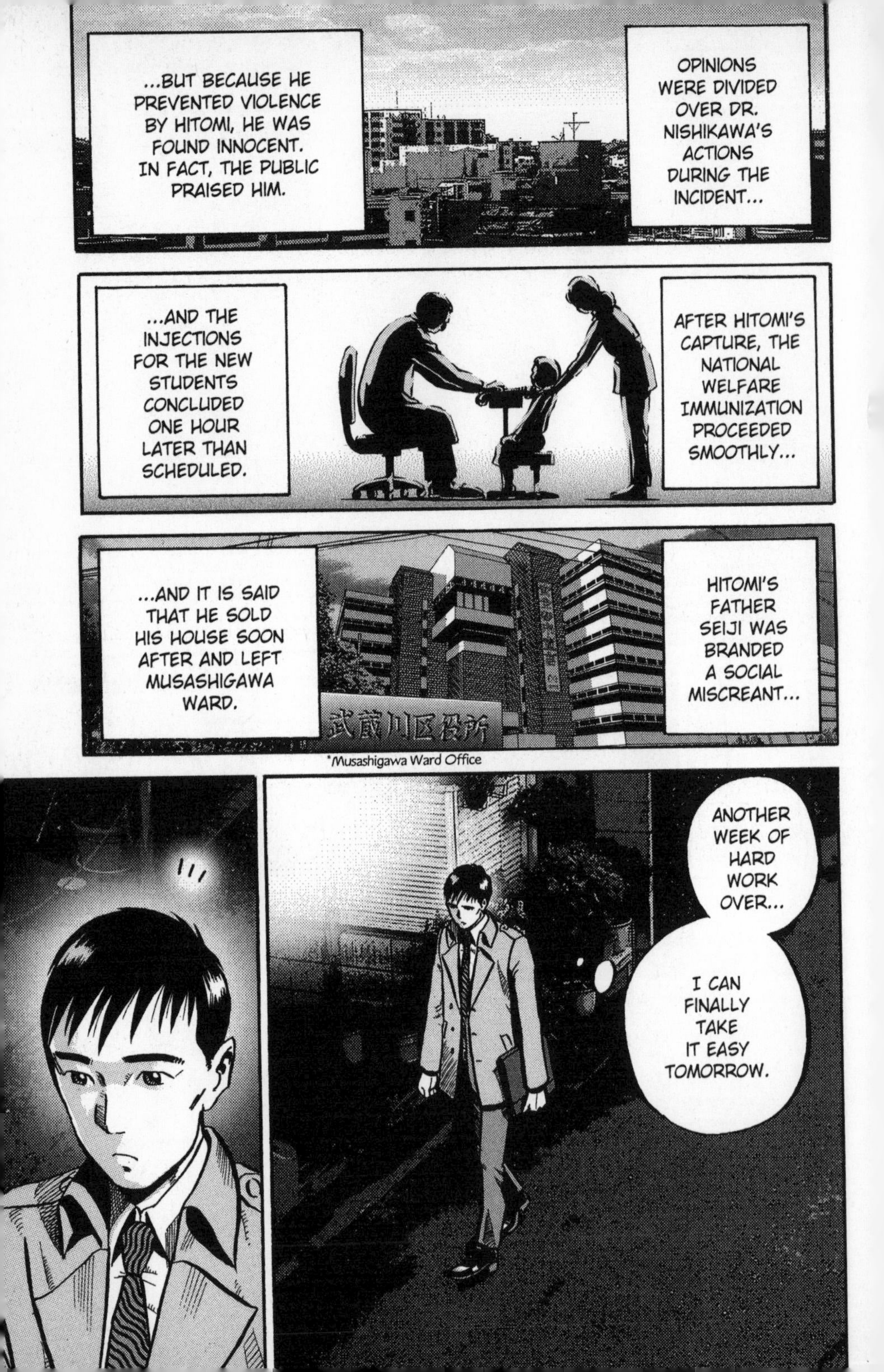
OPINIONS WERE DIVIDED OVER DR. NISHIKAWA'S ACTIONS DURING THE INCIDENT...
...BUT BECAUSE HE PREVENTED VIOLENCE BY HITOMI, HE WAS FOUND INNOCENT. IN FACT, THE PUBLIC PRAISED HIM.
AFTER HITOMI'S CAPTURE, THE NATIONAL WELFARE IMMUNIZATION PROCEEDED SMOOTHLY...
...AND THE INJECTIONS FOR THE NEW STUDENTS CONCLUDED ONE HOUR LATER THAN SCHEDULED.
HITOMI'S FATHER SEIJI WAS BRANDED A SOCIAL MISCREANT...
...AND IT IS SAID THAT HE SOLD HIS HOUSE SOON AFTER AND LEFT MUSASHIGAWA WARD.
武蔵川区役所
*Musashigawa Ward Office
ANOTHER WEEK OF HARD WORK OVER...
I CAN FINALLY TAKE IT EASY TOMORROW.

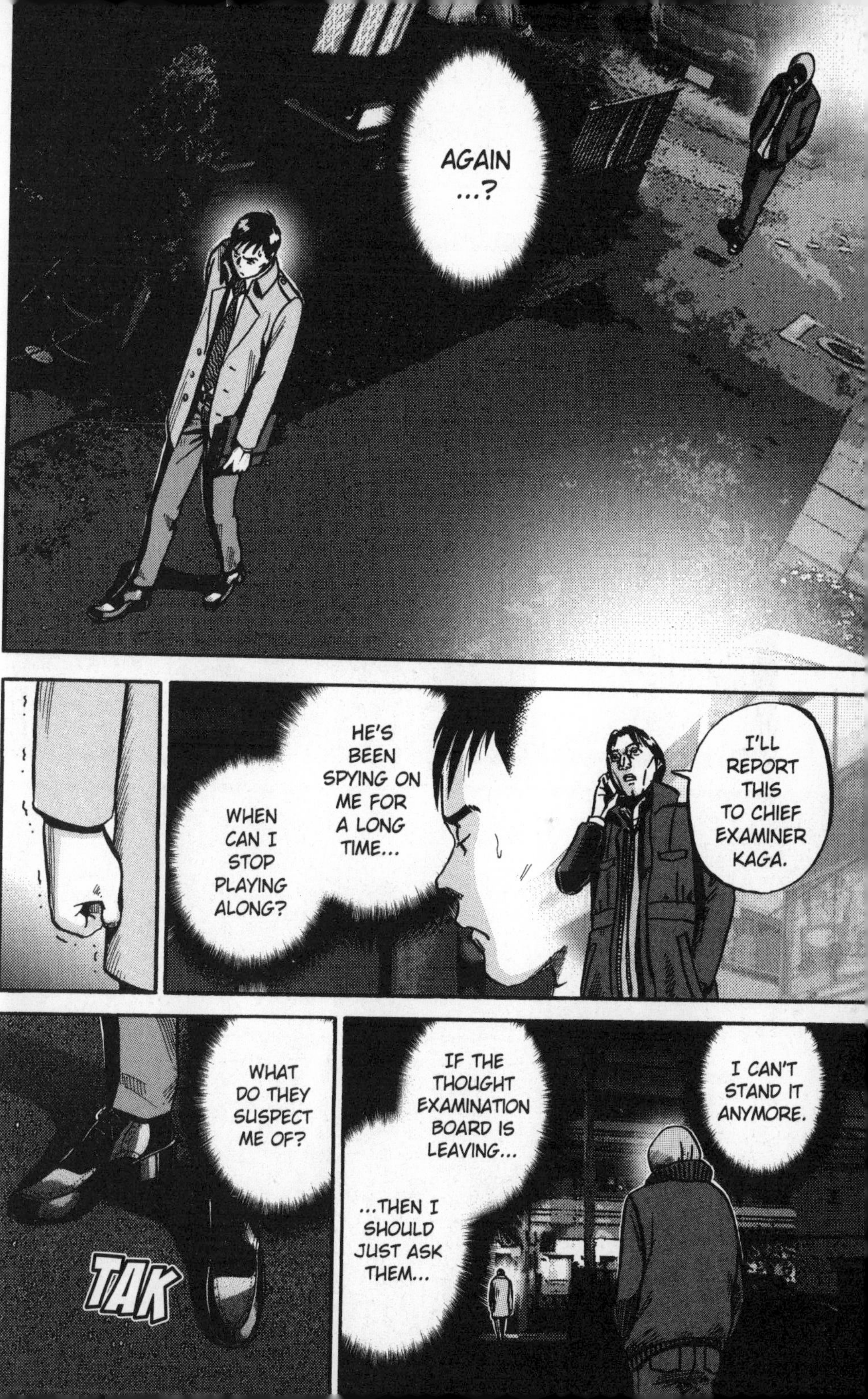
AGAIN ...?
I'LL REPORT THIS TO CHIEF EXAMINER KAGA.
HE'S BEEN SPYING ON ME FOR A LONG TIME...
WHEN CAN I STOP PLAYING ALONG?
I CAN'T STAND IT ANYMORE.
IF THE THOUGHT EXAMINATION BOARD IS LEAVING...
...THEN I SHOULD JUST ASK THEM...
WHAT DO THEY SUSPECT ME OF?
TAK

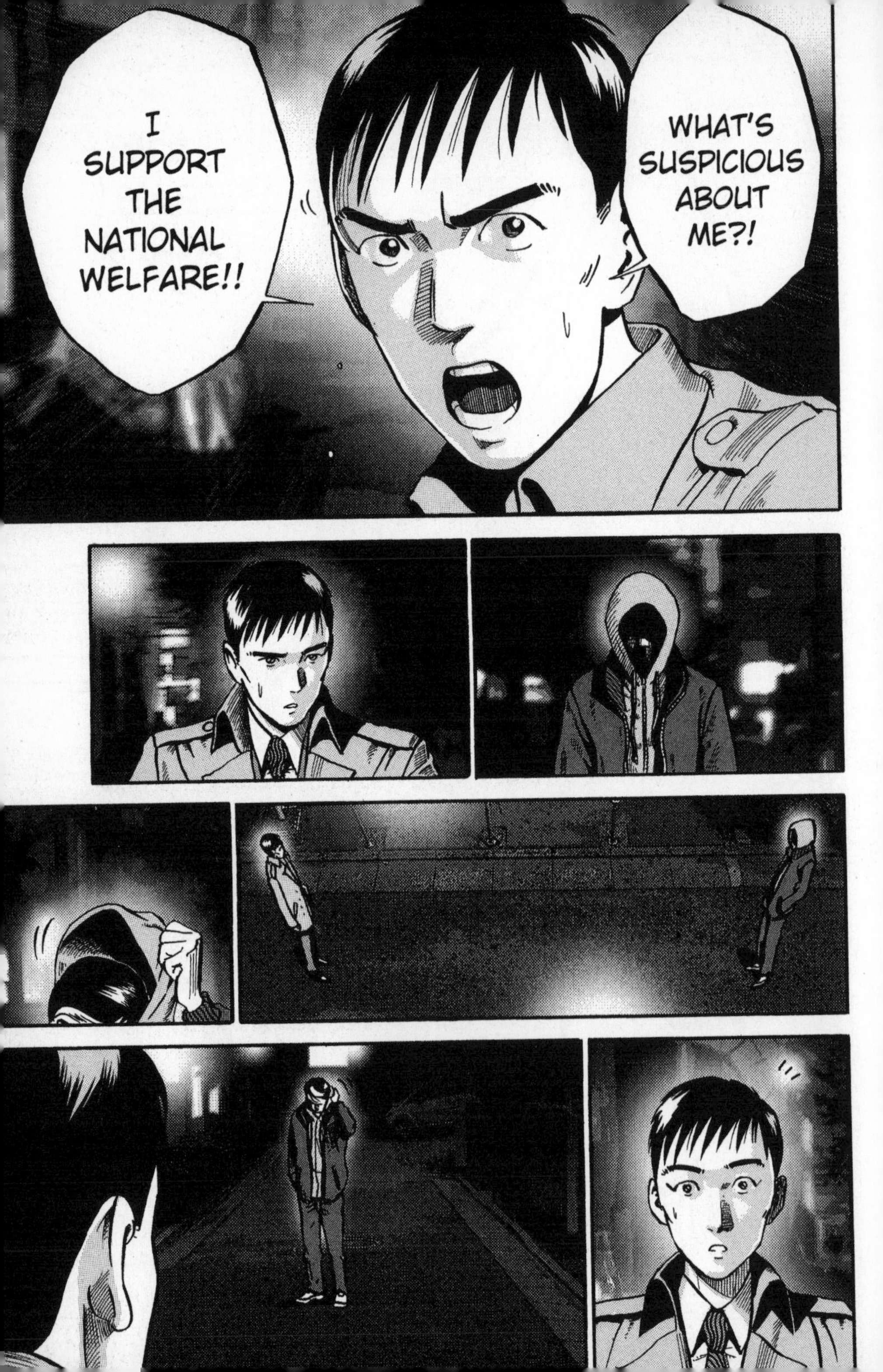
WHAT'S SUSPICIOUS ABOUT ME?!
I SUPPORT THE NATIONAL WELFARE!!

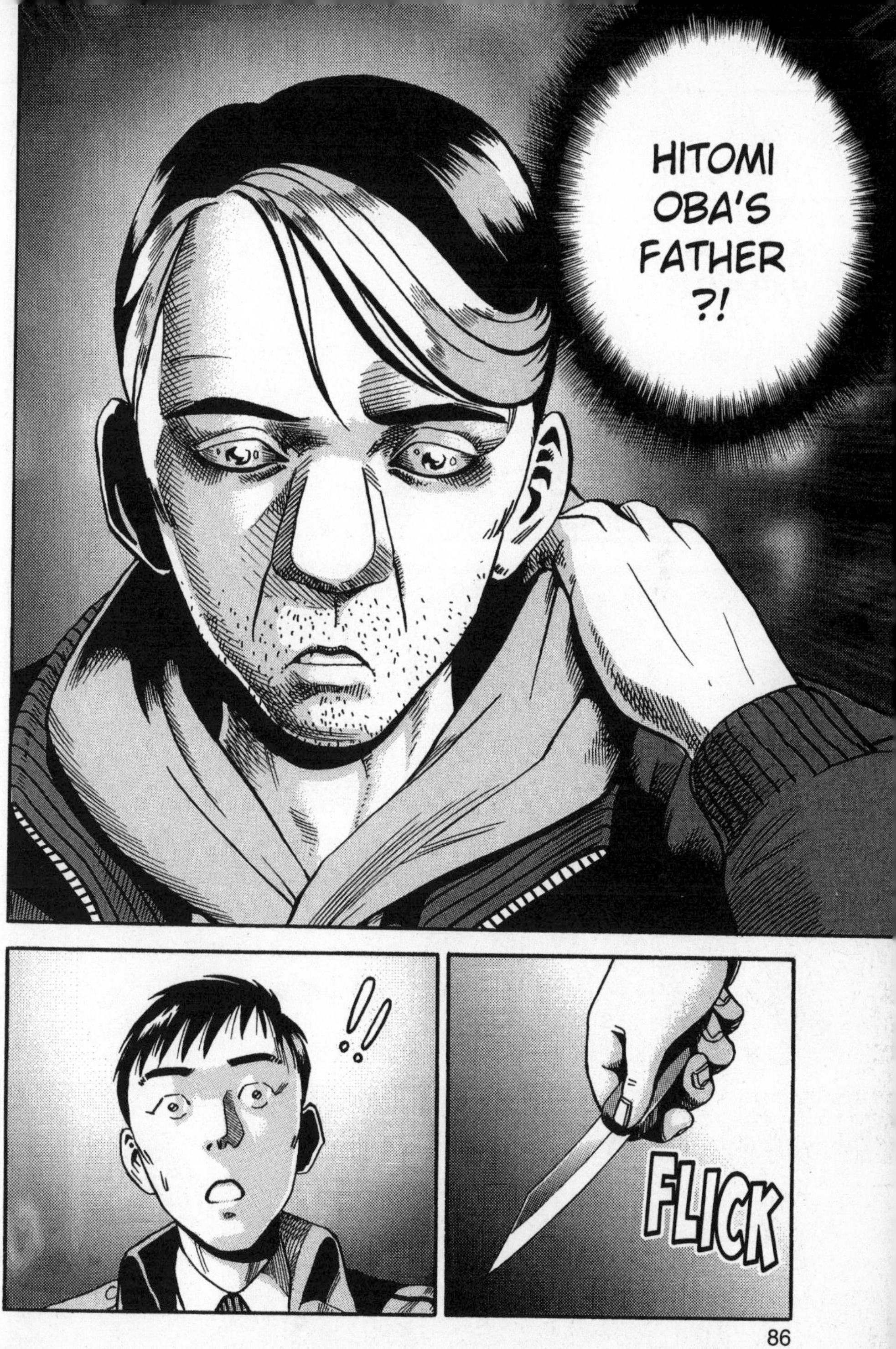
HITOMI OBA'S FATHER ?!
FLICK
!!

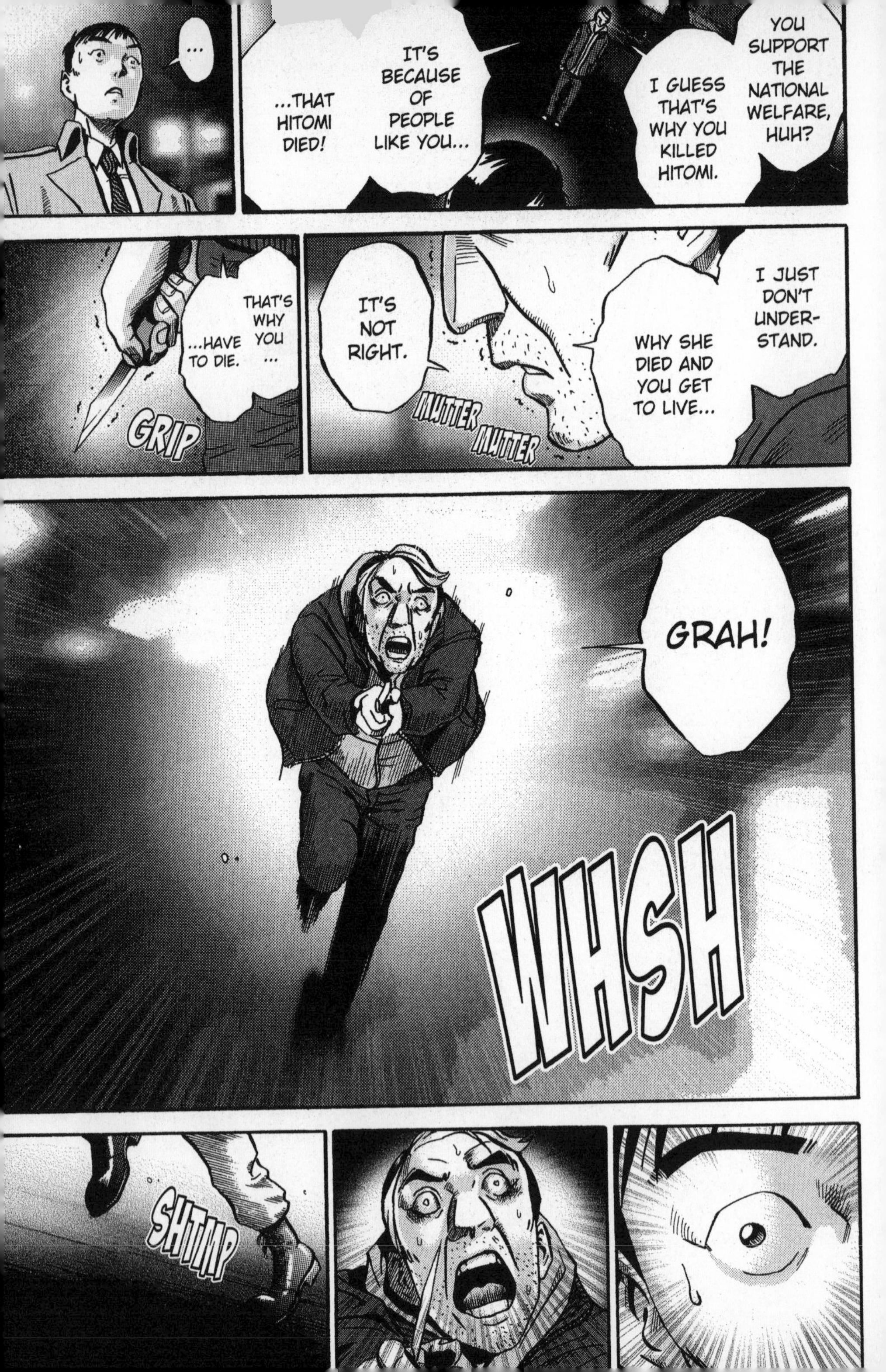
YOU SUPPORT THE NATIONAL WELFARE, HUH?
I GUESS THAT'S WHY YOU KILLED HITOMI.
IT'S BECAUSE OF PEOPLE LIKE YOU...
...THAT HITOMI DIED!
...
I JUST DON'T UNDER-STAND.
WHY SHE DIED AND YOU GET TO LIVE...
IT'S NOT RIGHT.
MUTTER MUTTER
THAT'S WHY YOU ...
...HAVE TO DIE.
GRIP
GRAH!
WHSH
SHTMP

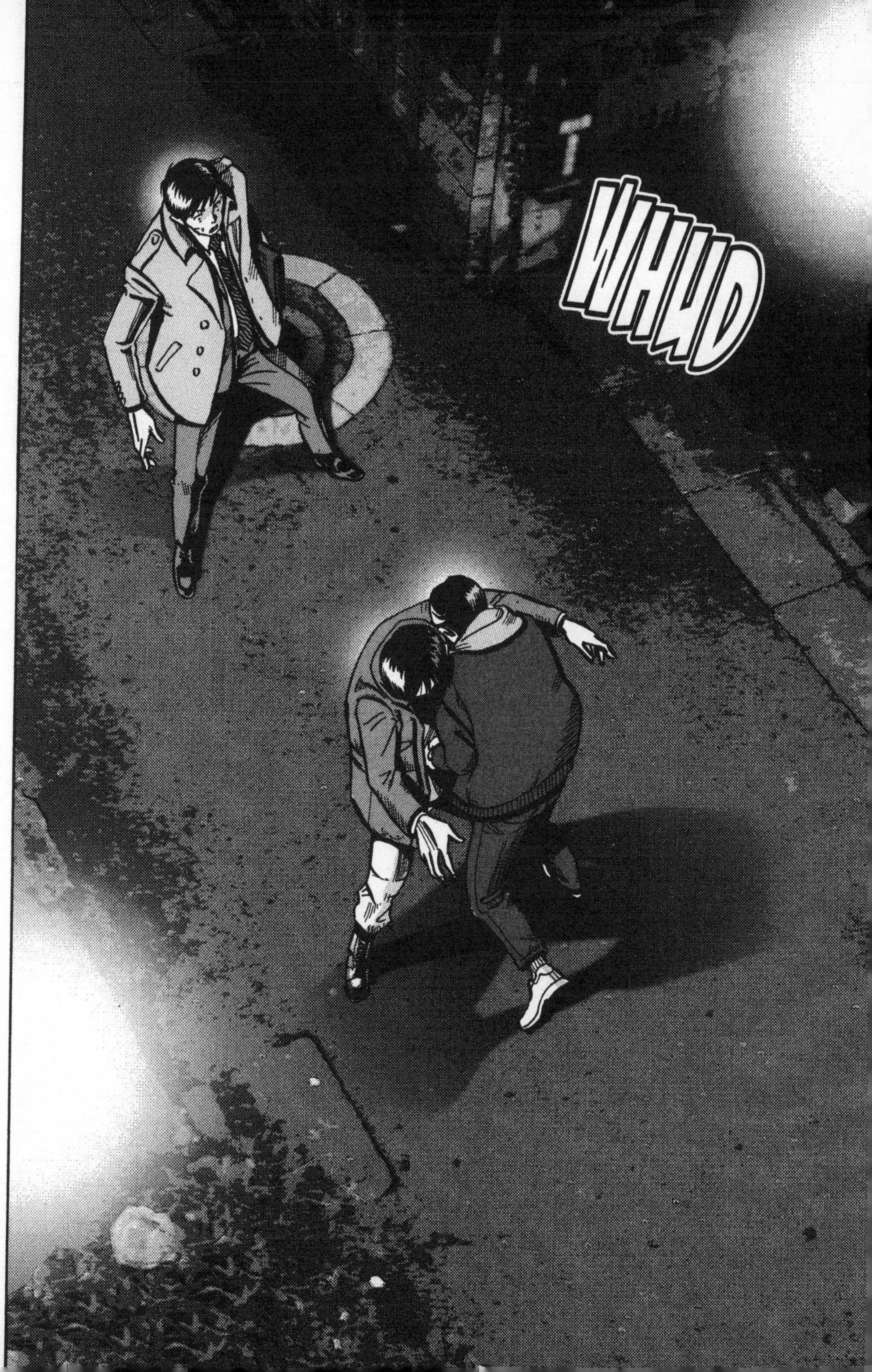
WHUD

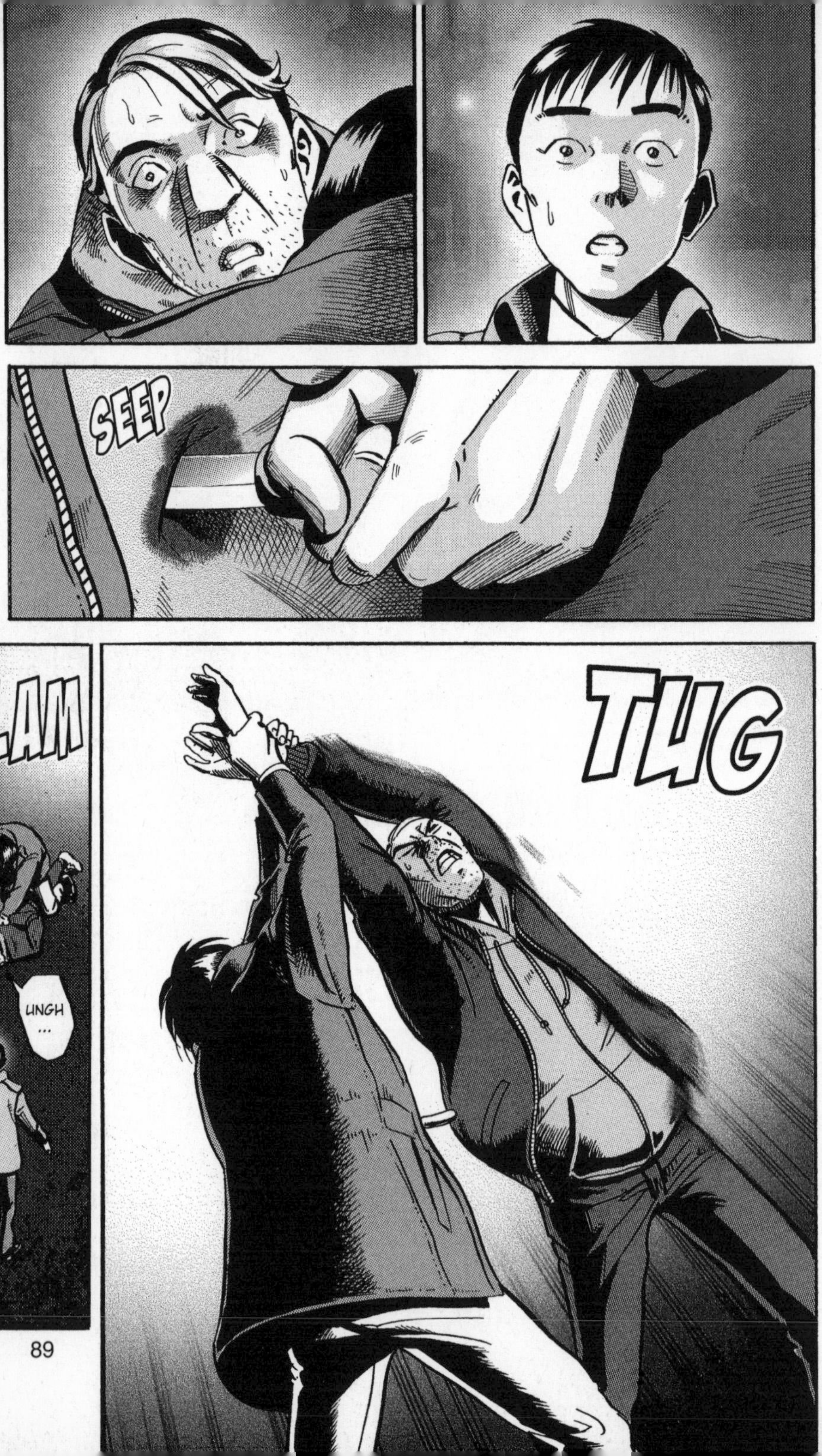
SEEP
TUG
SLAM
UNGH ...

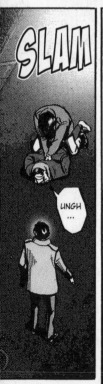

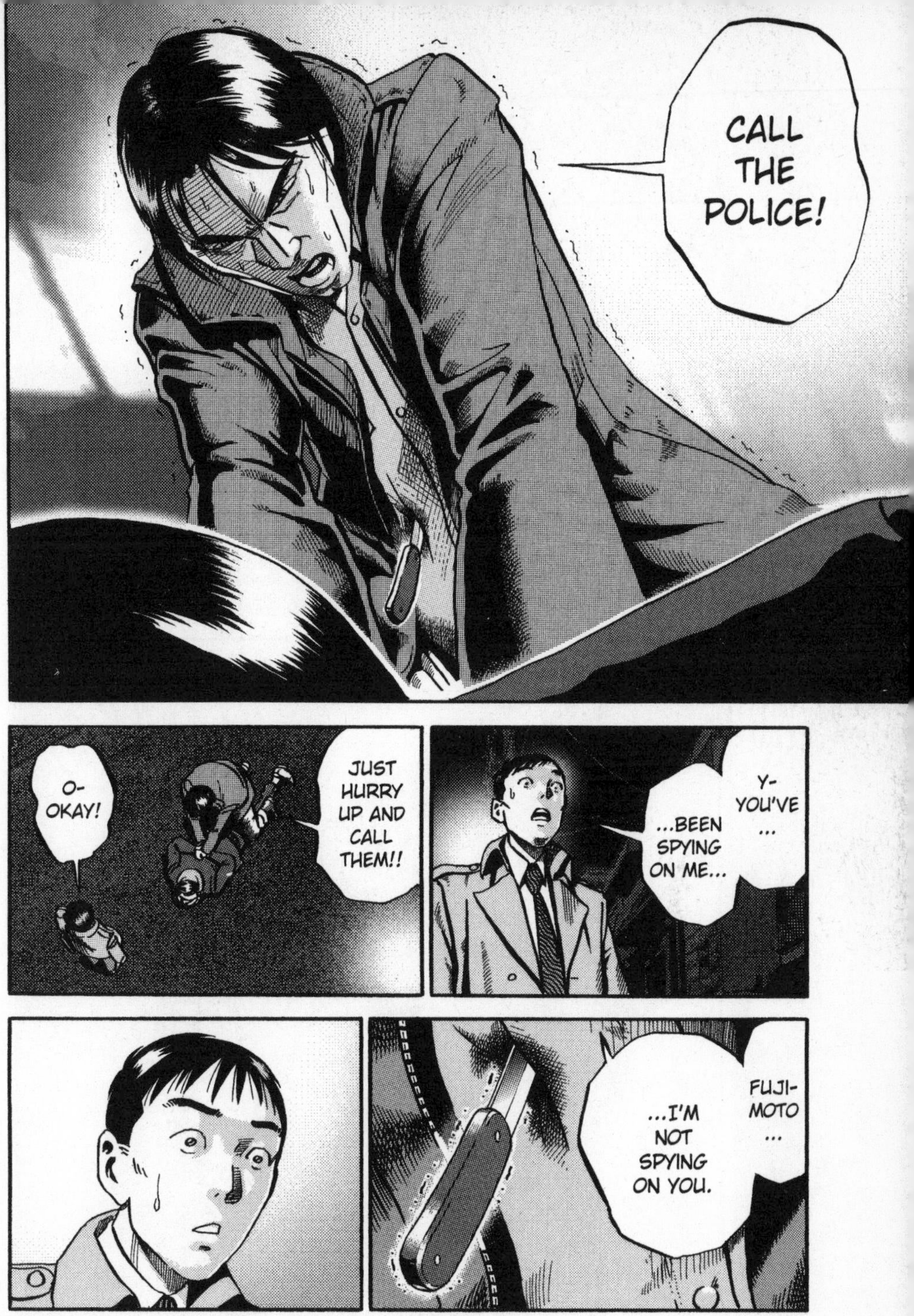
CALL THE POLICE!
Y-YOU'VE ...
...BEEN SPYING ON ME...
JUST HURRY UP AND CALL THEM!!
O-OKAY!
FUJI-MOTO ...
...I'M NOT SPYING ON YOU.

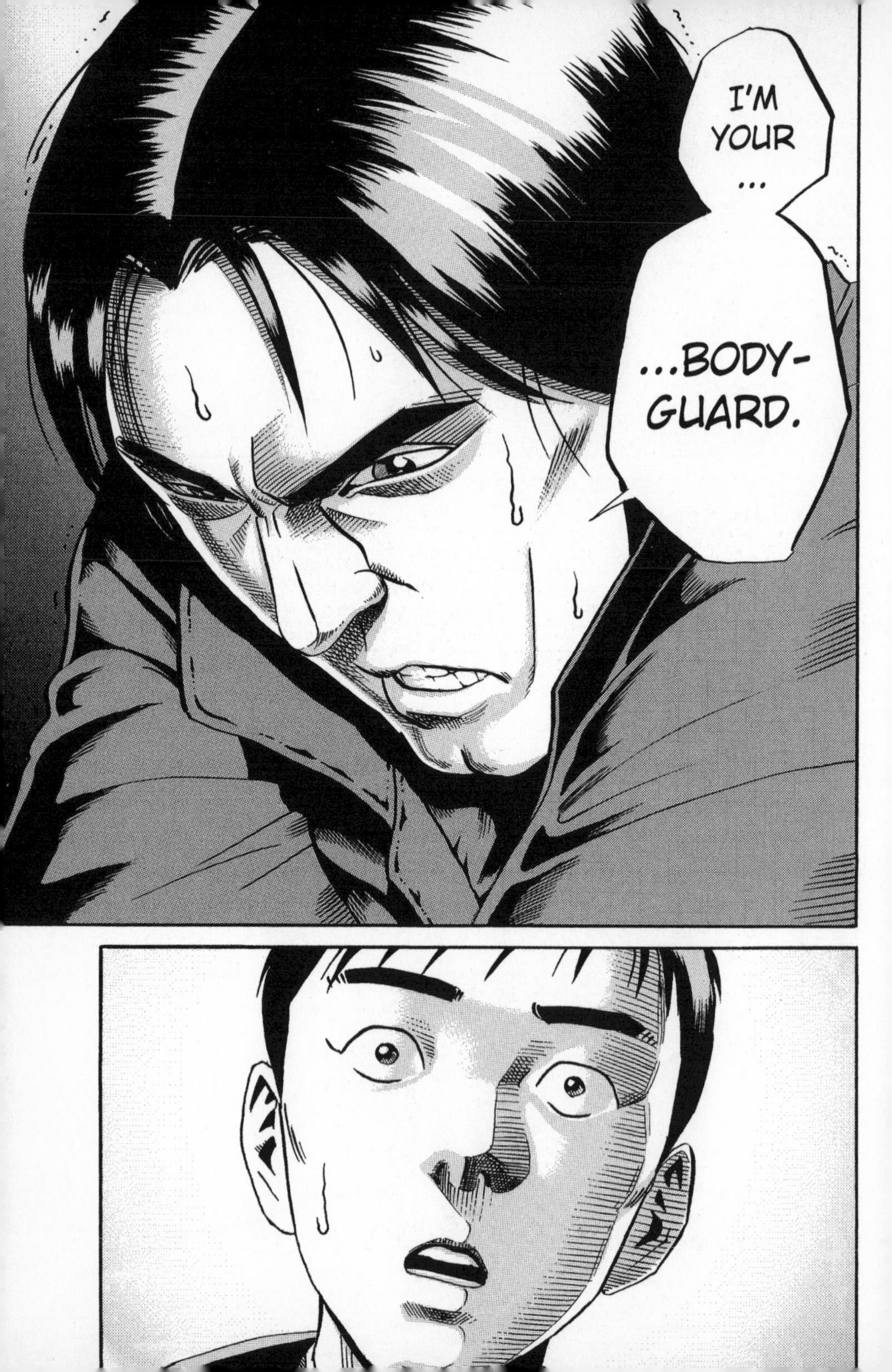
I'M YOUR ...
...BODY-GUARD.

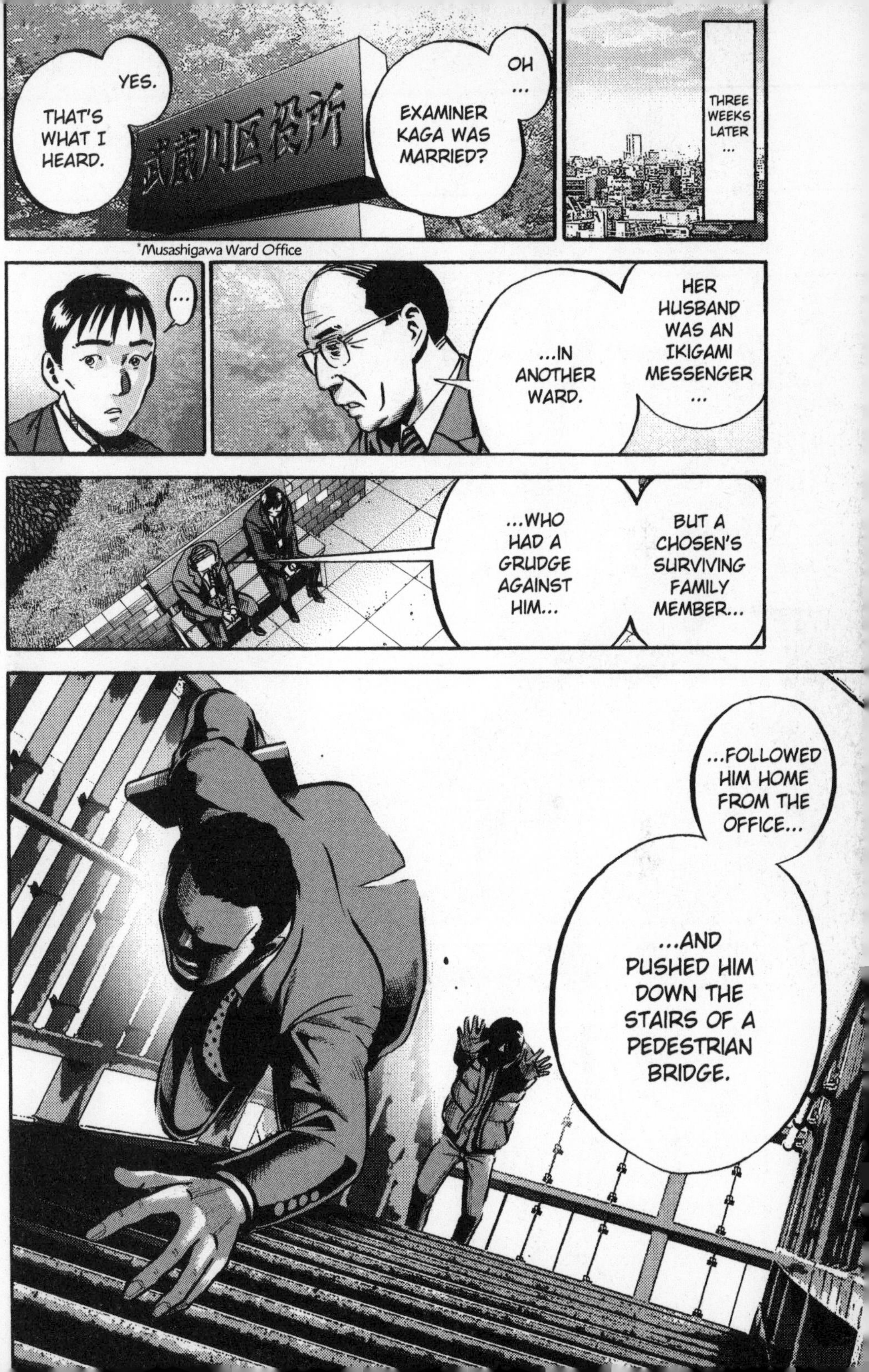
THREE WEEKS LATER ...
OH ... EXAMINER KAGA WAS MARRIED?
武蔵川区役所
YES. THAT'S WHAT I HEARD.
HER HUSBAND WAS AN IKIGAMI MESSENGER ...
...IN ANOTHER WARD.
...
BUT A CHOSEN'S SURVIVING FAMILY MEMBER...
...WHO HAD A GRUDGE AGAINST HIM...
...FOLLOWED HIM HOME FROM THE OFFICE...
...AND PUSHED HIM DOWN THE STAIRS OF A PEDESTRIAN BRIDGE.
*Musashigawa Ward Office

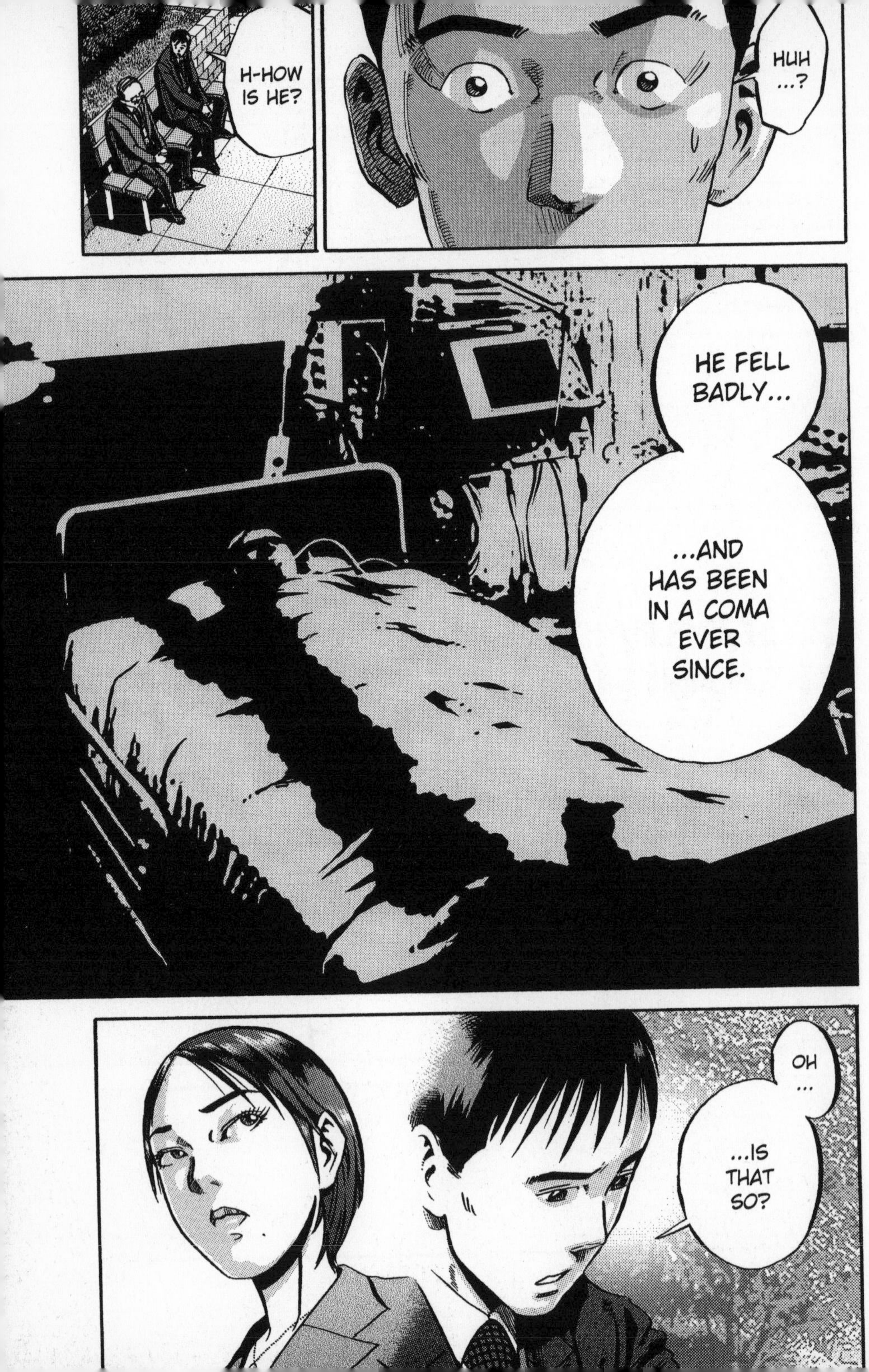
HUH ...?
H-HOW IS HE?
HE FELL BADLY...
...AND HAS BEEN IN A COMA EVER SINCE.
OH ...
...IS THAT SO?

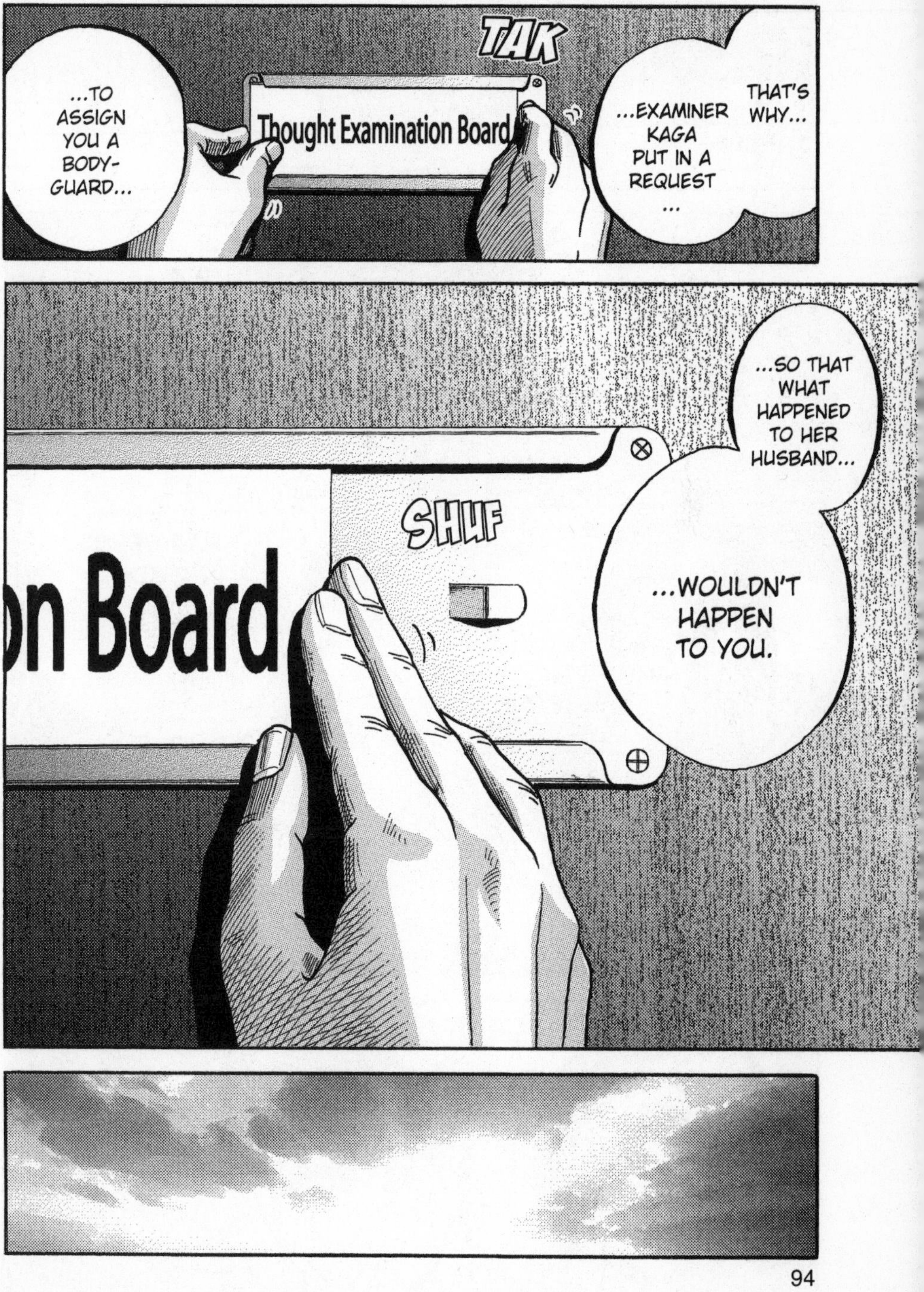
TAK
THAT'S WHY...
...EXAMINER KAGA PUT IN A REQUEST...
Thought Examination Board
...TO ASSIGN YOU A BODY-GUARD...
...SO THAT WHAT HAPPENED TO HER HUSBAND...
...WOULDN'T HAPPEN TO YOU.
SHUF
on Board

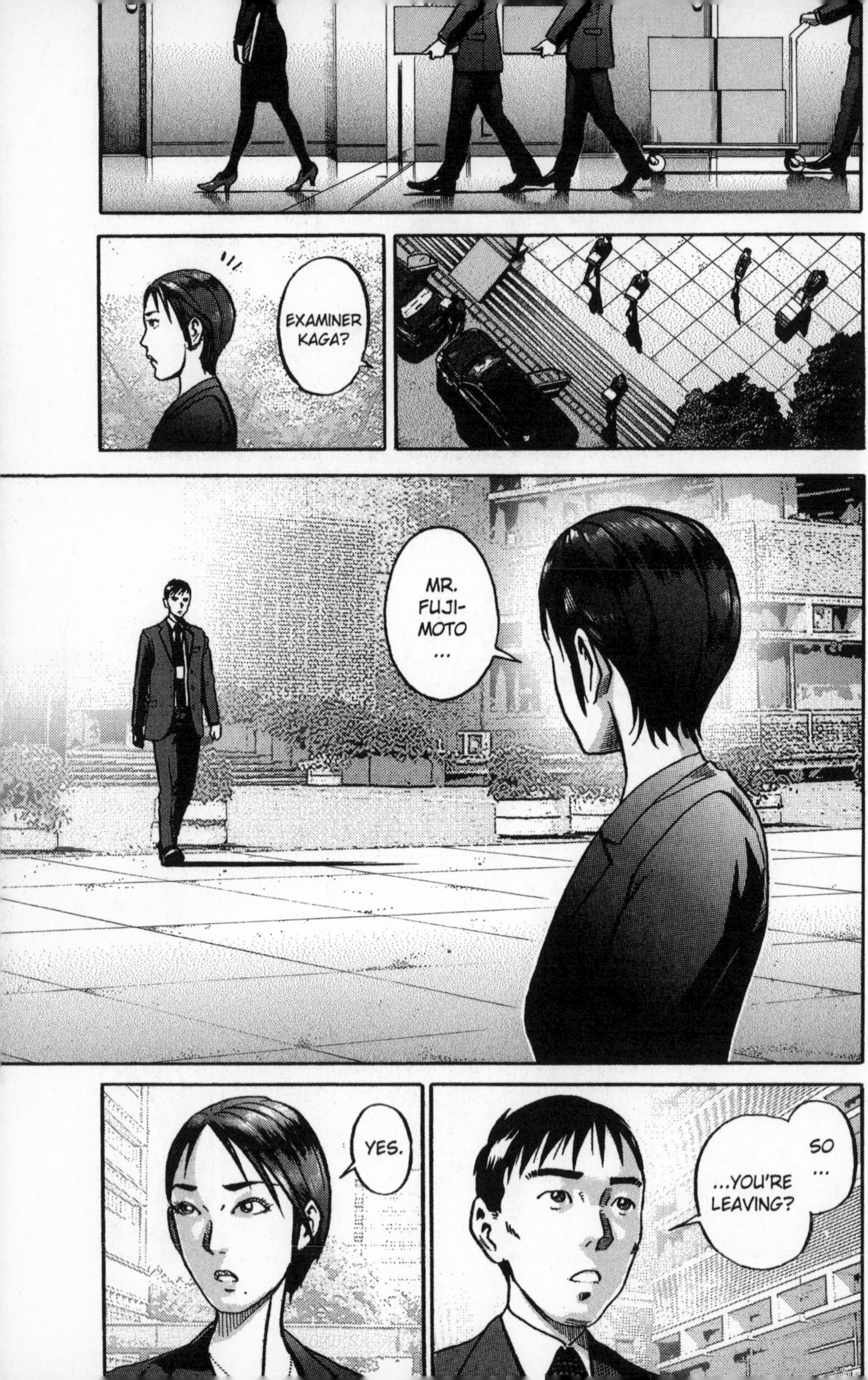
EXAMINER KAGA?
MR. FUJI-MOTO ...
SO ...
...YOU'RE LEAVING?
YES.

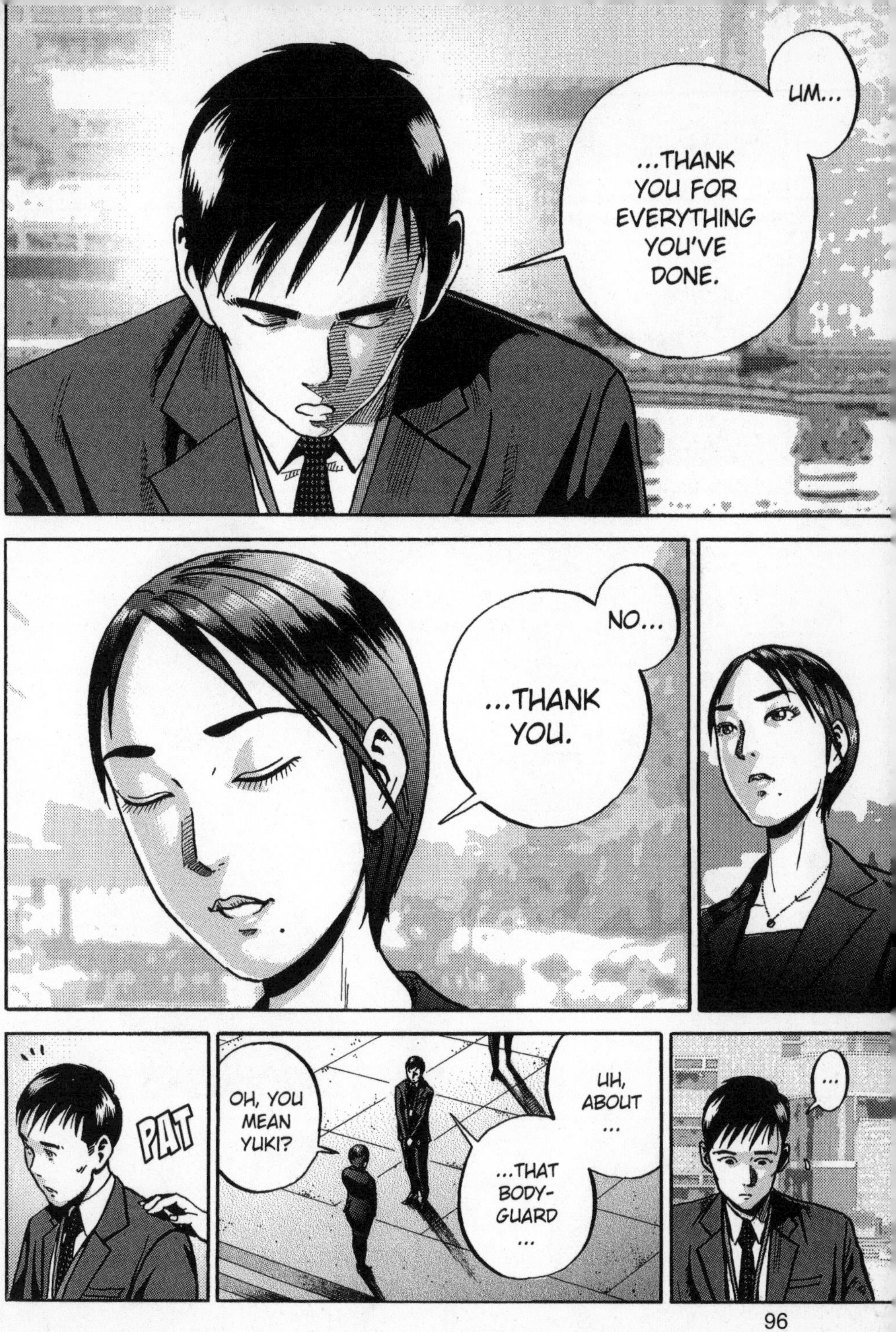
UM...
...THANK YOU FOR EVERYTHING YOU'VE DONE.
NO...
...THANK YOU.
...
UH, ABOUT ...
...THAT BODY-GUARD ...
OH, YOU MEAN YUKI?
PAT

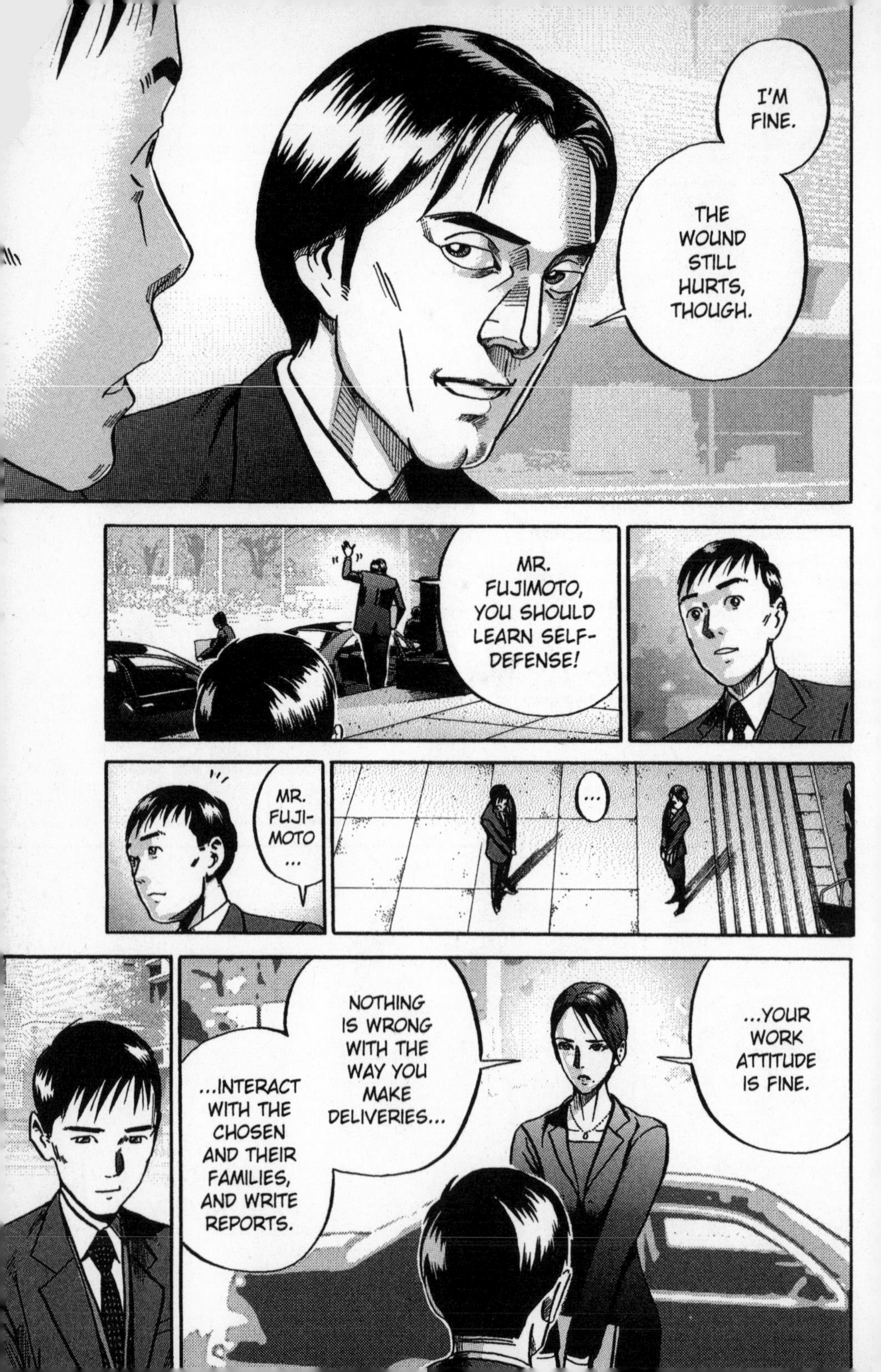
I'M FINE.
THE WOUND STILL HURTS, THOUGH.
MR. FUJIMOTO, YOU SHOULD LEARN SELF-DEFENSE!
...
MR. FUJI-MOTO ...
...YOUR WORK ATTITUDE IS FINE.
NOTHING IS WRONG WITH THE WAY YOU MAKE DELIVERIES...
...INTERACT WITH THE CHOSEN AND THEIR FAMILIES, AND WRITE REPORTS.

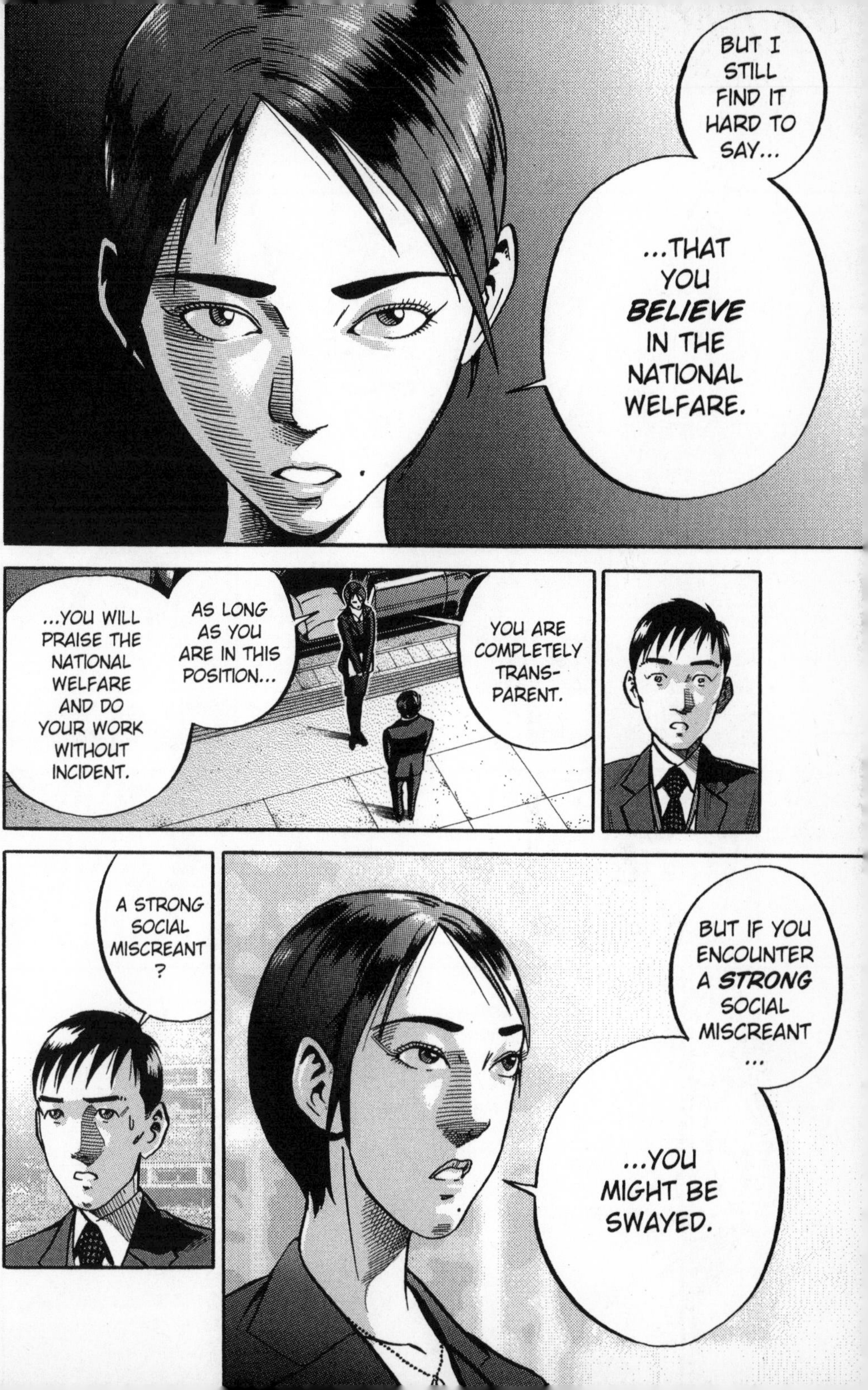
BUT I STILL FIND IT HARD TO SAY...
...THAT YOU *BELIEVE* IN THE NATIONAL WELFARE.
YOU ARE COMPLETELY TRANS-PARENT.
AS LONG AS YOU ARE IN THIS POSITION...
...YOU WILL PRAISE THE NATIONAL WELFARE AND DO YOUR WORK WITHOUT INCIDENT.
BUT IF YOU ENCOUNTER A *STRONG* SOCIAL MISCREANT...
...YOU MIGHT BE SWAYED.
A STRONG SOCIAL MISCREANT?

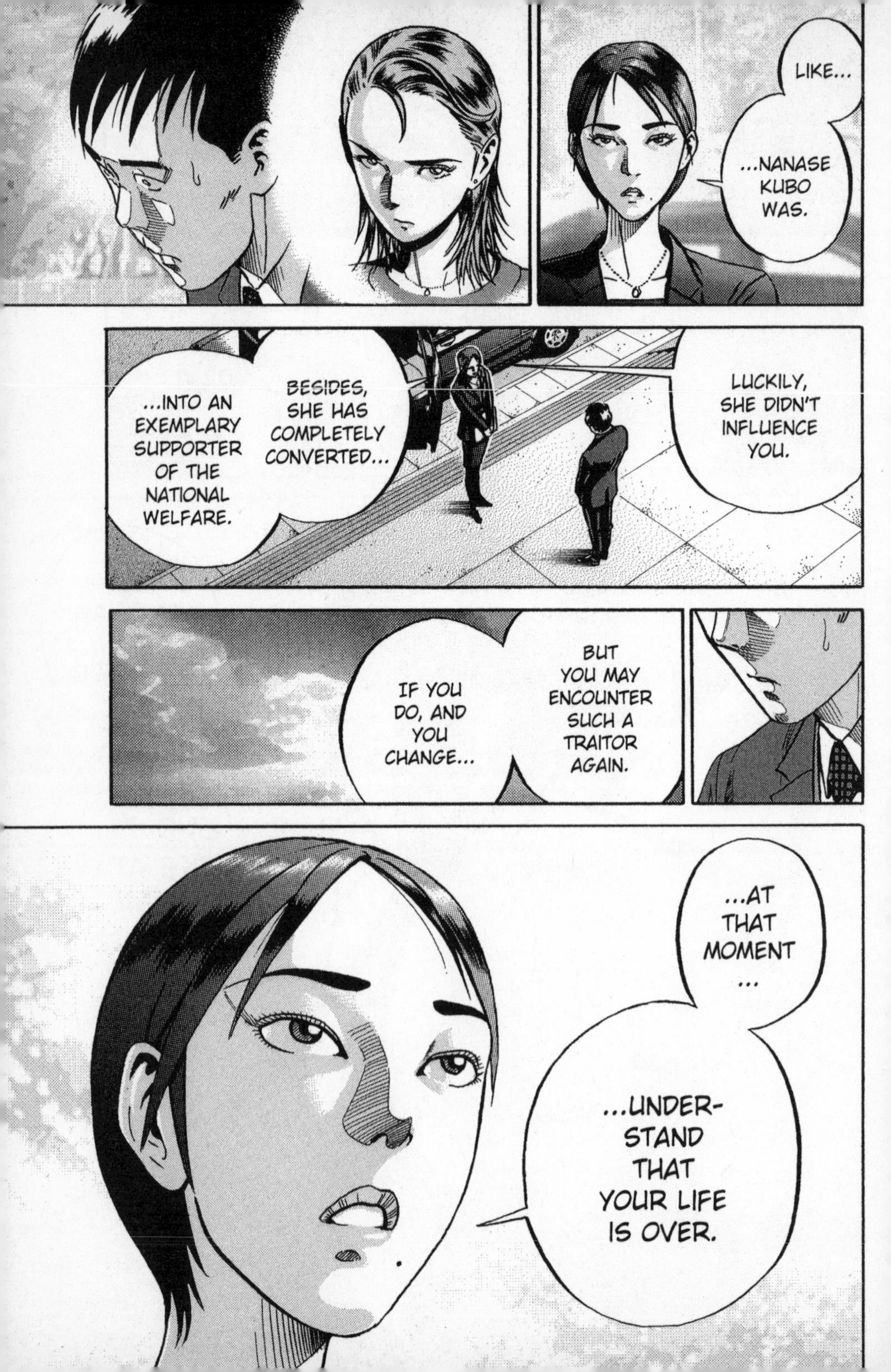
LIKE...
...NANASE KUBO WAS.
LUCKILY, SHE DIDN'T INFLUENCE YOU.
BESIDES, SHE HAS COMPLETELY CONVERTED...
...INTO AN EXEMPLARY SUPPORTER OF THE NATIONAL WELFARE.
BUT YOU MAY ENCOUNTER SUCH A TRAITOR AGAIN.
IF YOU DO, AND YOU CHANGE...
...AT THAT MOMENT...
...UNDERSTAND THAT YOUR LIFE IS OVER.

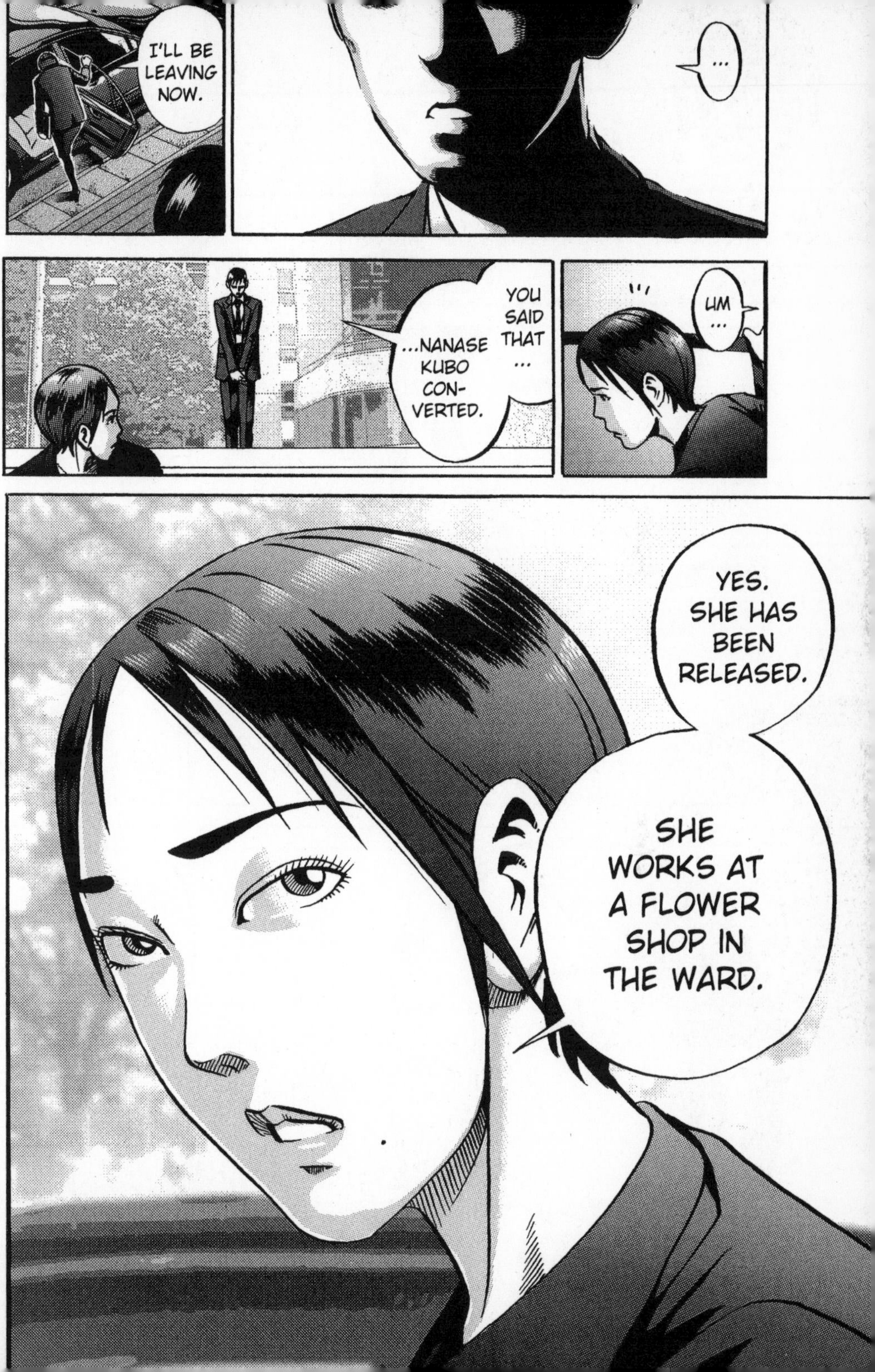
...
I'LL BE LEAVING NOW.
UM ...
YOU SAID THAT ...
...NANASE KUBO CON-VERTED.
YES. SHE HAS BEEN RELEASED.
SHE WORKS AT A FLOWER SHOP IN THE WARD.

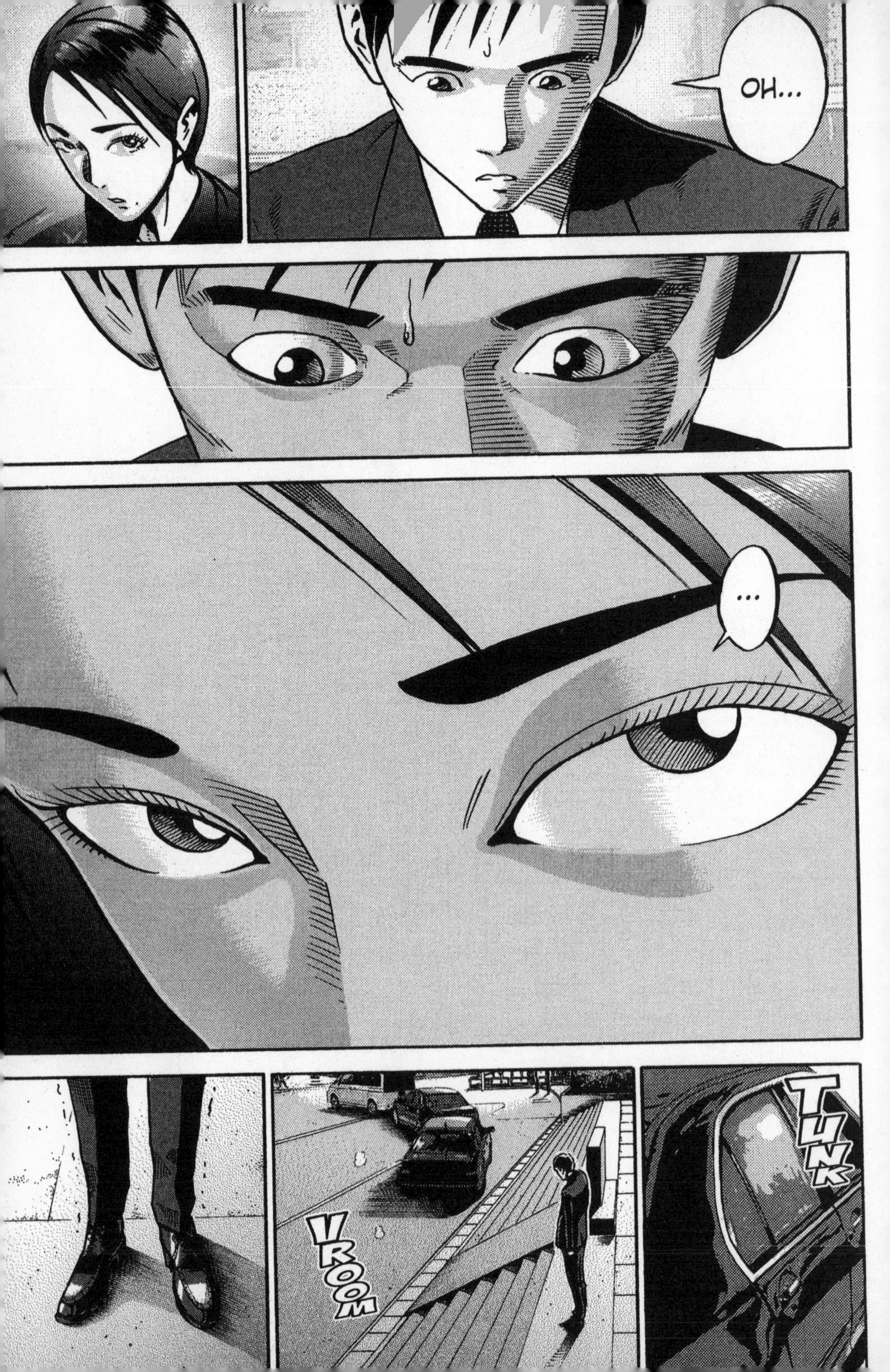
OH...
...
TUNK
VROOM

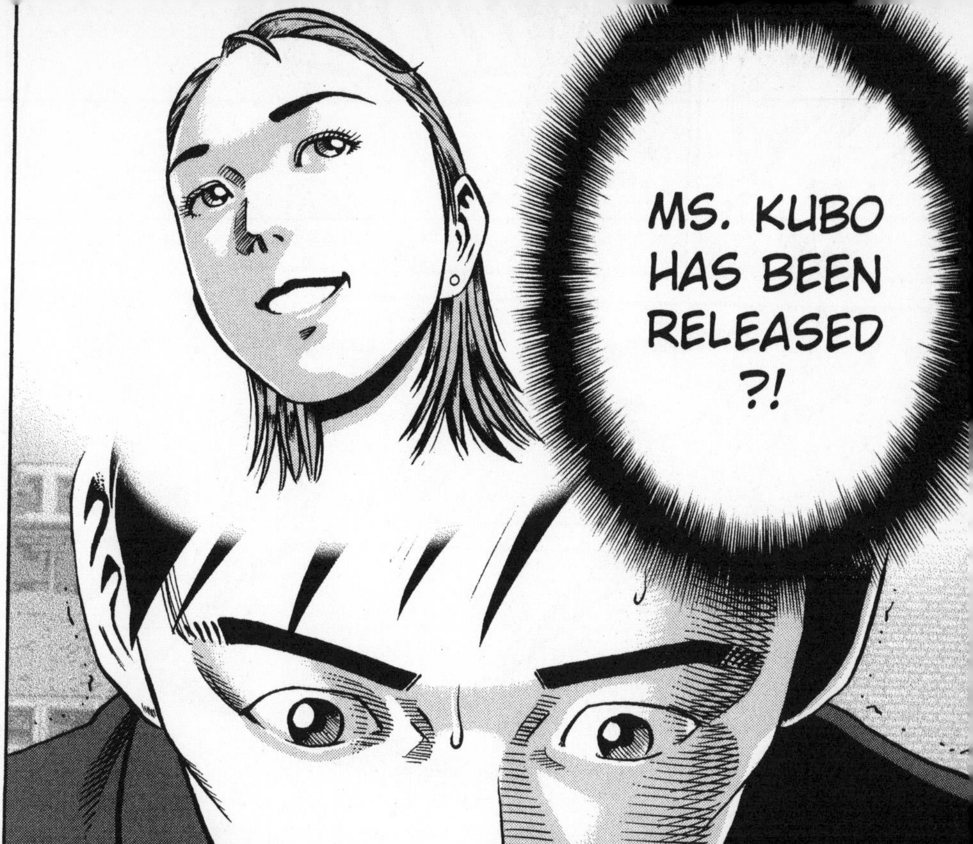
MS. KUBO HAS BEEN RELEASED ?!

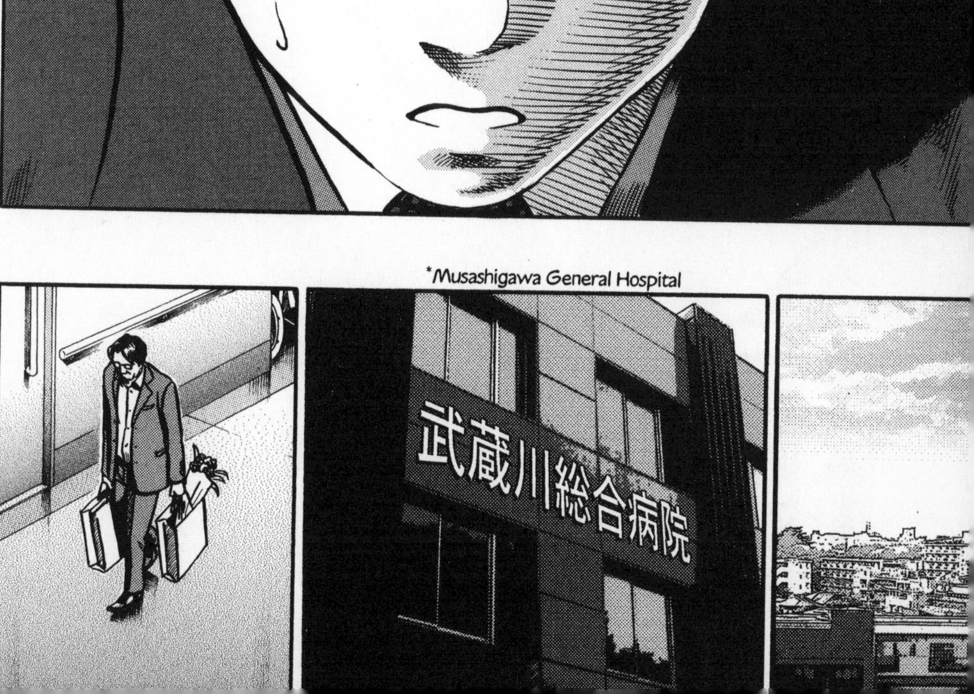
武蔵川総合病院

*Musashigawa General Hospital

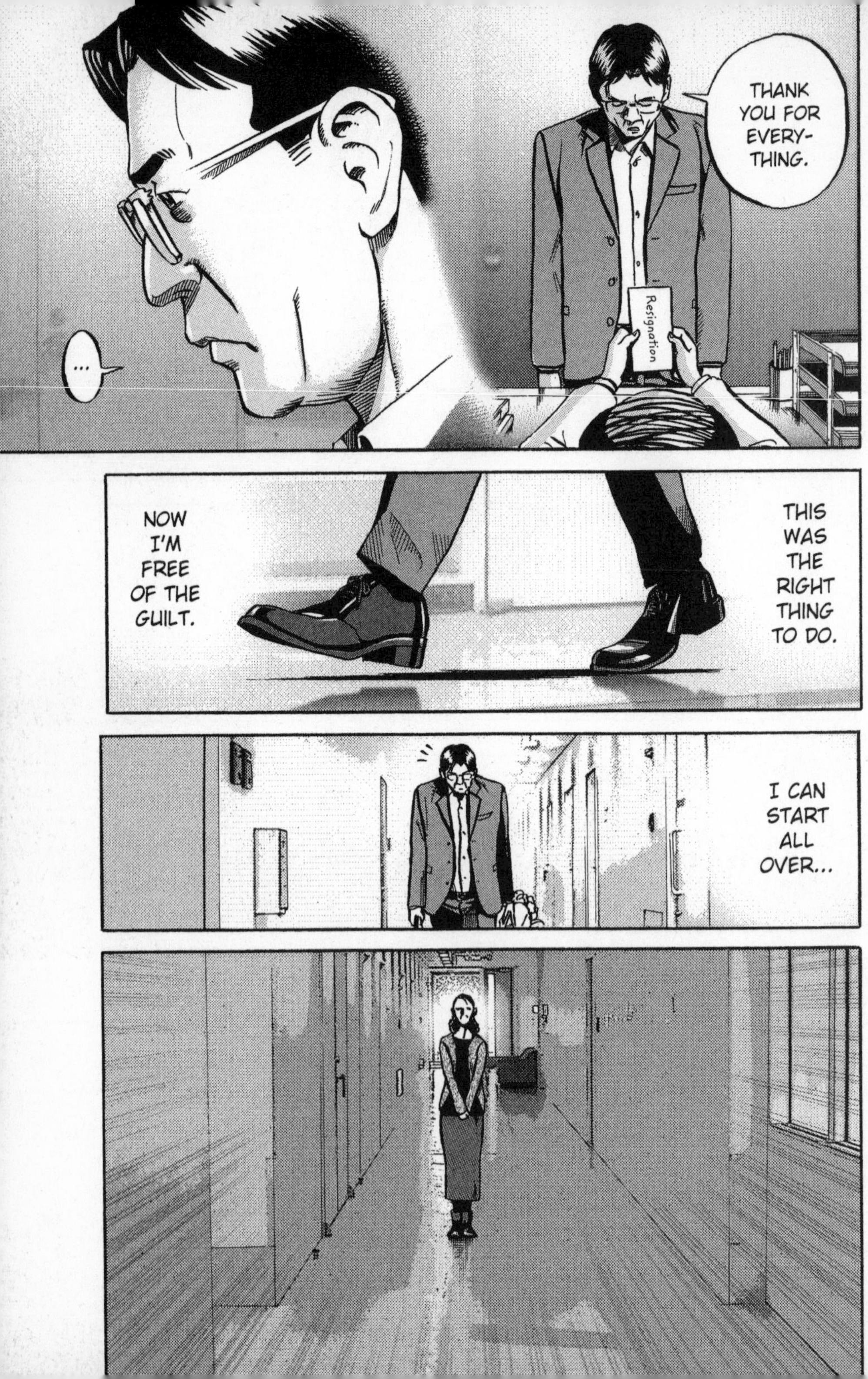
THANK YOU FOR EVERY-THING.
Resignation
...
THIS WAS THE RIGHT THING TO DO.
NOW I'M FREE OF THE GUILT.
I CAN START ALL OVER...

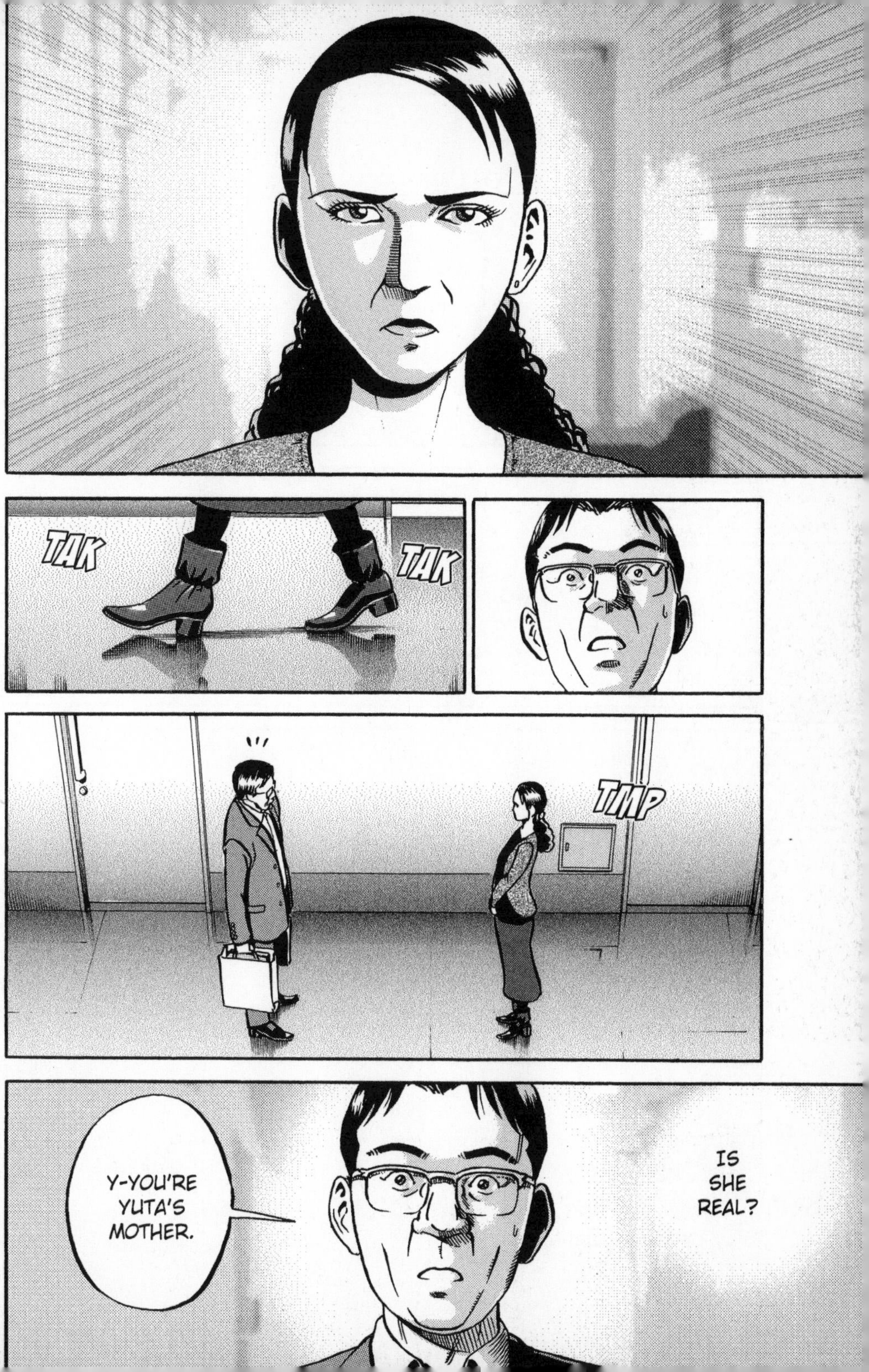
TAK
TAK
TMP
IS SHE REAL?
Y-YOU'RE YUTA'S MOTHER.

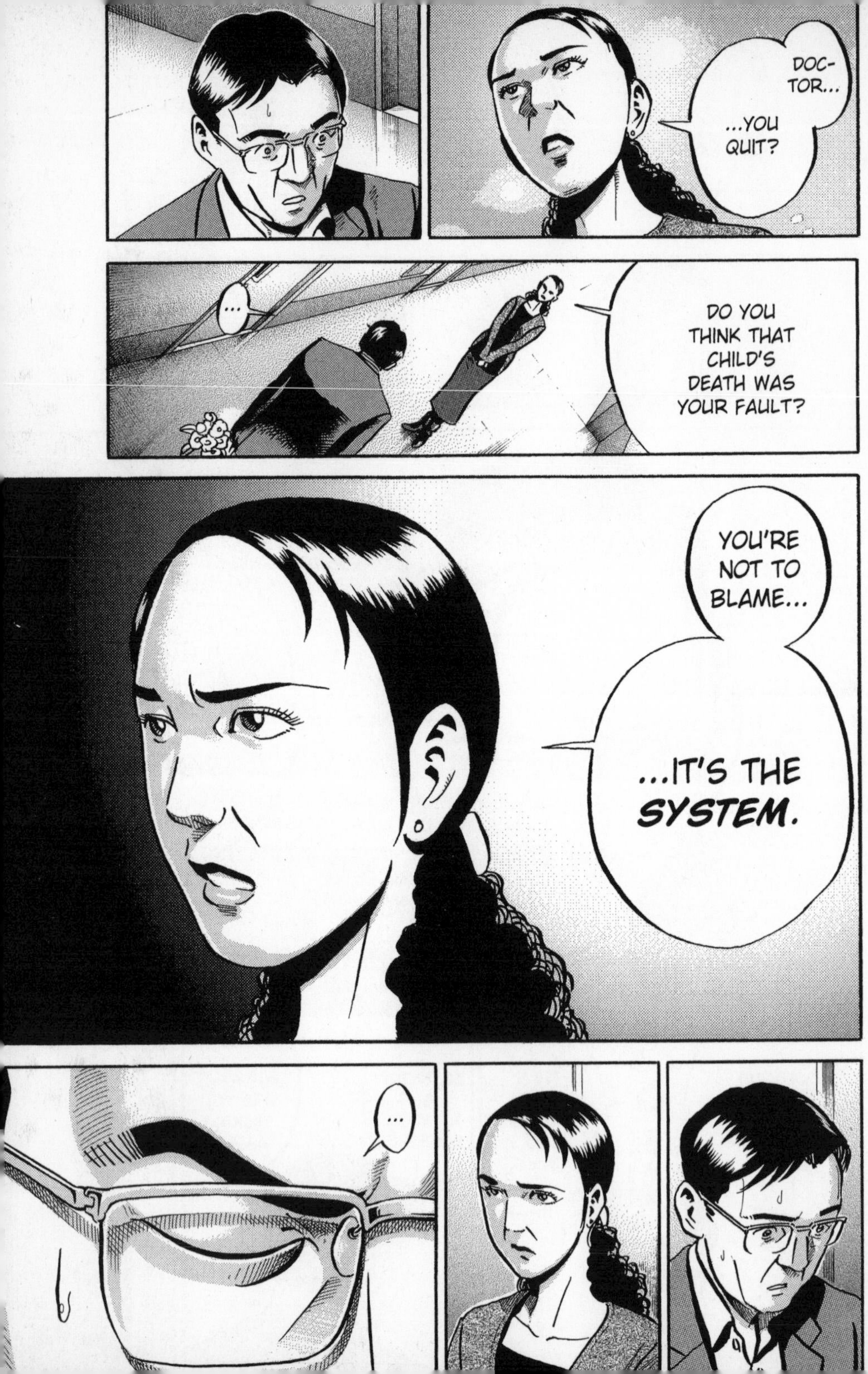
DOCTOR...
...YOU QUIT?
DO YOU THINK THAT CHILD'S DEATH WAS YOUR FAULT?
...
YOU'RE NOT TO BLAME...
...IT'S THE *SYSTEM.*
...

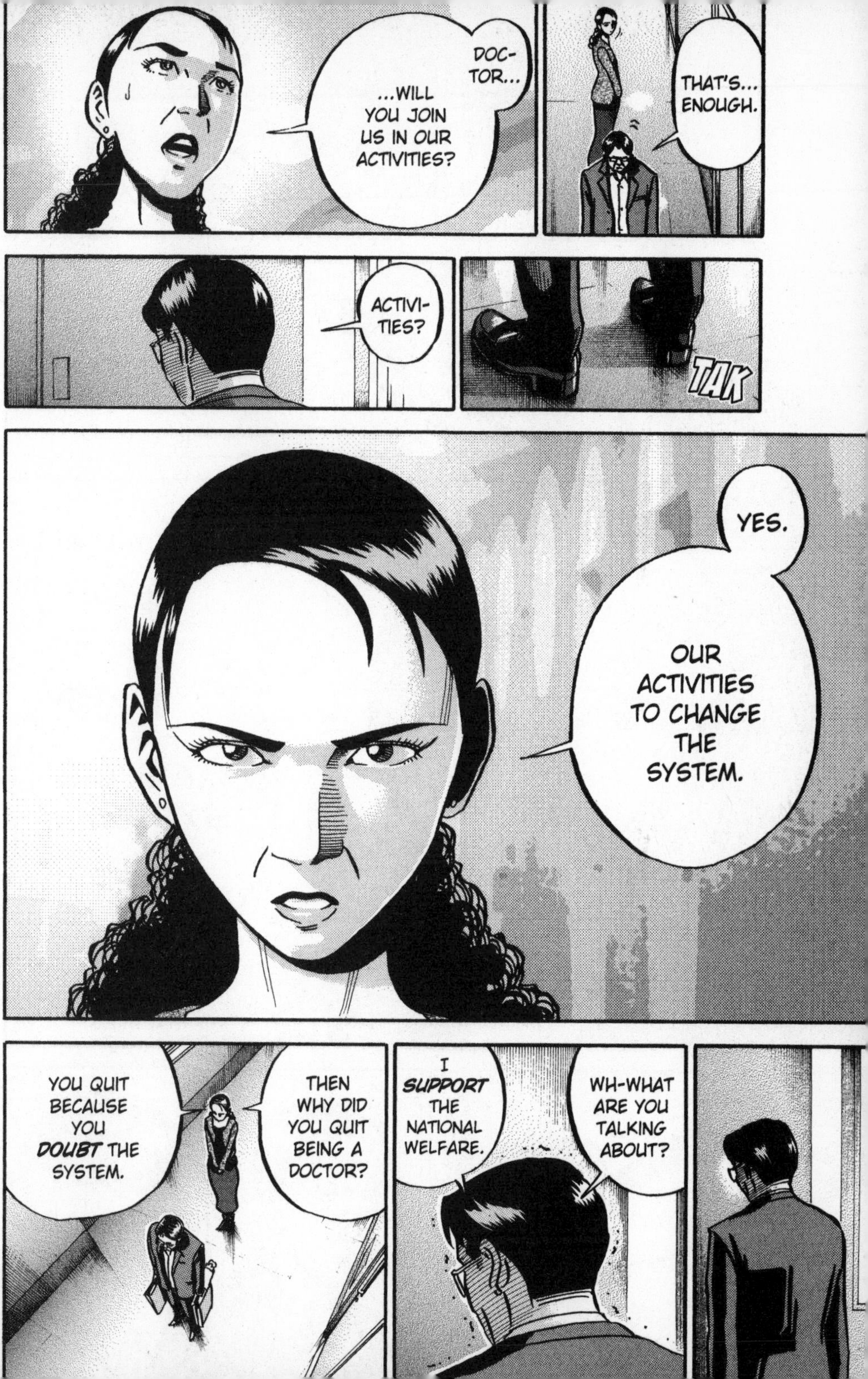
THAT'S... ENOUGH.
DOC-TOR...
...WILL YOU JOIN US IN OUR ACTIVITIES?
TAK
ACTIVI-TIES?
YES.
OUR ACTIVITIES TO CHANGE THE SYSTEM.
WH-WHAT ARE YOU TALKING ABOUT?
I *SUPPORT* THE NATIONAL WELFARE.
THEN WHY DID YOU QUIT BEING A DOCTOR?
YOU QUIT BECAUSE YOU *DOUBT* THE SYSTEM.

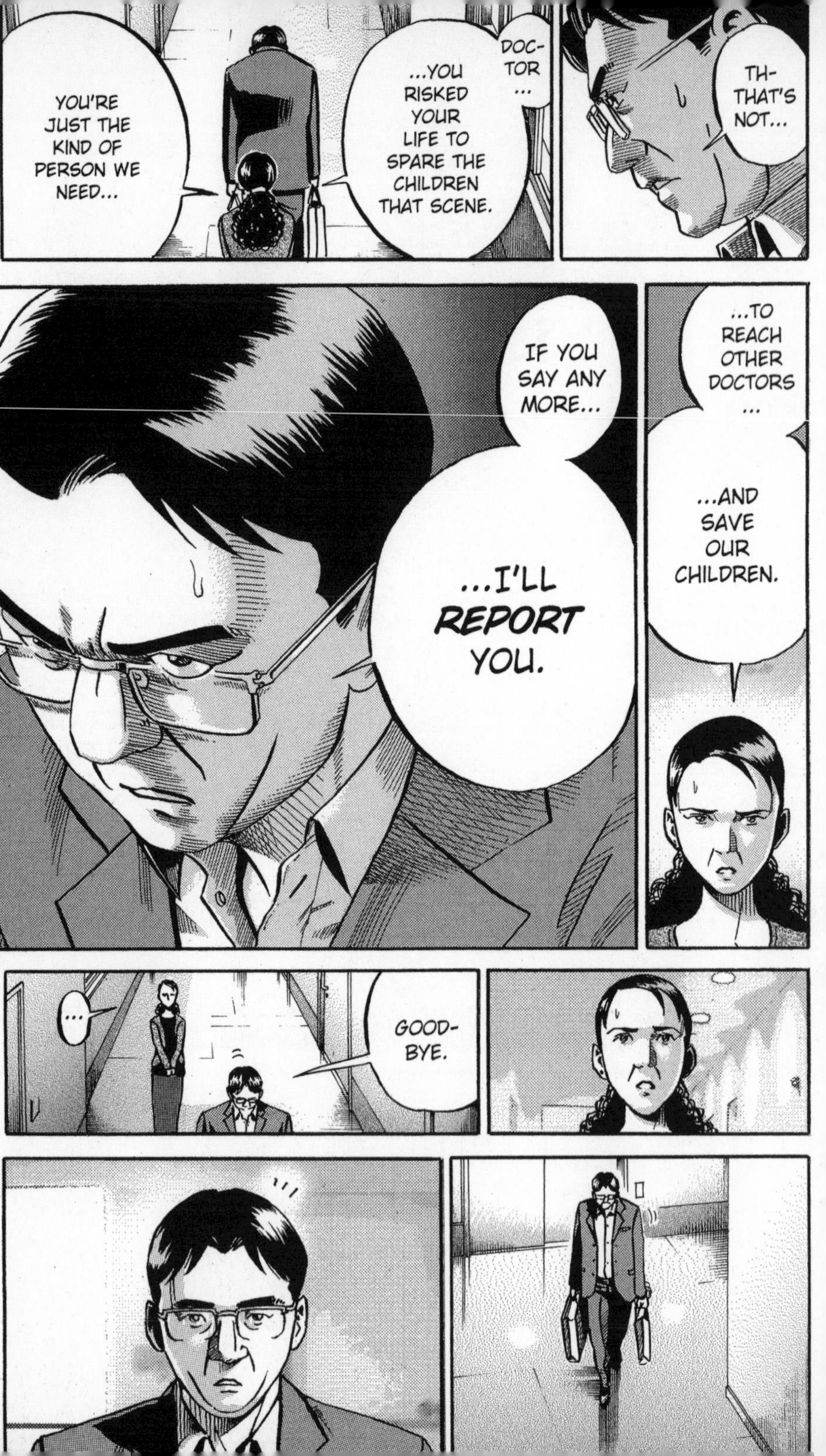
TH- THAT'S NOT...
DOC- TOR ...
...YOU RISKED YOUR LIFE TO SPARE THE CHILDREN THAT SCENE.
YOU'RE JUST THE KIND OF PERSON WE NEED...
...TO REACH OTHER DOCTORS ...
...AND SAVE OUR CHILDREN.
IF YOU SAY ANY MORE...
...I'LL **REPORT** YOU.
GOOD- BYE.
...

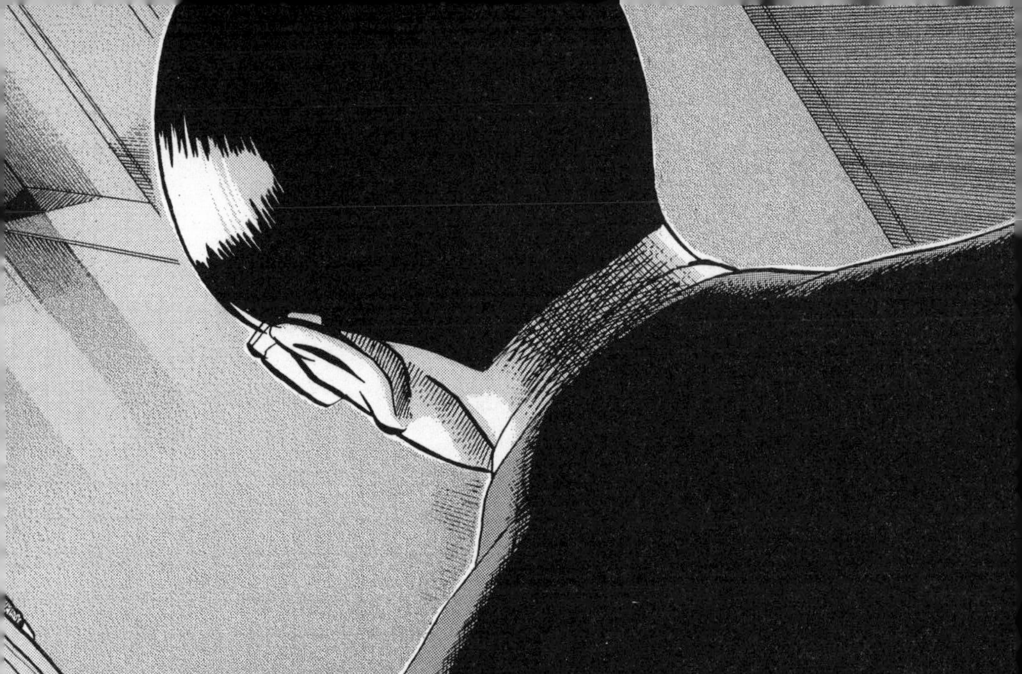

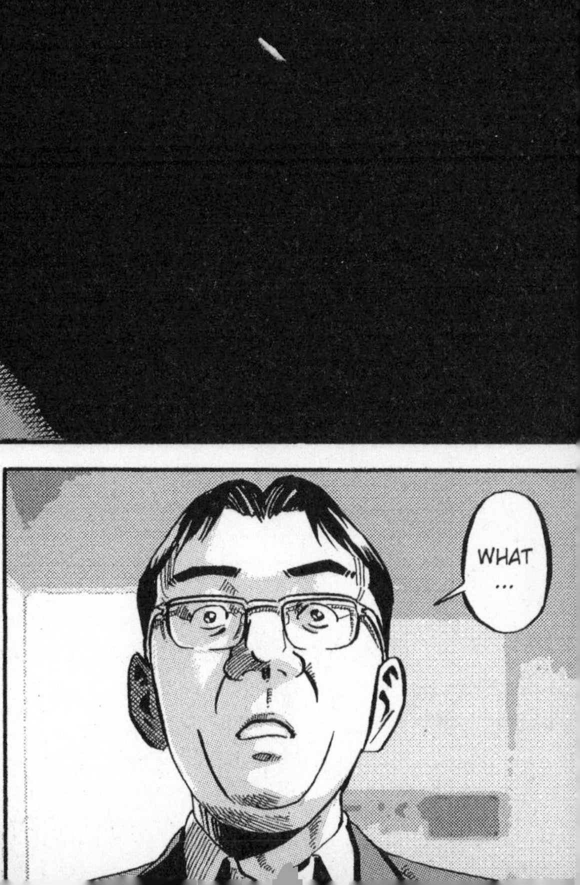
WHAT ...

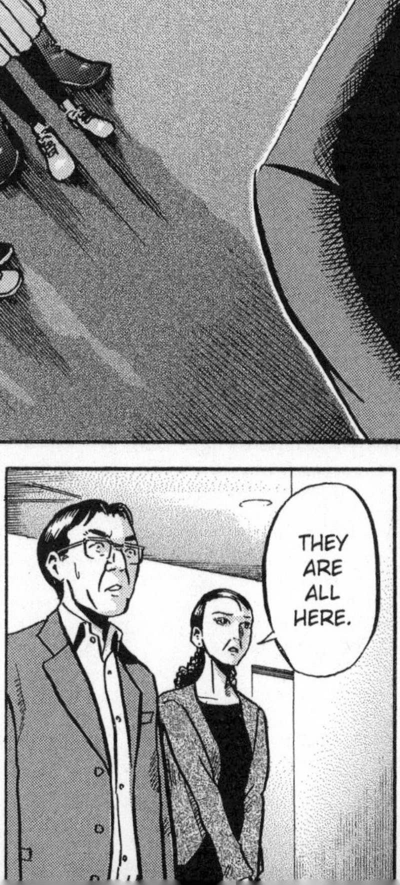
THEY ARE ALL HERE.

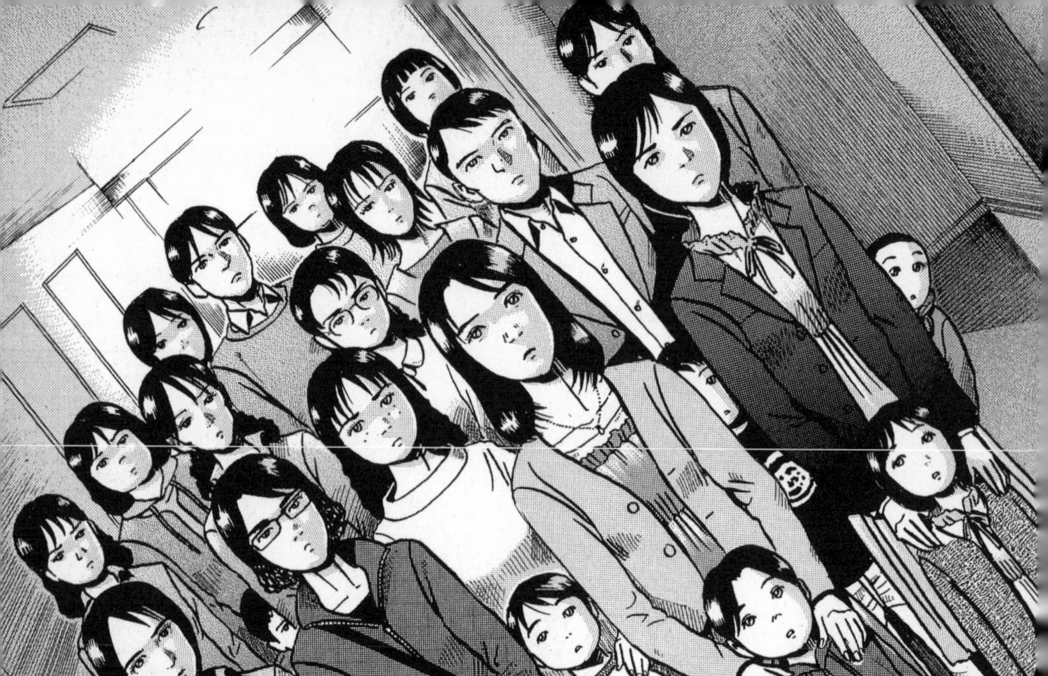

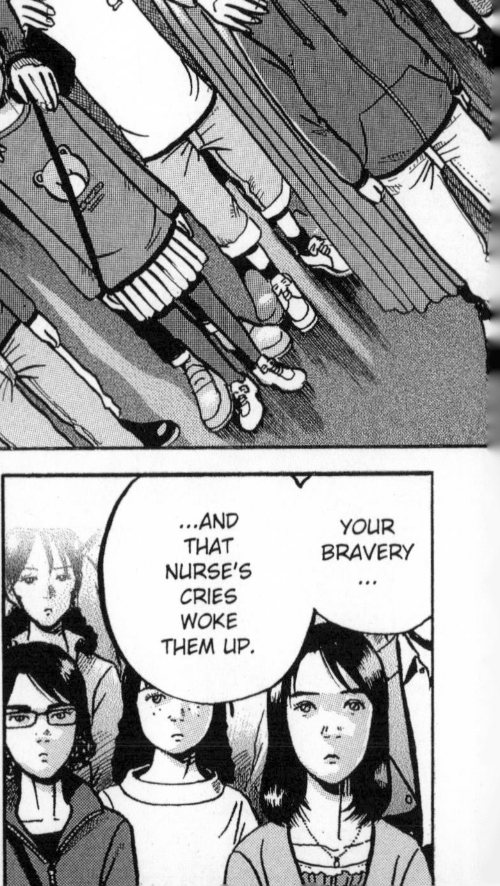
YOUR BRAVERY ...
...AND THAT NURSE'S CRIES WOKE THEM UP.

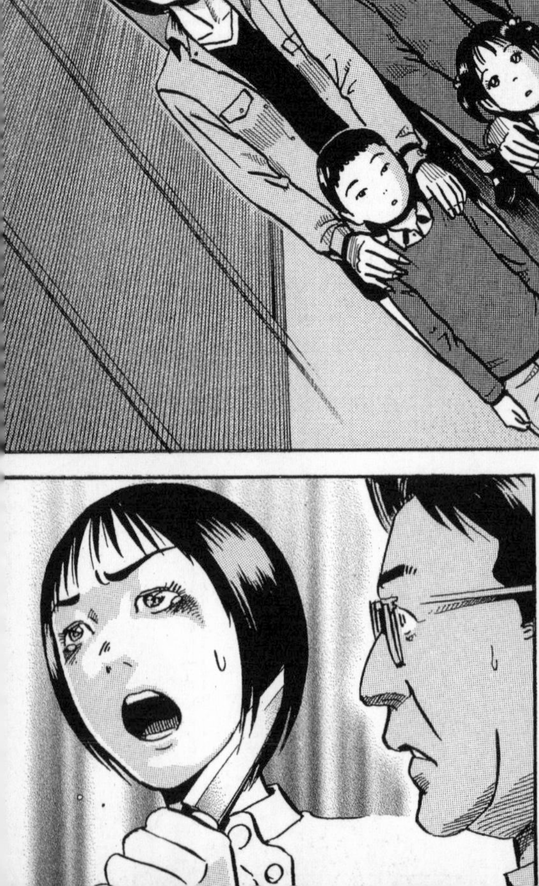

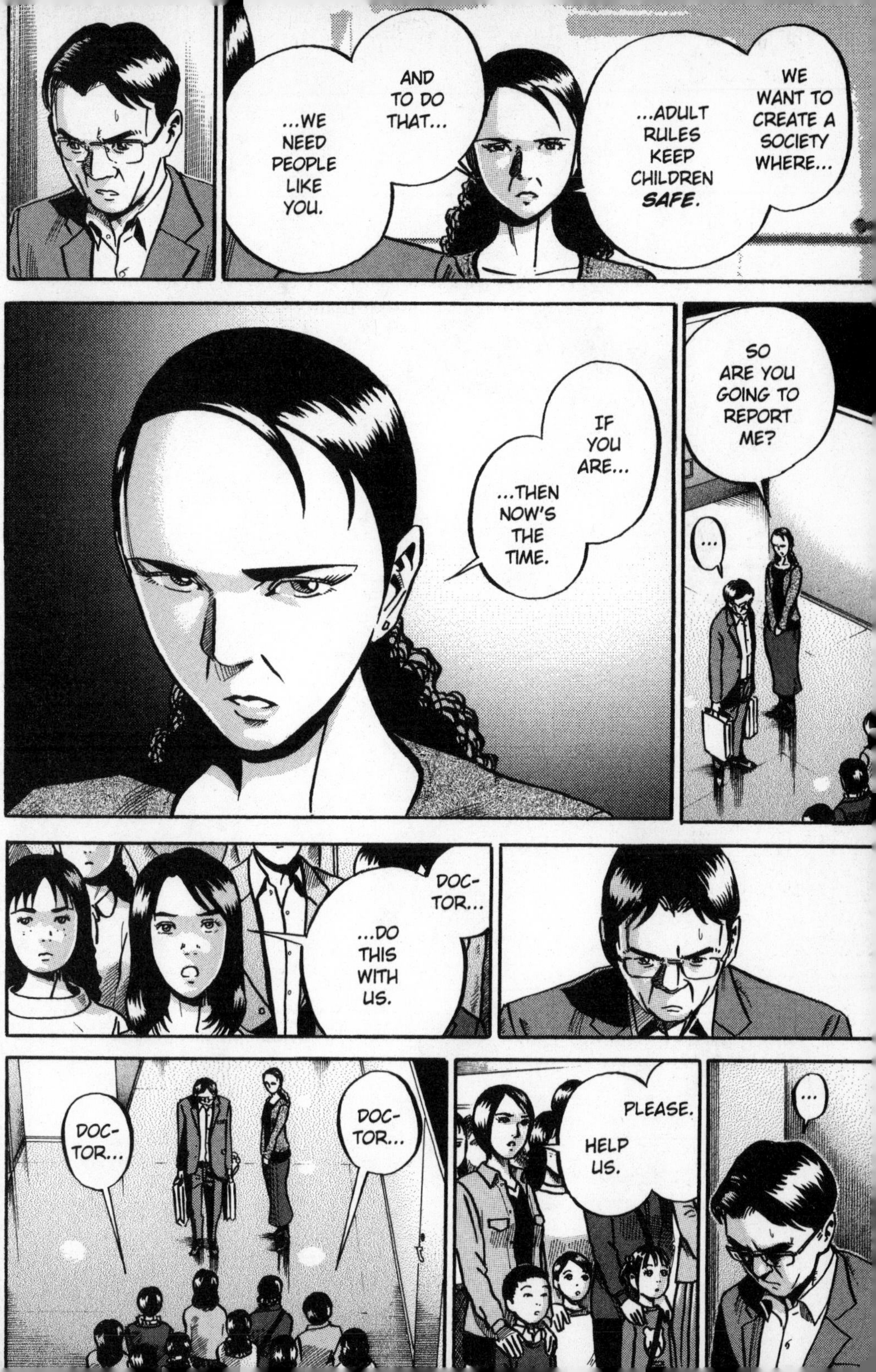
WE WANT TO CREATE A SOCIETY WHERE...
...ADULT RULES KEEP CHILDREN *SAFE*.
AND TO DO THAT...
...WE NEED PEOPLE LIKE YOU.
SO ARE YOU GOING TO REPORT ME?
...
IF YOU ARE...
...THEN NOW'S THE TIME.
DOC-TOR...
...DO THIS WITH US.
...
PLEASE.
HELP US.
DOC-TOR...
DOC-TOR...

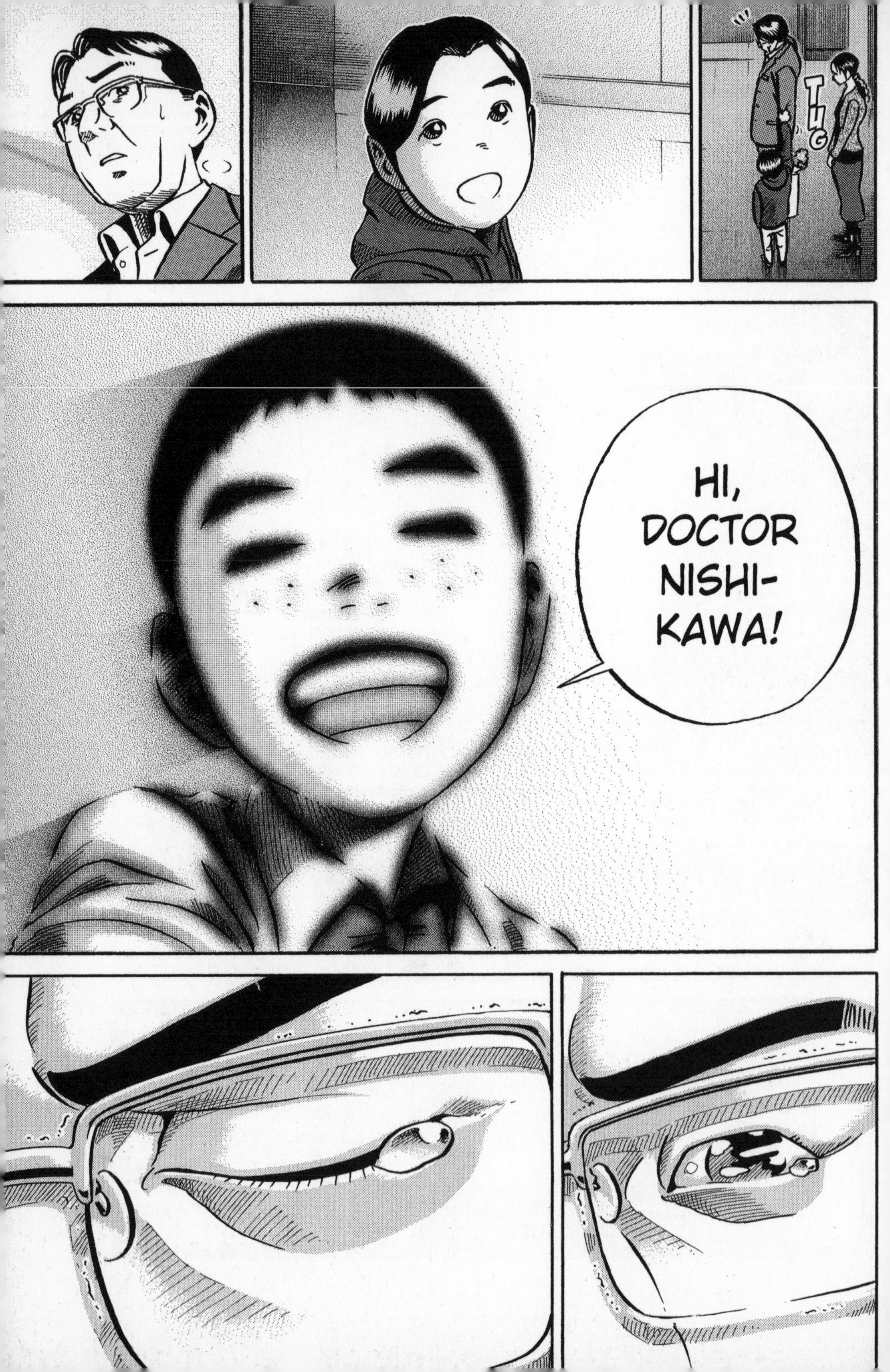
TUG
HI, DOCTOR NISHI-KAWA!

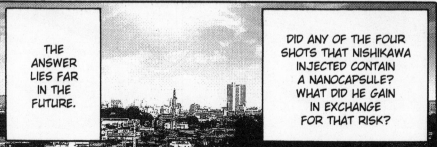

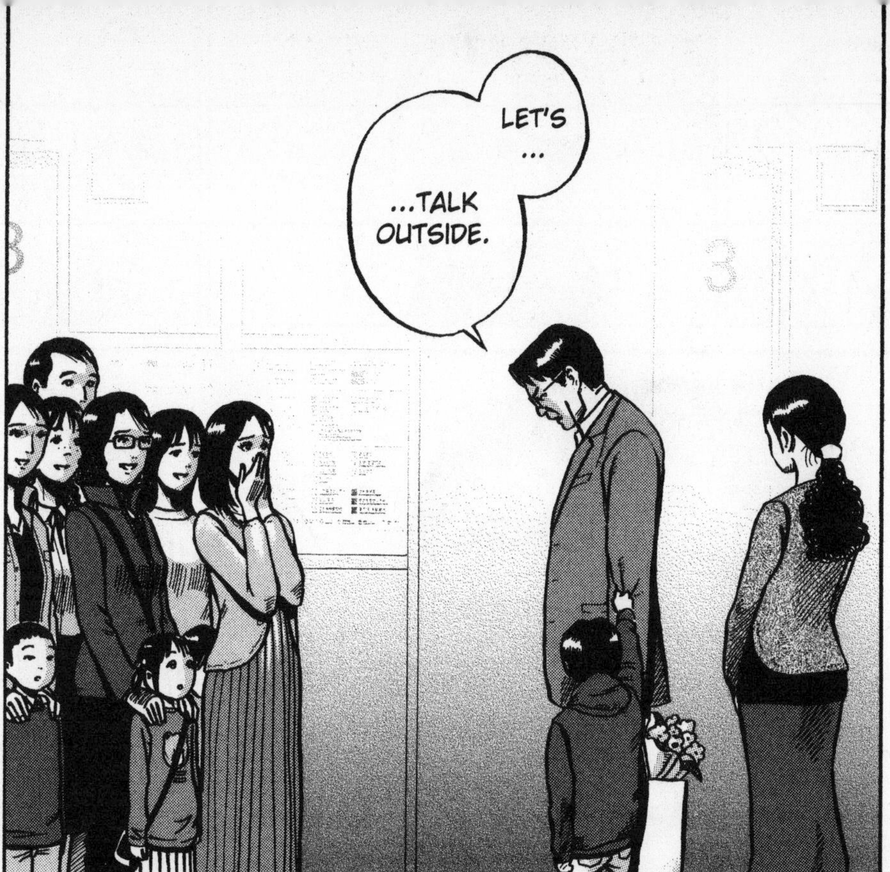
LET'S ...
...TALK OUTSIDE.

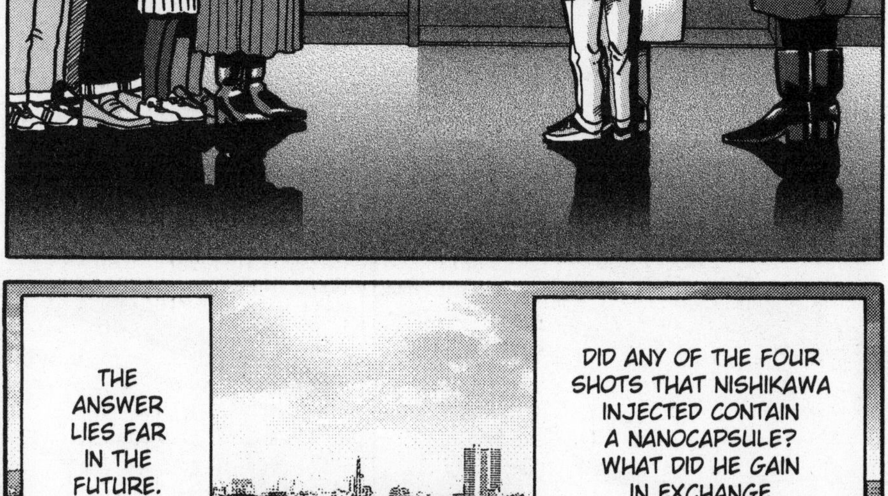
DID ANY OF THE FOUR SHOTS THAT NISHIKAWA INJECTED CONTAIN A NANOCAPSULE? WHAT DID HE GAIN IN EXCHANGE FOR THAT RISK?
THE ANSWER LIES FAR IN THE FUTURE.

Episode 18 Two Fallen in War Act 1

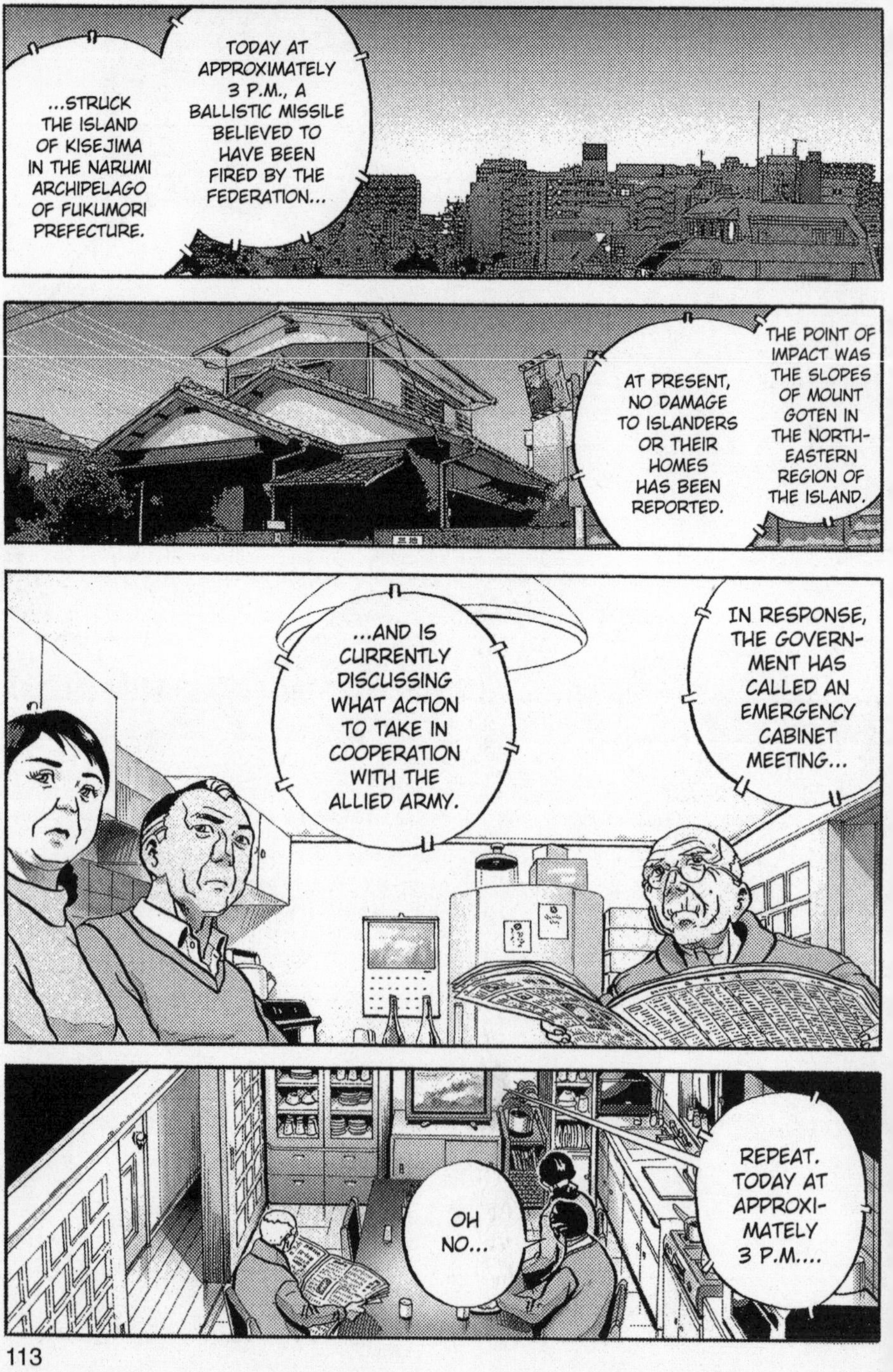
TODAY AT APPROXIMATELY 3 P.M., A BALLISTIC MISSILE BELIEVED TO HAVE BEEN FIRED BY THE FEDERATION...
...STRUCK THE ISLAND OF KISEJIMA IN THE NARUMI ARCHIPELAGO OF FUKUMORI PREFECTURE.
THE POINT OF IMPACT WAS THE SLOPES OF MOUNT GOTEN IN THE NORTH-EASTERN REGION OF THE ISLAND.
AT PRESENT, NO DAMAGE TO ISLANDERS OR THEIR HOMES HAS BEEN REPORTED.
IN RESPONSE, THE GOVERNMENT HAS CALLED AN EMERGENCY CABINET MEETING...
...AND IS CURRENTLY DISCUSSING WHAT ACTION TO TAKE IN COOPERATION WITH THE ALLIED ARMY.
REPEAT. TODAY AT APPROXIMATELY 3 P.M....
OH NO...

*Today approx. 3 P.M.

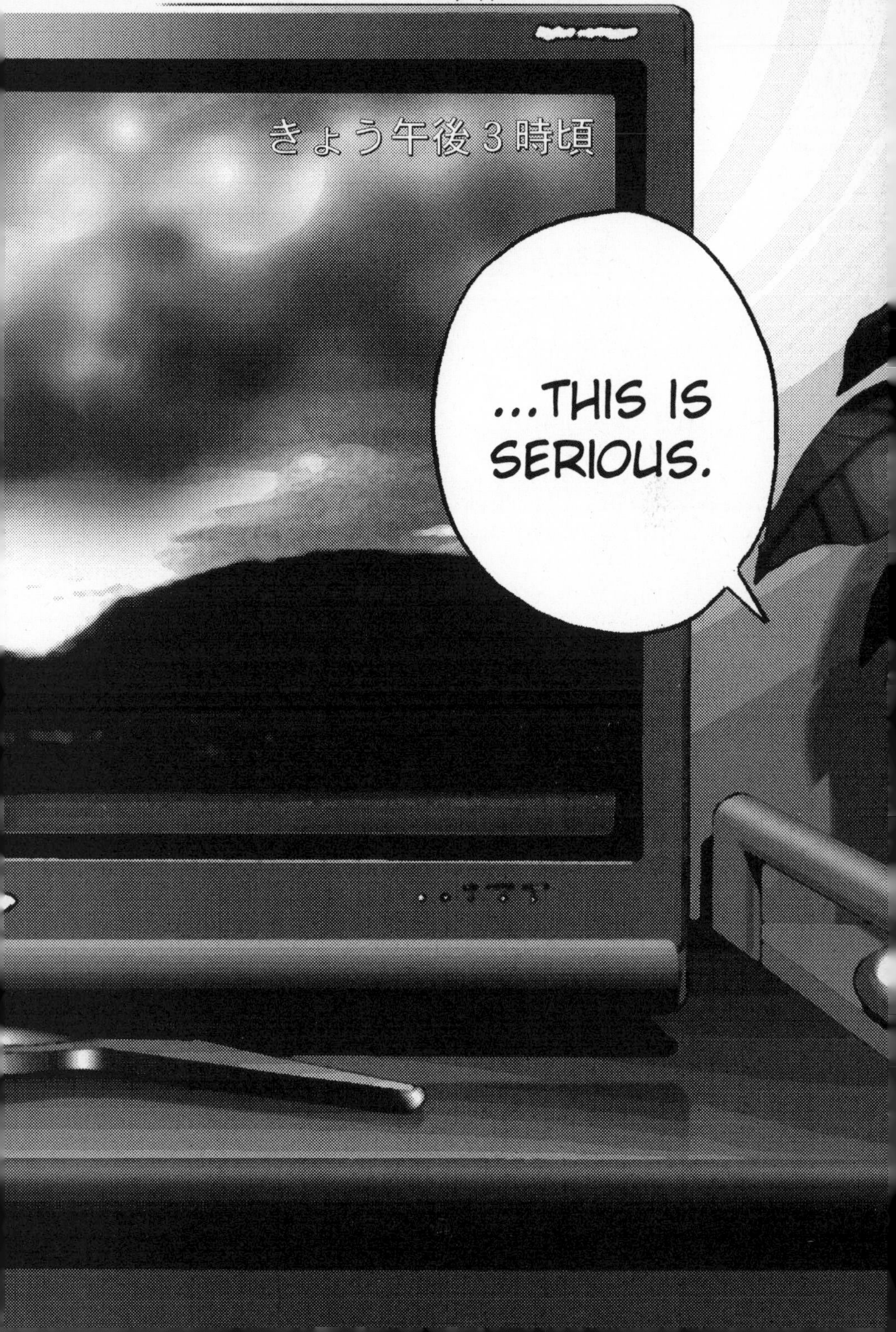
きょう午後３時頃
...THIS IS SERIOUS.

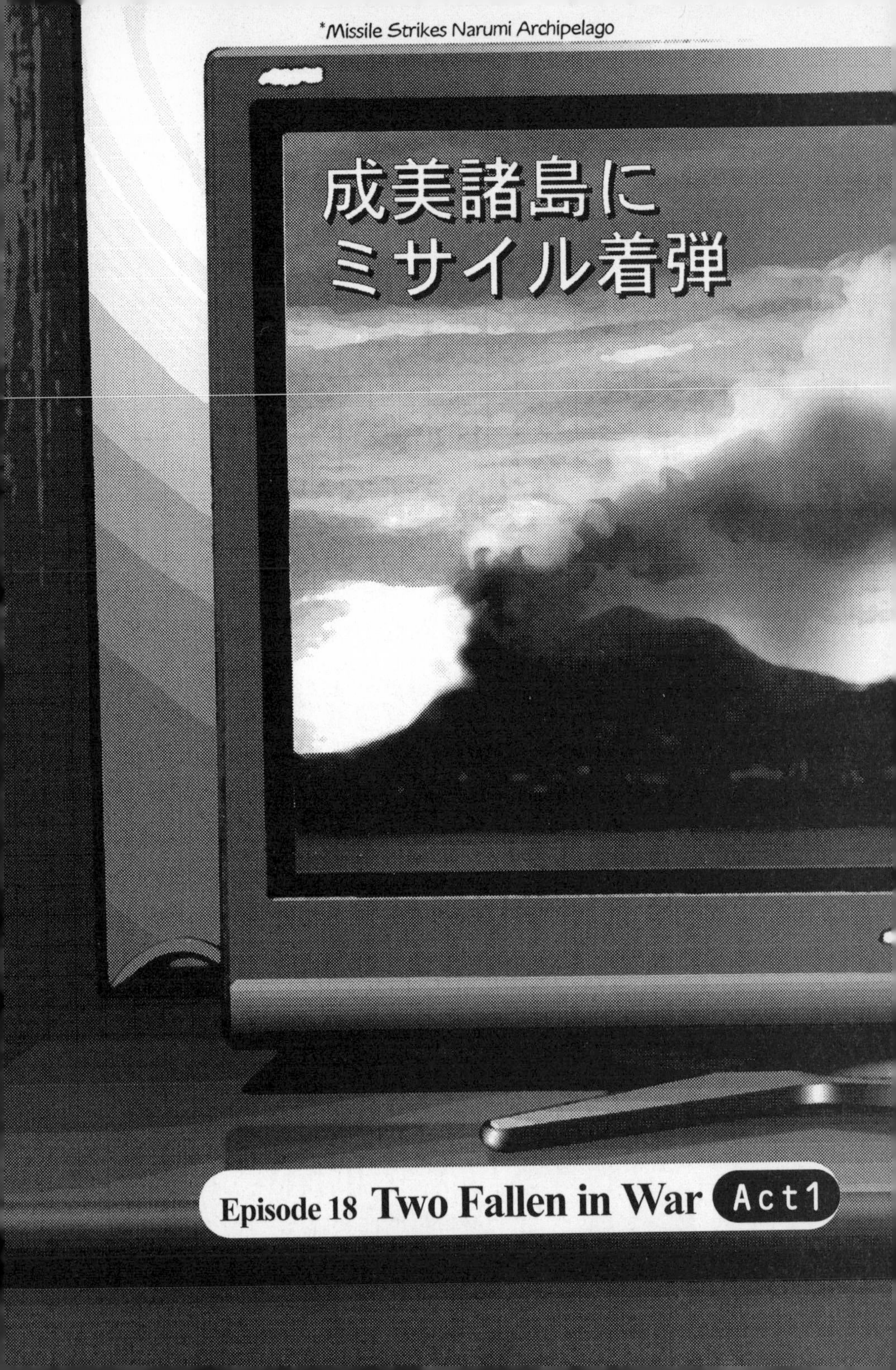
*Missile Strikes Narumi Archipelago
成美諸島に
ミサイル着弾
Episode 18 Two Fallen in War Act1

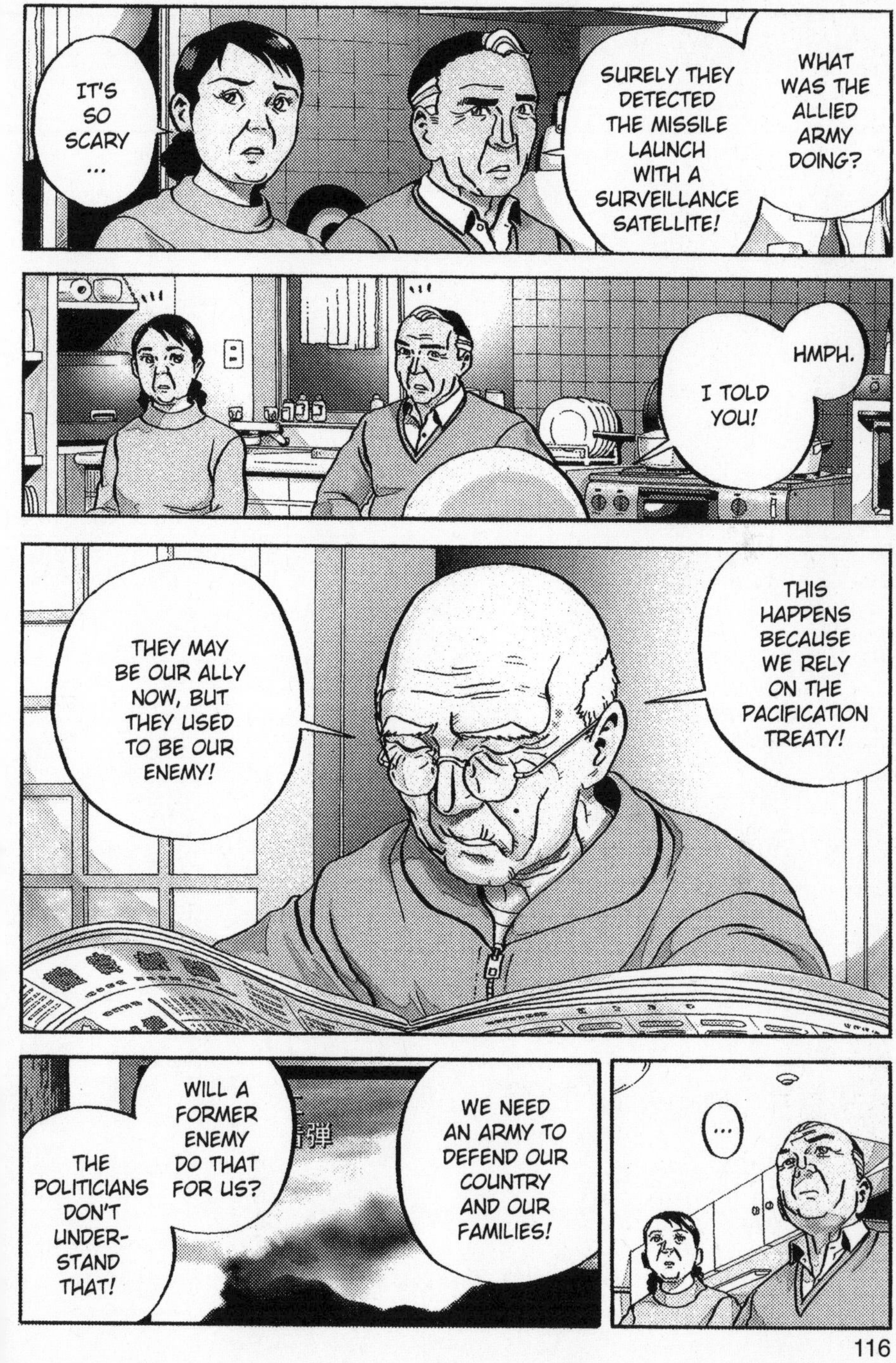
WHAT WAS THE ALLIED ARMY DOING?
SURELY THEY DETECTED THE MISSILE LAUNCH WITH A SURVEILLANCE SATELLITE!
IT'S SO SCARY ...
HMPH.
I TOLD YOU!
THIS HAPPENS BECAUSE WE RELY ON THE PACIFICATION TREATY!
THEY MAY BE OUR ALLY NOW, BUT THEY USED TO BE OUR ENEMY!
...
WE NEED AN ARMY TO DEFEND OUR COUNTRY AND OUR FAMILIES!
WILL A FORMER ENEMY DO THAT FOR US?
THE POLITICIANS DON'T UNDER-STAND THAT!

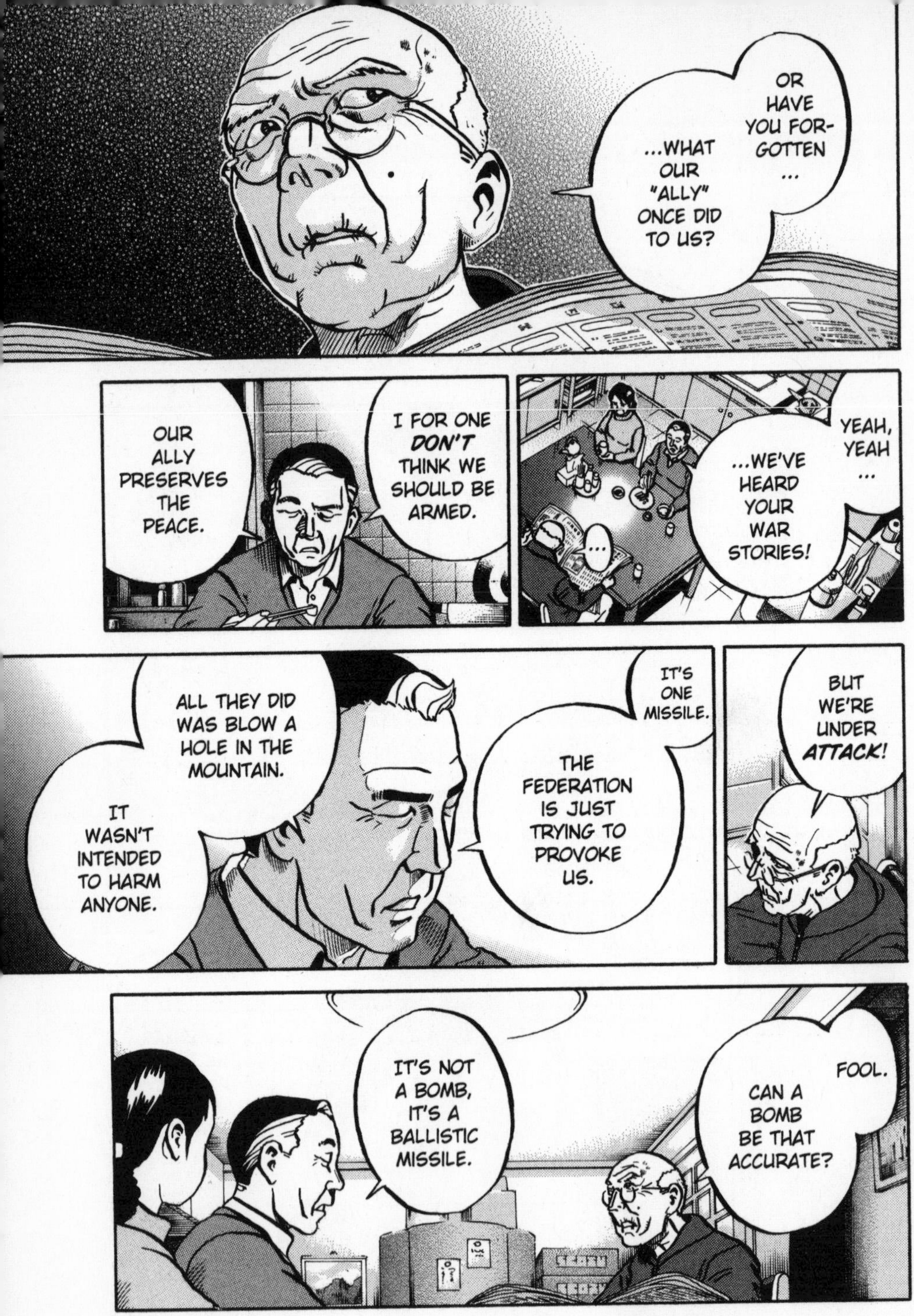
OR HAVE YOU FORGOTTEN ...
...WHAT OUR "ALLY" ONCE DID TO US?
YEAH, YEAH ...
...WE'VE HEARD YOUR WAR STORIES!
...
I FOR ONE DON'T THINK WE SHOULD BE ARMED.
OUR ALLY PRESERVES THE PEACE.
BUT WE'RE UNDER ATTACK!
IT'S ONE MISSILE.
THE FEDERATION IS JUST TRYING TO PROVOKE US.
ALL THEY DID WAS BLOW A HOLE IN THE MOUNTAIN.
IT WASN'T INTENDED TO HARM ANYONE.
FOOL.
CAN A BOMB BE THAT ACCURATE?
IT'S NOT A BOMB, IT'S A BALLISTIC MISSILE.

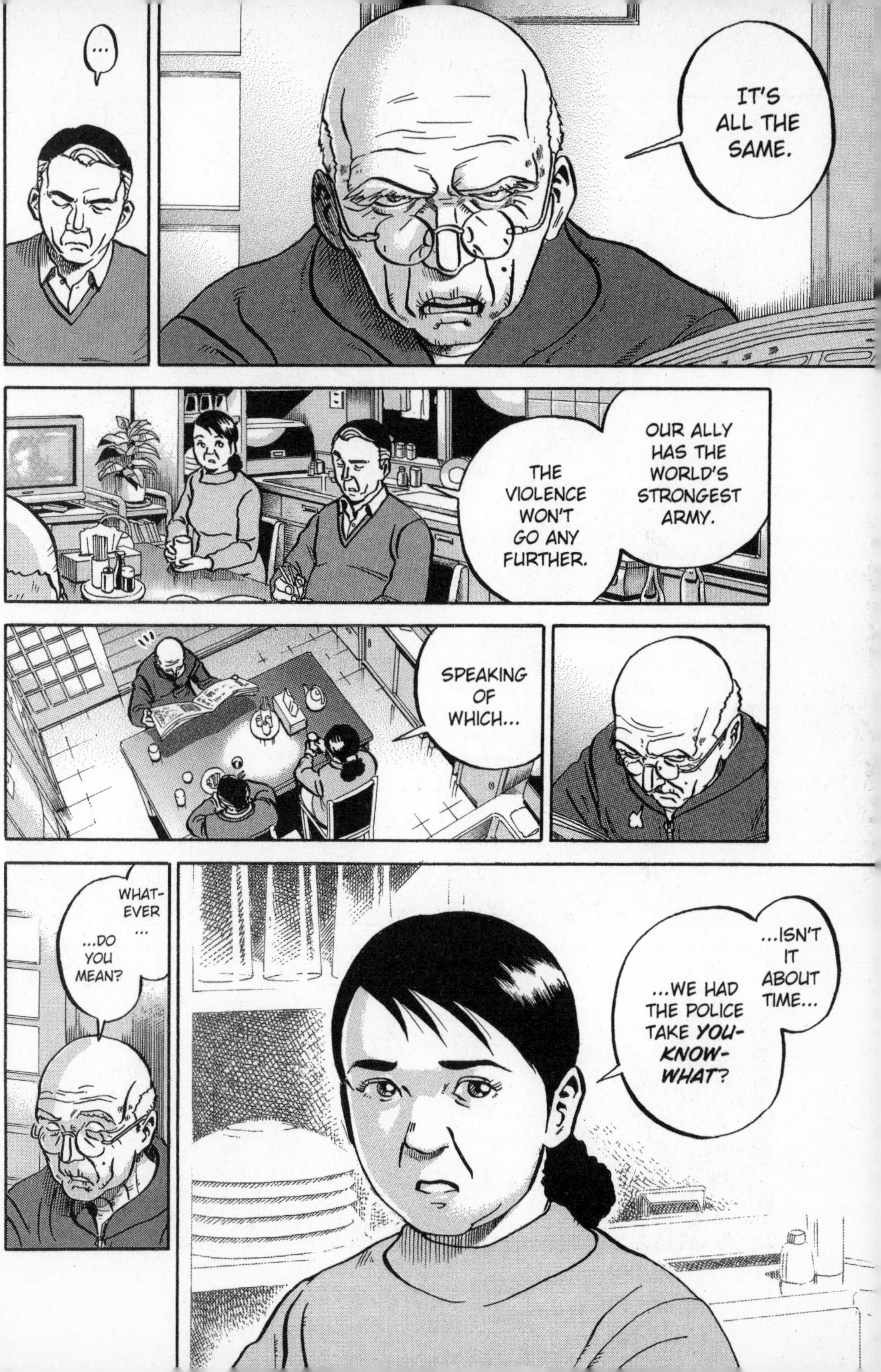
IT'S ALL THE SAME.
...
OUR ALLY HAS THE WORLD'S STRONGEST ARMY.
THE VIOLENCE WON'T GO ANY FURTHER.
SPEAKING OF WHICH...
...ISN'T IT ABOUT TIME...
...WE HAD THE POLICE TAKE *YOU-KNOW-WHAT*?
WHAT-EVER ...
...DO YOU MEAN?

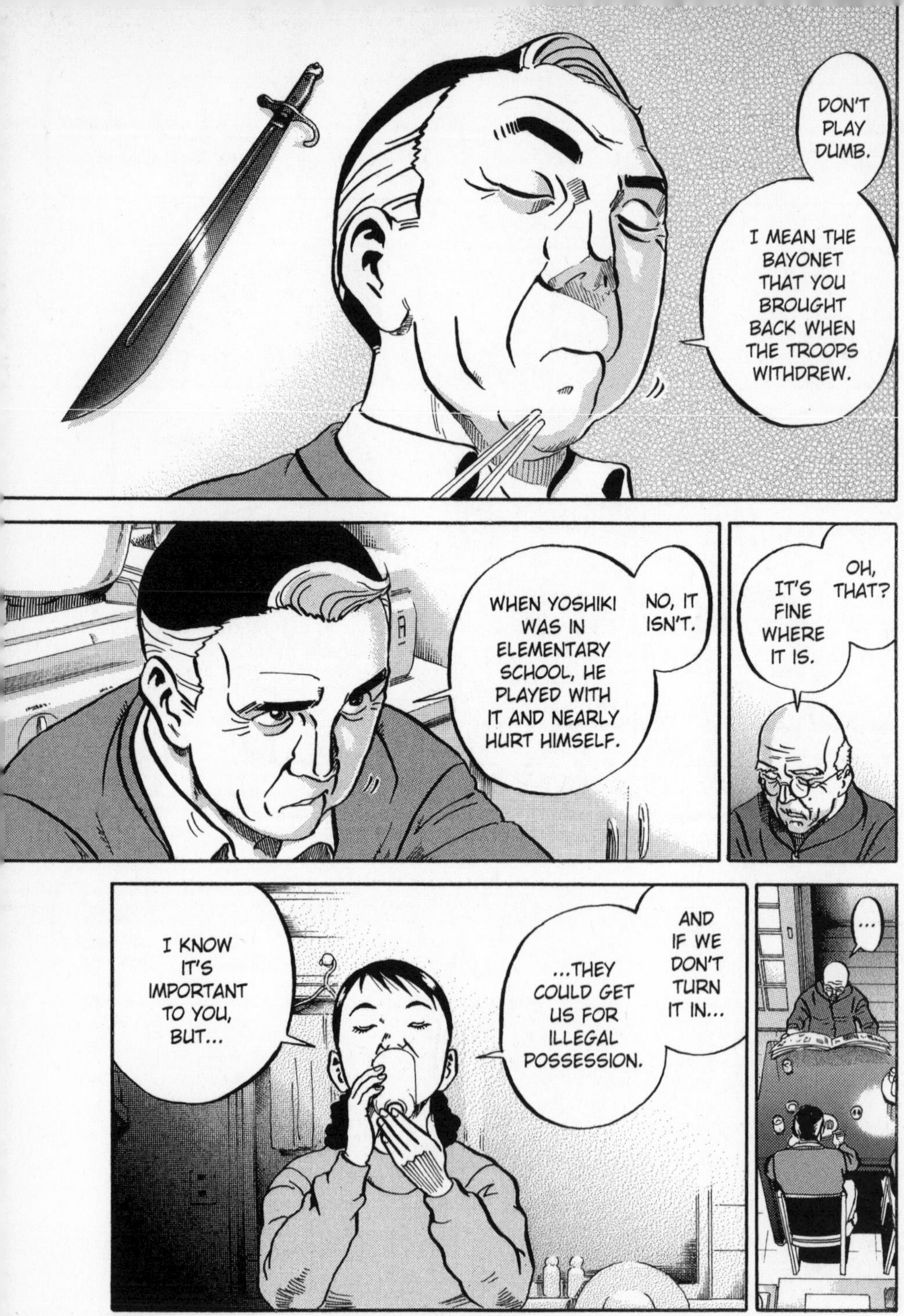
DON'T PLAY DUMB.
I MEAN THE BAYONET THAT YOU BROUGHT BACK WHEN THE TROOPS WITHDREW.
OH, THAT?
IT'S FINE WHERE IT IS.
NO, IT ISN'T.
WHEN YOSHIKI WAS IN ELEMENTARY SCHOOL, HE PLAYED WITH IT AND NEARLY HURT HIMSELF.
...
AND IF WE DON'T TURN IT IN...
...THEY COULD GET US FOR ILLEGAL POSSESSION.
I KNOW IT'S IMPORTANT TO YOU, BUT...

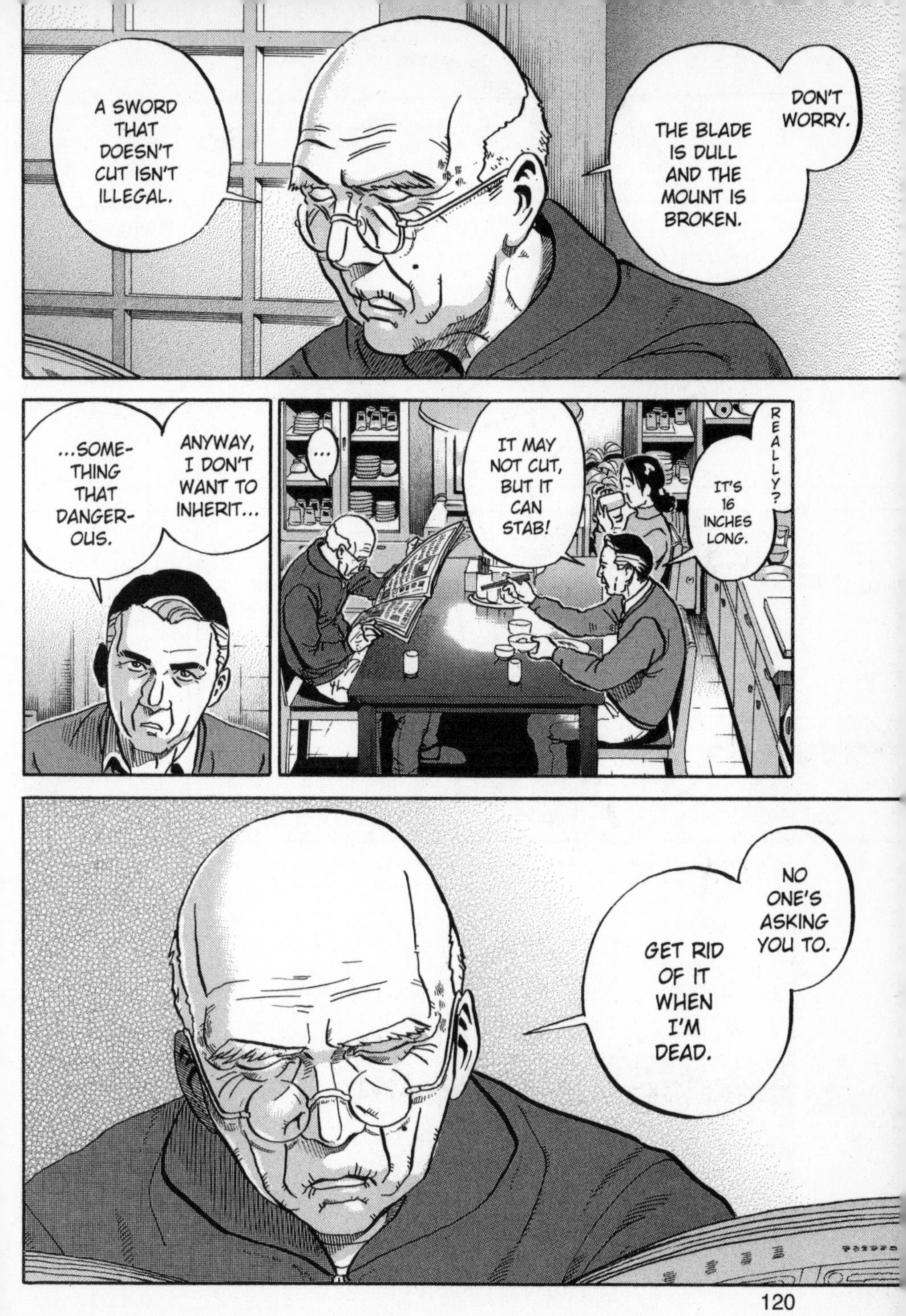
DON'T WORRY.
THE BLADE IS DULL AND THE MOUNT IS BROKEN.
A SWORD THAT DOESN'T CUT ISN'T ILLEGAL.
REALLY?
IT'S 16 INCHES LONG.
IT MAY NOT CUT, BUT IT CAN STAB!
...
ANYWAY, I DON'T WANT TO INHERIT...
...SOME-THING THAT DANGER-OUS.
NO ONE'S ASKING YOU TO.
GET RID OF IT WHEN I'M DEAD.

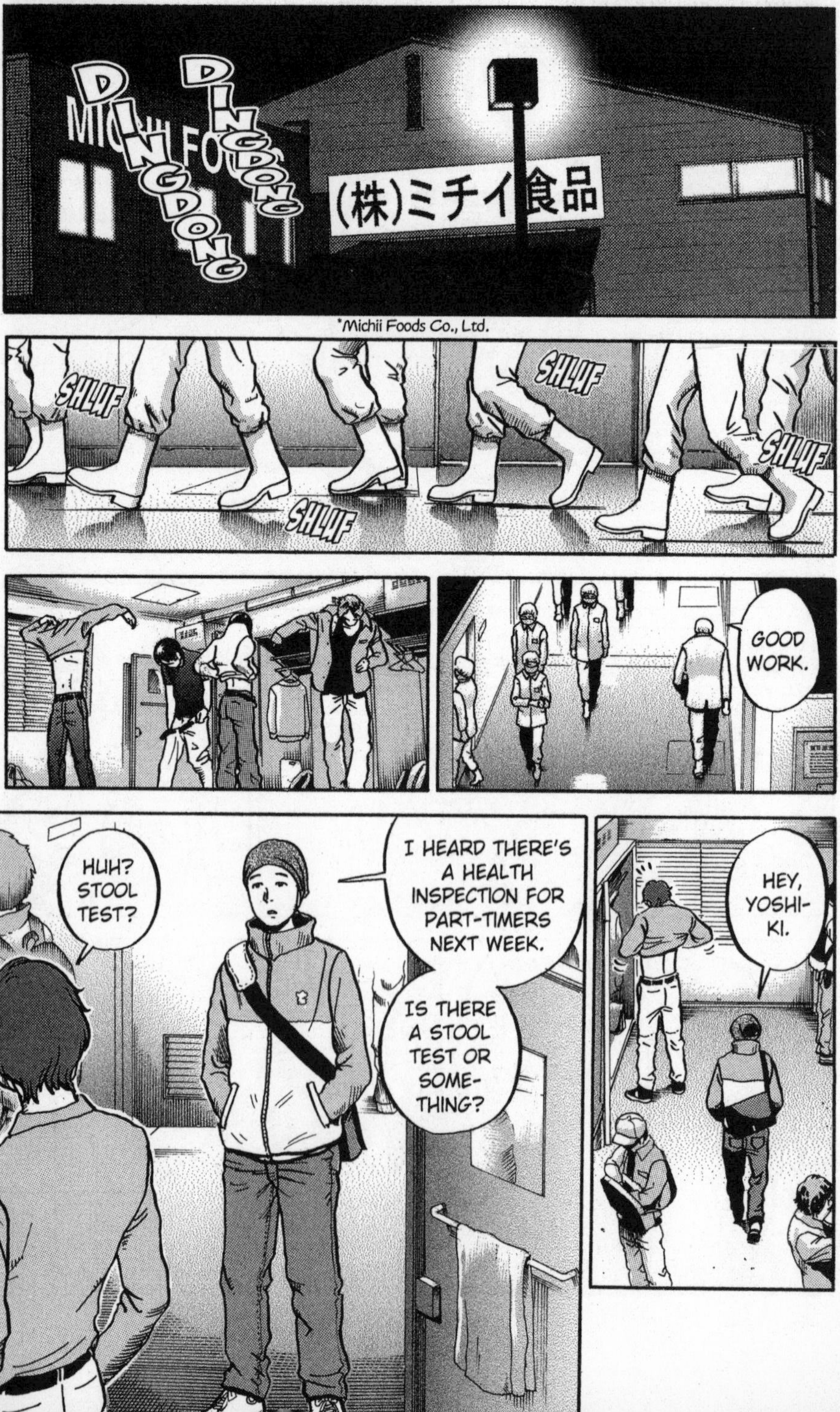
DING DONG
DING DONG
(株)ミチイ食品
*Michii Foods Co., Ltd.
SHLUF
SHLUF
SHLUF
SHLUF
GOOD WORK.
HEY, YOSHI-KI.
I HEARD THERE'S A HEALTH INSPECTION FOR PART-TIMERS NEXT WEEK.
IS THERE A STOOL TEST OR SOME-THING?
HUH? STOOL TEST?

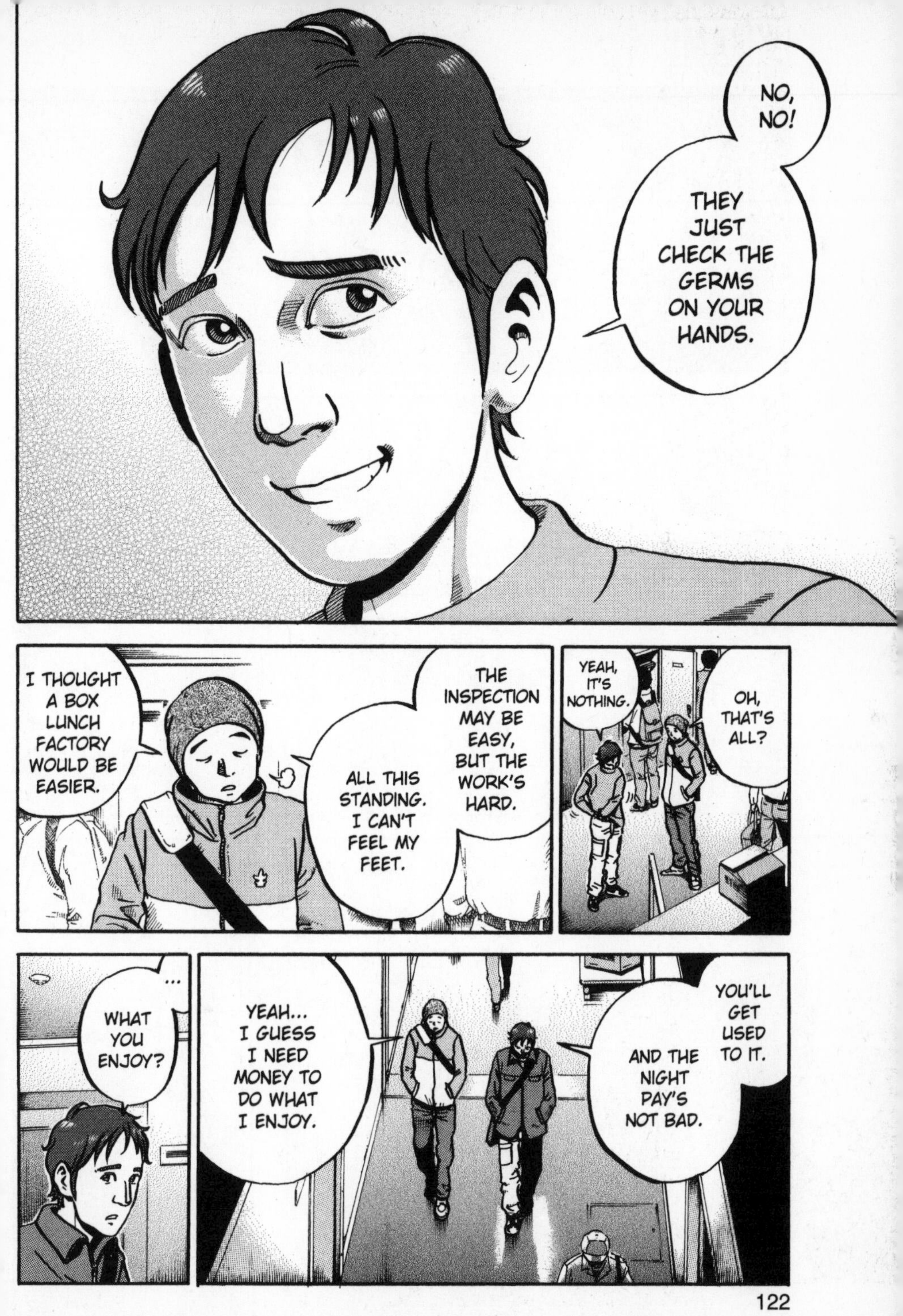
NO, NO!
THEY JUST CHECK THE GERMS ON YOUR HANDS.
OH, THAT'S ALL?
YEAH, IT'S NOTHING.
THE INSPECTION MAY BE EASY, BUT THE WORK'S HARD.
ALL THIS STANDING. I CAN'T FEEL MY FEET.
I THOUGHT A BOX LUNCH FACTORY WOULD BE EASIER.
YOU'LL GET USED TO IT.
AND THE NIGHT PAY'S NOT BAD.
YEAH... I GUESS I NEED MONEY TO DO WHAT I ENJOY.
...
WHAT YOU ENJOY?

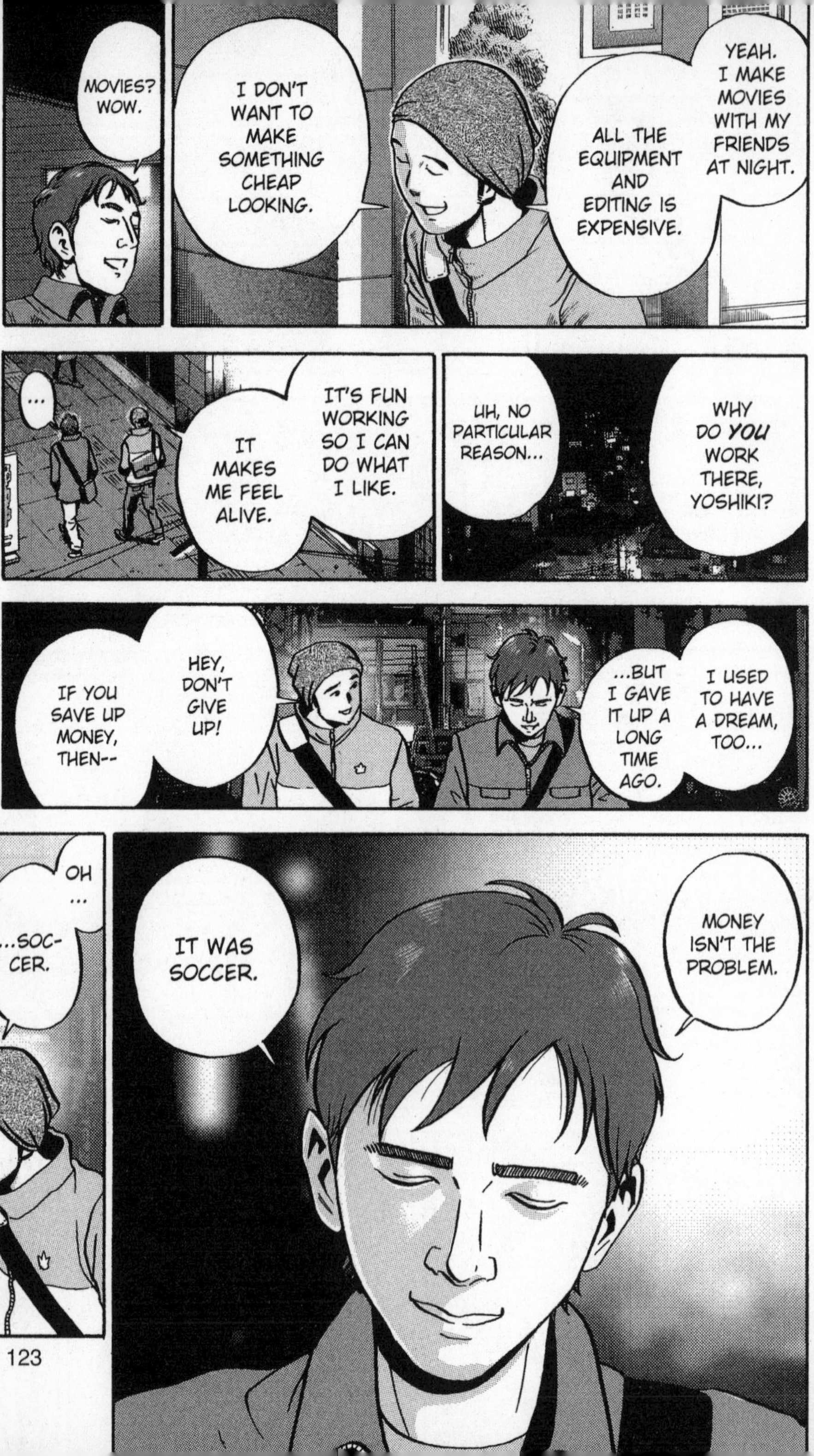
YEAH. I MAKE MOVIES WITH MY FRIENDS AT NIGHT.
ALL THE EQUIPMENT AND EDITING IS EXPENSIVE.
I DON'T WANT TO MAKE SOMETHING CHEAP LOOKING.
MOVIES? WOW.
WHY DO *YOU* WORK THERE, YOSHIKI?
UH, NO PARTICULAR REASON...
IT'S FUN WORKING SO I CAN DO WHAT I LIKE.
IT MAKES ME FEEL ALIVE.
...
I USED TO HAVE A DREAM, TOO...
...BUT I GAVE IT UP A LONG TIME AGO.
HEY, DON'T GIVE UP!
IF YOU SAVE UP MONEY, THEN--
MONEY ISN'T THE PROBLEM.
IT WAS SOCCER.
OH...
...SOC-CER.

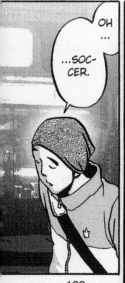

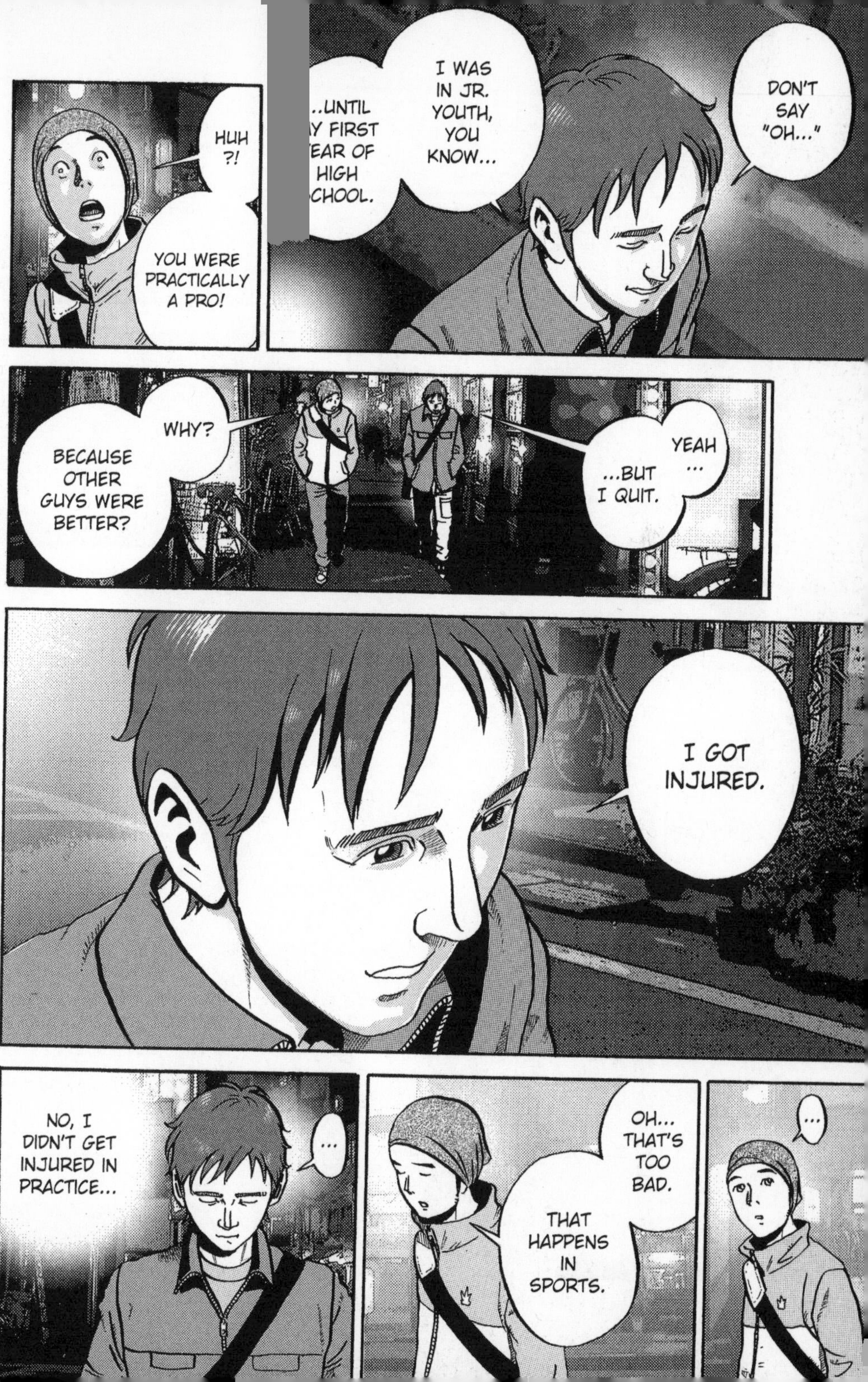
DON'T SAY "OH..."
I WAS IN JR. YOUTH, YOU KNOW...
...UNTIL Y FIRST EAR OF HIGH CHOOL.
HUH ?!
YOU WERE PRACTICALLY A PRO!
YEAH ...
...BUT I QUIT.
WHY?
BECAUSE OTHER GUYS WERE BETTER?
I GOT INJURED.
...
OH... THAT'S TOO BAD.
THAT HAPPENS IN SPORTS.
...
NO, I DIDN'T GET INJURED IN PRACTICE...

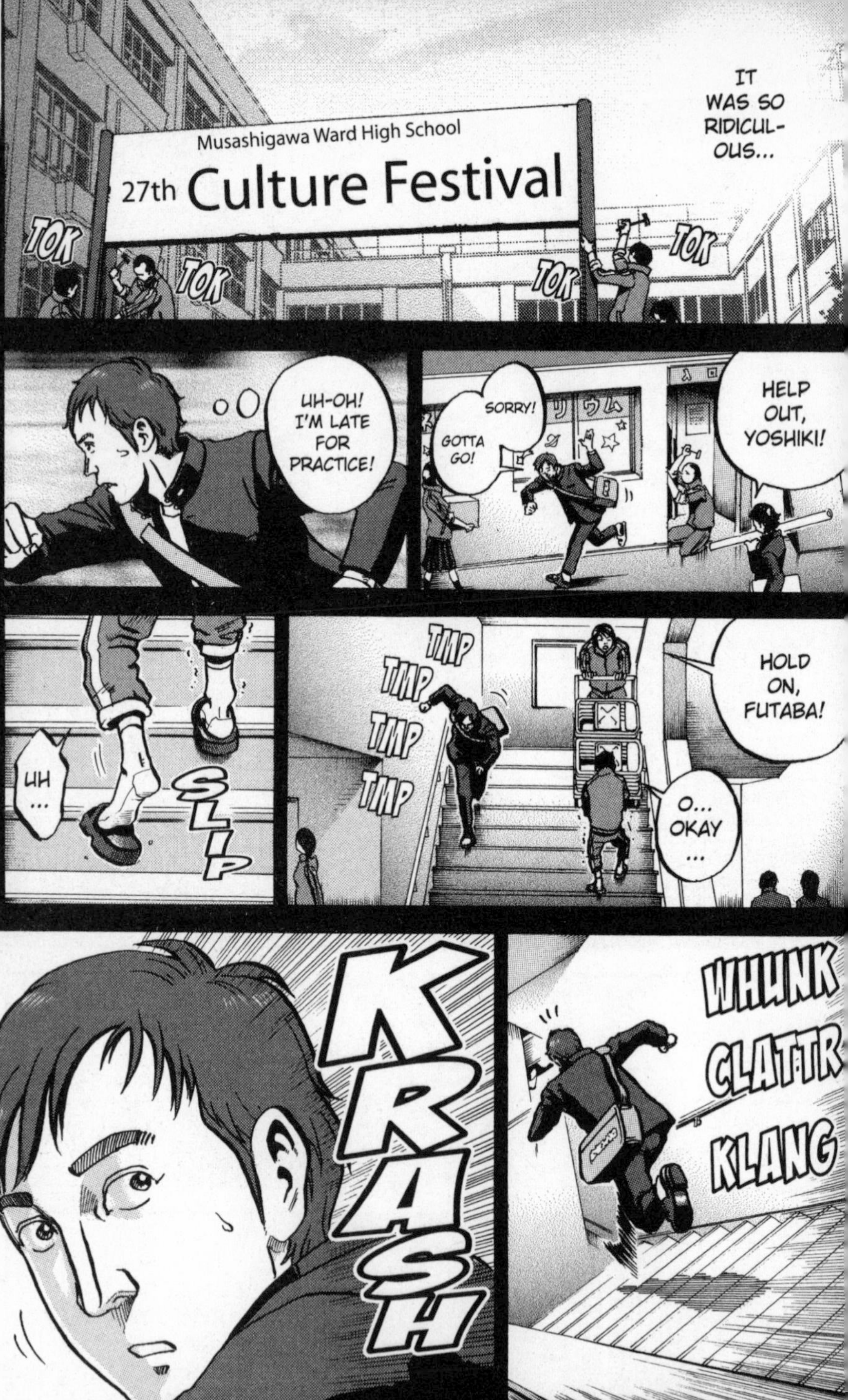
IT WAS SO RIDICUL-OUS...
Musashigawa Ward High School
27th Culture Festival
TOK
TOK
TOK
TOK
HELP OUT, YOSHIKI!
SORRY!
GOTTA GO!
UH-OH! I'M LATE FOR PRACTICE!
HOLD ON, FUTABA!
TMP
TMP
TMP
TMP
O... OKAY ...
UH ...
SLIP
WHUNK
CLATTR
KLANG
KRASH

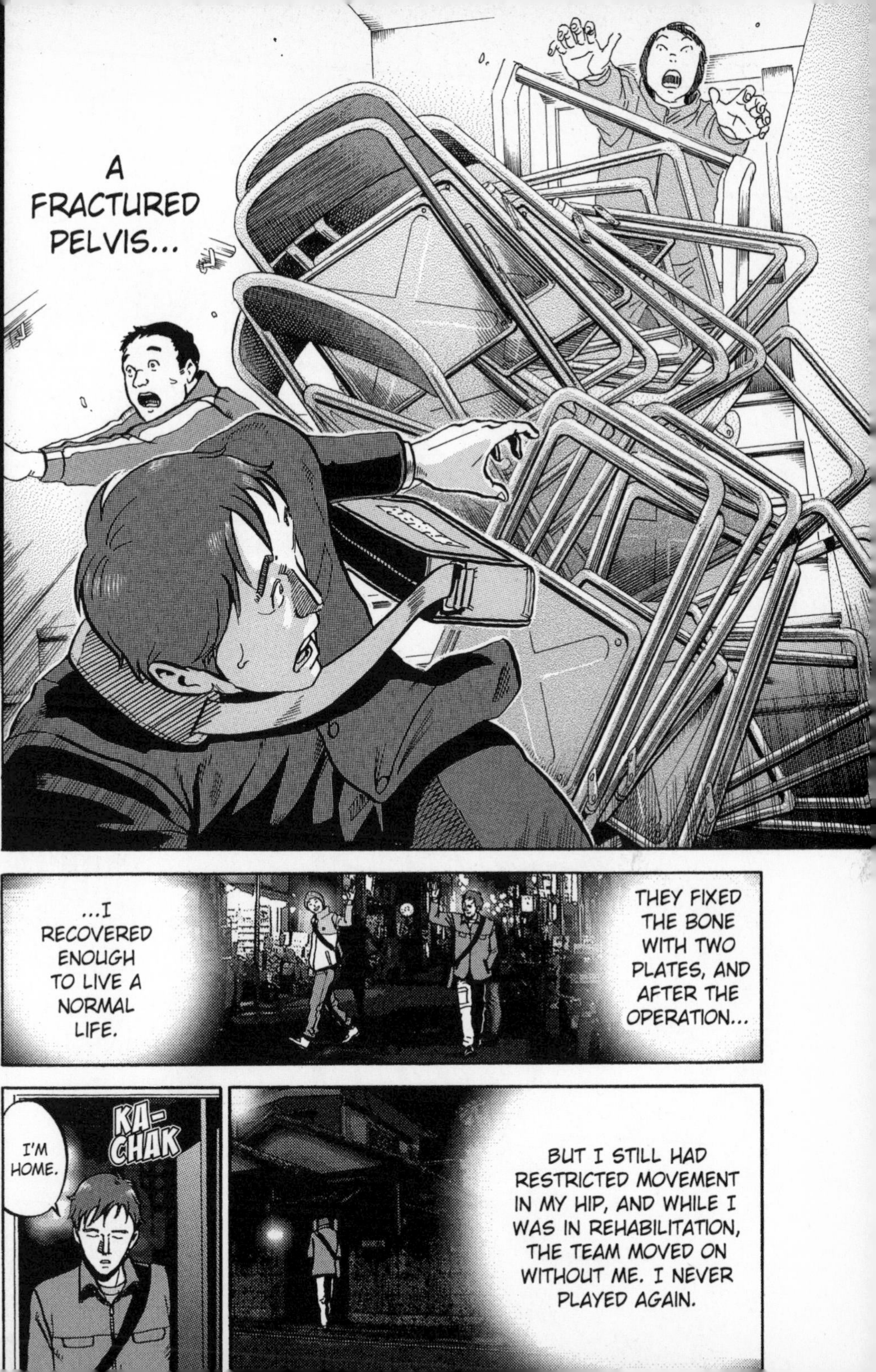
A FRACTURED PELVIS...
THEY FIXED THE BONE WITH TWO PLATES, AND AFTER THE OPERATION...
...I RECOVERED ENOUGH TO LIVE A NORMAL LIFE.
BUT I STILL HAD RESTRICTED MOVEMENT IN MY HIP, AND WHILE I WAS IN REHABILITATION, THE TEAM MOVED ON WITHOUT ME. I NEVER PLAYED AGAIN.
KA-CHAK
I'M HOME.

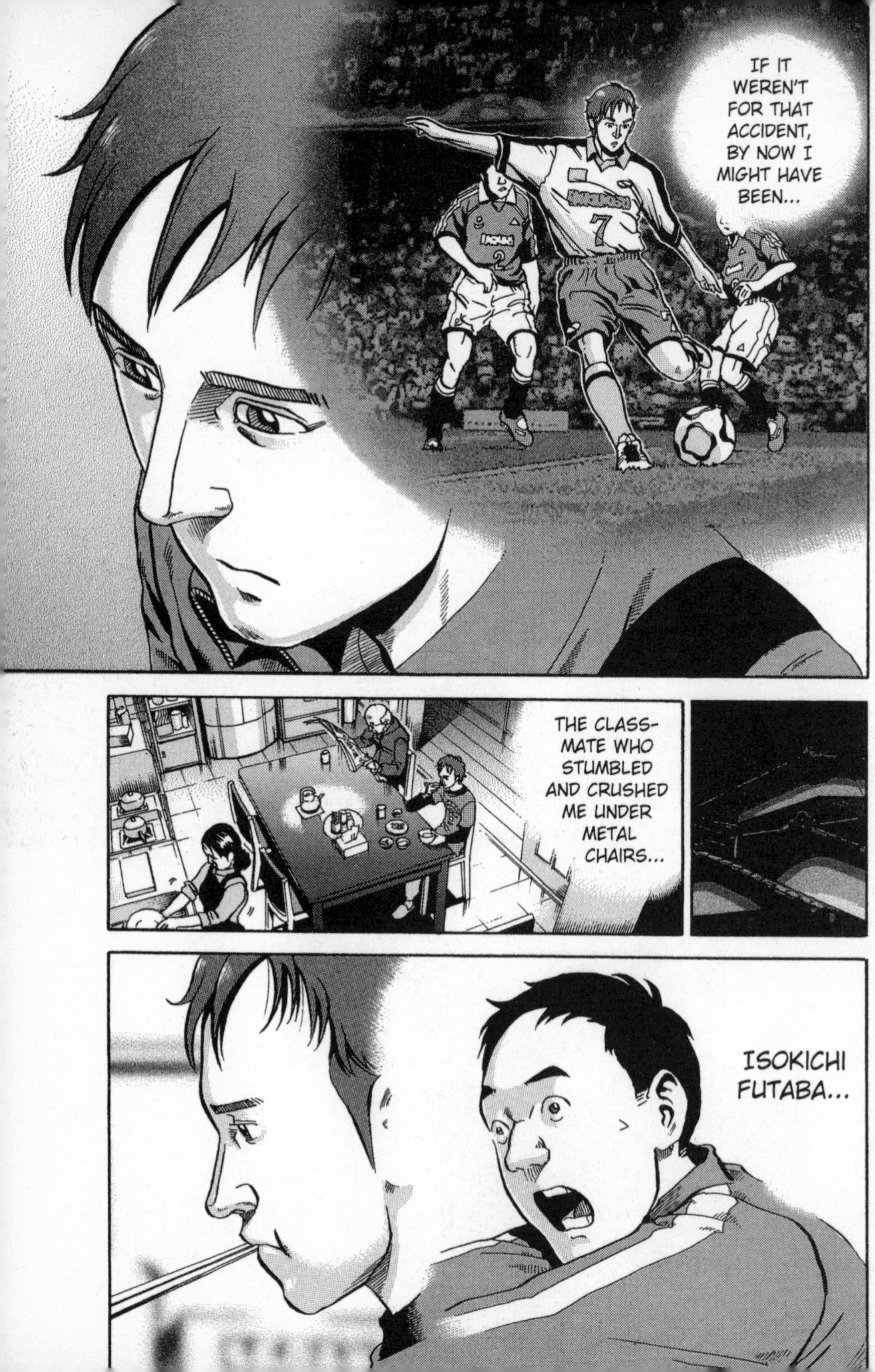
IF IT WEREN'T FOR THAT ACCIDENT, BY NOW I MIGHT HAVE BEEN...
THE CLASS-MATE WHO STUMBLED AND CRUSHED ME UNDER METAL CHAIRS...
ISOKICHI FUTABA...

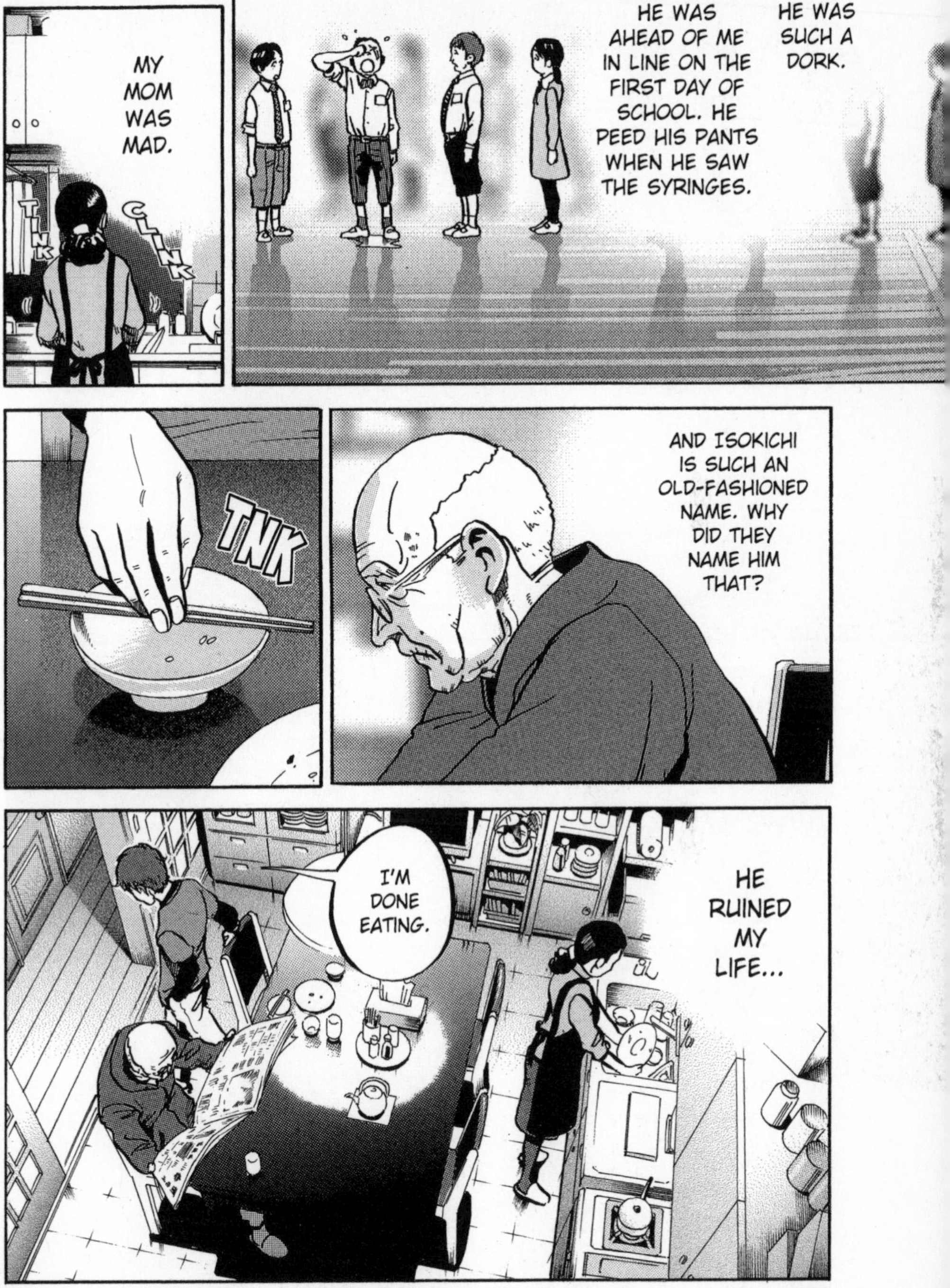
HE WAS SUCH A DORK.
HE WAS AHEAD OF ME IN LINE ON THE FIRST DAY OF SCHOOL. HE PEED HIS PANTS WHEN HE SAW THE SYRINGES.
MY MOM WAS MAD.
CLINK
TINK
AND ISOKICHI IS SUCH AN OLD-FASHIONED NAME. WHY DID THEY NAME HIM THAT?
TNK
HE RUINED MY LIFE...
I'M DONE EATING.

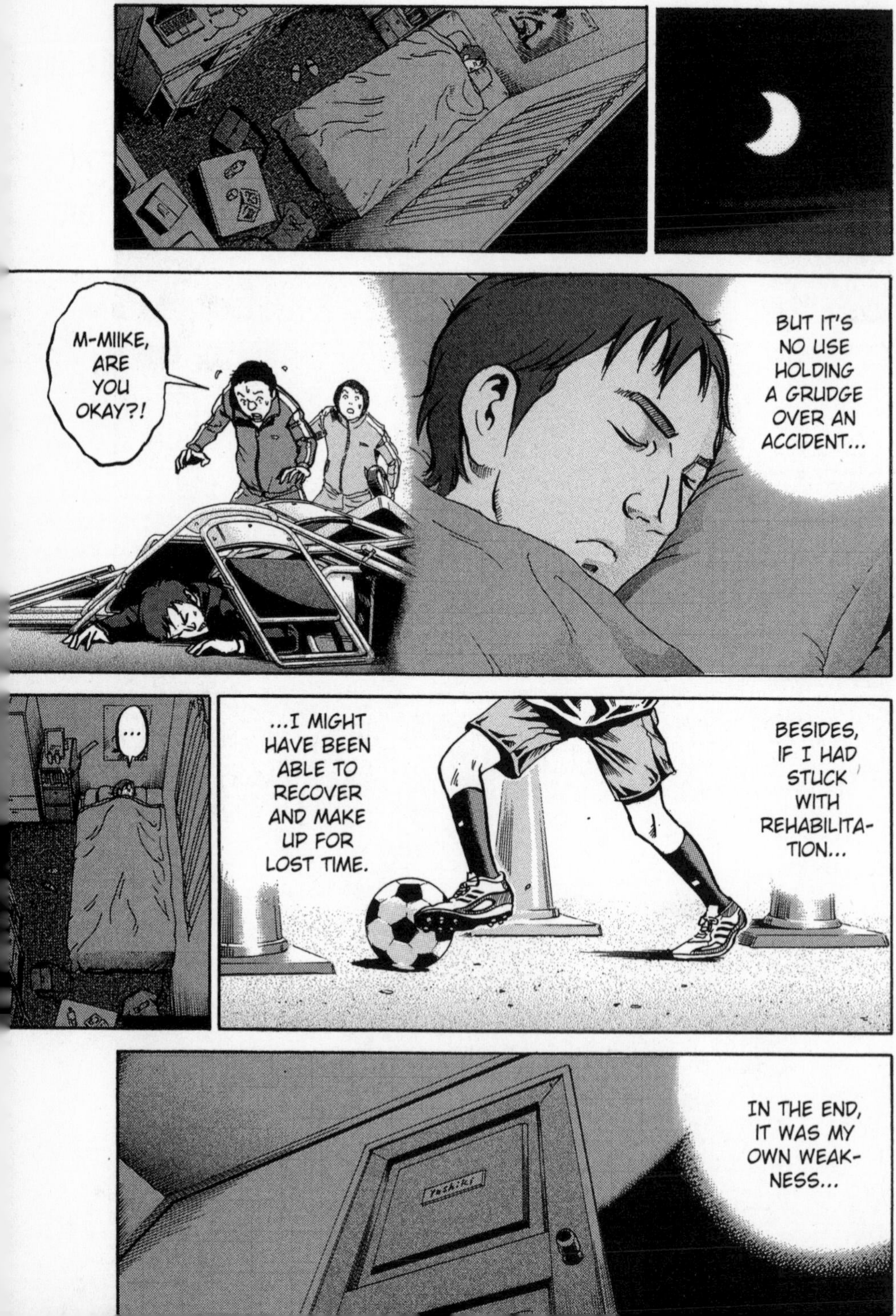
BUT IT'S NO USE HOLDING A GRUDGE OVER AN ACCIDENT...
M-MIIKE, ARE YOU OKAY?!
BESIDES, IF I HAD STUCK WITH REHABILITA-TION...
...I MIGHT HAVE BEEN ABLE TO RECOVER AND MAKE UP FOR LOST TIME.
...
IN THE END, IT WAS MY OWN WEAK-NESS...

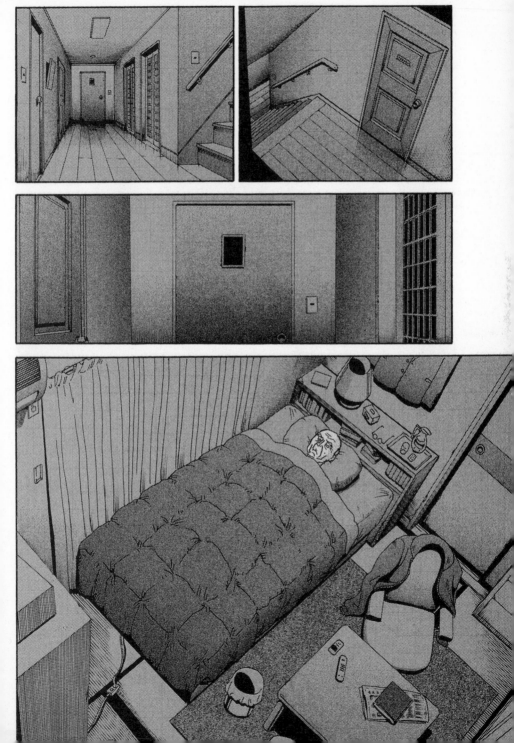

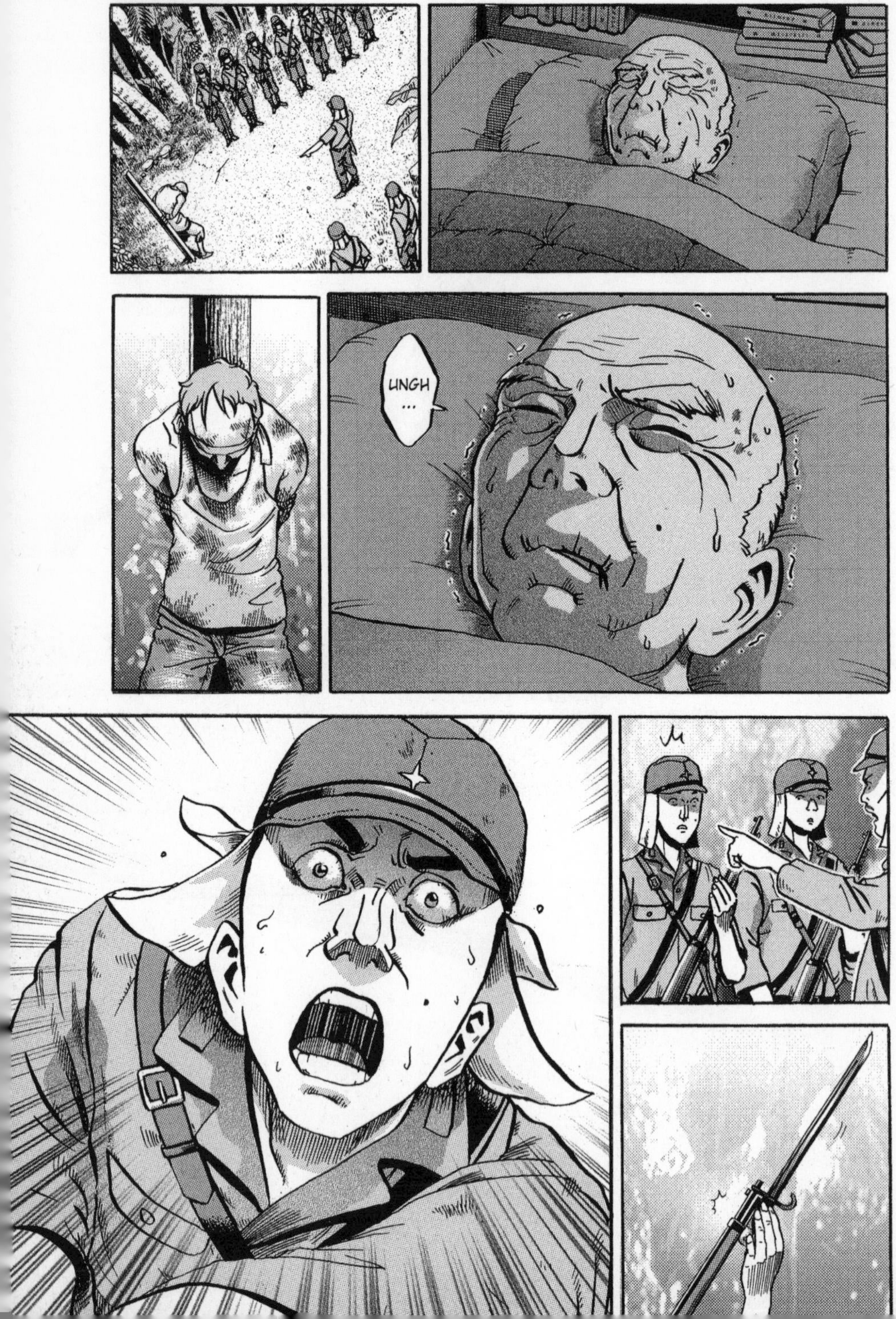
UNGH ...

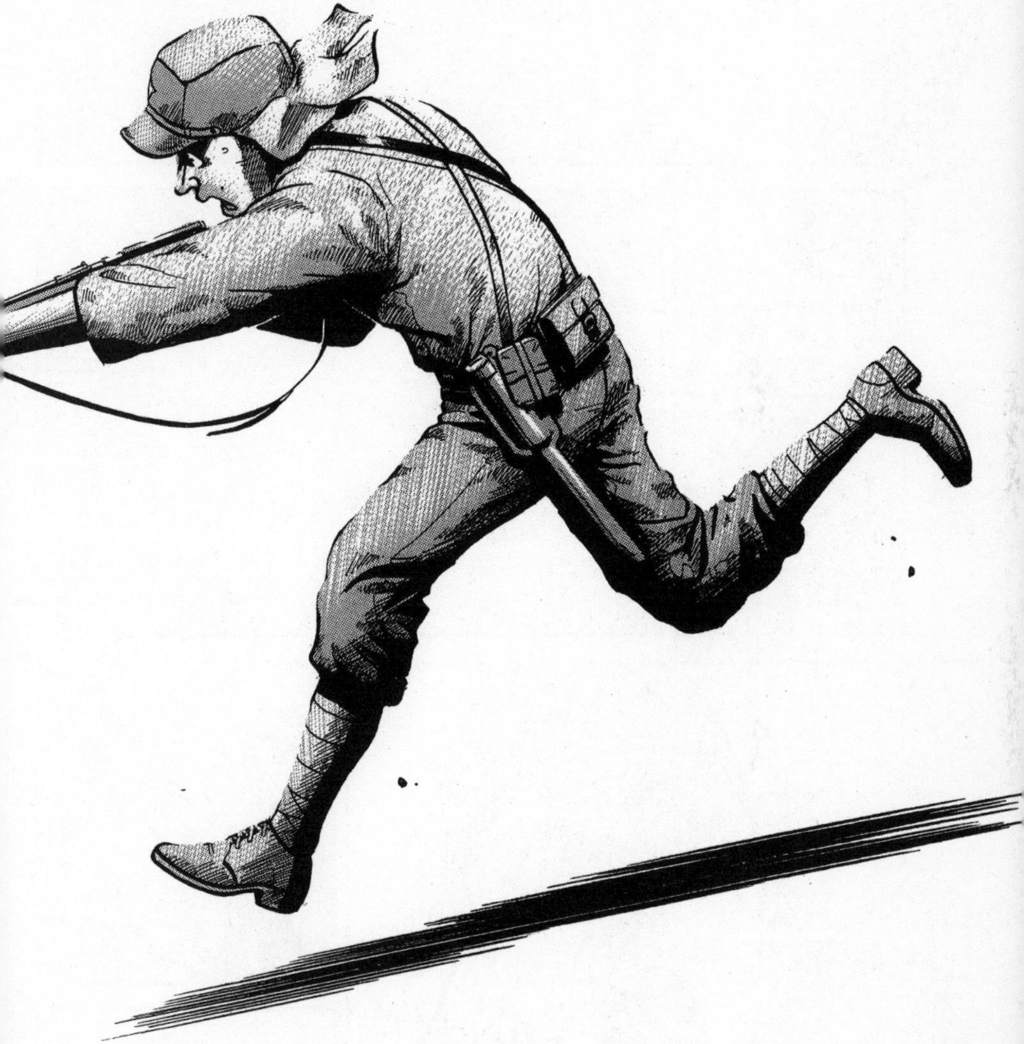

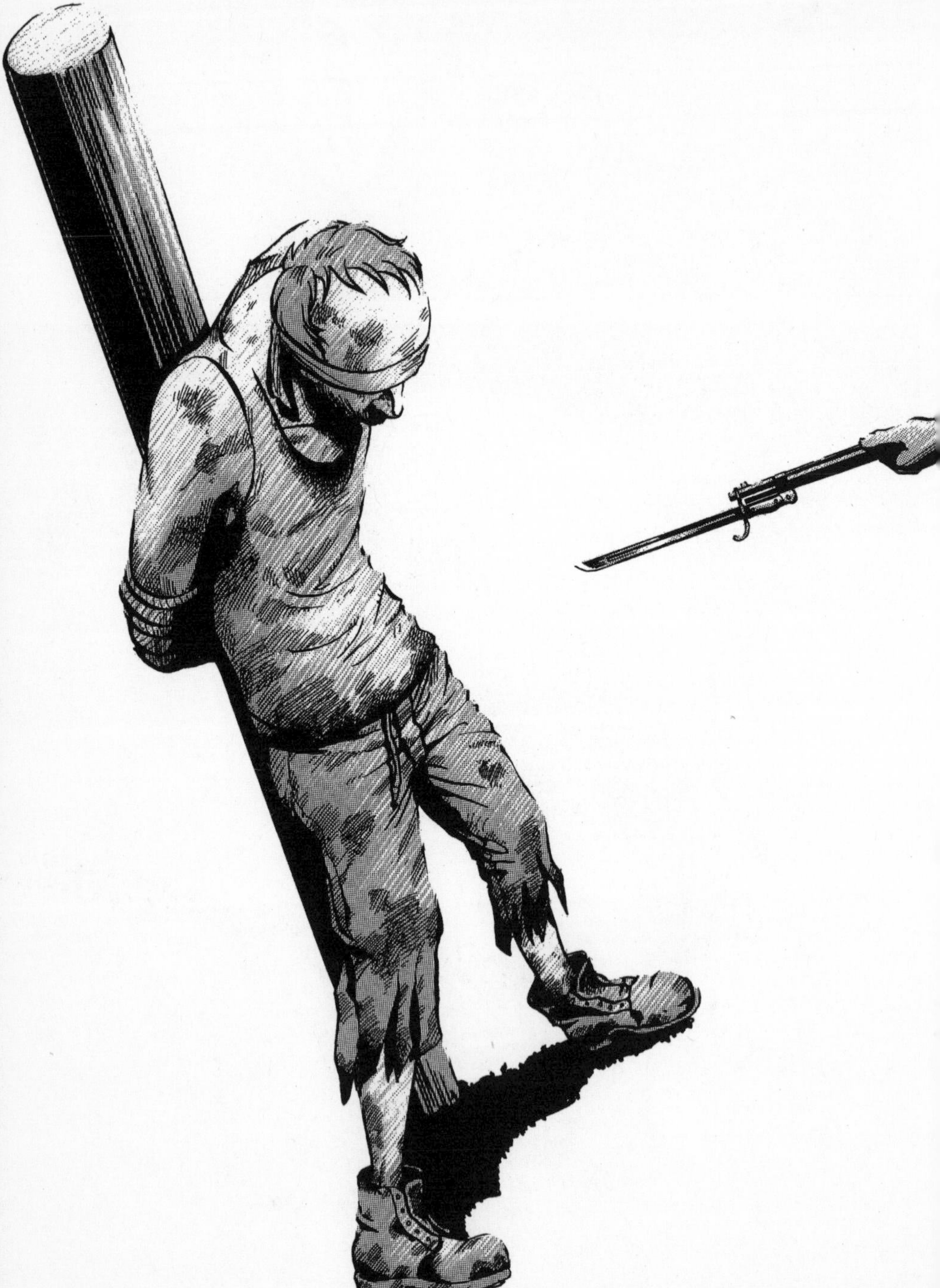

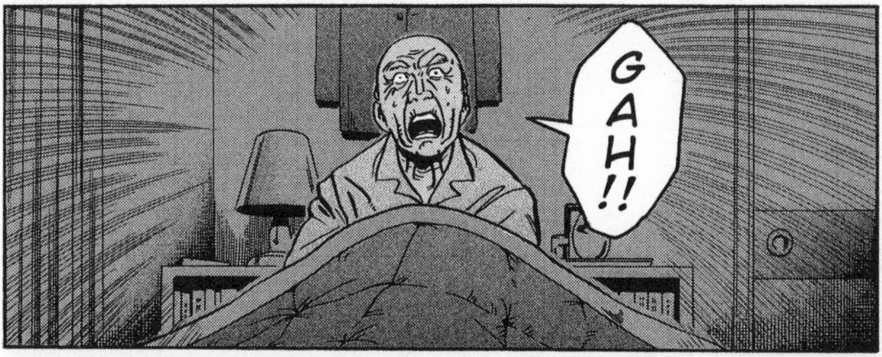
GAH!!
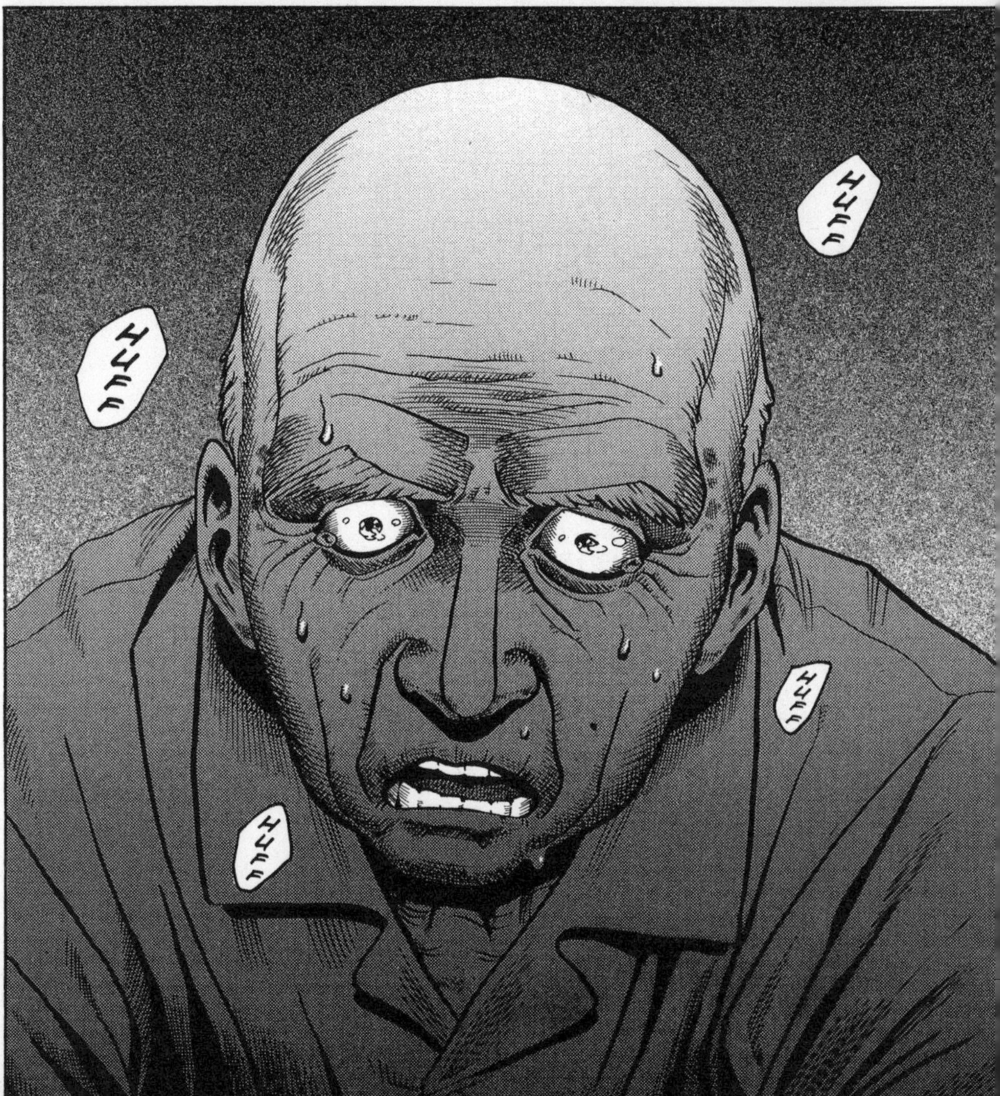
HUFF
HUFF
HUFF
HUFF

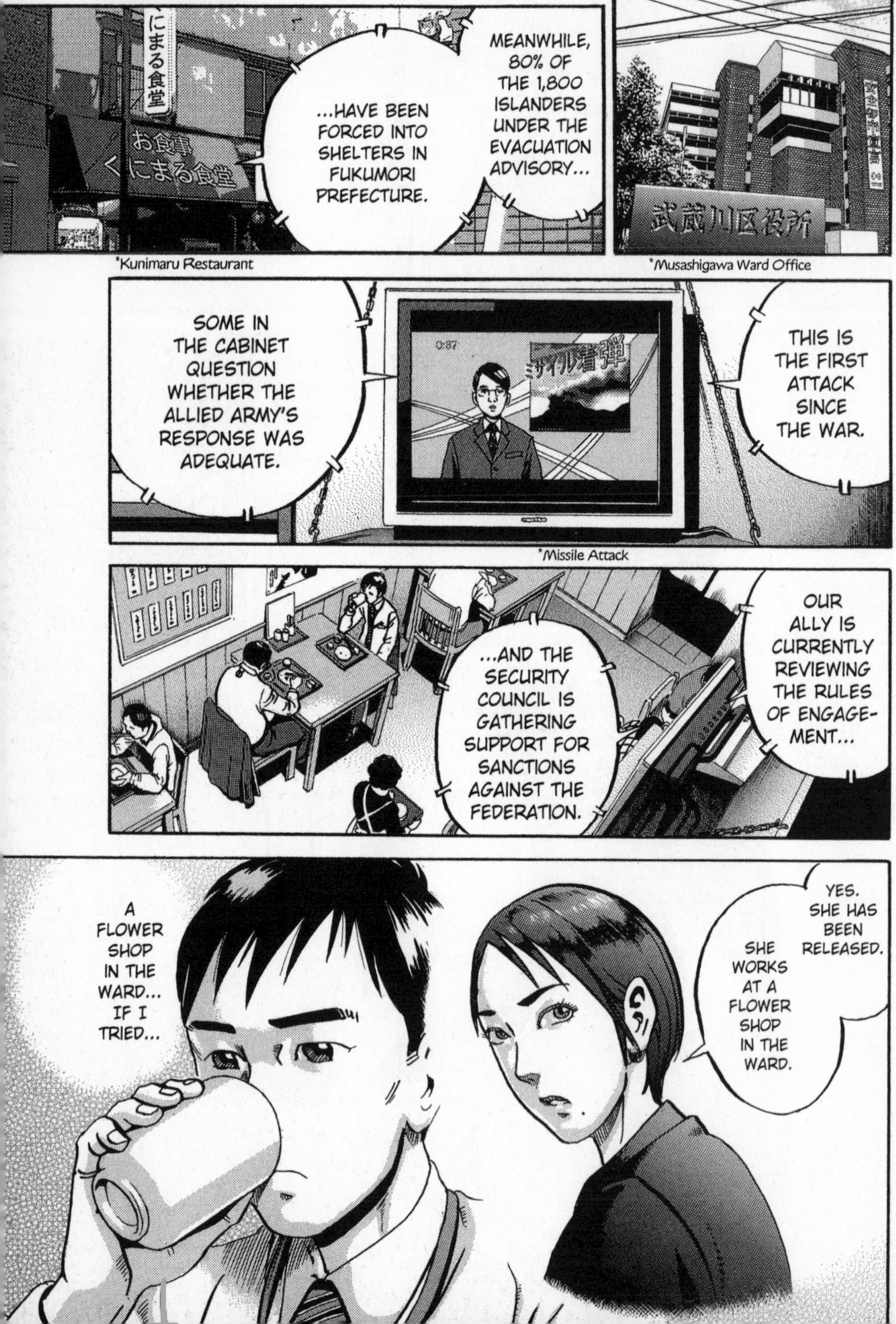
武蔵川区役所
にまる食堂
お食事
くにまる食堂
MEANWHILE, 80% OF THE 1,800 ISLANDERS UNDER THE EVACUATION ADVISORY...
...HAVE BEEN FORCED INTO SHELTERS IN FUKUMORI PREFECTURE.
ミサイル着弾
THIS IS THE FIRST ATTACK SINCE THE WAR.
SOME IN THE CABINET QUESTION WHETHER THE ALLIED ARMY'S RESPONSE WAS ADEQUATE.
OUR ALLY IS CURRENTLY REVIEWING THE RULES OF ENGAGE-MENT...
...AND THE SECURITY COUNCIL IS GATHERING SUPPORT FOR SANCTIONS AGAINST THE FEDERATION.
YES. SHE HAS BEEN RELEASED.
SHE WORKS AT A FLOWER SHOP IN THE WARD.
A FLOWER SHOP IN THE WARD... IF I TRIED...

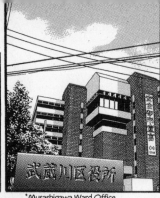

*Musashigawa Ward Office

*Kunimaru Restaurant

*Missile Attack

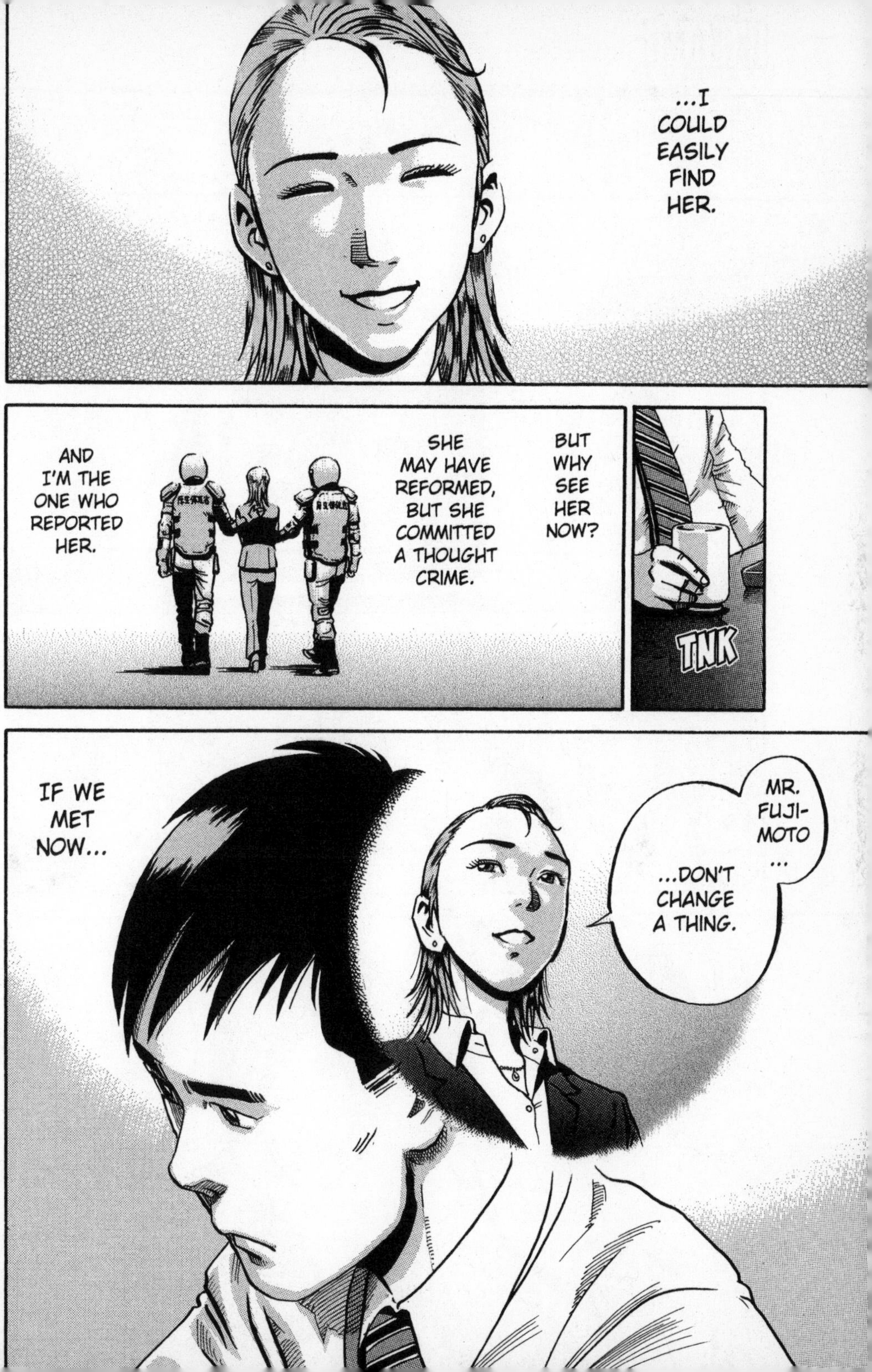
...I COULD EASILY FIND HER.
TNK
BUT WHY SEE HER NOW?
SHE MAY HAVE REFORMED, BUT SHE COMMITTED A THOUGHT CRIME.
AND I'M THE ONE WHO REPORTED HER.
MR. FUJI-MOTO ...
...DON'T CHANGE A THING.
IF WE MET NOW...

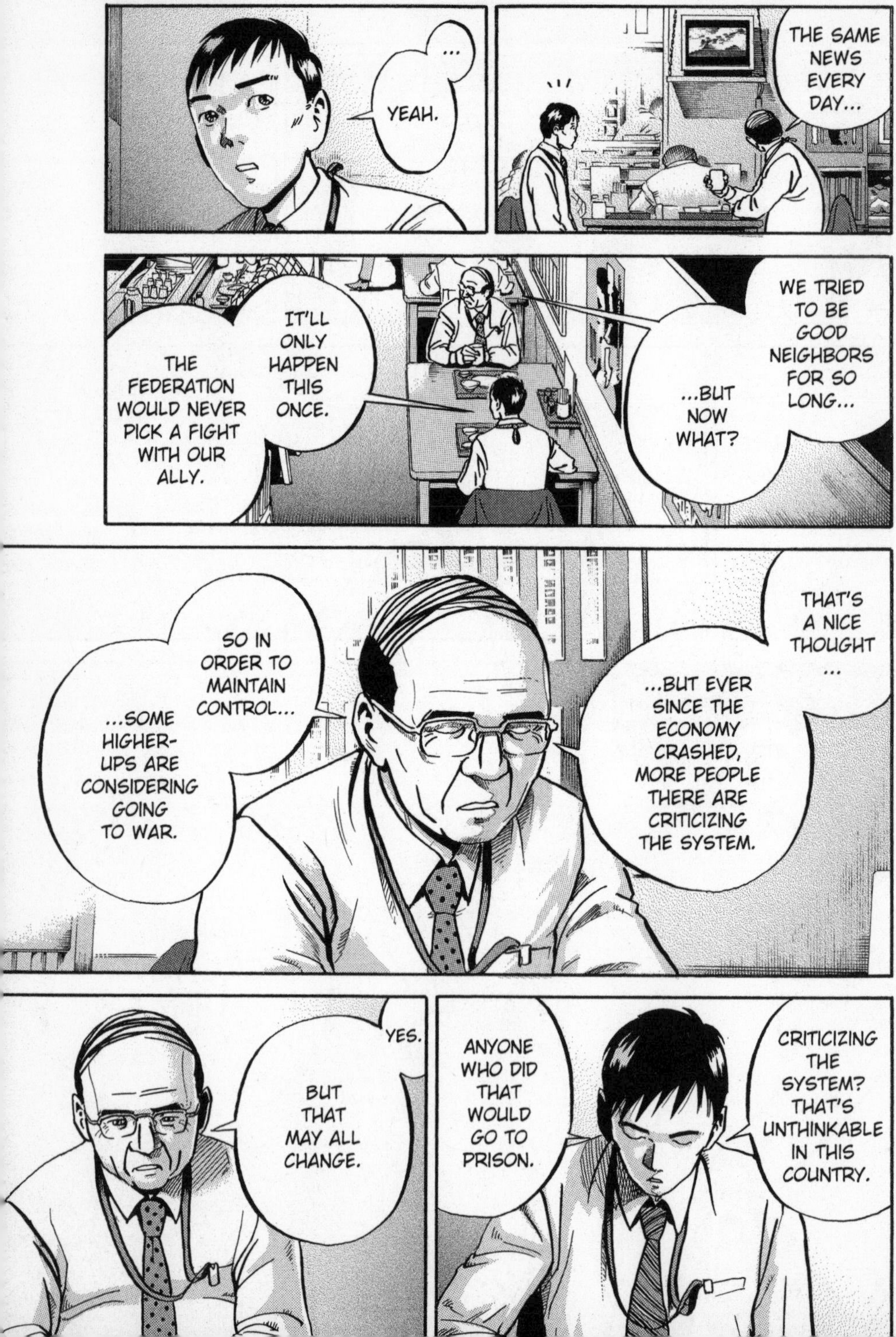
THE SAME NEWS EVERY DAY...
...
YEAH.
WE TRIED TO BE GOOD NEIGHBORS FOR SO LONG...
...BUT NOW WHAT?
IT'LL ONLY HAPPEN THIS ONCE.
THE FEDERATION WOULD NEVER PICK A FIGHT WITH OUR ALLY.
THAT'S A NICE THOUGHT...
...BUT EVER SINCE THE ECONOMY CRASHED, MORE PEOPLE THERE ARE CRITICIZING THE SYSTEM.
SO IN ORDER TO MAINTAIN CONTROL...
...SOME HIGHER-UPS ARE CONSIDERING GOING TO WAR.
CRITICIZING THE SYSTEM? THAT'S UNTHINKABLE IN THIS COUNTRY.
ANYONE WHO DID THAT WOULD GO TO PRISON.
YES.
BUT THAT MAY ALL CHANGE.

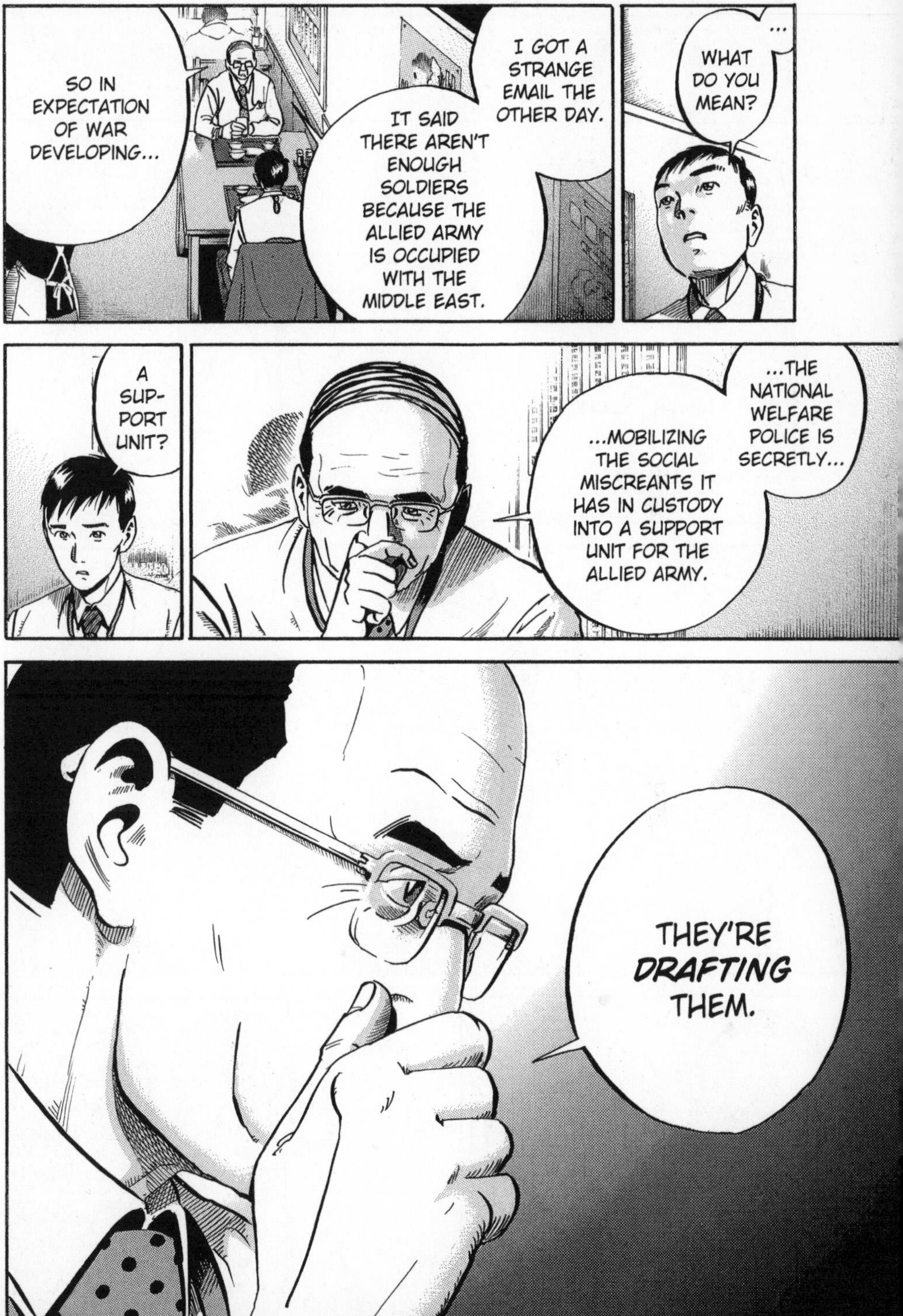
...
WHAT DO YOU MEAN?
I GOT A STRANGE EMAIL THE OTHER DAY.
IT SAID THERE AREN'T ENOUGH SOLDIERS BECAUSE THE ALLIED ARMY IS OCCUPIED WITH THE MIDDLE EAST.
SO IN EXPECTATION OF WAR DEVELOPING...
...THE NATIONAL WELFARE POLICE IS SECRETLY...
...MOBILIZING THE SOCIAL MISCREANTS IT HAS IN CUSTODY INTO A SUPPORT UNIT FOR THE ALLIED ARMY.
A SUP-PORT UNIT?
THEY'RE *DRAFTING* THEM.

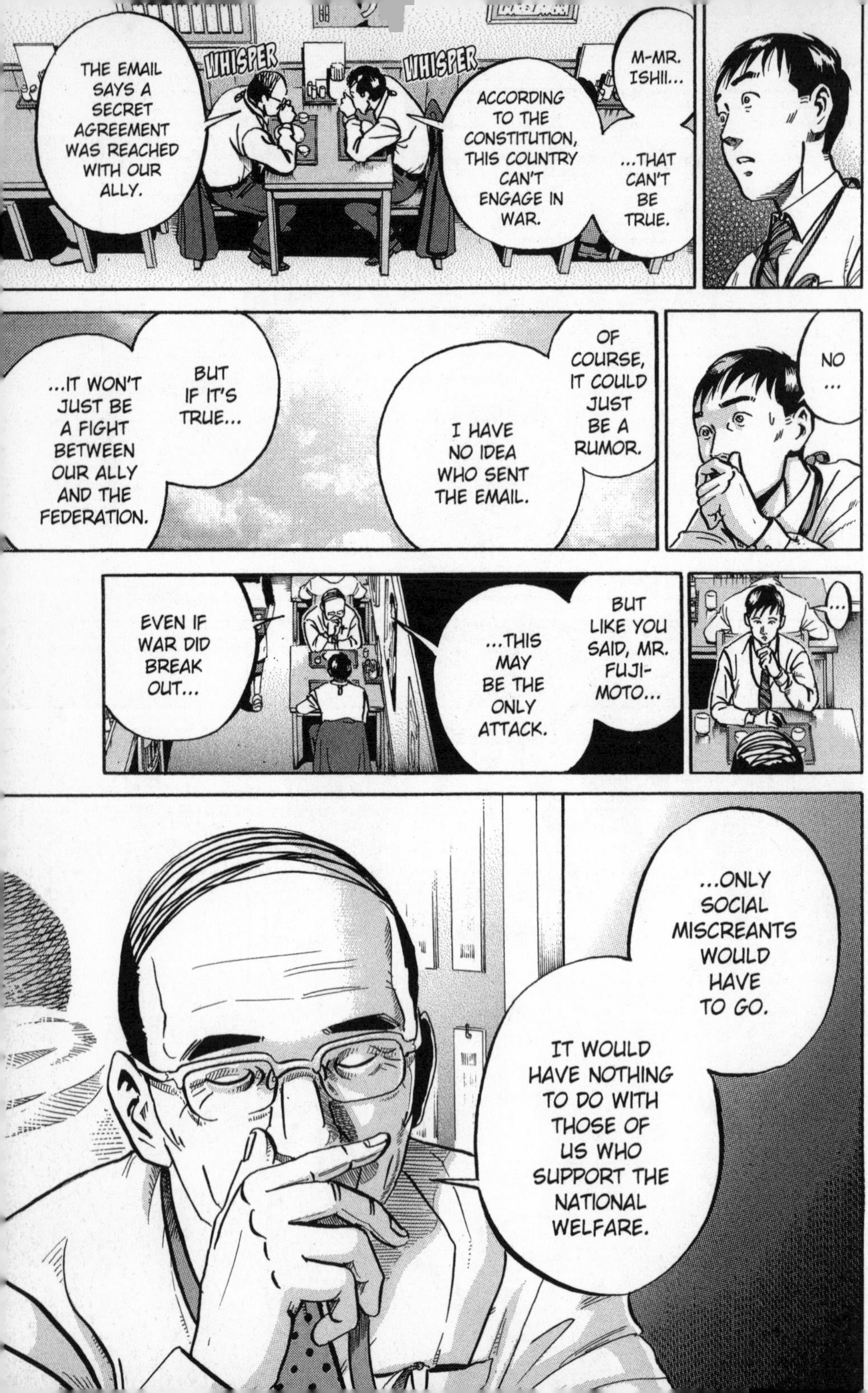
M-MR. ISHII... ...THAT CAN'T BE TRUE.
ACCORDING TO THE CONSTITUTION, THIS COUNTRY CAN'T ENGAGE IN WAR.
WHISPER
WHISPER
THE EMAIL SAYS A SECRET AGREEMENT WAS REACHED WITH OUR ALLY.
NO ...
OF COURSE, IT COULD JUST BE A RUMOR.
I HAVE NO IDEA WHO SENT THE EMAIL.
BUT IF IT'S TRUE...
...IT WON'T JUST BE A FIGHT BETWEEN OUR ALLY AND THE FEDERATION.
...
BUT LIKE YOU SAID, MR. FUJI-MOTO...
...THIS MAY BE THE ONLY ATTACK.
EVEN IF WAR DID BREAK OUT...
...ONLY SOCIAL MISCREANTS WOULD HAVE TO GO.
IT WOULD HAVE NOTHING TO DO WITH THOSE OF US WHO SUPPORT THE NATIONAL WELFARE.

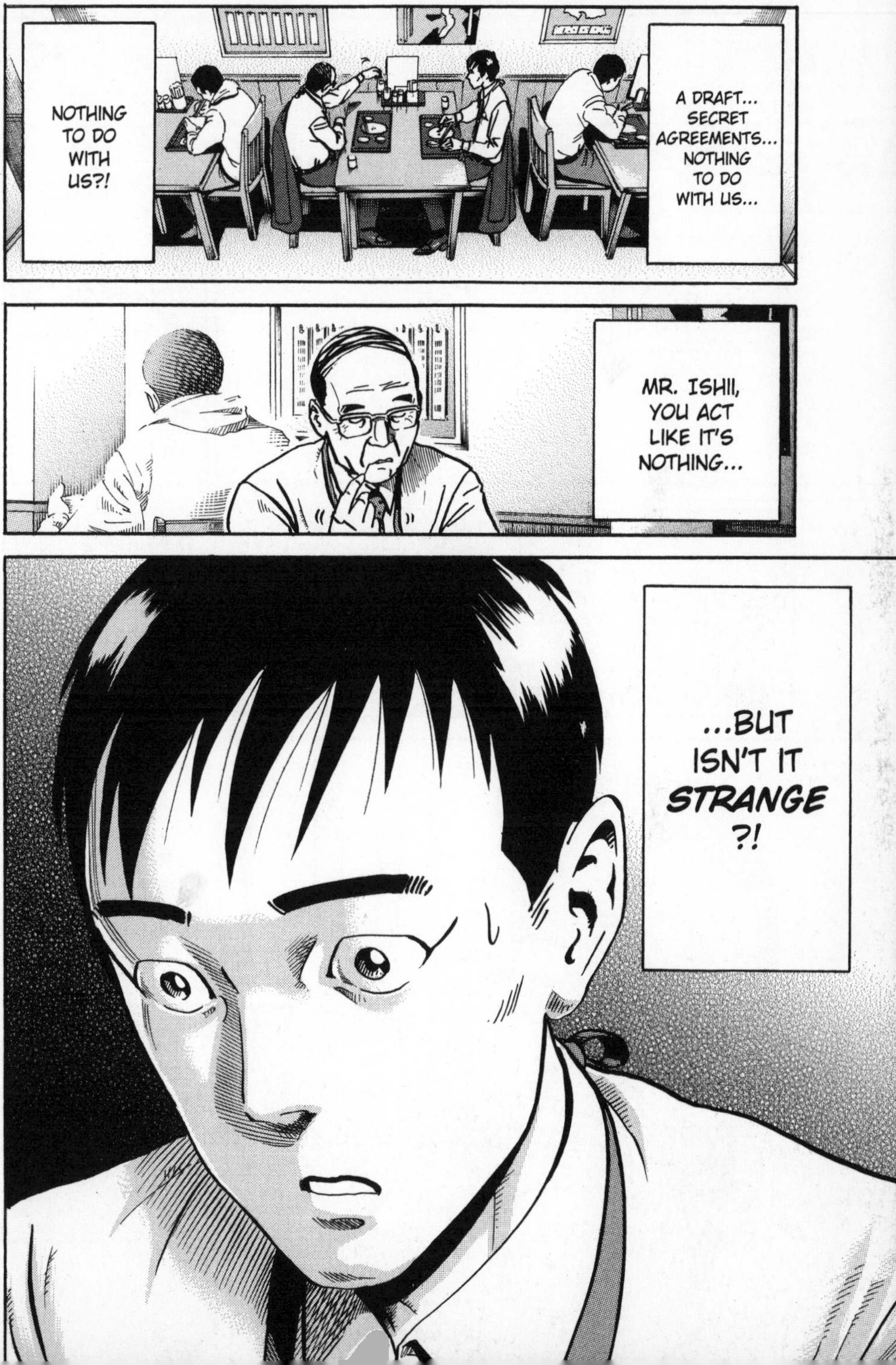
A DRAFT... SECRET AGREEMENTS... NOTHING TO DO WITH US...
NOTHING TO DO WITH US?!
MR. ISHII, YOU ACT LIKE IT'S NOTHING...
...BUT ISN'T IT *STRANGE* ?!

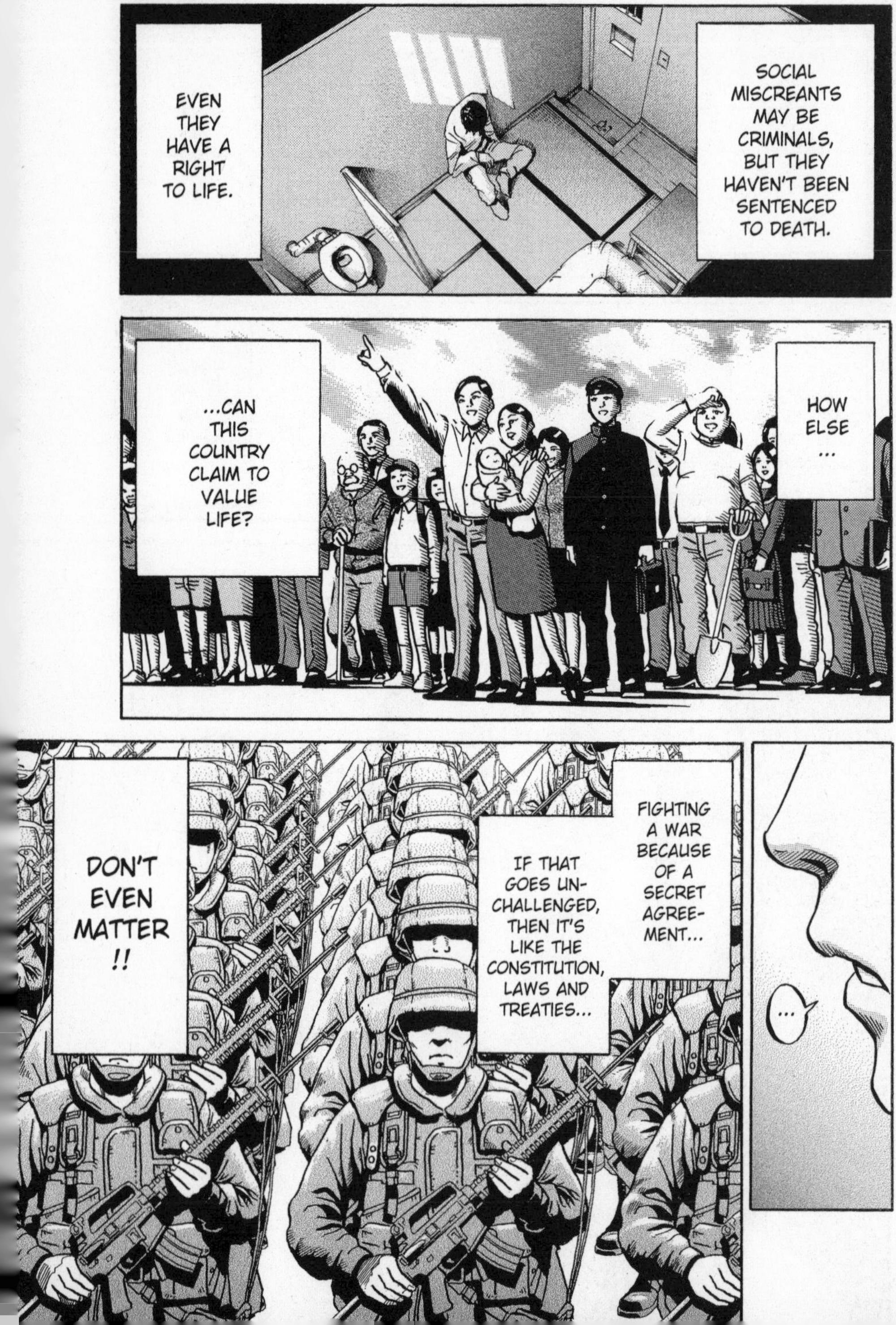
SOCIAL MISCREANTS MAY BE CRIMINALS, BUT THEY HAVEN'T BEEN SENTENCED TO DEATH.
EVEN THEY HAVE A RIGHT TO LIFE.
HOW ELSE ...
...CAN THIS COUNTRY CLAIM TO VALUE LIFE?
...
FIGHTING A WAR BECAUSE OF A SECRET AGREE-MENT...
IF THAT GOES UN-CHALLENGED, THEN IT'S LIKE THE CONSTITUTION, LAWS AND TREATIES...
DON'T EVEN MATTER !!

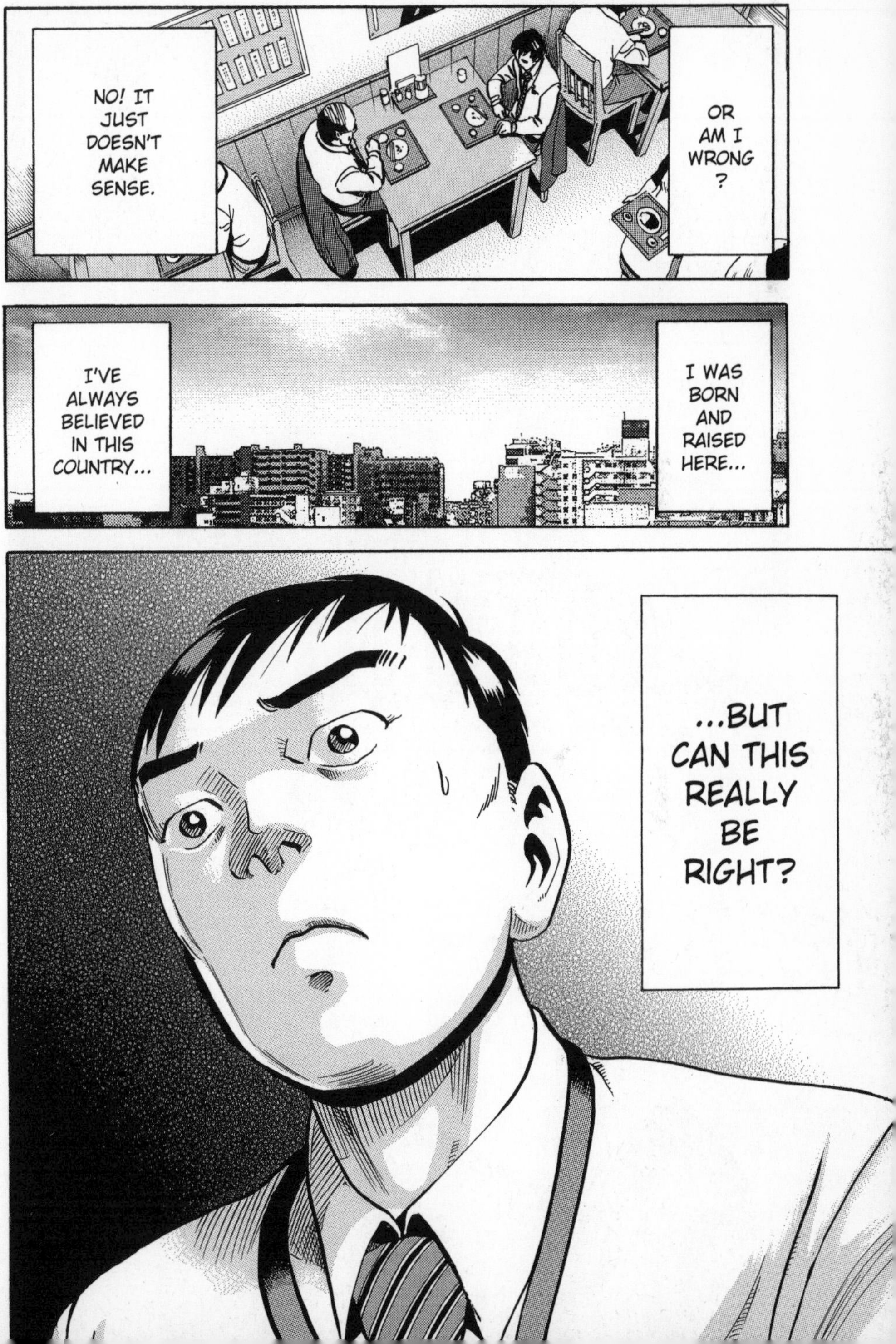
OR AM I WRONG ?
NO! IT JUST DOESN'T MAKE SENSE.
I WAS BORN AND RAISED HERE...
I'VE ALWAYS BELIEVED IN THIS COUNTRY...
...BUT CAN THIS REALLY BE RIGHT?

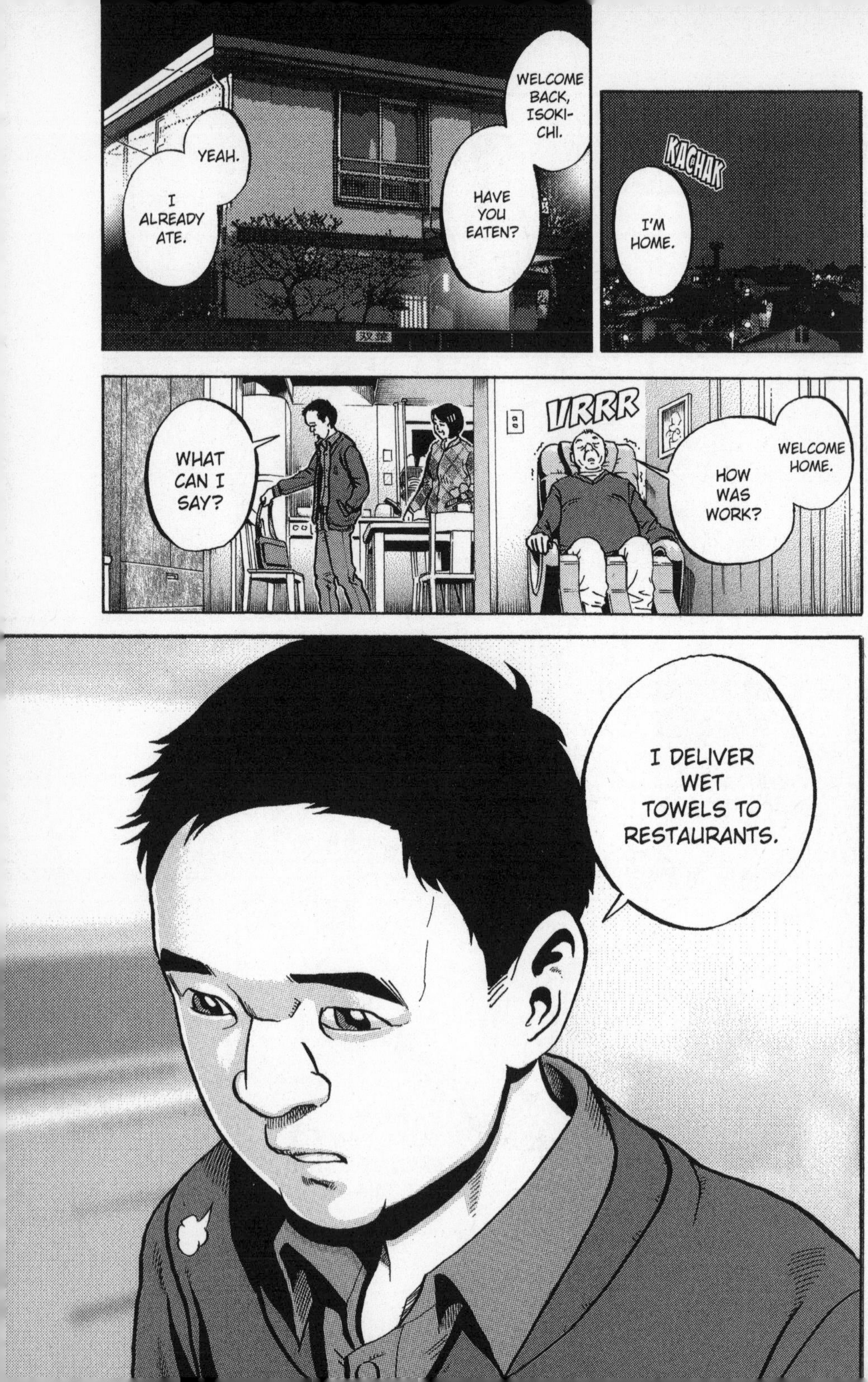
KACHAK
I'M HOME.
WELCOME BACK, ISOKI-CHI.
HAVE YOU EATEN?
YEAH.
I ALREADY ATE.
URRR
WELCOME HOME.
HOW WAS WORK?
WHAT CAN I SAY?
I DELIVER WET TOWELS TO RESTAURANTS.

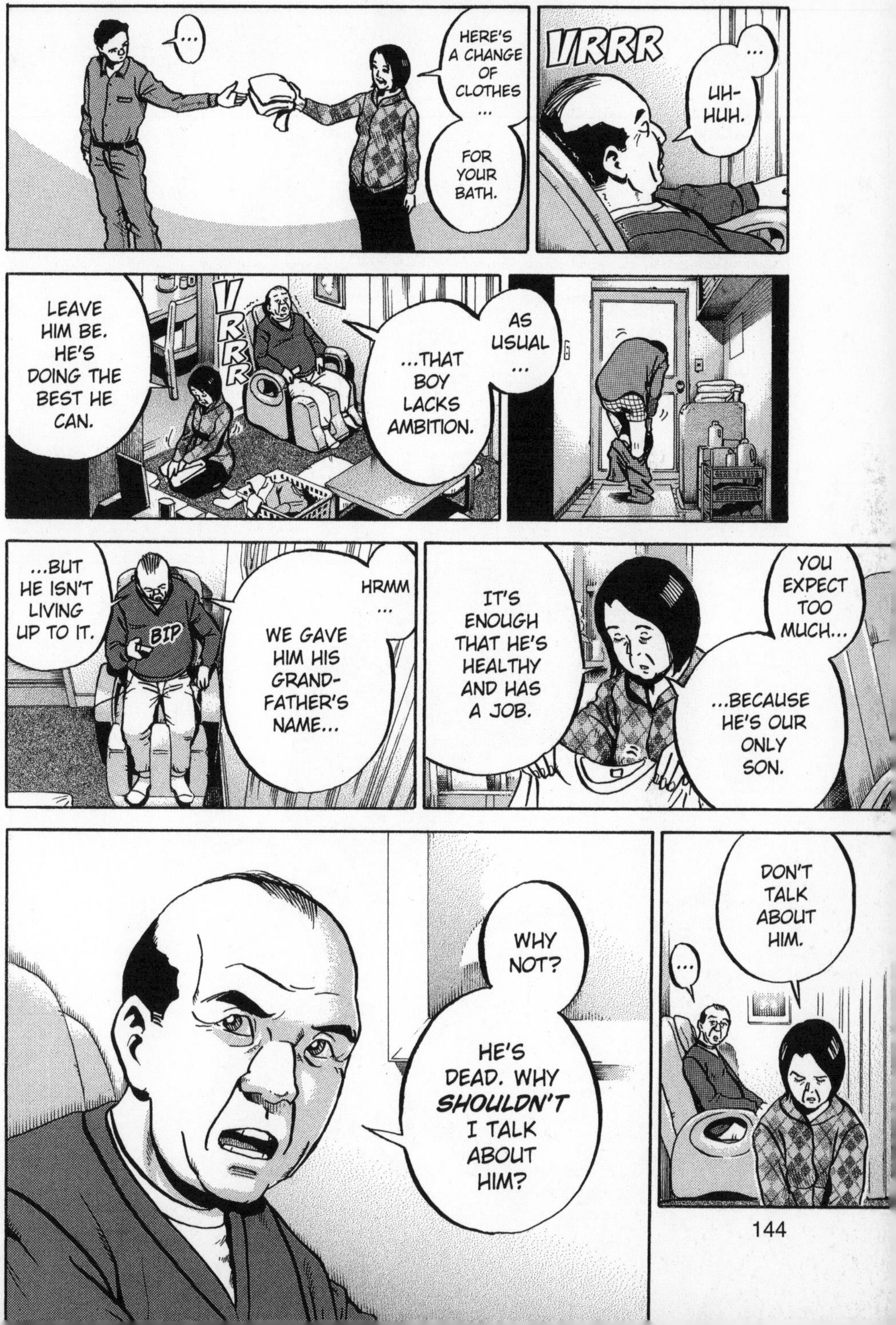
VRRR
...
UH-HUH.
HERE'S A CHANGE OF CLOTHES ...
FOR YOUR BATH.
...
AS USUAL ...
...THAT BOY LACKS AMBITION.
VRRR
LEAVE HIM BE. HE'S DOING THE BEST HE CAN.
YOU EXPECT TOO MUCH...
...BECAUSE HE'S OUR ONLY SON.
IT'S ENOUGH THAT HE'S HEALTHY AND HAS A JOB.
HRMM ...
WE GAVE HIM HIS GRAND-FATHER'S NAME...
BIP
...BUT HE ISN'T LIVING UP TO IT.
DON'T TALK ABOUT HIM.
...
WHY NOT?
HE'S DEAD. WHY *SHOULDN'T* I TALK ABOUT HIM?

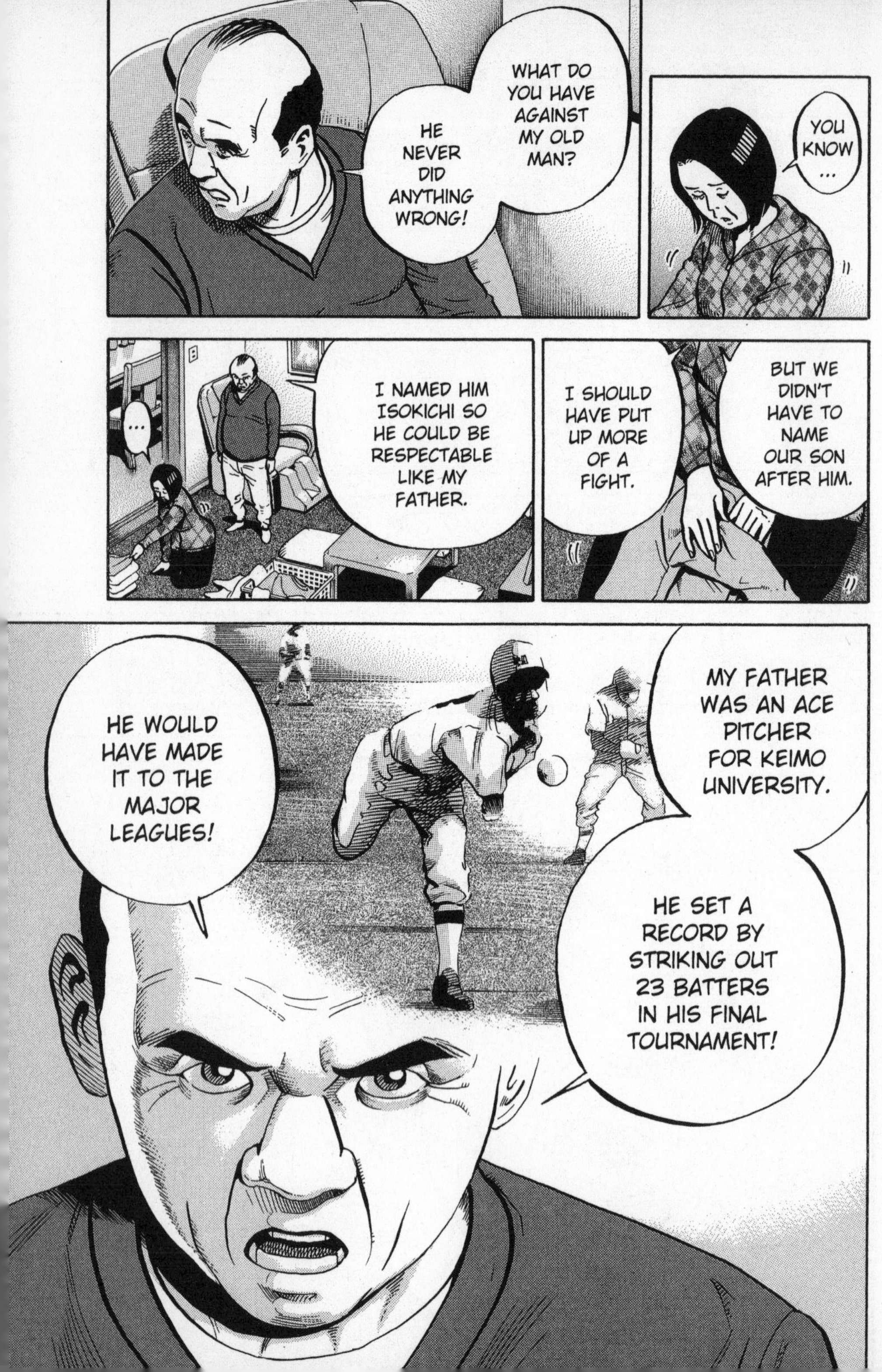
YOU KNOW ...
WHAT DO YOU HAVE AGAINST MY OLD MAN?
HE NEVER DID ANYTHING WRONG!
BUT WE DIDN'T HAVE TO NAME OUR SON AFTER HIM.
I SHOULD HAVE PUT UP MORE OF A FIGHT.
I NAMED HIM ISOKICHI SO HE COULD BE RESPECTABLE LIKE MY FATHER.
...
MY FATHER WAS AN ACE PITCHER FOR KEIMO UNIVERSITY.
HE SET A RECORD BY STRIKING OUT 23 BATTERS IN HIS FINAL TOURNAMENT!
HE WOULD HAVE MADE IT TO THE MAJOR LEAGUES!

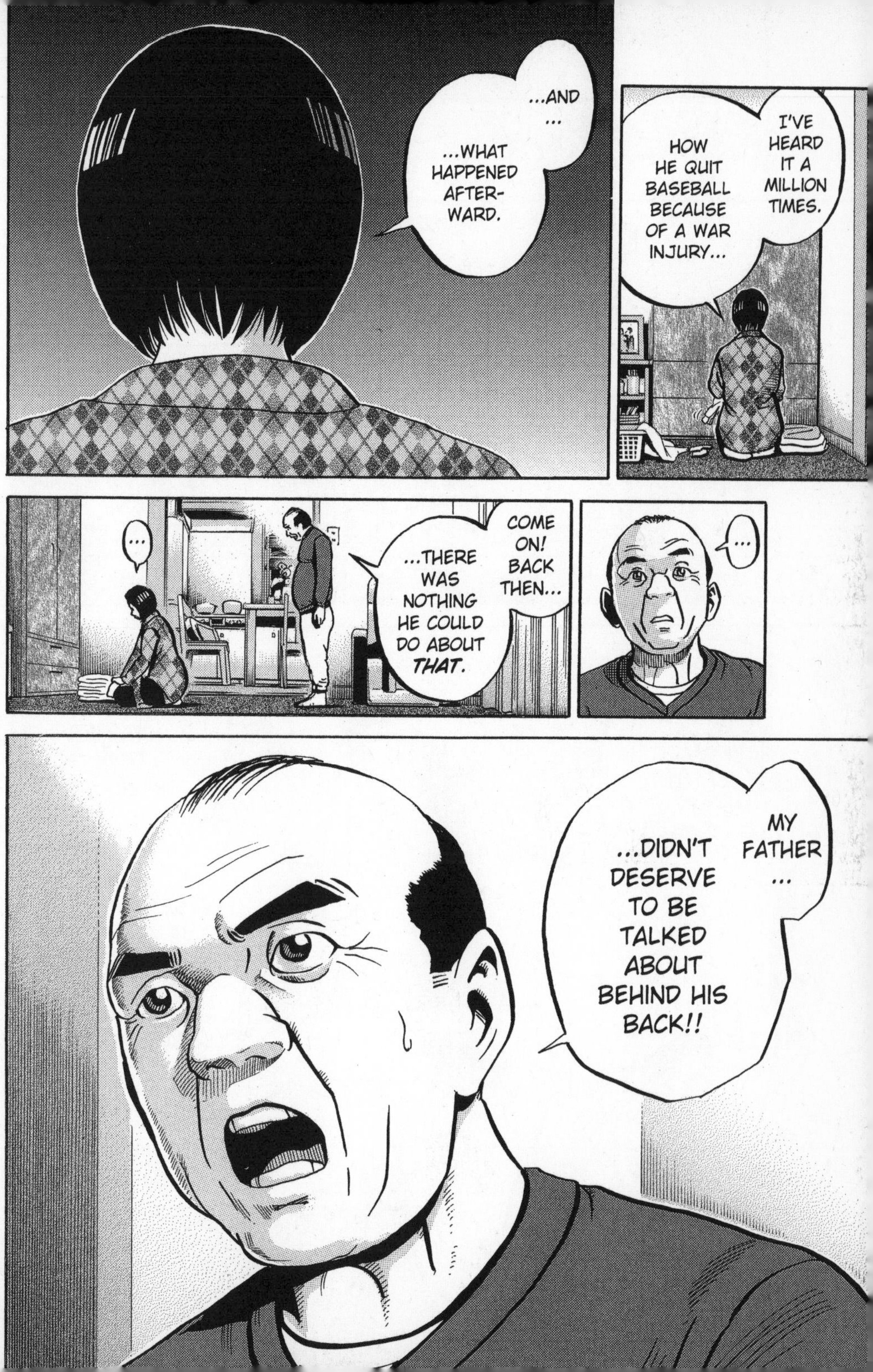
I'VE HEARD IT A MILLION TIMES. HOW HE QUIT BASEBALL BECAUSE OF A WAR INJURY...
...AND ... ...WHAT HAPPENED AFTER-WARD.
...
COME ON! BACK THEN... ...THERE WAS NOTHING HE COULD DO ABOUT *THAT*.
...
MY FATHER ... ...DIDN'T DESERVE TO BE TALKED ABOUT BEHIND HIS BACK!!

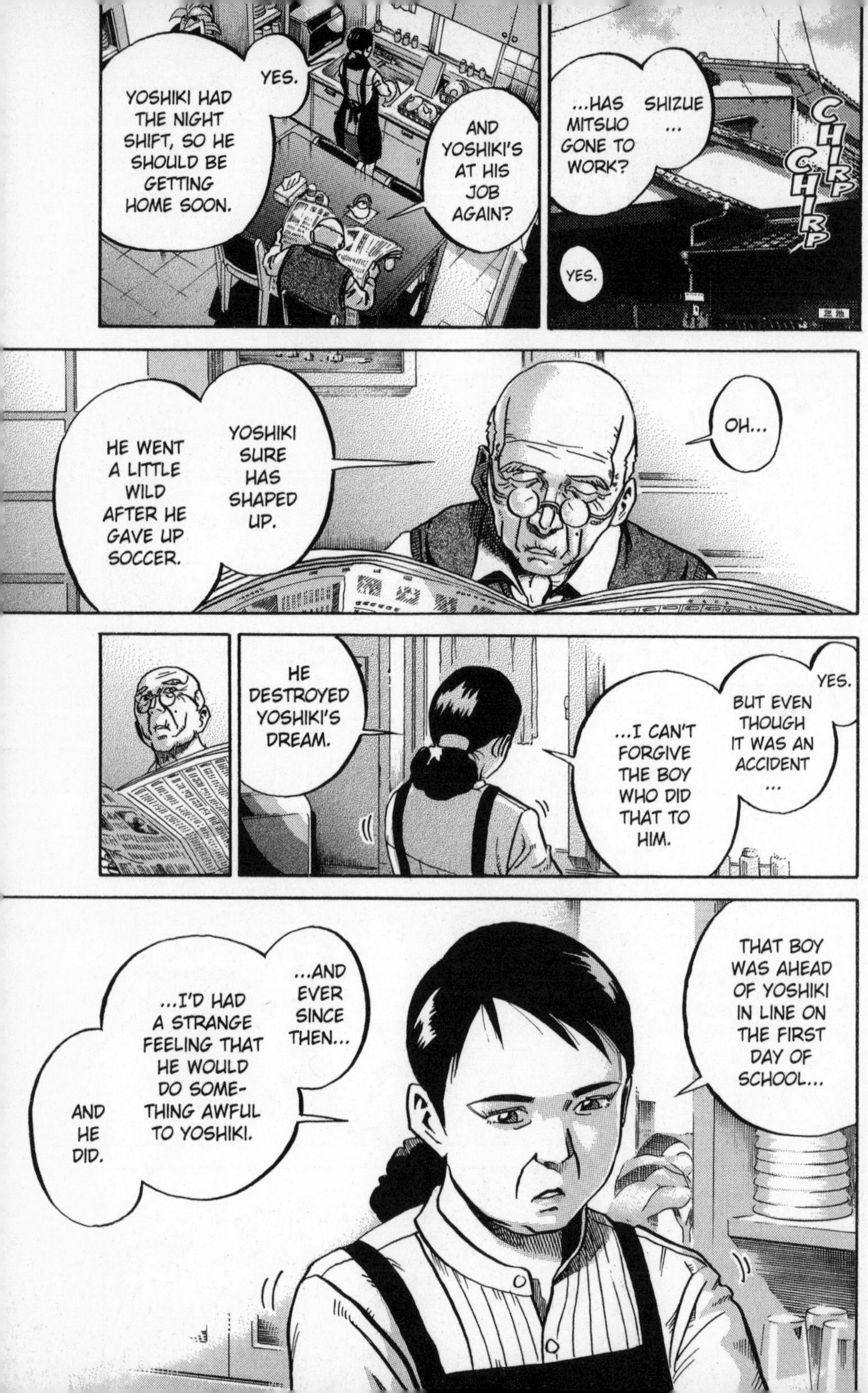
SHIZUE ...
...HAS MITSUO GONE TO WORK?
CHIRP CHIRP
YES.
AND YOSHIKI'S AT HIS JOB AGAIN?
YES.
YOSHIKI HAD THE NIGHT SHIFT, SO HE SHOULD BE GETTING HOME SOON.
OH...
YOSHIKI SURE HAS SHAPED UP.
HE WENT A LITTLE WILD AFTER HE GAVE UP SOCCER.
YES.
BUT EVEN THOUGH IT WAS AN ACCIDENT ...
...I CAN'T FORGIVE THE BOY WHO DID THAT TO HIM.
HE DESTROYED YOSHIKI'S DREAM.
THAT BOY WAS AHEAD OF YOSHIKI IN LINE ON THE FIRST DAY OF SCHOOL...
...AND EVER SINCE THEN...
...I'D HAD A STRANGE FEELING THAT HE WOULD DO SOME-THING AWFUL TO YOSHIKI.
AND HE DID.

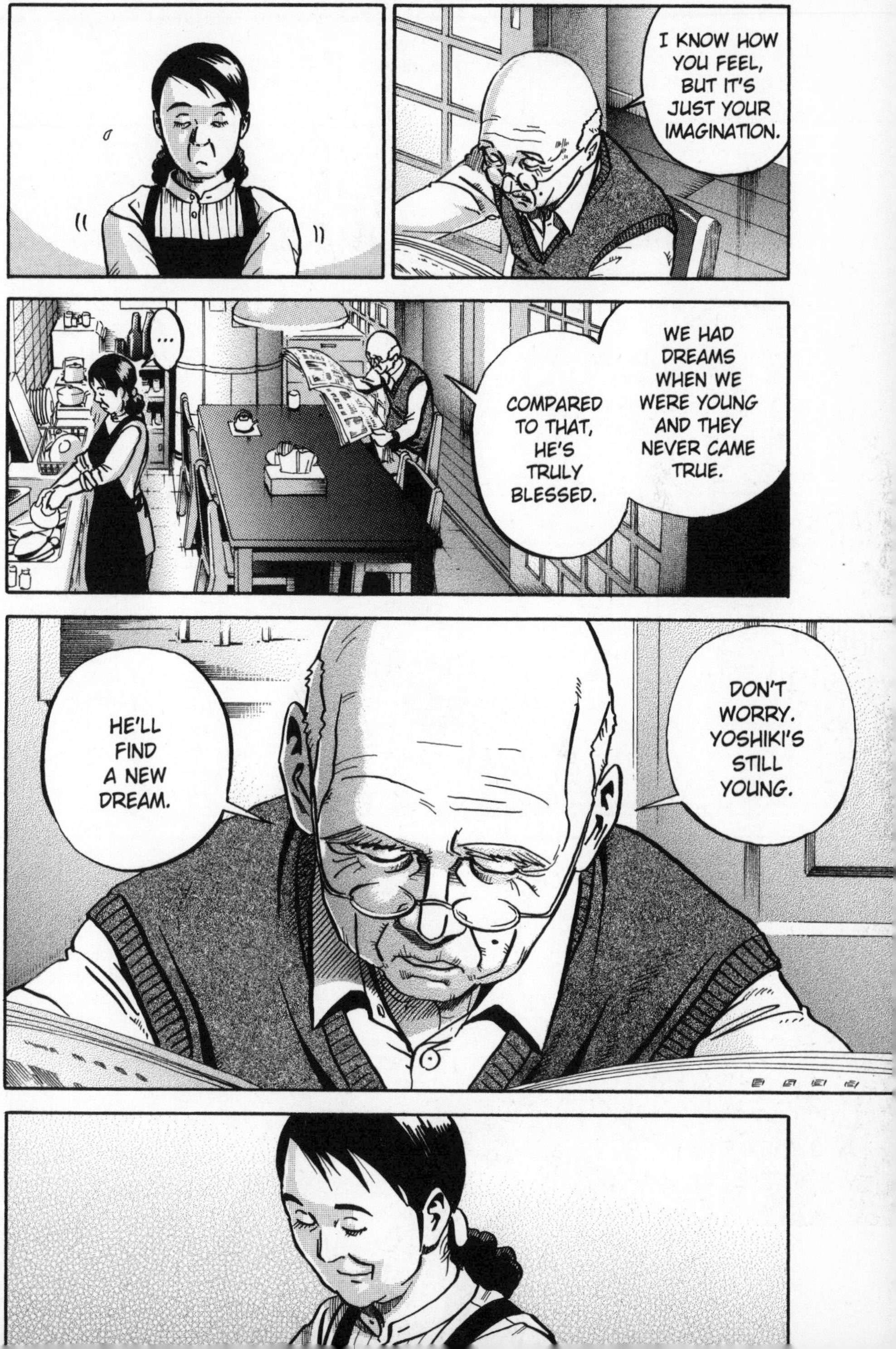
I KNOW HOW YOU FEEL, BUT IT'S JUST YOUR IMAGINATION.
WE HAD DREAMS WHEN WE WERE YOUNG AND THEY NEVER CAME TRUE.
COMPARED TO THAT, HE'S TRULY BLESSED.
...
DON'T WORRY. YOSHIKI'S STILL YOUNG.
HE'LL FIND A NEW DREAM.

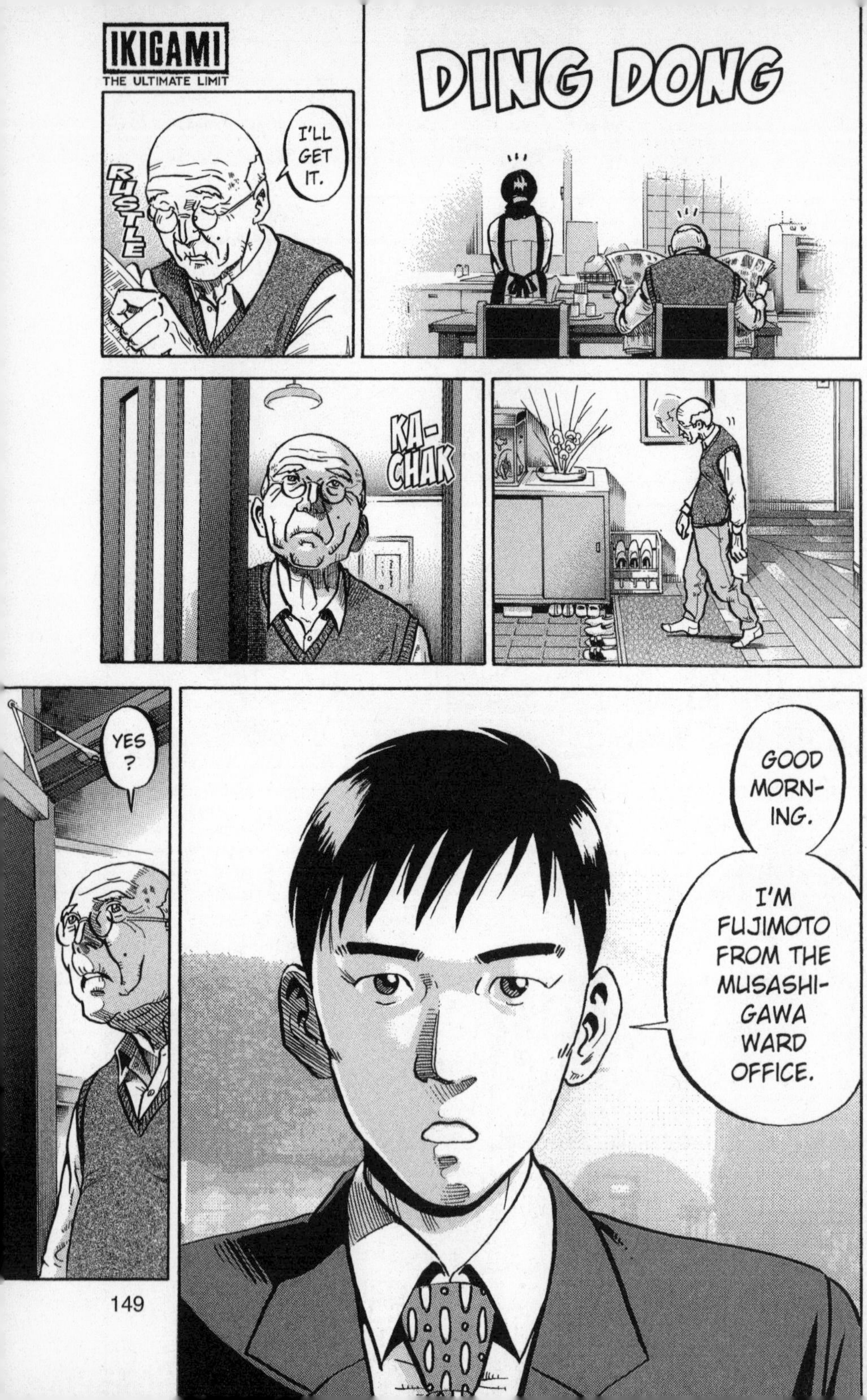
DING DONG
RUSTLE
I'LL GET IT.
KA-CHAK
GOOD MORNING.
I'M FUJIMOTO FROM THE MUSASHIGAWA WARD OFFICE.
YES?

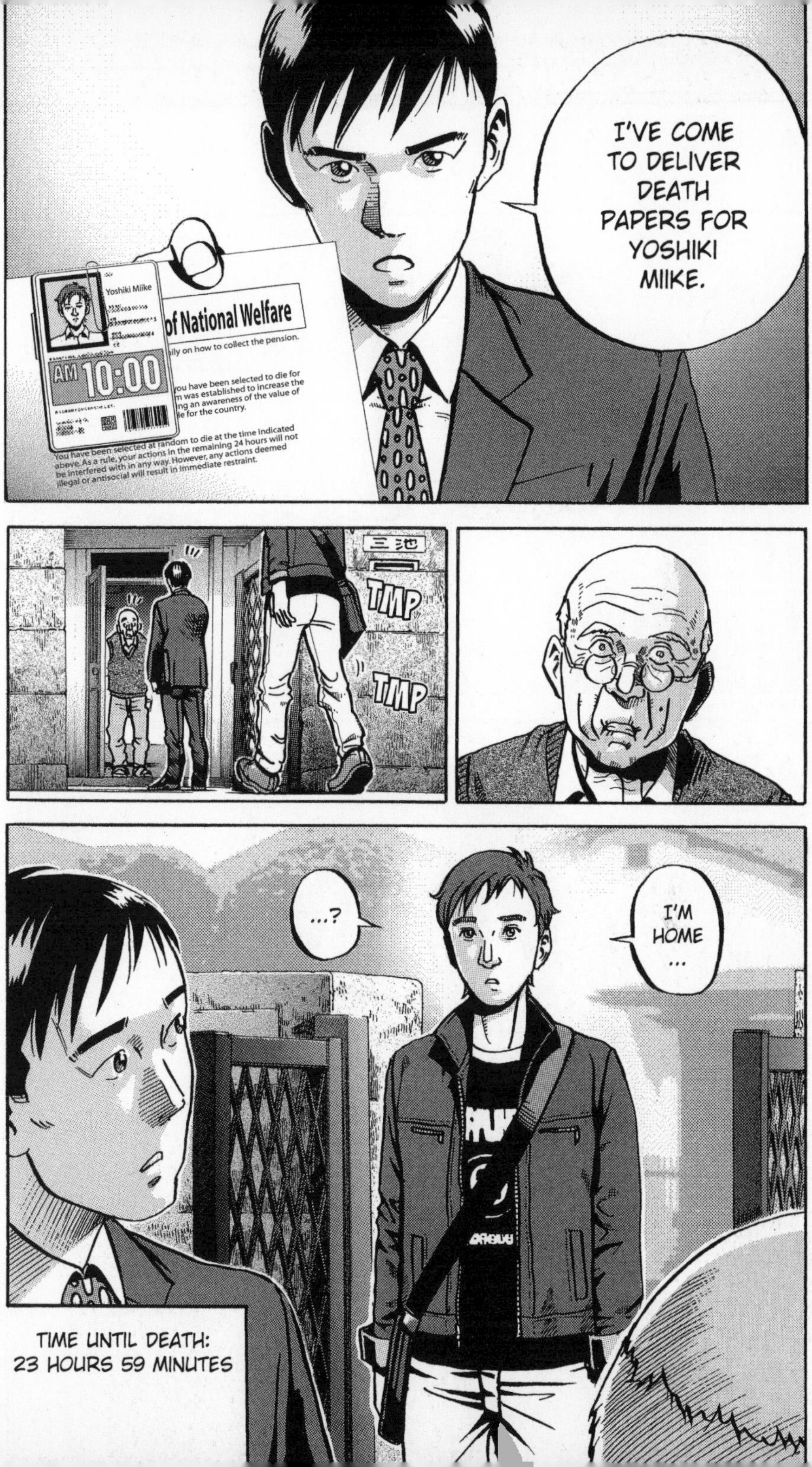
I'VE COME TO DELIVER DEATH PAPERS FOR YOSHIKI MIIKE.
Yoshiki Miike
AM 10:00
of National Welfare
ily on how to collect the pension.
you have been selected to die for
m was established to increase the
ng an awareness of the value of
le for the country.
You have been selected at random to die at the time indicated above. As a rule, your actions in the remaining 24 hours will not be interfered with in any way. However, any actions deemed illegal or antisocial will result in immediate restraint.
三池
TMP
TMP
I'M HOME ...
...?
TIME UNTIL DEATH: 23 HOURS 59 MINUTES

Episode 18 Two Fallen in War Act2

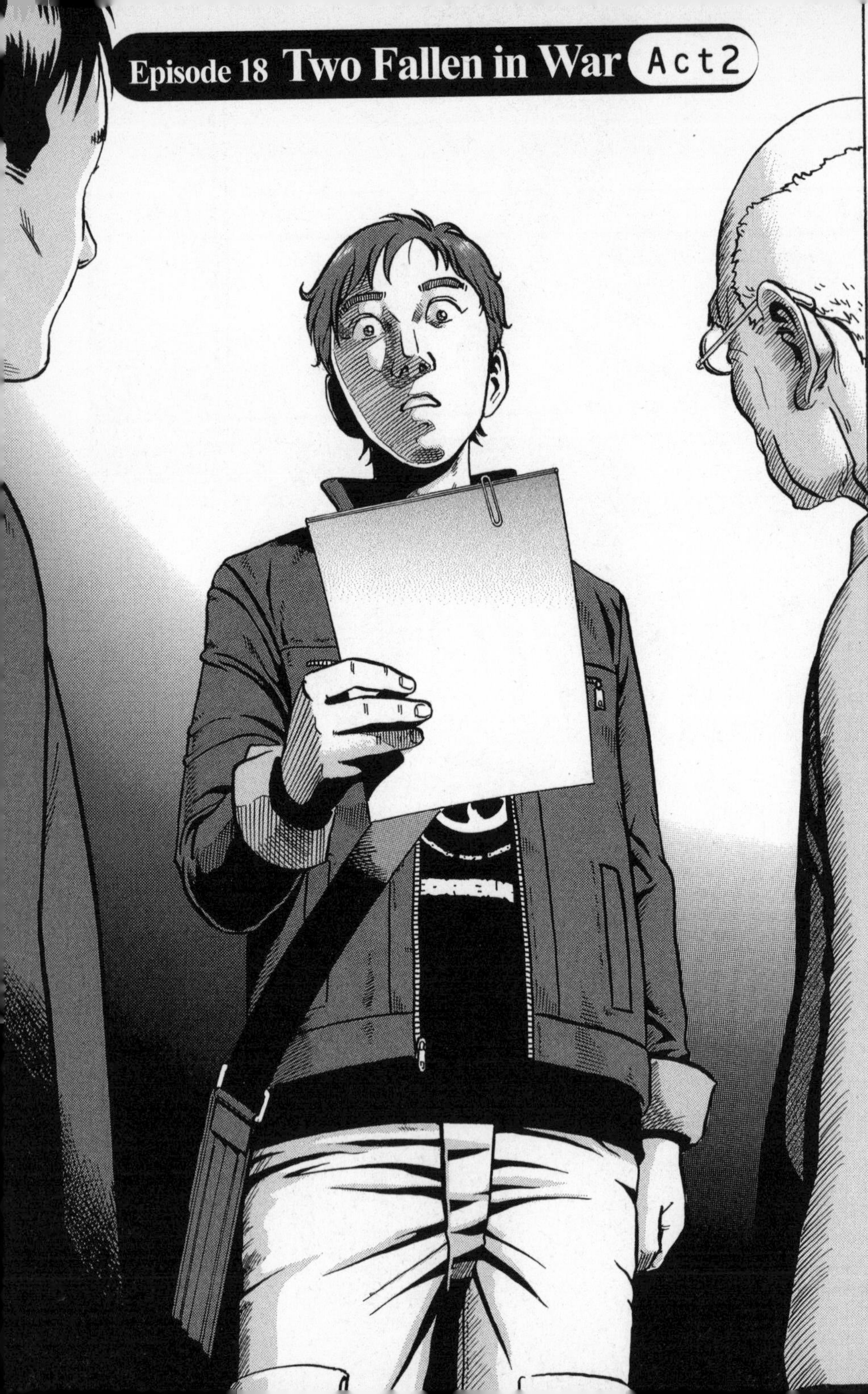

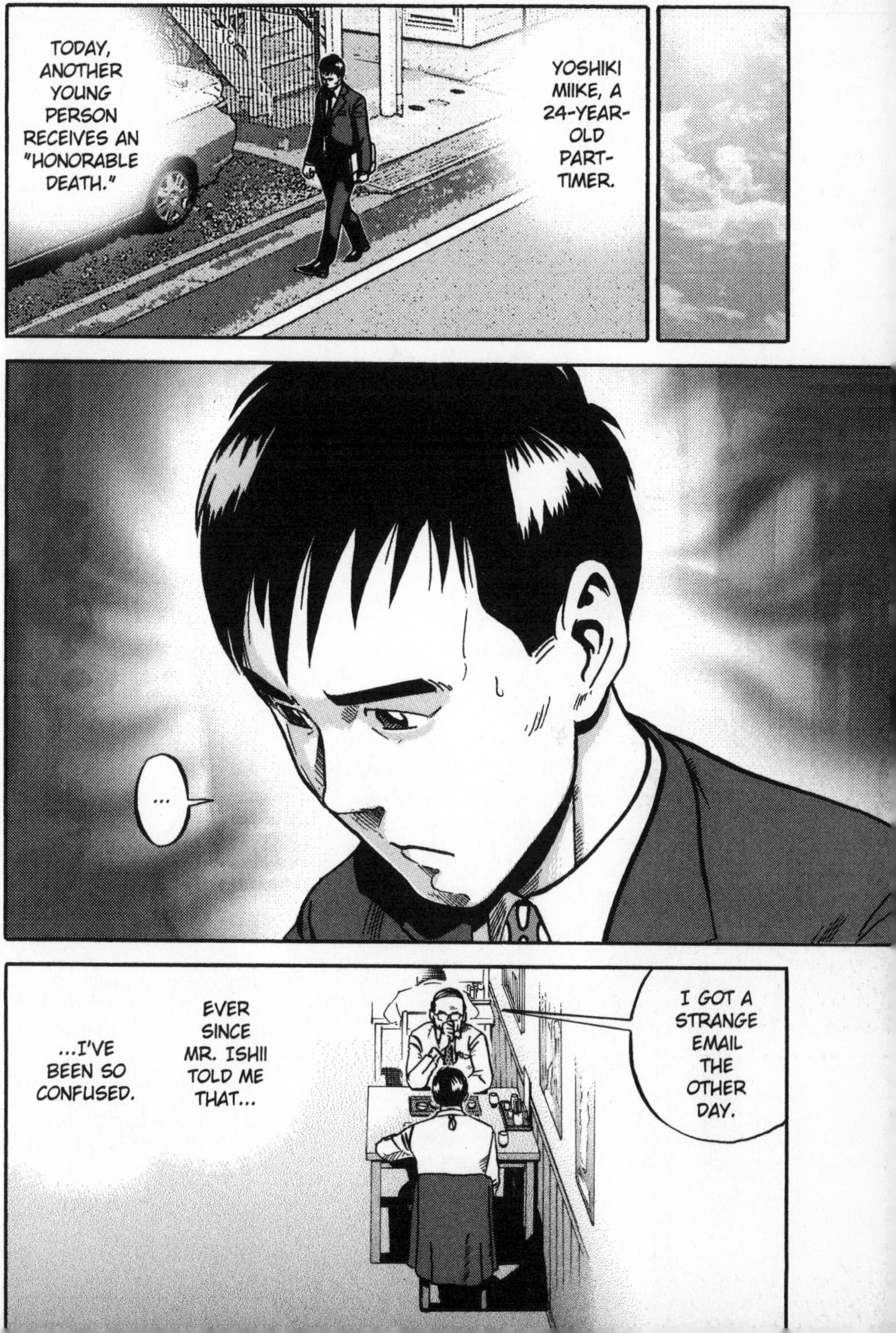
YOSHIKI MIIKE, A 24-YEAR-OLD PART-TIMER.
TODAY, ANOTHER YOUNG PERSON RECEIVES AN "HONORABLE DEATH."
...
I GOT A STRANGE EMAIL THE OTHER DAY.
EVER SINCE MR. ISHII TOLD ME THAT...
...I'VE BEEN SO CONFUSED.

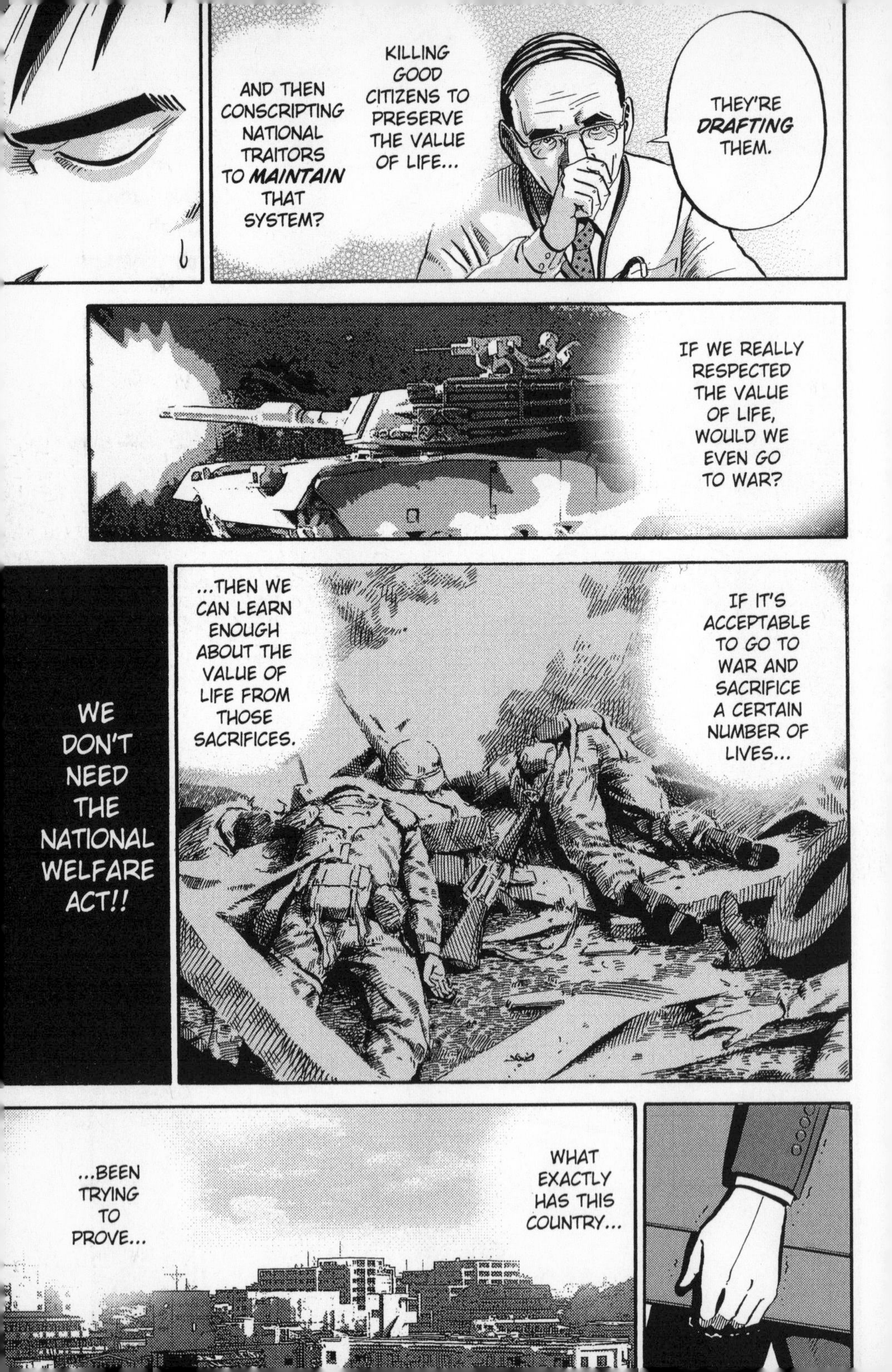
THEY'RE *DRAFTING* THEM.
KILLING GOOD CITIZENS TO PRESERVE THE VALUE OF LIFE...
AND THEN CONSCRIPTING NATIONAL TRAITORS TO *MAINTAIN* THAT SYSTEM?
IF WE REALLY RESPECTED THE VALUE OF LIFE, WOULD WE EVEN GO TO WAR?
IF IT'S ACCEPTABLE TO GO TO WAR AND SACRIFICE A CERTAIN NUMBER OF LIVES...
...THEN WE CAN LEARN ENOUGH ABOUT THE VALUE OF LIFE FROM THOSE SACRIFICES.
WE DON'T NEED THE NATIONAL WELFARE ACT!!
WHAT EXACTLY HAS THIS COUNTRY...
...BEEN TRYING TO PROVE...

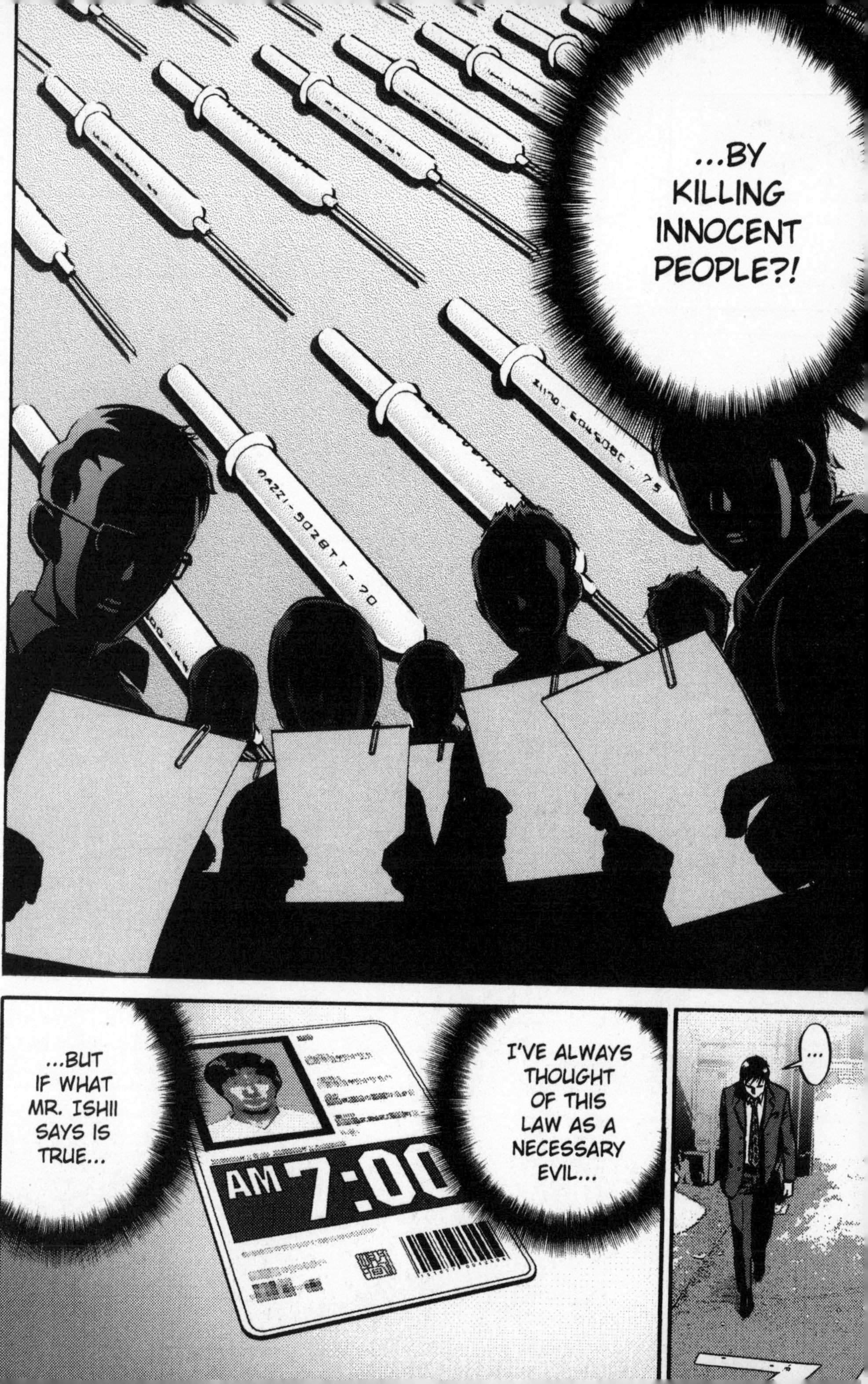
...BY KILLING INNOCENT PEOPLE?!
...
I'VE ALWAYS THOUGHT OF THIS LAW AS A NECESSARY EVIL...
AM 7:00
...BUT IF WHAT MR. ISHII SAYS IS TRUE...

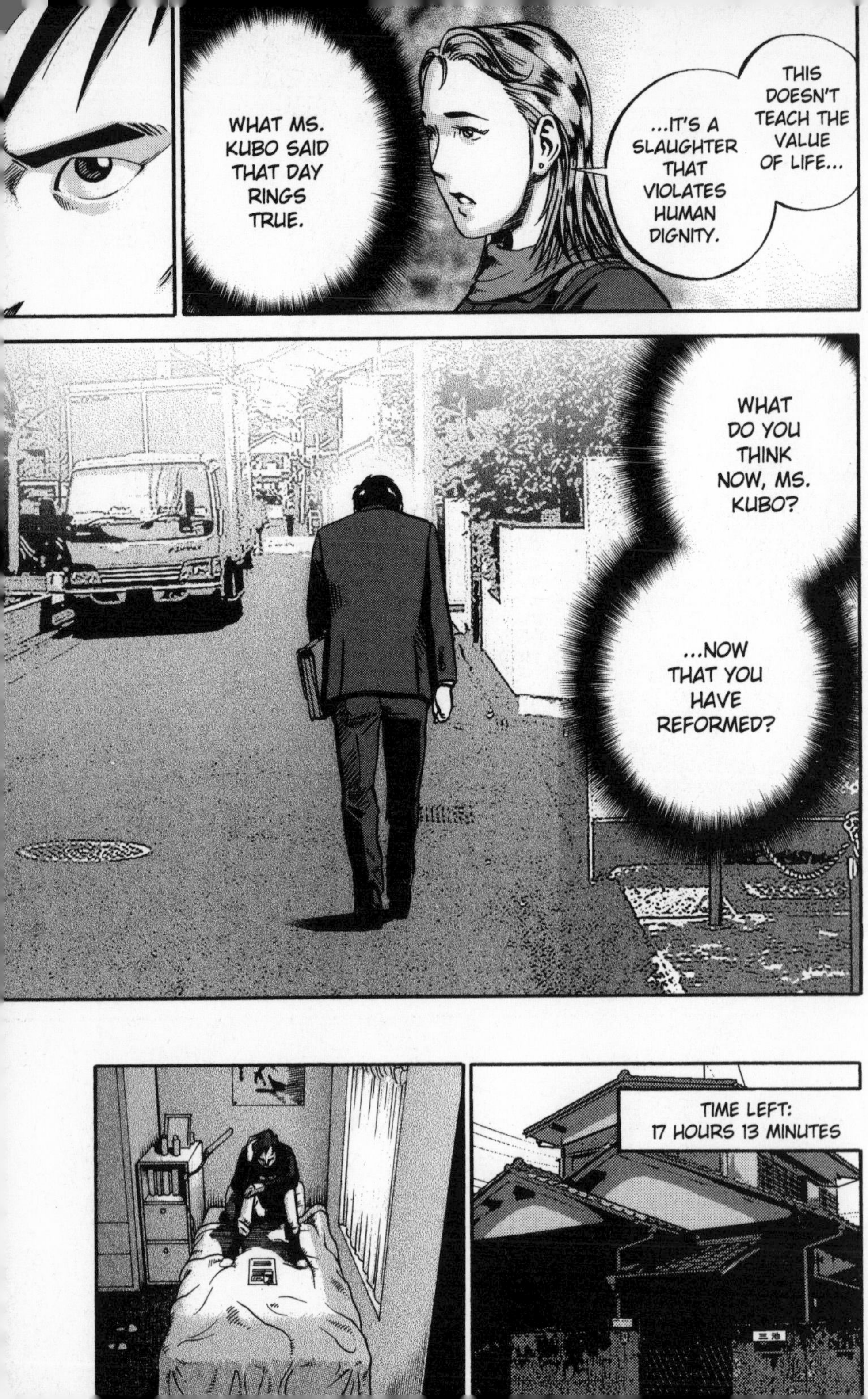
THIS DOESN'T TEACH THE VALUE OF LIFE...
...IT'S A SLAUGHTER THAT VIOLATES HUMAN DIGNITY.
WHAT MS. KUBO SAID THAT DAY RINGS TRUE.
WHAT DO YOU THINK NOW, MS. KUBO?
...NOW THAT YOU HAVE REFORMED?
TIME LEFT: 17 HOURS 13 MINUTES
三池

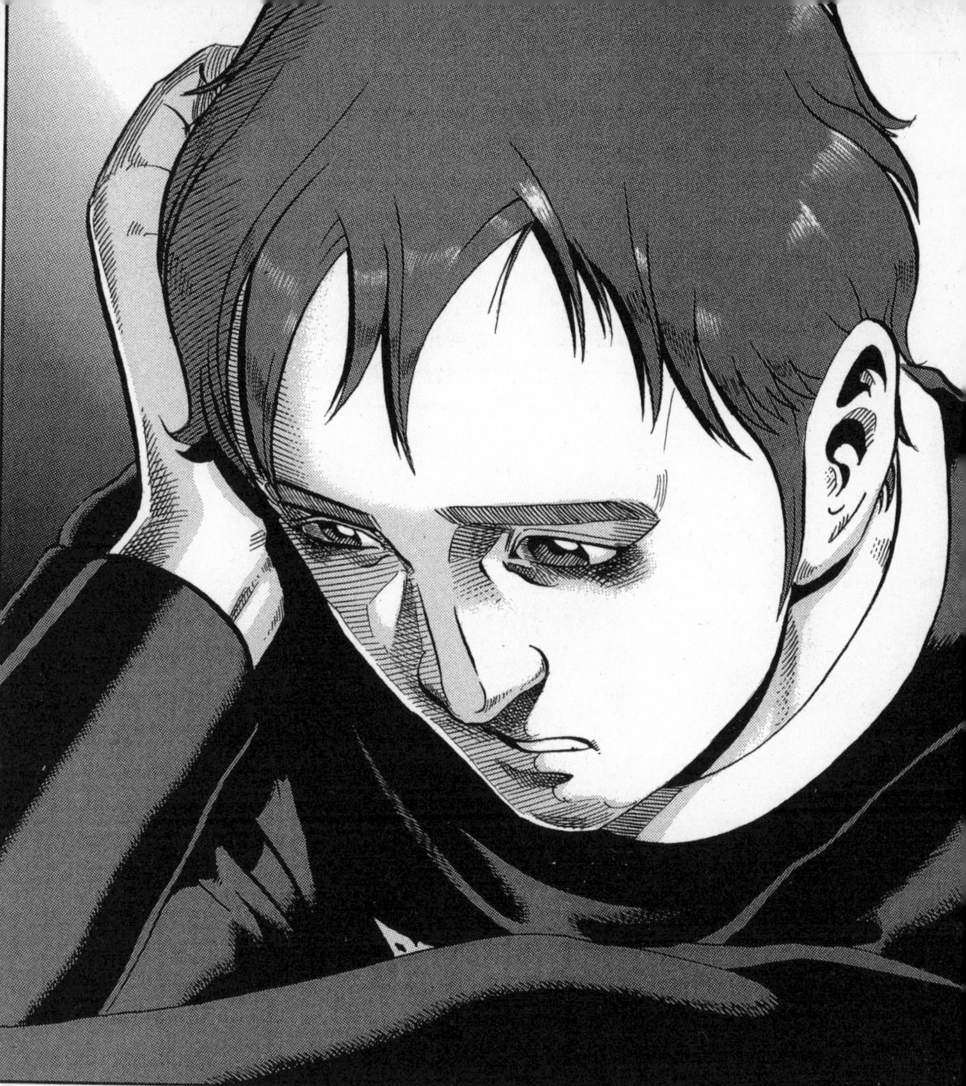

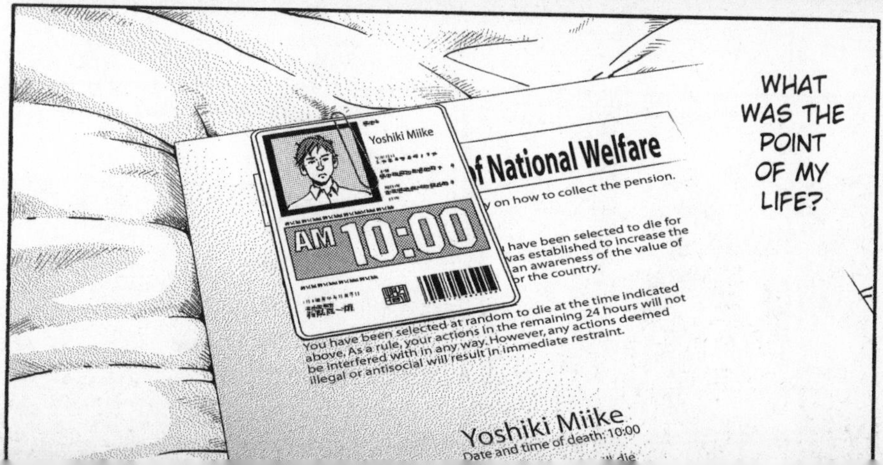
WHAT WAS THE POINT OF MY LIFE?
Yoshiki Miike
AM 10:00
of National Welfare
y on how to collect the pension.
have been selected to die for
was established to increase the
an awareness of the value of
or the country.
You have been selected at random to die at the time indicated above. As a rule, your actions in the remaining 24 hours will not be interfered with in any way. However, any actions deemed illegal or antisocial will result in immediate restraint.
Yoshiki Miike
Date and time of death: 10:00

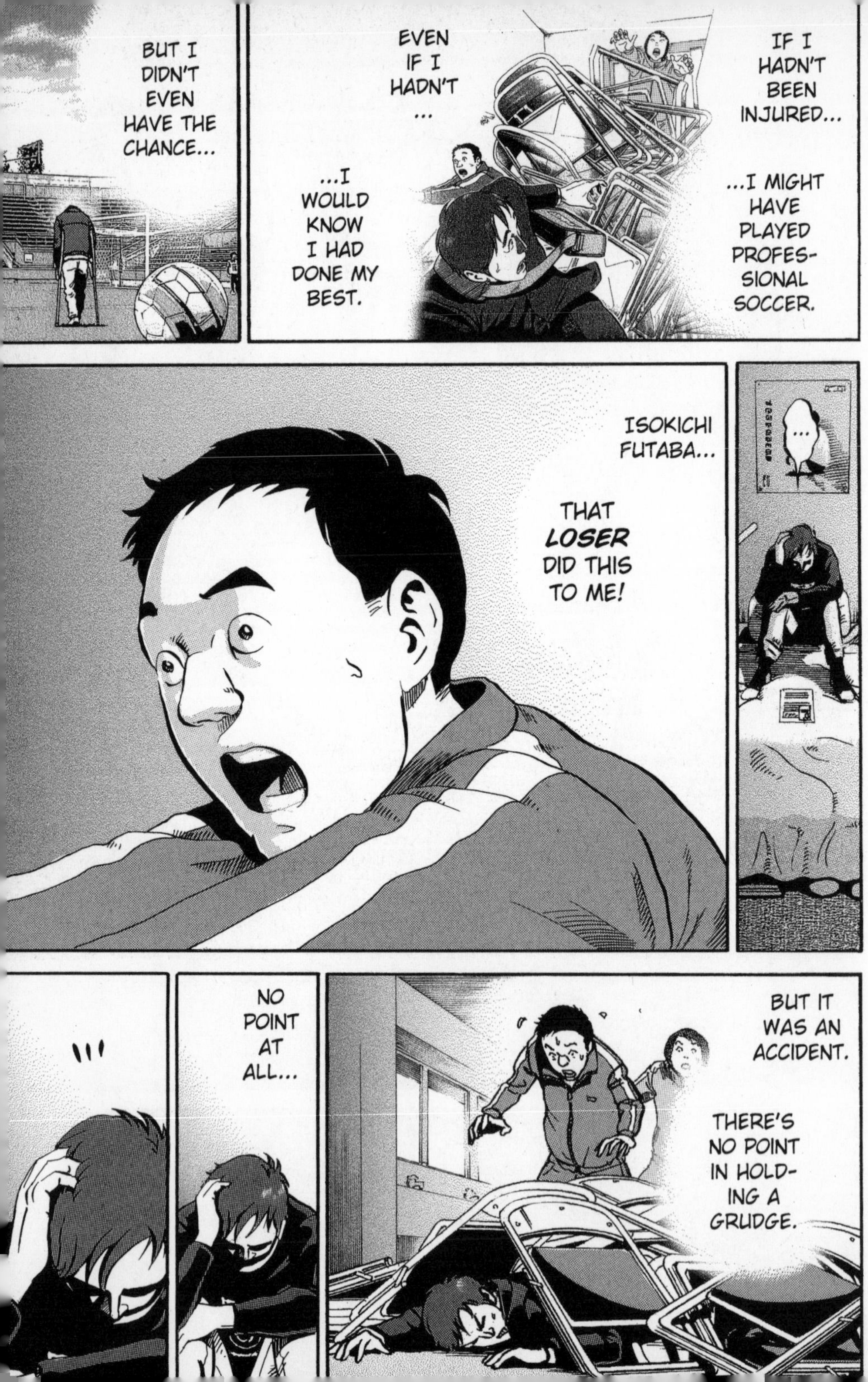
IF I HADN'T BEEN INJURED...
...I MIGHT HAVE PLAYED PROFES-SIONAL SOCCER.
EVEN IF I HADN'T ...
...I WOULD KNOW I HAD DONE MY BEST.
BUT I DIDN'T EVEN HAVE THE CHANCE...
...
ISOKICHI FUTABA...
THAT LOSER DID THIS TO ME!
BUT IT WAS AN ACCIDENT.
THERE'S NO POINT IN HOLD-ING A GRUDGE.
NO POINT AT ALL...

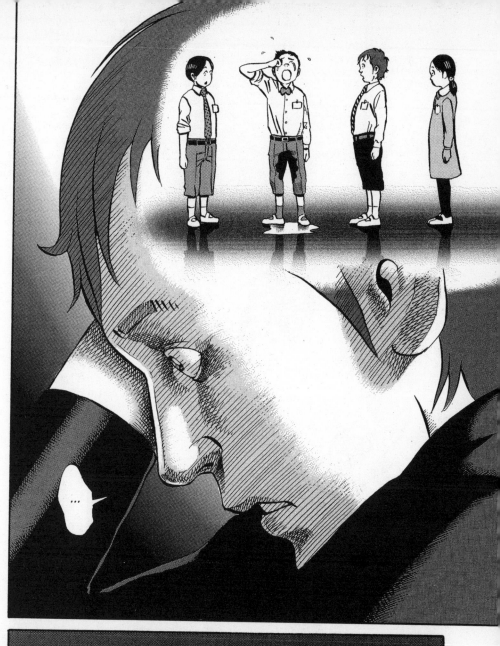

…

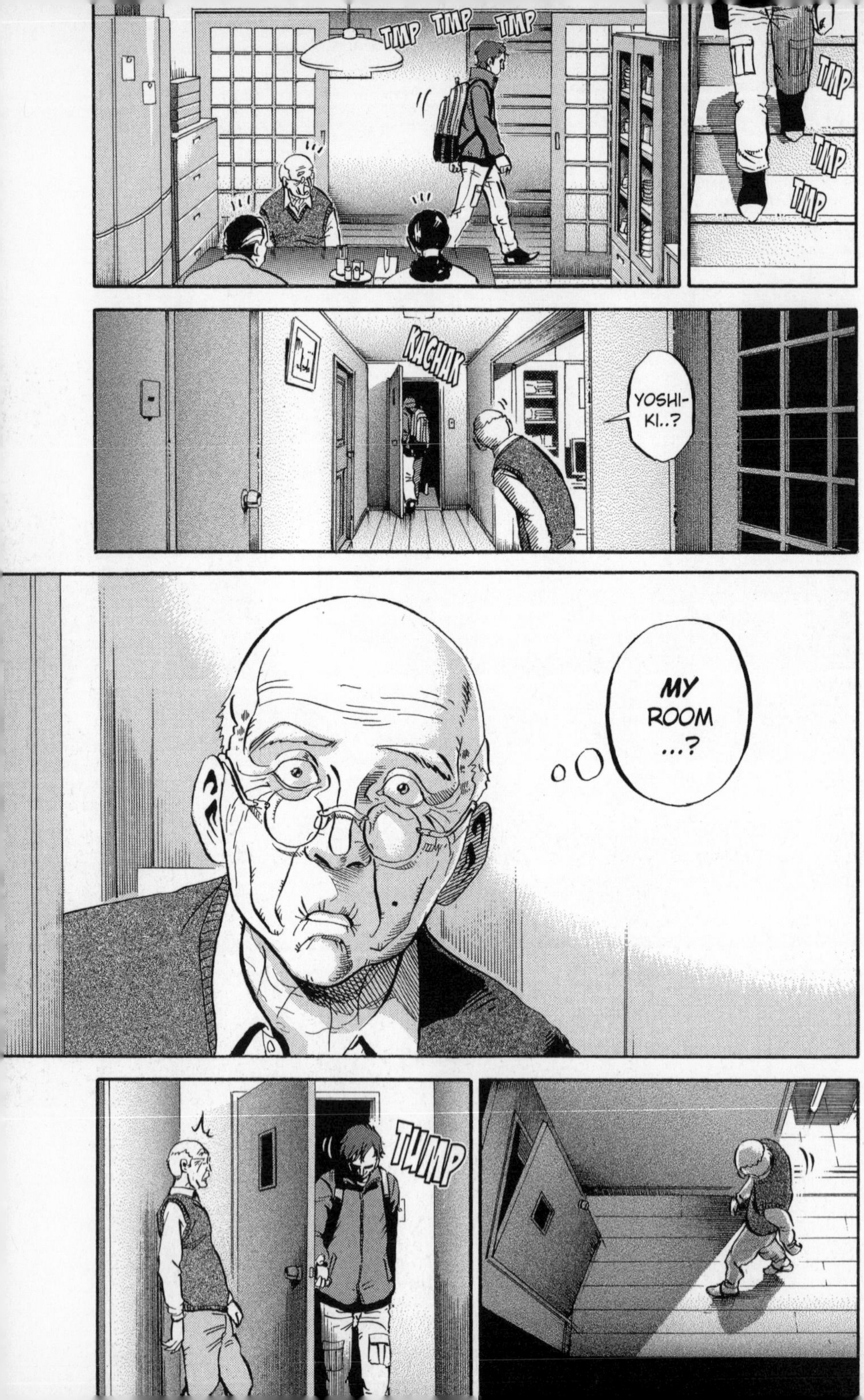
TMP
TMP
TMP
TMP
TMP
TMP
YOSHI-KI..?
KACHAK
MY ROOM ...?
TUMP

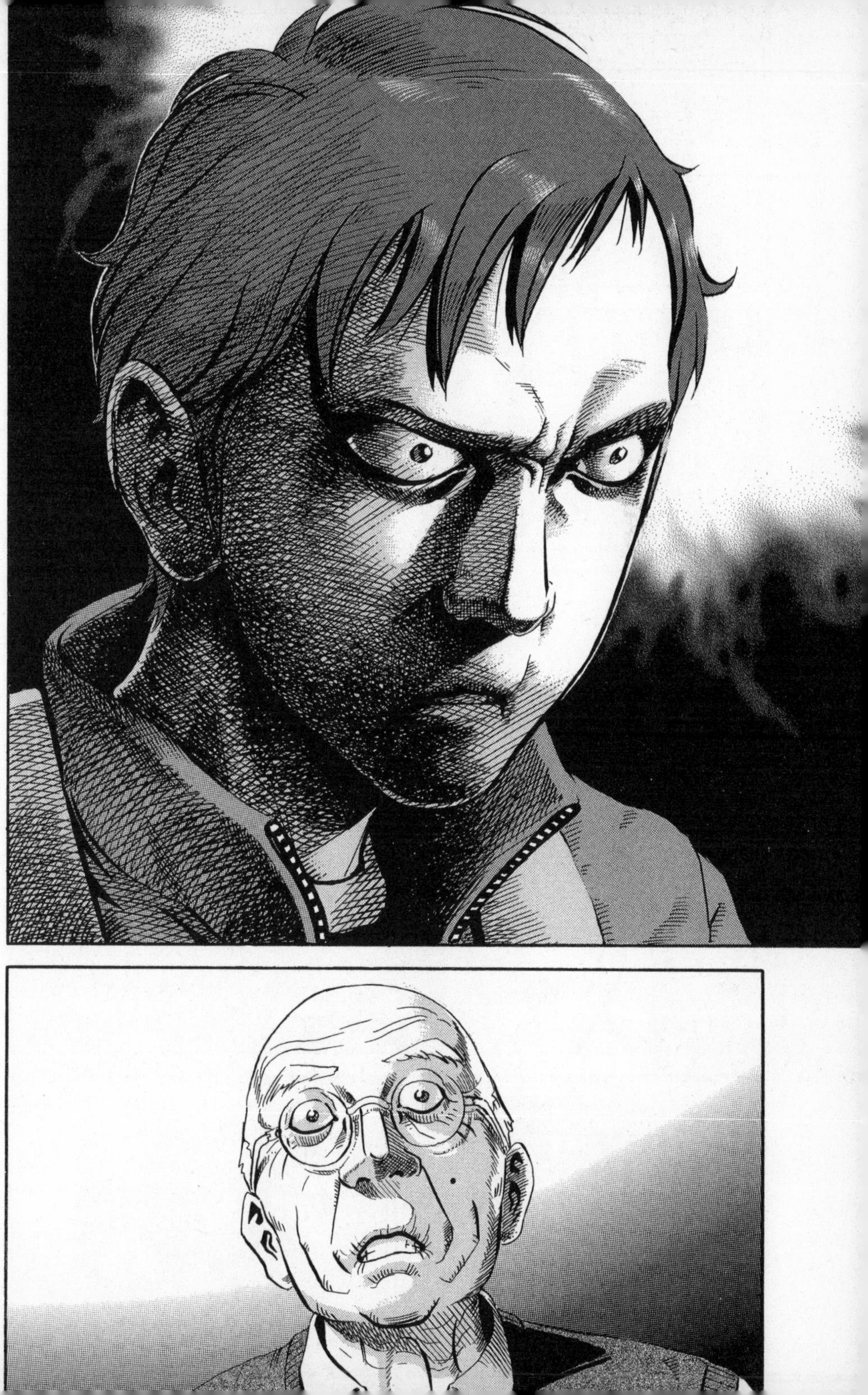

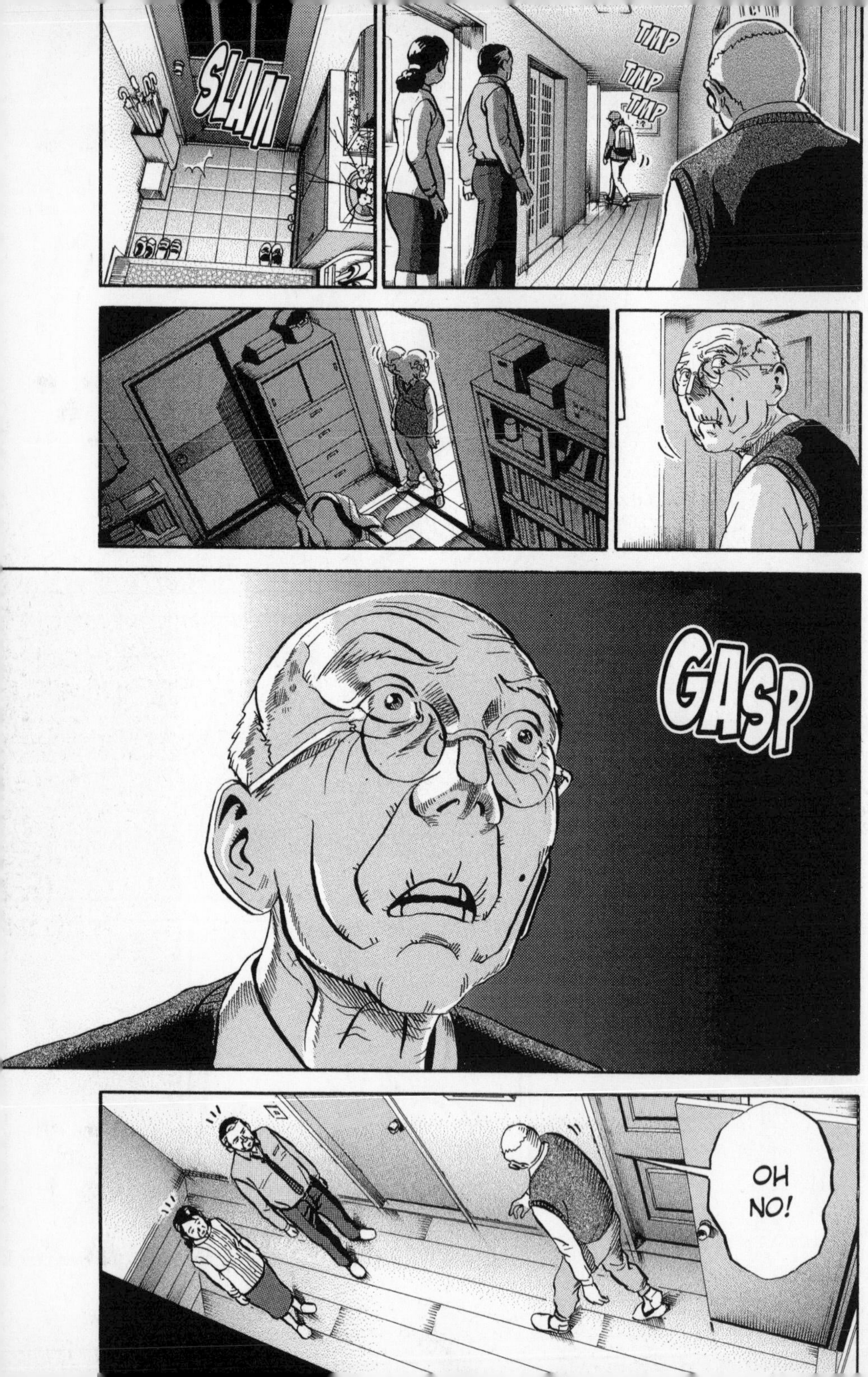
TMP
TMP
TMP
SLAM
GASP
OH NO!

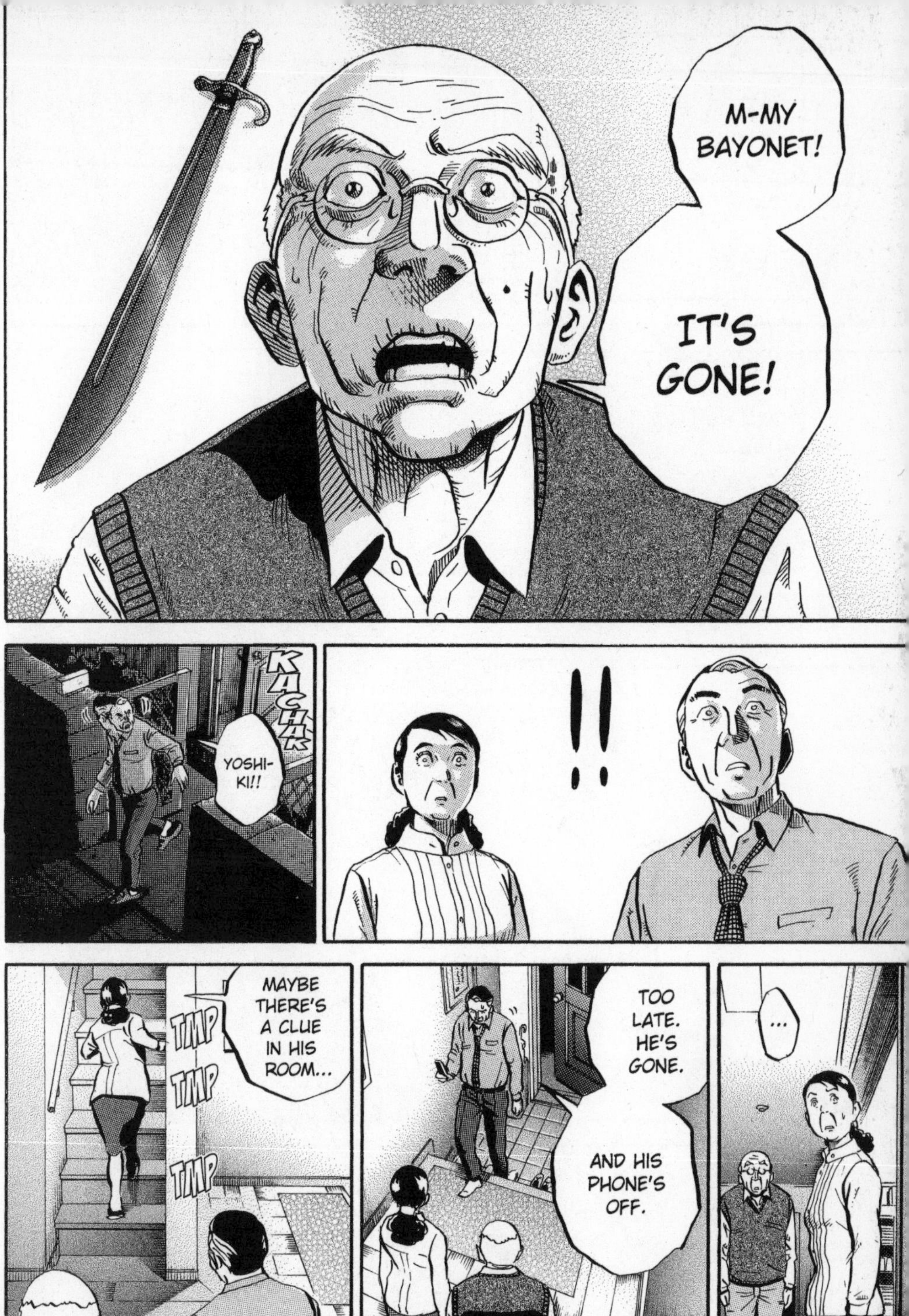
M-MY BAYONET!
IT'S GONE!
!!
KACHAK
YOSHIKI!!
...
TOO LATE. HE'S GONE.
AND HIS PHONE'S OFF.
MAYBE THERE'S A CLUE IN HIS ROOM...
TMP
TMP
TMP

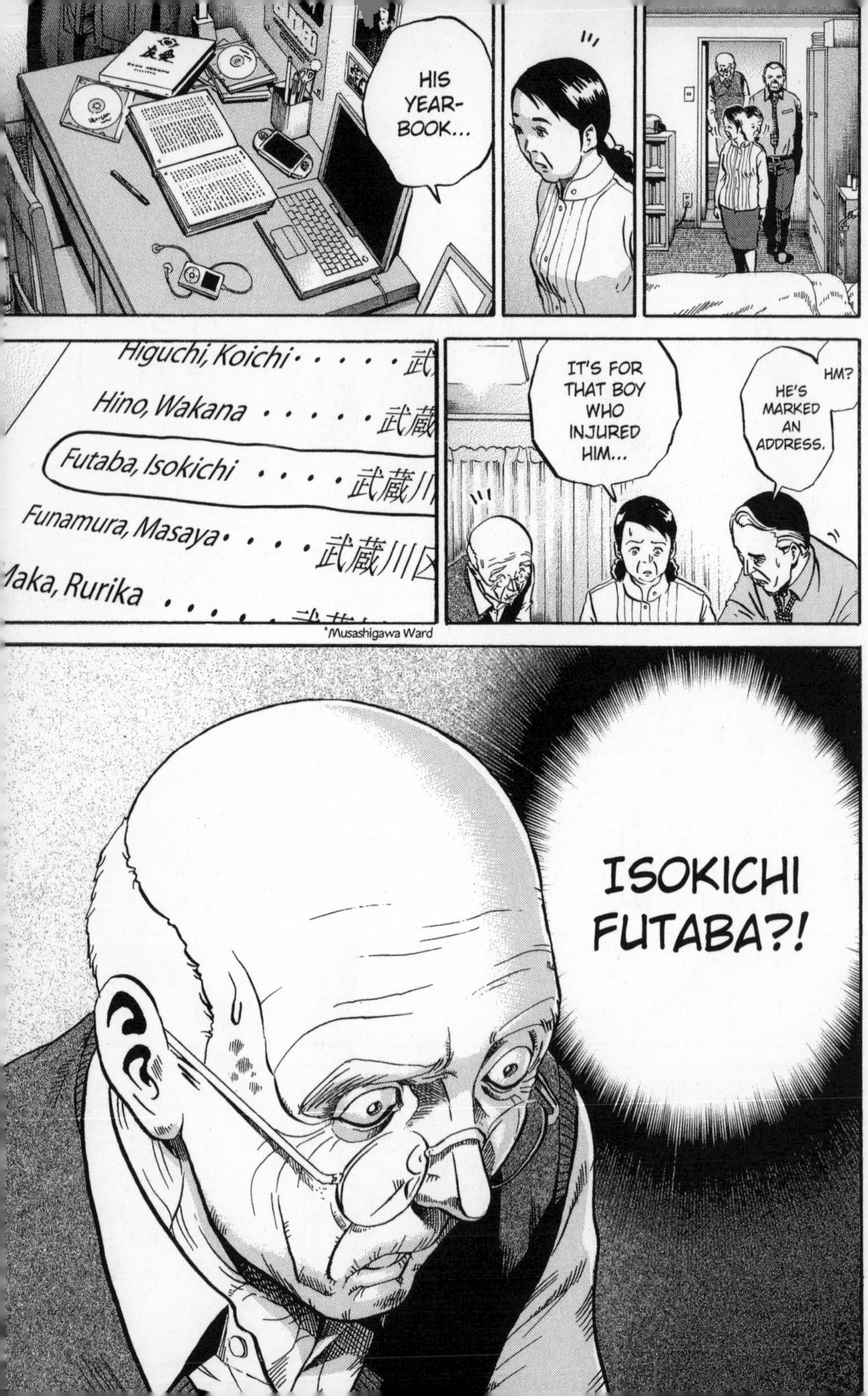
HIS YEAR-BOOK...
HM?
HE'S MARKED AN ADDRESS.
IT'S FOR THAT BOY WHO INJURED HIM...
Higuchi, Koichi · · · · · ·武
Hino, Wakana · · · · · ·武蔵
Futaba, Isokichi · · · · ·武蔵川
Funamura, Masaya · · · · ·武蔵川区
aka, Rurika
ISOKICHI FUTABA?!
*Musashigawa Ward

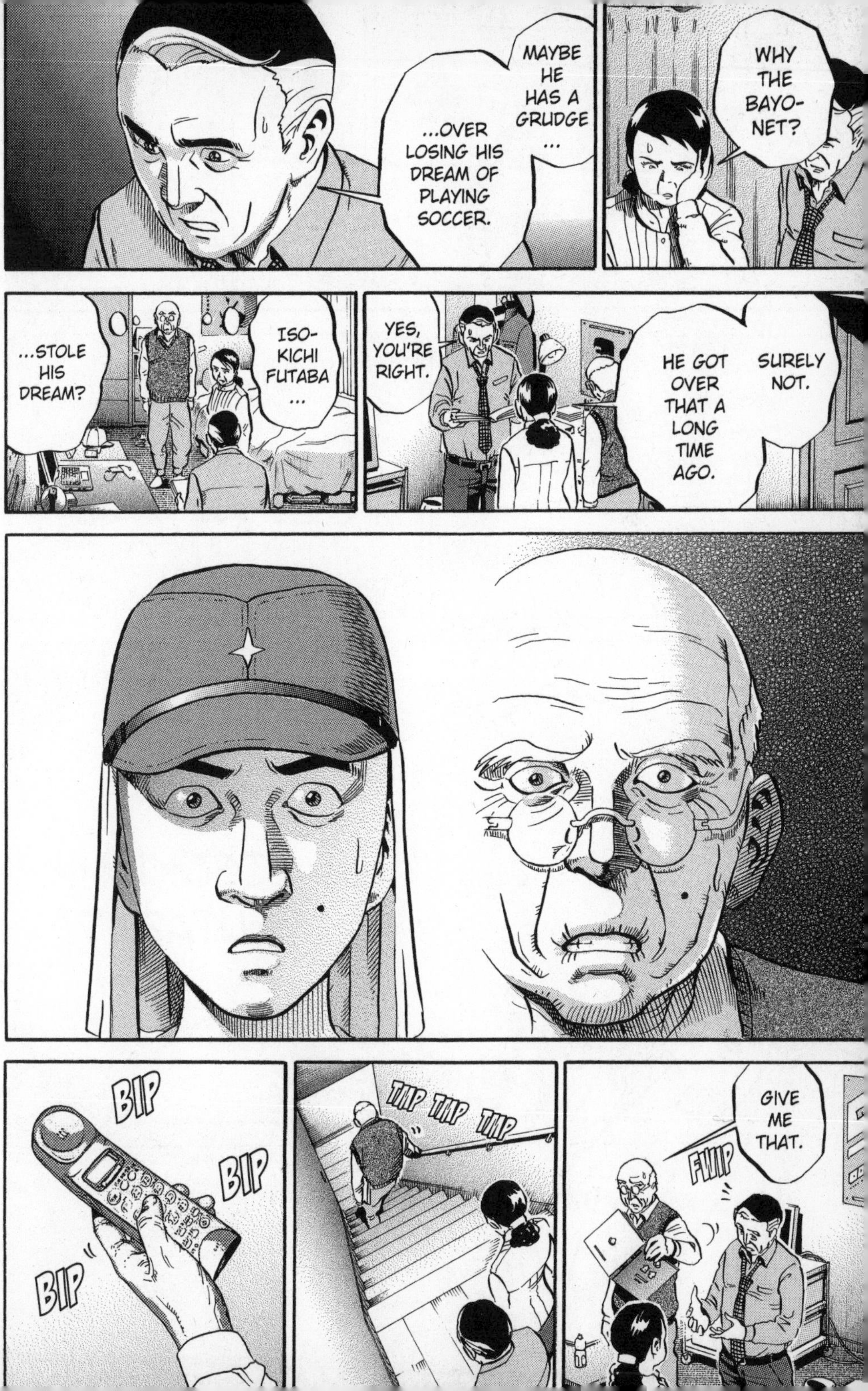
WHY THE BAYO-NET?
MAYBE HE HAS A GRUDGE ...
...OVER LOSING HIS DREAM OF PLAYING SOCCER.
SURELY NOT.
HE GOT OVER THAT A LONG TIME AGO.
YES, YOU'RE RIGHT.
ISO-KICHI FUTABA ...
...STOLE HIS DREAM?
GIVE ME THAT.
FWIP
TMP TMP TMP
BIP
BIP
BIP

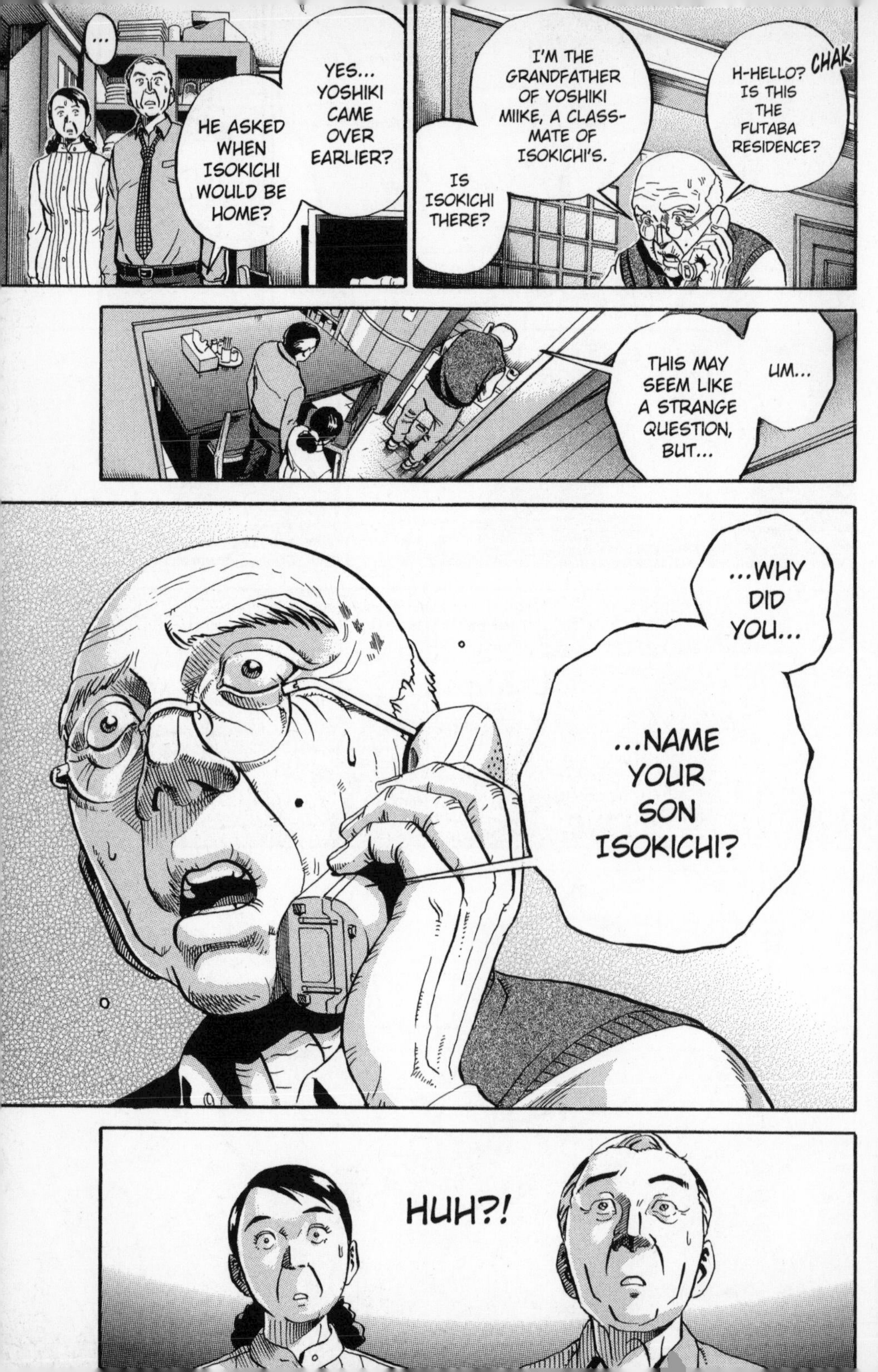
CHAK
H-HELLO? IS THIS THE FUTABA RESIDENCE?
I'M THE GRANDFATHER OF YOSHIKI MIIKE, A CLASS-MATE OF ISOKICHI'S.
IS ISOKICHI THERE?
YES... YOSHIKI CAME OVER EARLIER?
HE ASKED WHEN ISOKICHI WOULD BE HOME?
...
UM...
THIS MAY SEEM LIKE A STRANGE QUESTION, BUT...
...WHY DID YOU...
...NAME YOUR SON ISOKICHI?
HUH?!

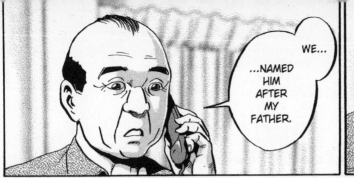

WE...

...NAMED HIM AFTER MY FATHER.

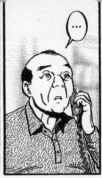

...

YES.

SO YOUR FATHER'S NAME WAS ISOKICHI FUTABA?

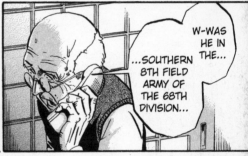

THE 68TH DIVISION'S 19TH REGIMENT OF FOOT SOLDIERS ...

W-WAS HE IN THE...

...SOUTHERN 8TH FIELD ARMY OF THE 68TH DIVISION...

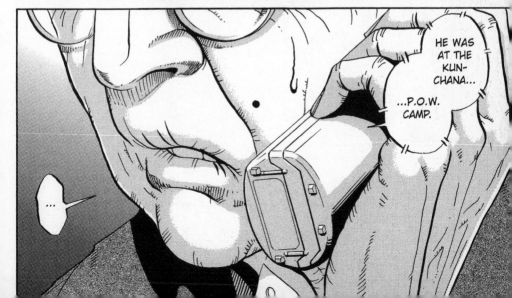

HE WAS AT THE KUN-CHANA...

...P.O.W. CAMP.

...

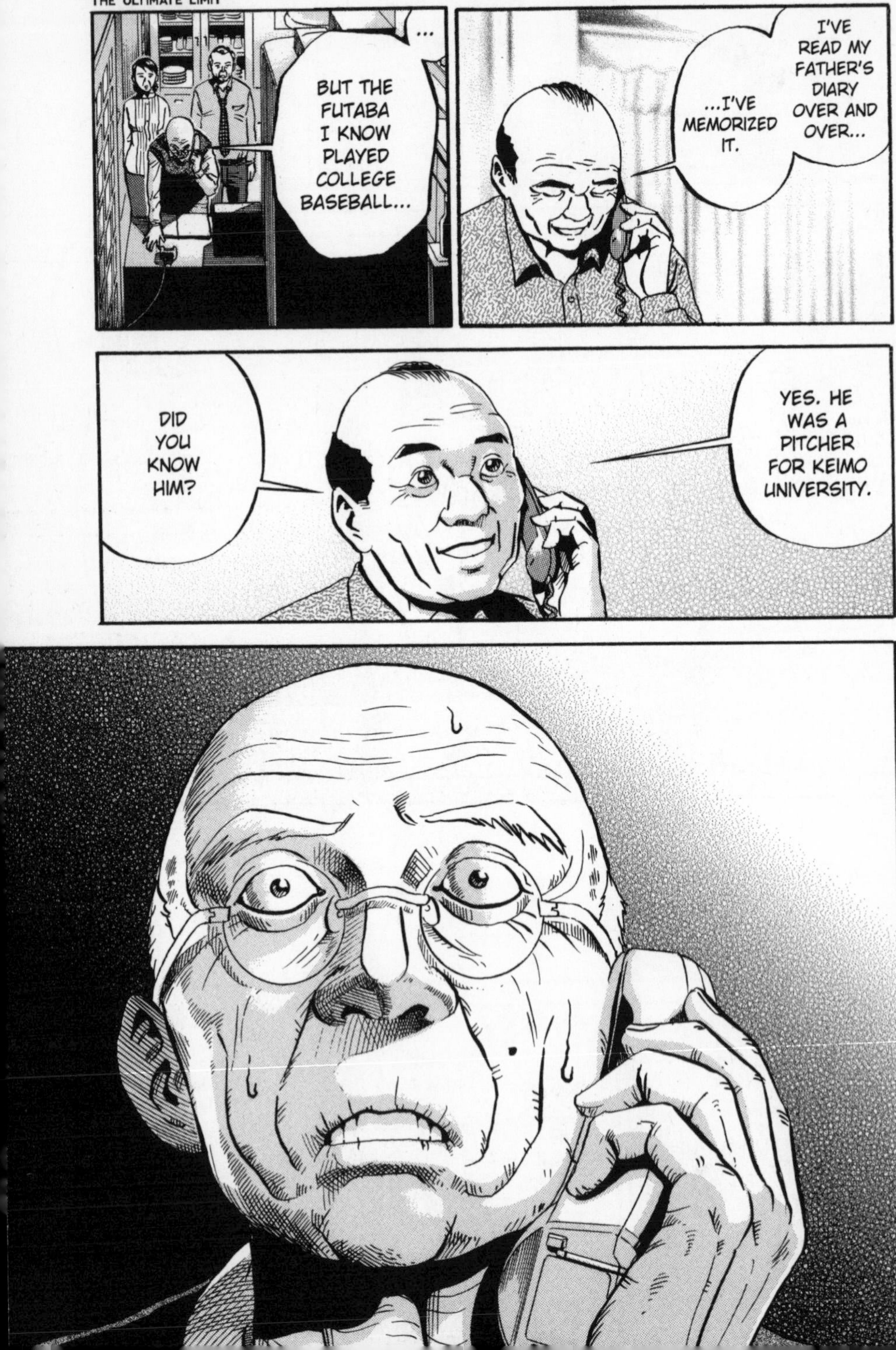
I'VE READ MY FATHER'S DIARY OVER AND OVER...
...I'VE MEMORIZED IT.
...
BUT THE FUTABA I KNOW PLAYED COLLEGE BASEBALL...
YES. HE WAS A PITCHER FOR KEIMO UNIVERSITY.
DID YOU KNOW HIM?

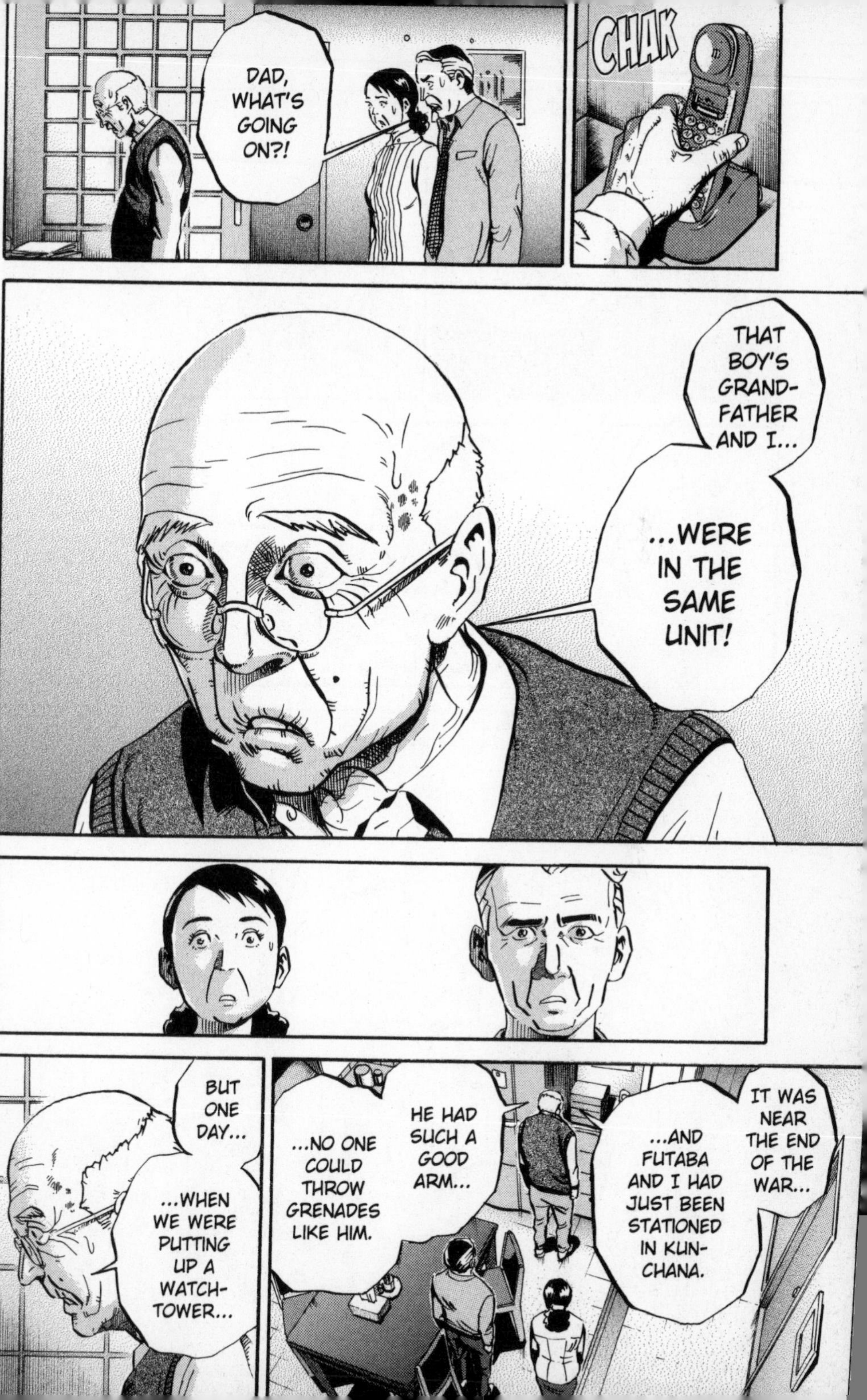
CHAK
DAD, WHAT'S GOING ON?!
THAT BOY'S GRAND-FATHER AND I...
...WERE IN THE SAME UNIT!
IT WAS NEAR THE END OF THE WAR...
...AND FUTABA AND I HAD JUST BEEN STATIONED IN KUN-CHANA.
HE HAD SUCH A GOOD ARM...
...NO ONE COULD THROW GRENADES LIKE HIM.
BUT ONE DAY...
...WHEN WE WERE PUTTING UP A WATCH-TOWER...

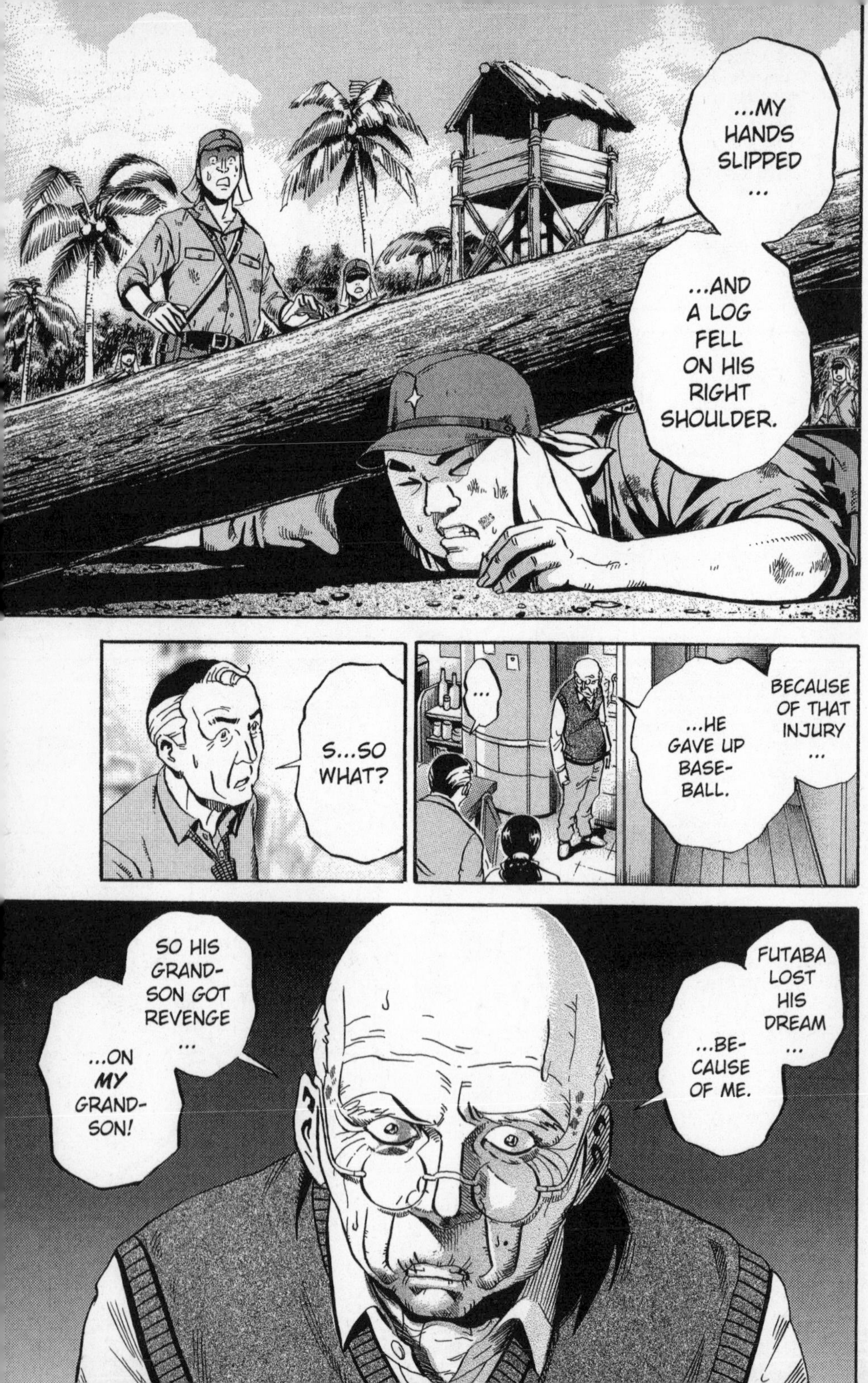
...MY HANDS SLIPPED ...
...AND A LOG FELL ON HIS RIGHT SHOULDER.
BECAUSE OF THAT INJURY ...
...HE GAVE UP BASE-BALL.
...
S...SO WHAT?
FUTABA LOST HIS DREAM ...
...BE-CAUSE OF ME.
SO HIS GRAND-SON GOT REVENGE ...
...ON *MY* GRAND-SON!

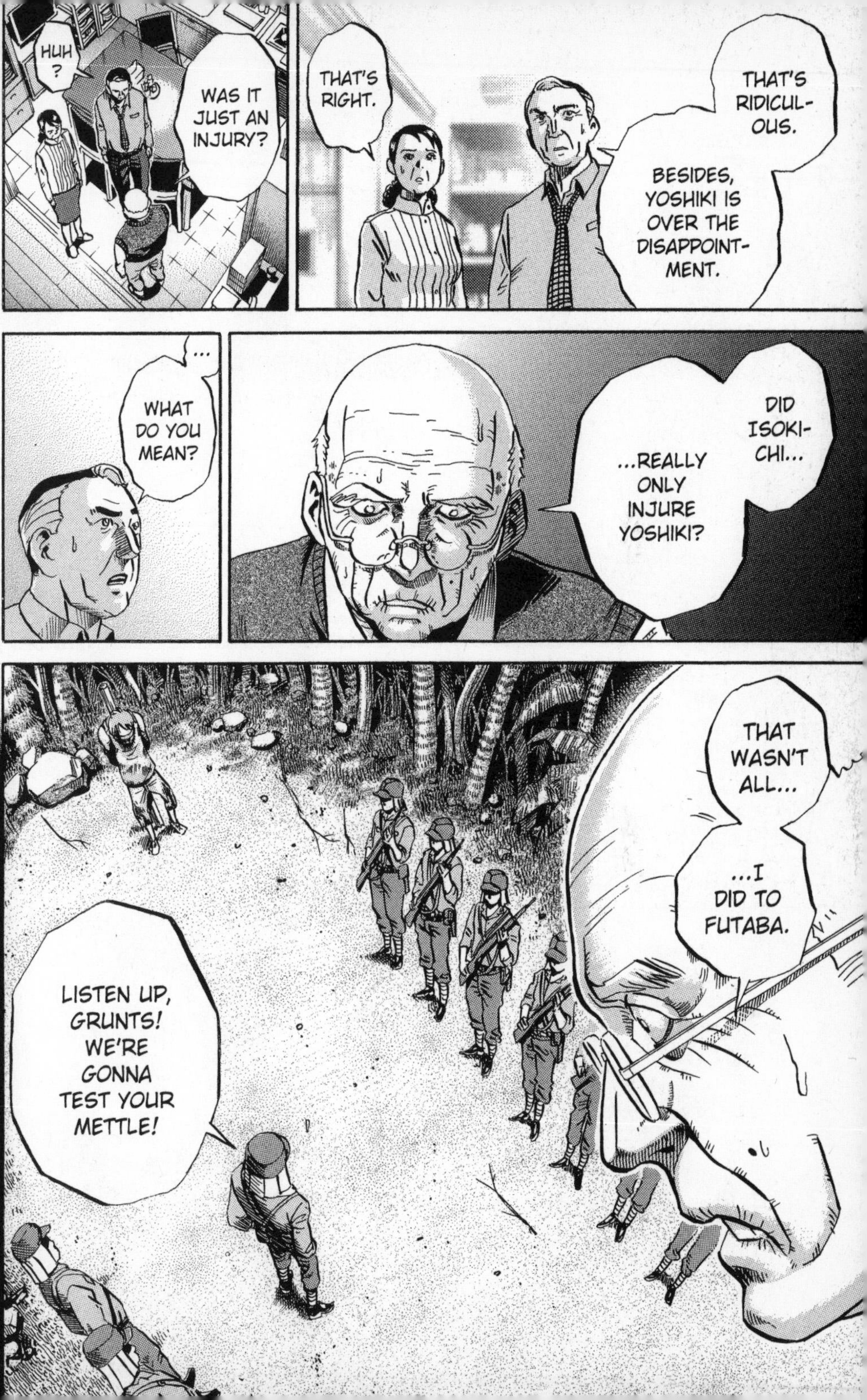
THAT'S RIDICULOUS.
BESIDES, YOSHIKI IS OVER THE DISAPPOINTMENT.
THAT'S RIGHT.
WAS IT JUST AN INJURY?
HUH?
DID ISOKICHI...
...REALLY ONLY INJURE YOSHIKI?
...
WHAT DO YOU MEAN?
THAT WASN'T ALL...
...I DID TO FUTABA.
LISTEN UP, GRUNTS! WE'RE GONNA TEST YOUR METTLE!

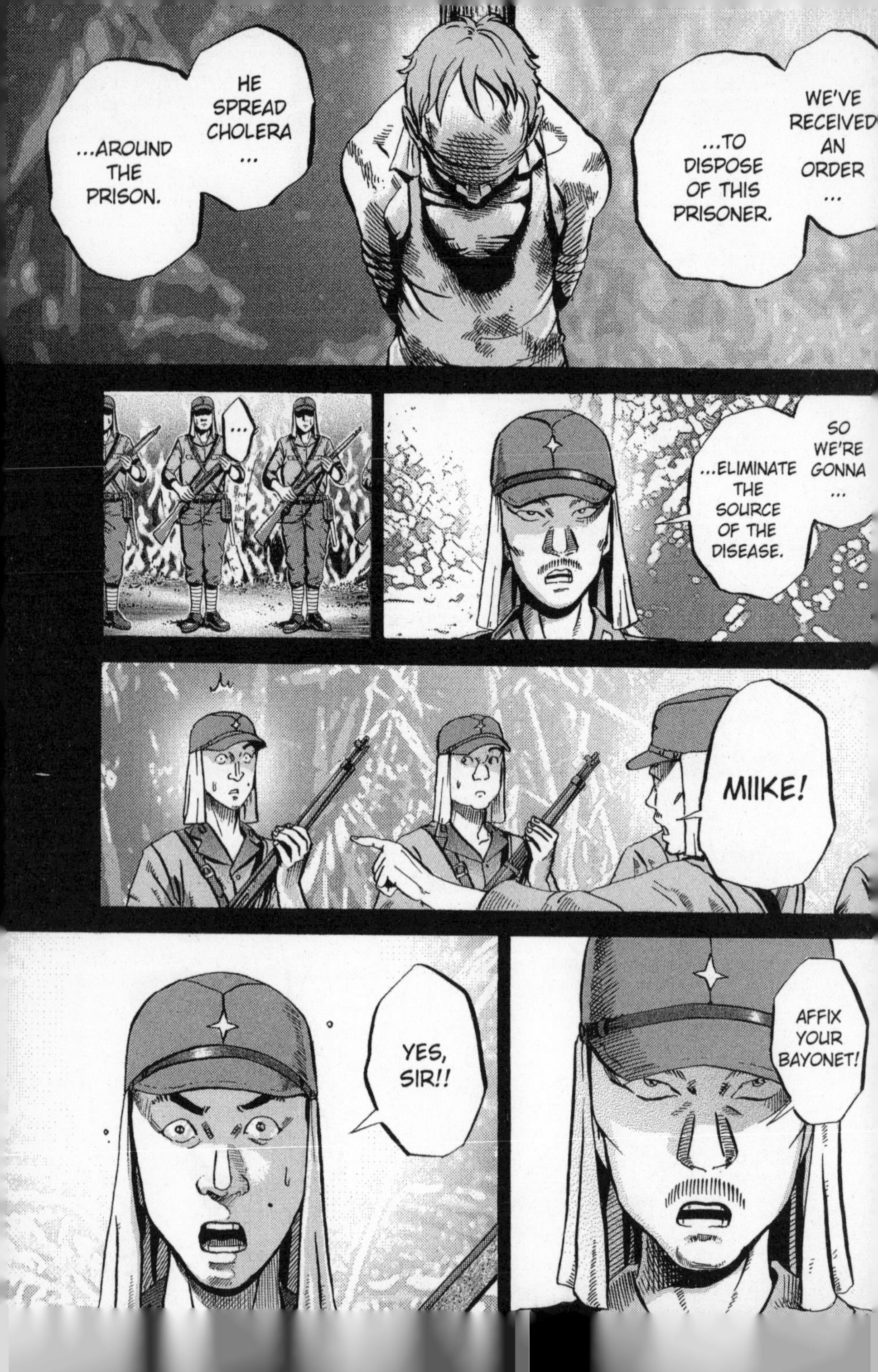
WE'VE RECEIVED AN ORDER ...
...TO DISPOSE OF THIS PRISONER.
HE SPREAD CHOLERA ...
...AROUND THE PRISON.
SO WE'RE GONNA ...
...ELIMINATE THE SOURCE OF THE DISEASE.
...
MIIKE!
AFFIX YOUR BAYONET!
YES, SIR!!

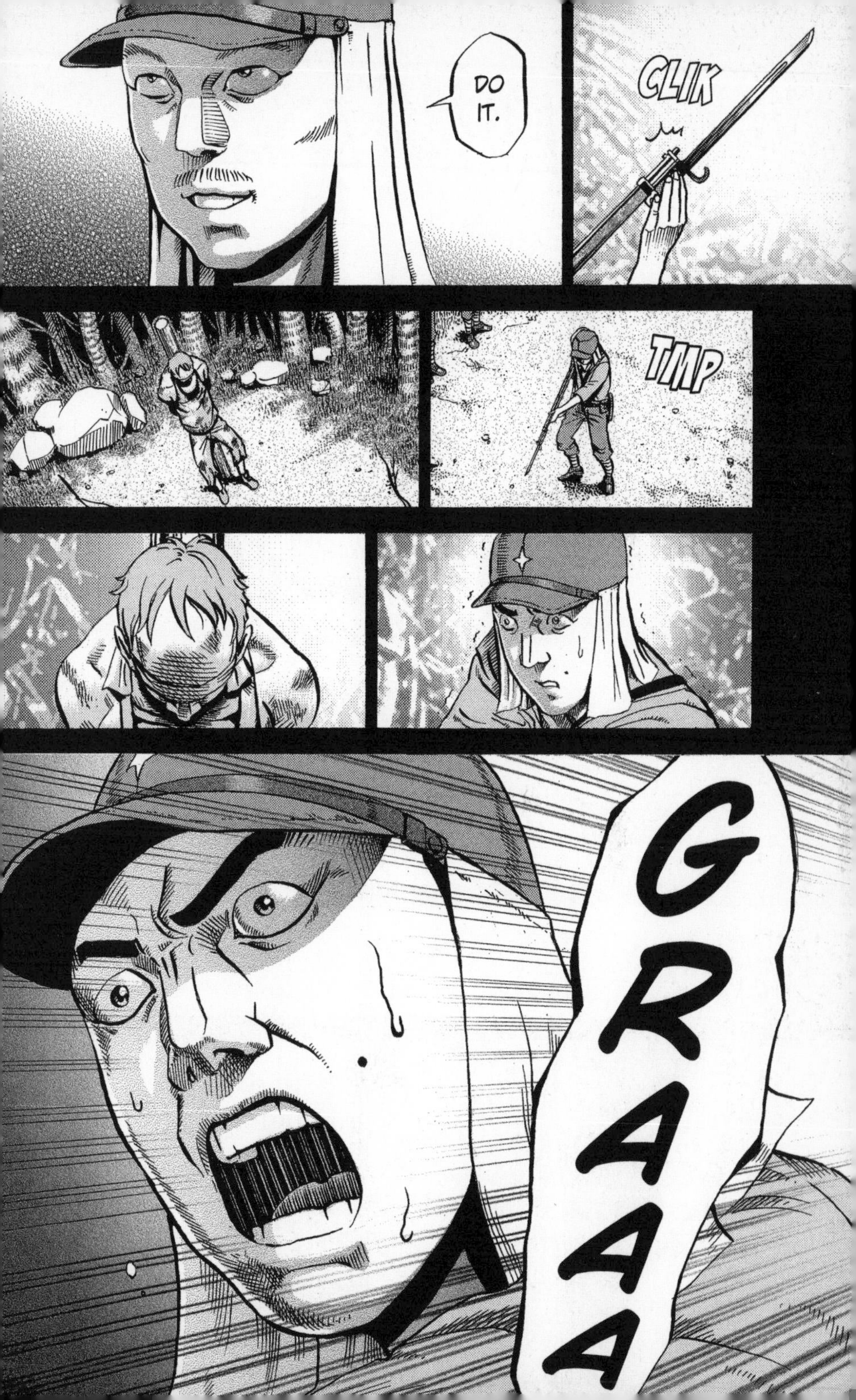
CLIK
DO IT.
TMP
GRAAAA

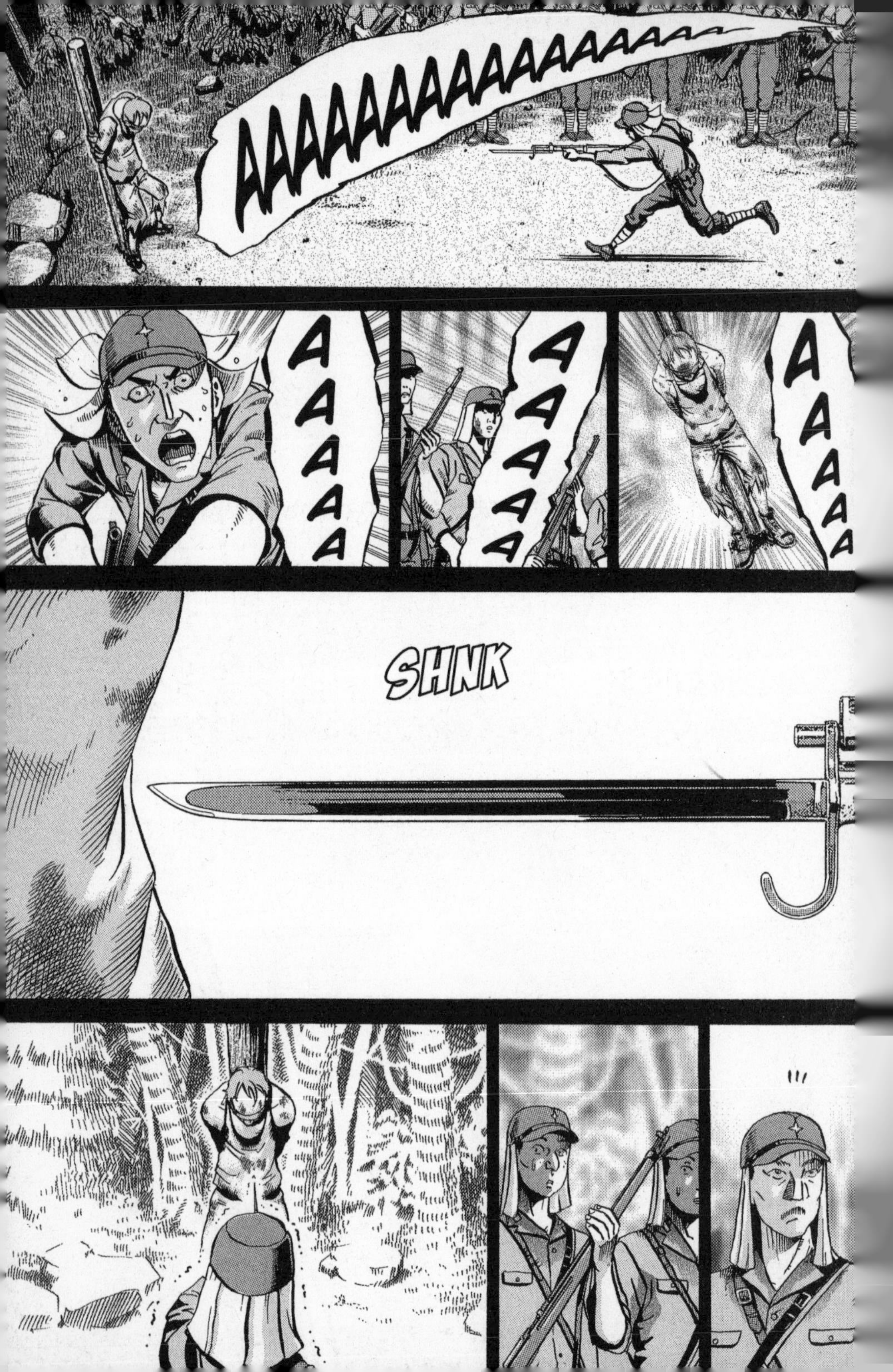
AAAAAAAAAAAAAAAA
AAAAA
AAAAA
AAAAA
SHNK

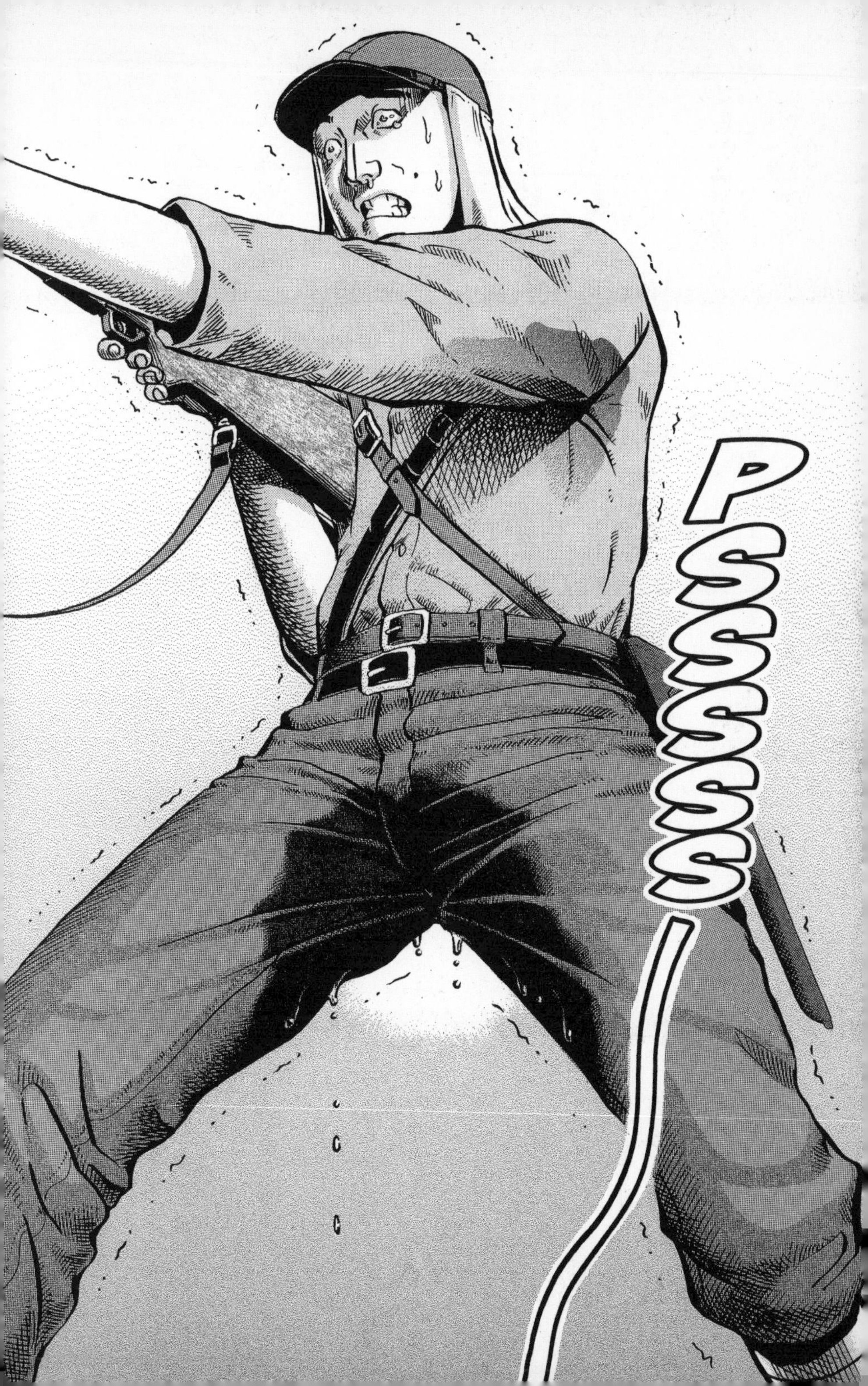
PSSSSS

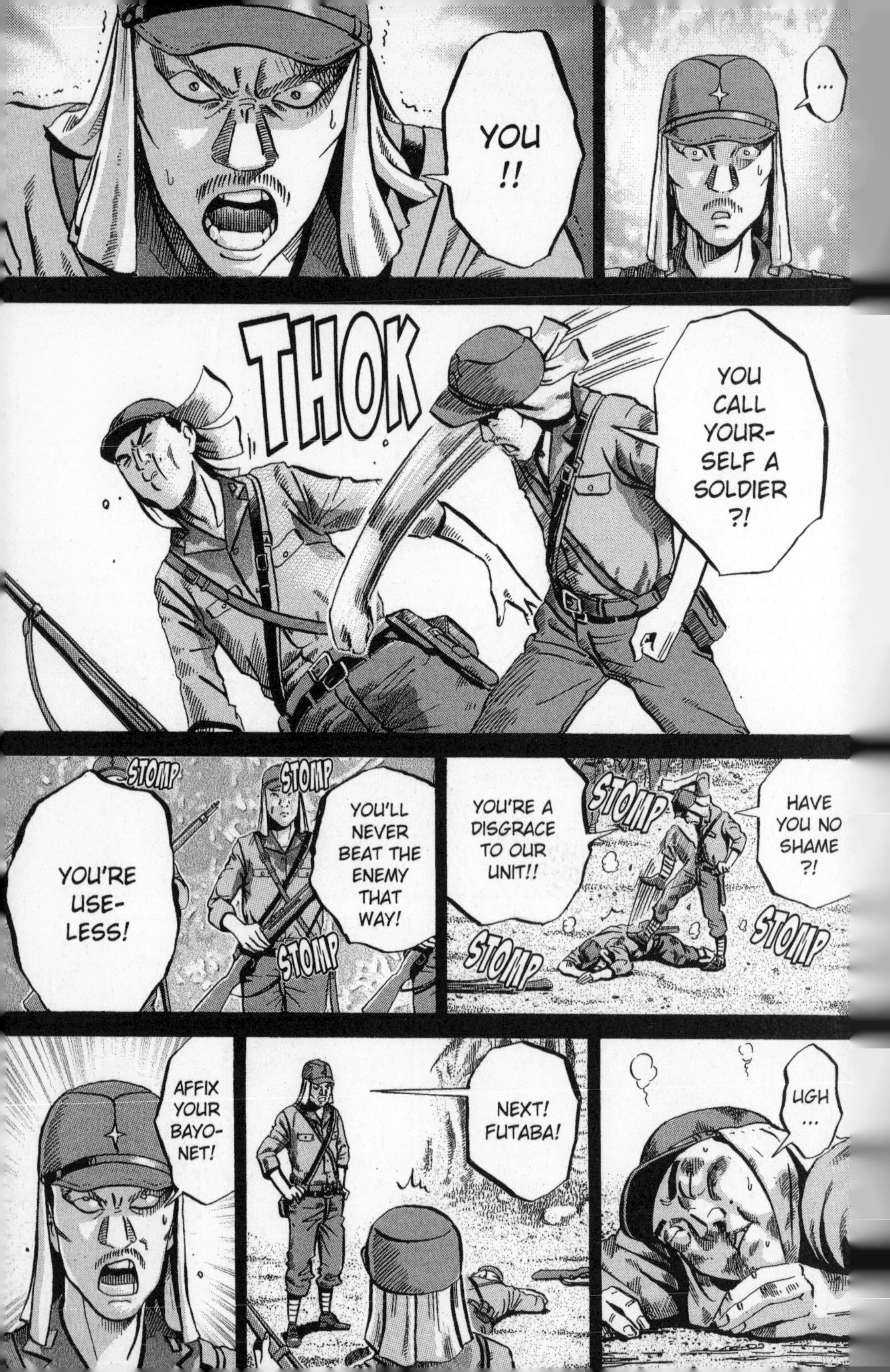
...
YOU !!
THOK
YOU CALL YOURSELF A SOLDIER ?!
HAVE YOU NO SHAME ?!
STOMP
YOU'RE A DISGRACE TO OUR UNIT!!
STOMP
STOMP
STOMP
YOU'LL NEVER BEAT THE ENEMY THAT WAY!
STOMP
YOU'RE USELESS!
STOMP
UGH ...
NEXT! FUTABA!
AFFIX YOUR BAYONET!

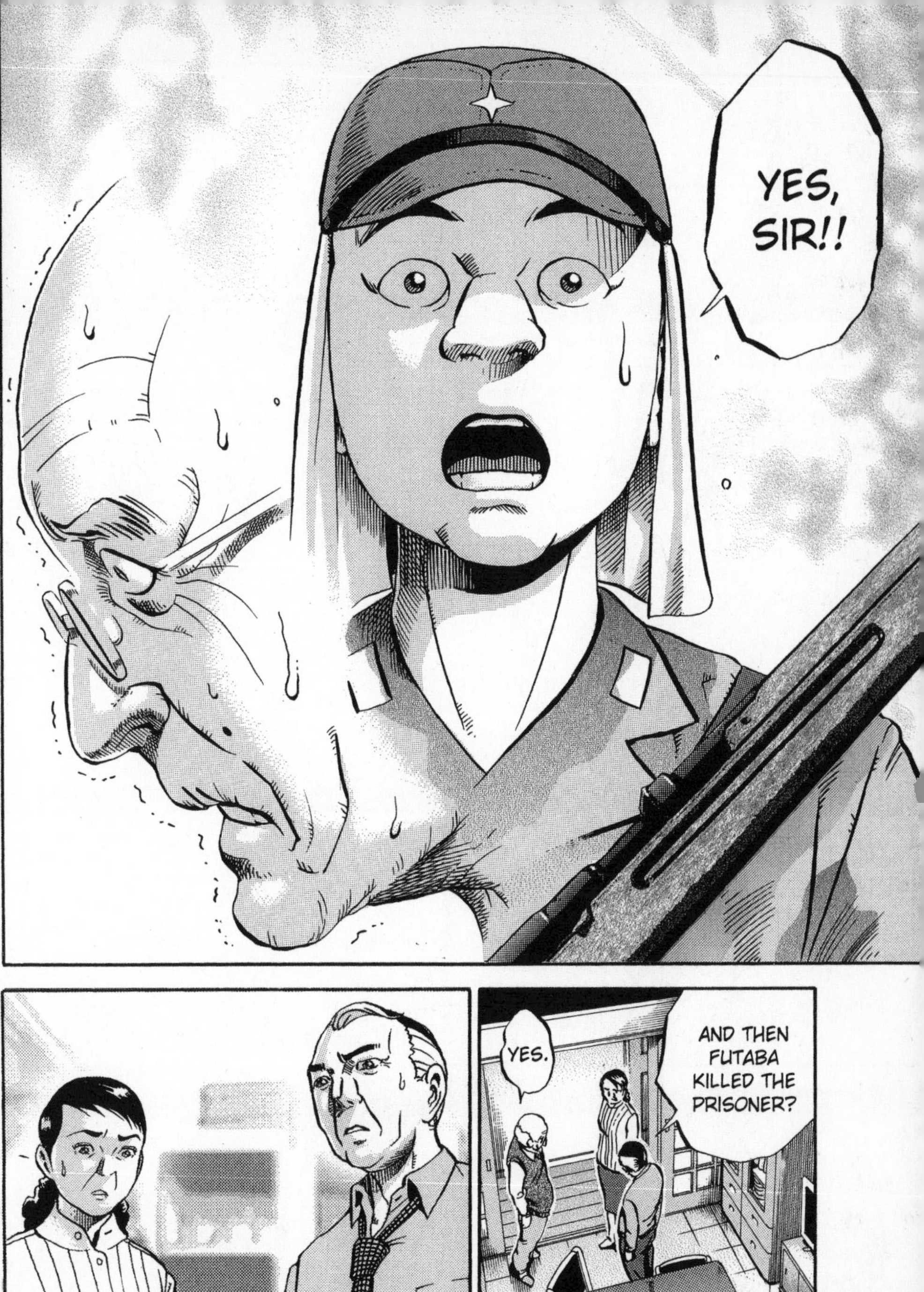
YES, SIR!!
AND THEN FUTABA KILLED THE PRISONER?
YES.

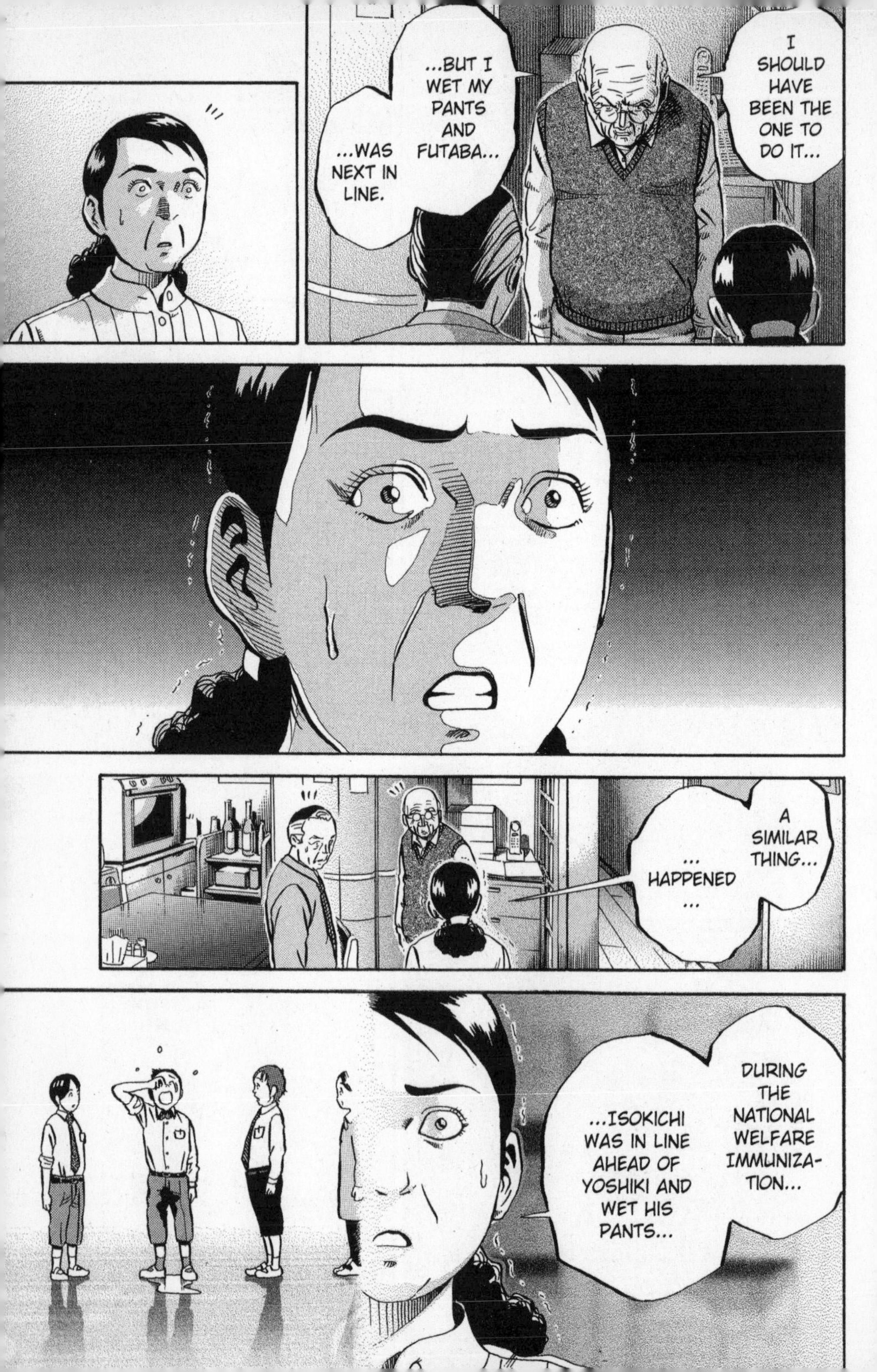
I SHOULD HAVE BEEN THE ONE TO DO IT...
...BUT I WET MY PANTS AND FUTABA...
...WAS NEXT IN LINE.
A SIMILAR THING...
...HAPPENED...
DURING THE NATIONAL WELFARE IMMUNIZATION...
...ISOKICHI WAS IN LINE AHEAD OF YOSHIKI AND WET HIS PANTS...

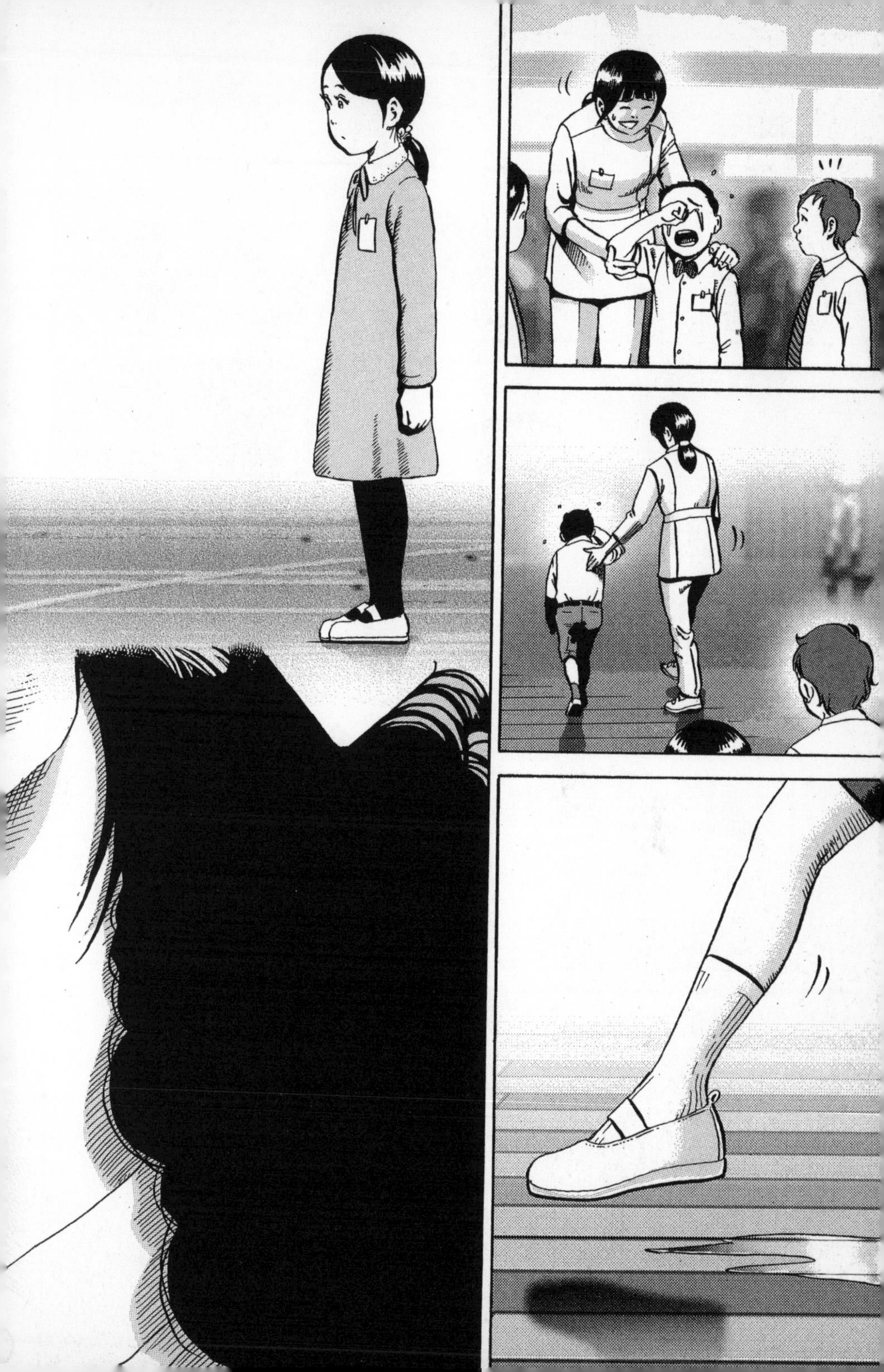

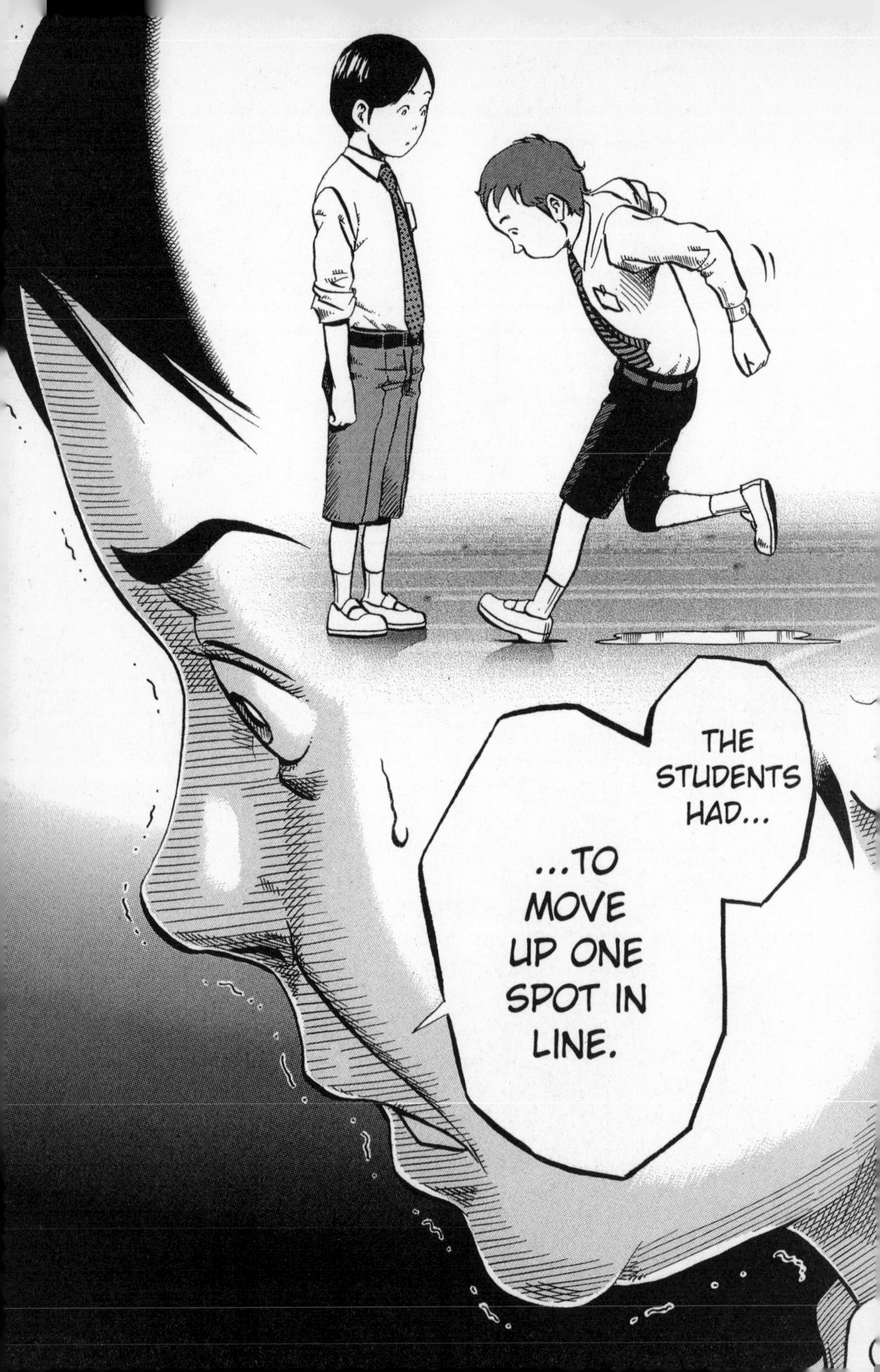
THE STUDENTS HAD...
...TO MOVE UP ONE SPOT IN LINE.

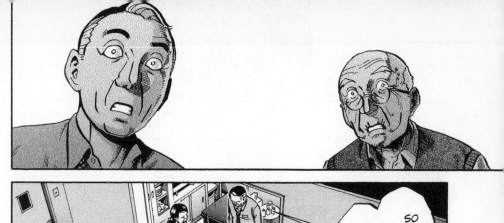

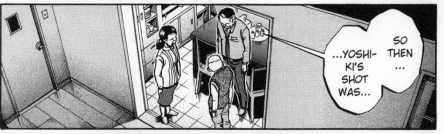

...YOSHI-KI'S SHOT WAS...

SO THEN...

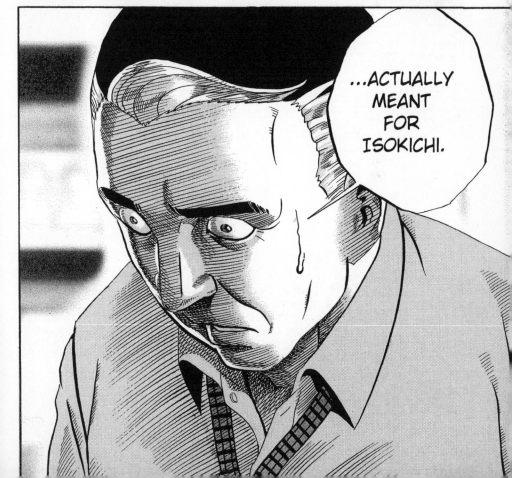

...ACTUALLY MEANT FOR ISOKICHI.

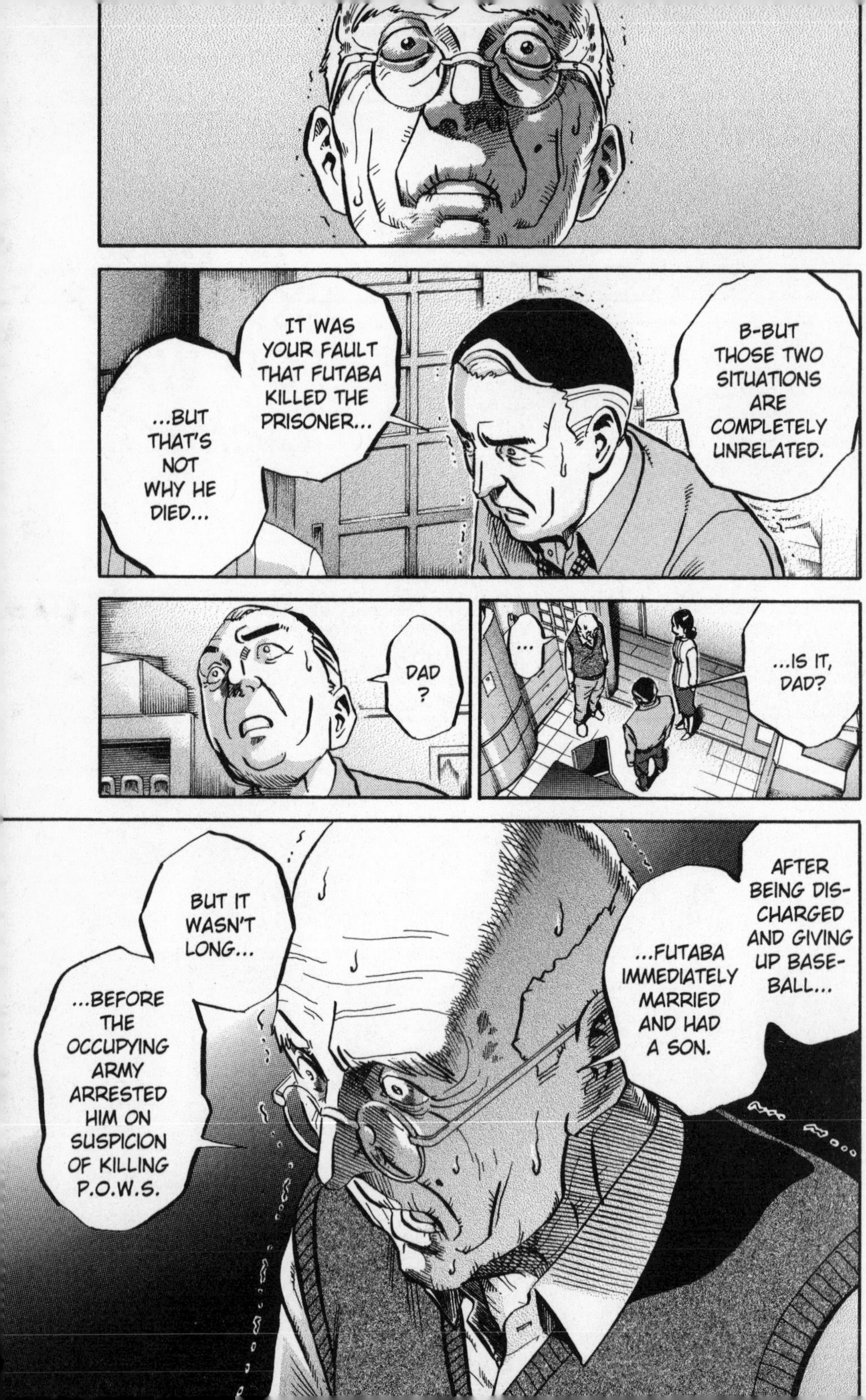
B-BUT THOSE TWO SITUATIONS ARE COMPLETELY UNRELATED.
IT WAS YOUR FAULT THAT FUTABA KILLED THE PRISONER...
...BUT THAT'S NOT WHY HE DIED...
...IS IT, DAD?
...
DAD ?
AFTER BEING DIS-CHARGED AND GIVING UP BASE-BALL...
...FUTABA IMMEDIATELY MARRIED AND HAD A SON.
BUT IT WASN'T LONG...
...BEFORE THE OCCUPYING ARMY ARRESTED HIM ON SUSPICION OF KILLING P.O.W.S.

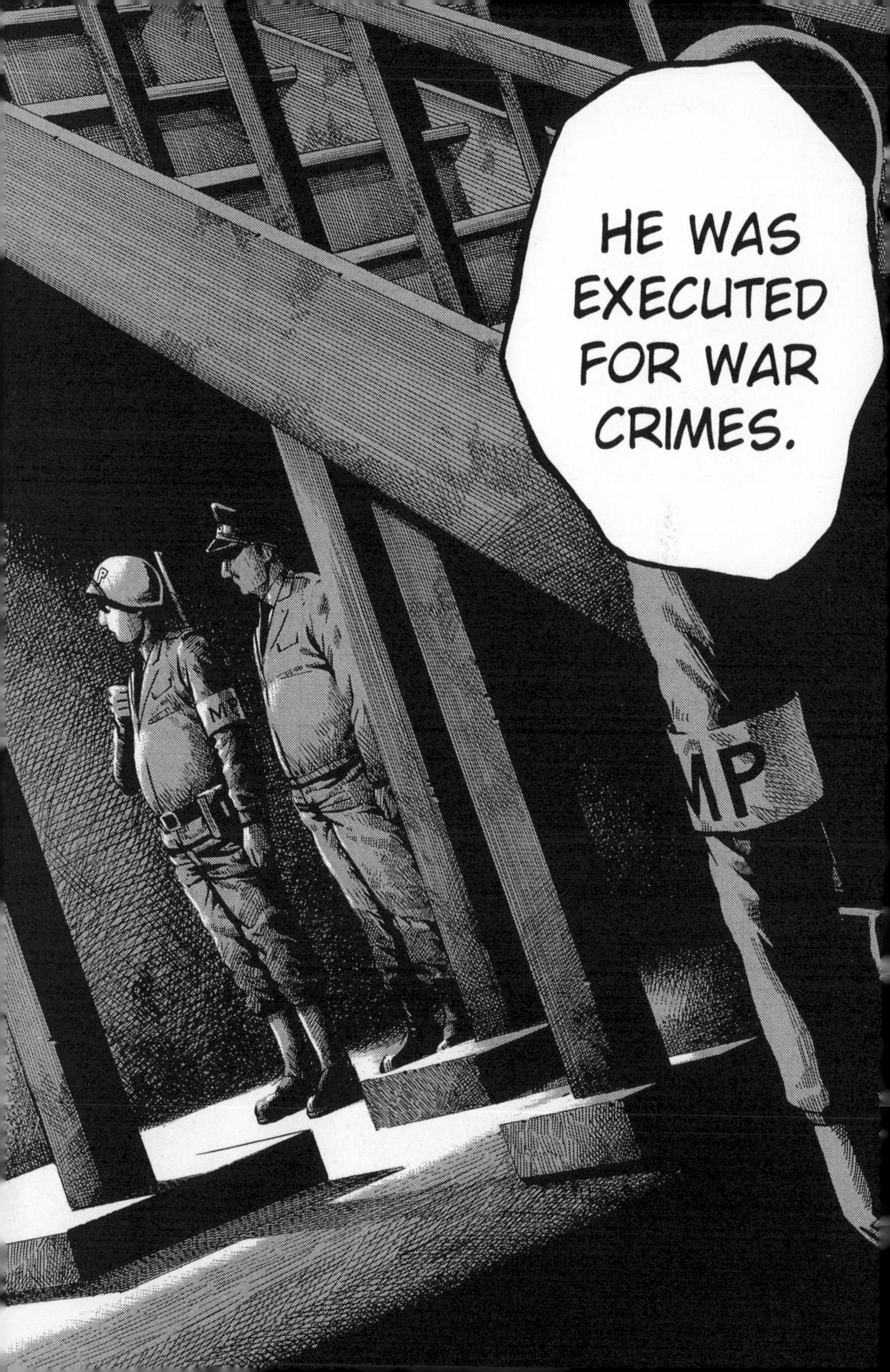
HE WAS EXECUTED FOR WAR CRIMES.
MP
MP

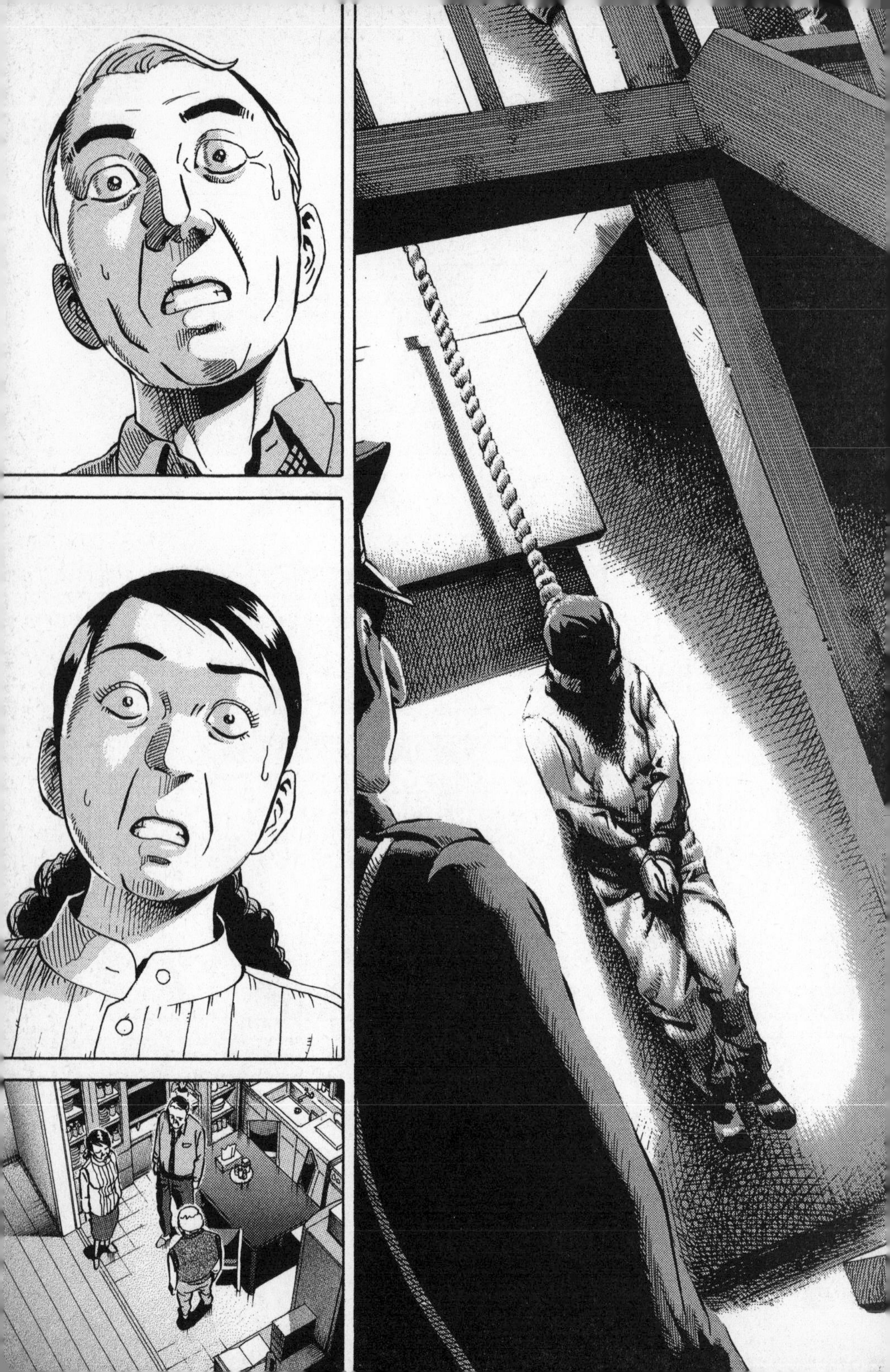

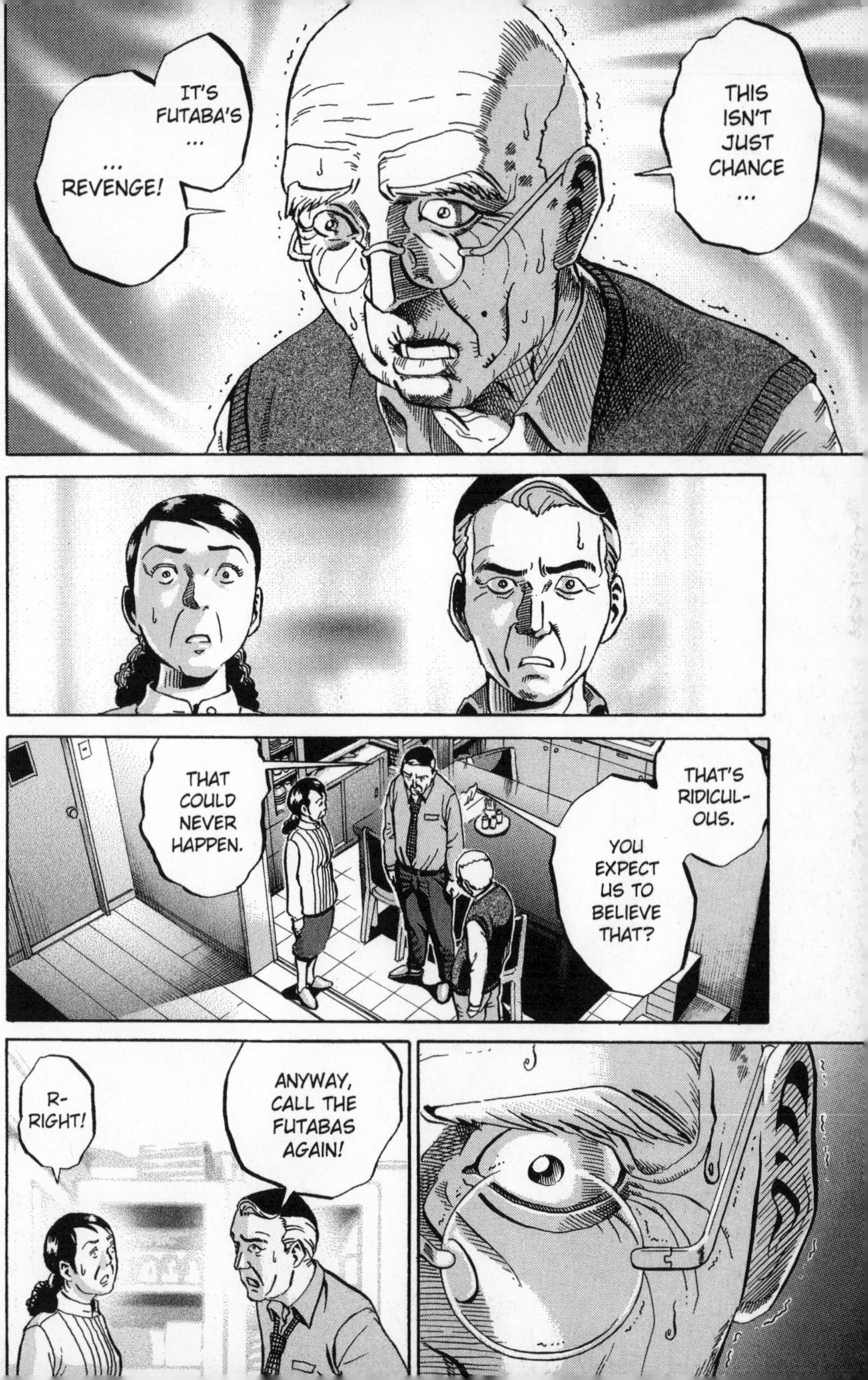
THIS ISN'T JUST CHANCE ...
IT'S FUTABA'S ... ... REVENGE!
THAT'S RIDICUL-OUS.
YOU EXPECT US TO BELIEVE THAT?
THAT COULD NEVER HAPPEN.
ANYWAY, CALL THE FUTABAS AGAIN!
R-RIGHT!

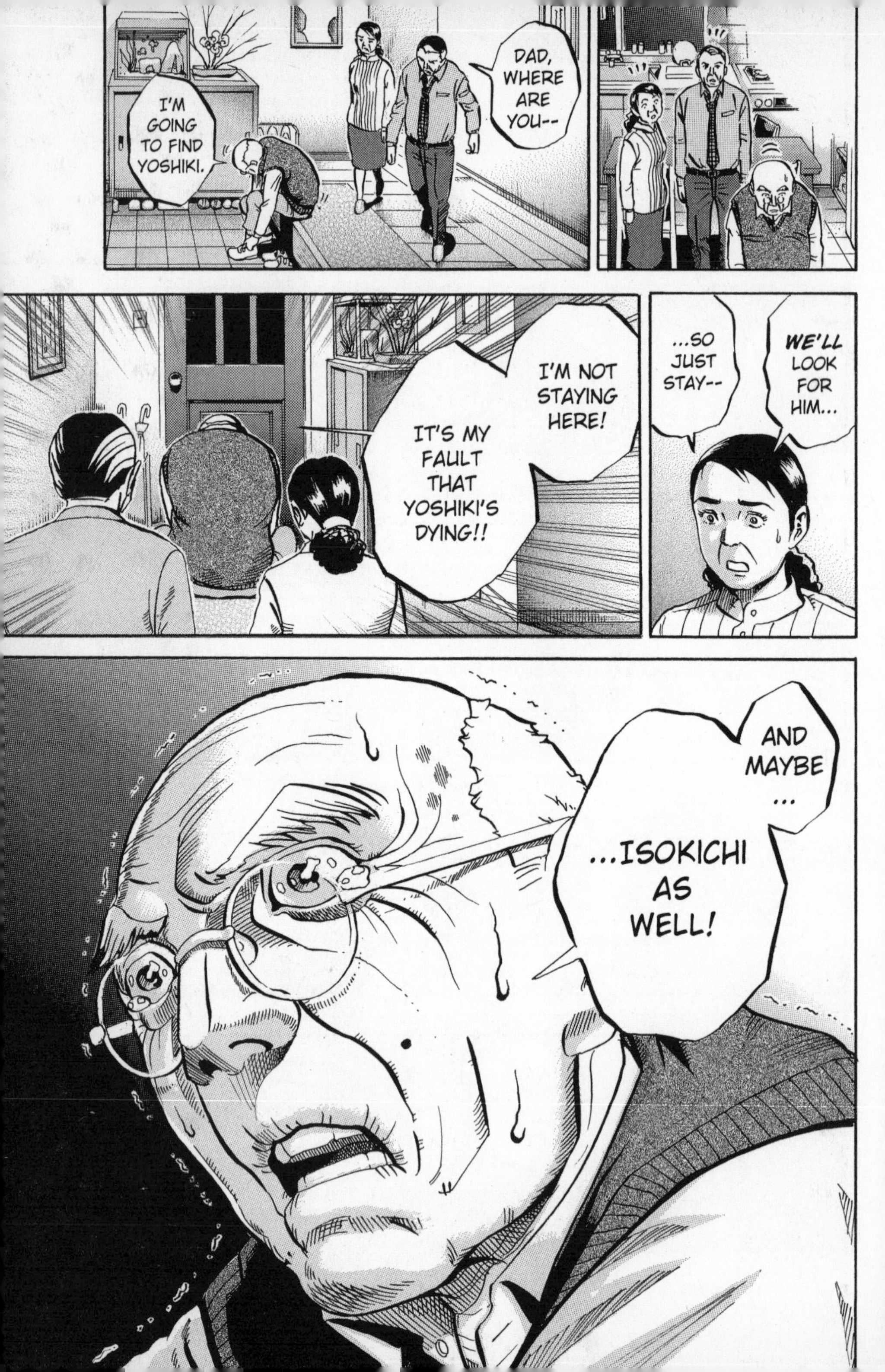
DAD, WHERE ARE YOU--
I'M GOING TO FIND YOSHIKI.
WE'LL LOOK FOR HIM...
...SO JUST STAY--
I'M NOT STAYING HERE!
IT'S MY FAULT THAT YOSHIKI'S DYING!!
AND MAYBE ...
...ISOKICHI AS WELL!

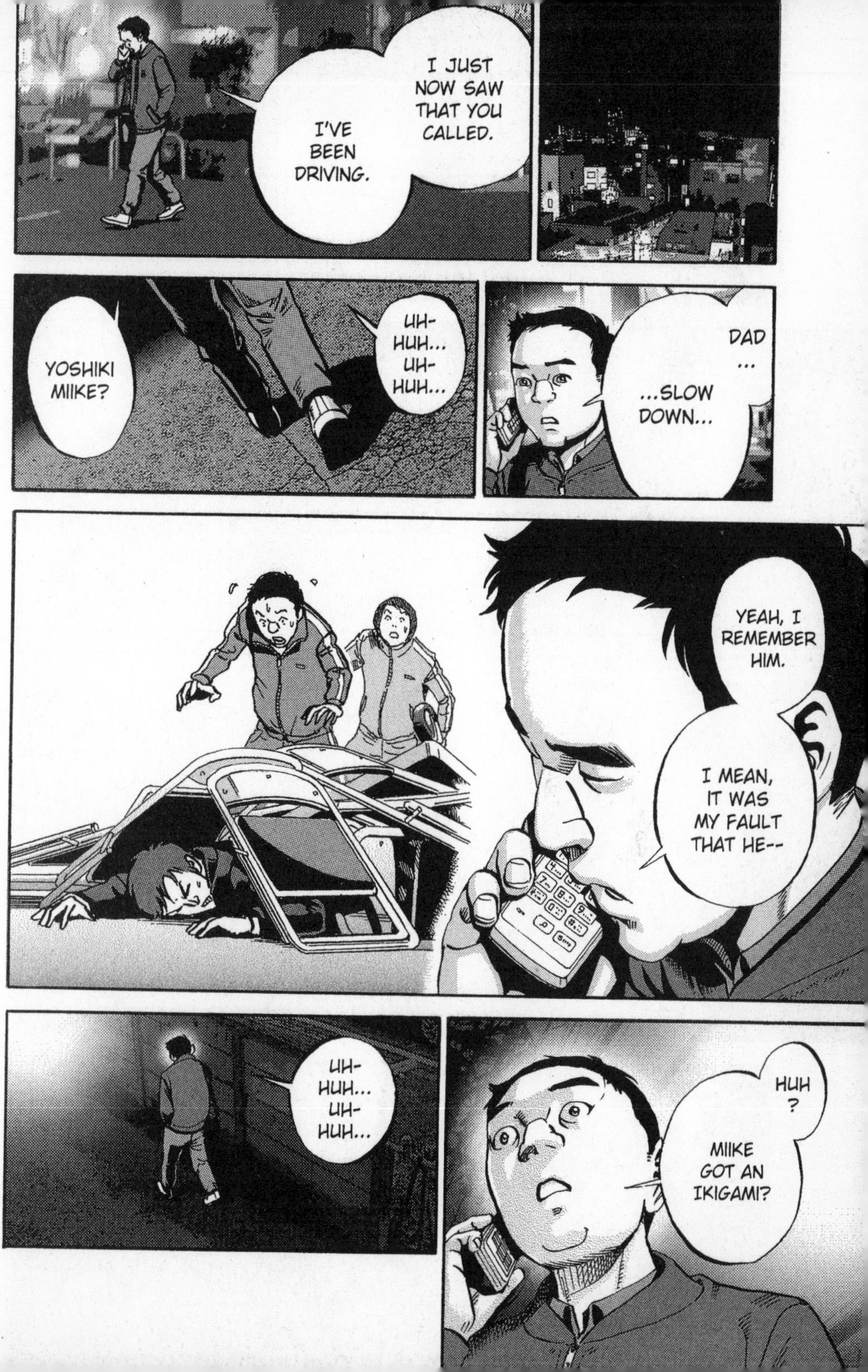
I JUST NOW SAW THAT YOU CALLED.
I'VE BEEN DRIVING.
DAD ...
...SLOW DOWN...
UH-HUH... UH-HUH...
YOSHIKI MIIKE?
YEAH, I REMEMBER HIM.
I MEAN, IT WAS MY FAULT THAT HE--
HUH ?
MIIKE GOT AN IKIGAMI?
UH-HUH... UH-HUH...

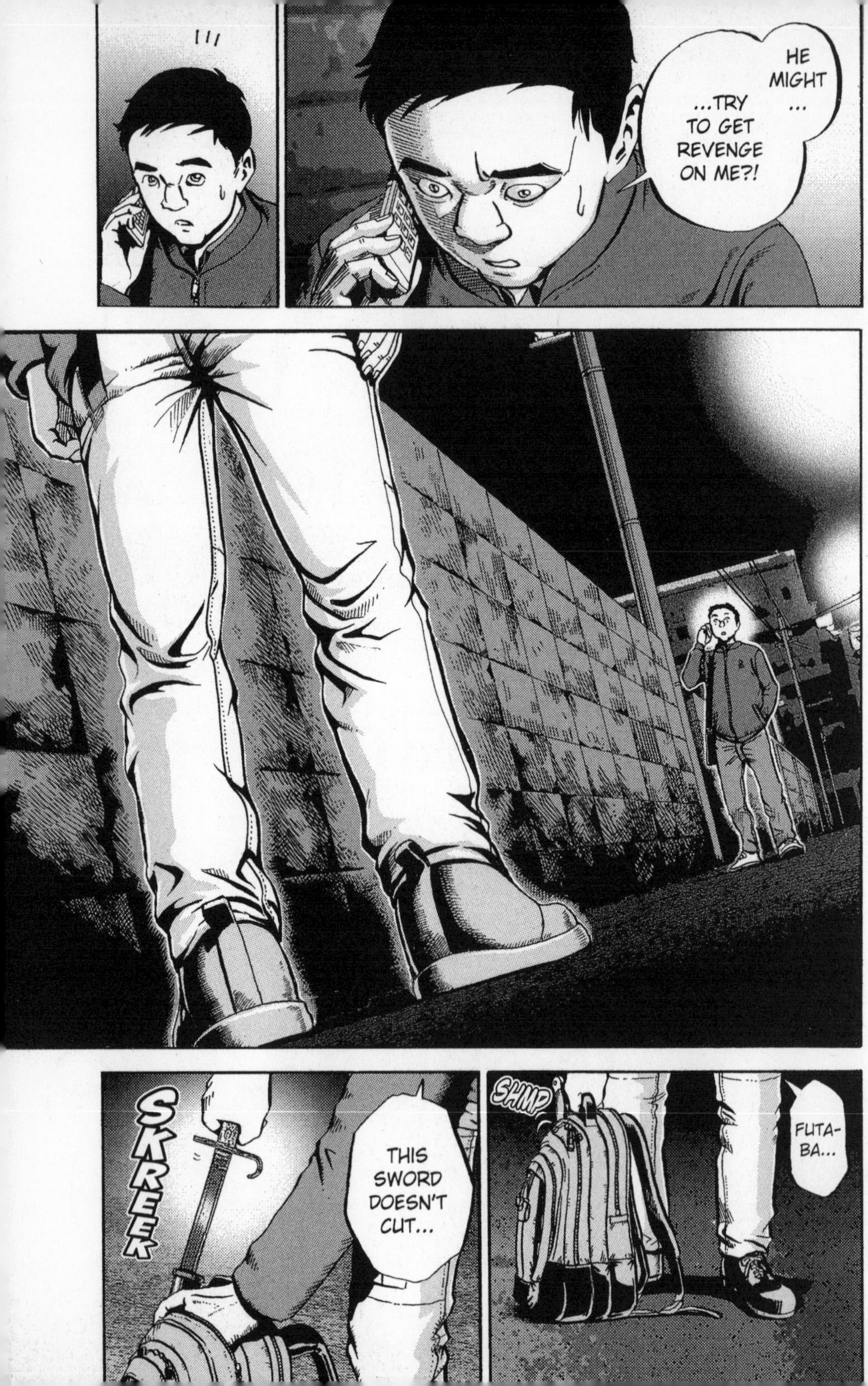
HE MIGHT ...
...TRY TO GET REVENGE ON ME?!
SHMP
FUTA-BA...
SKREEK
THIS SWORD DOESN'T CUT...

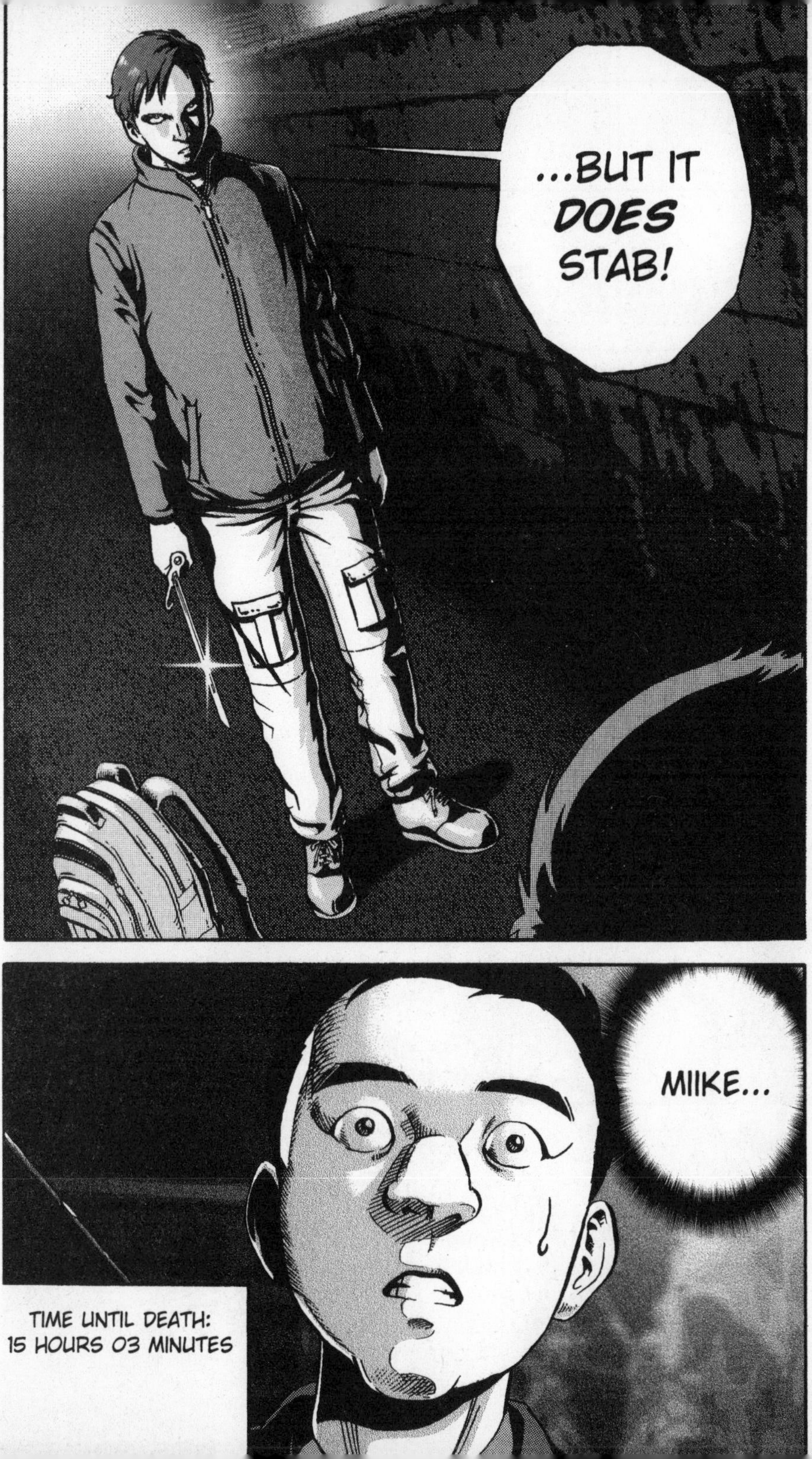
...BUT IT DOES STAB!
MIIKE...
TIME UNTIL DEATH: 15 HOURS 03 MINUTES

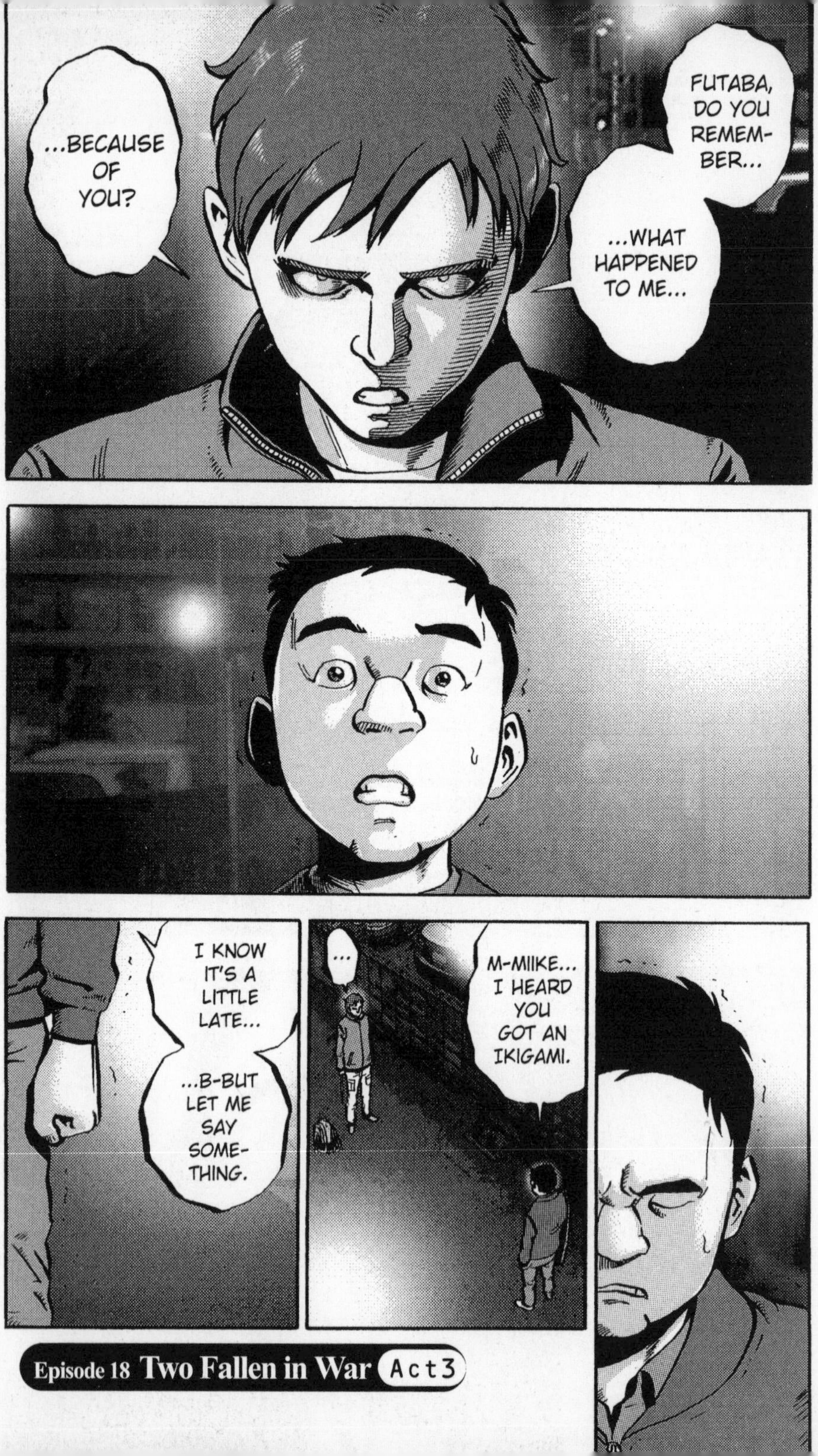
FUTABA, DO YOU REMEMBER...
...WHAT HAPPENED TO ME...
...BECAUSE OF YOU?
M-MIIKE... I HEARD YOU GOT AN IKIGAMI.
...
I KNOW IT'S A LITTLE LATE...
...B-BUT LET ME SAY SOMETHING.

Episode 18 Two Fallen in War Act3

Episode 18 Two Fallen in War Act3

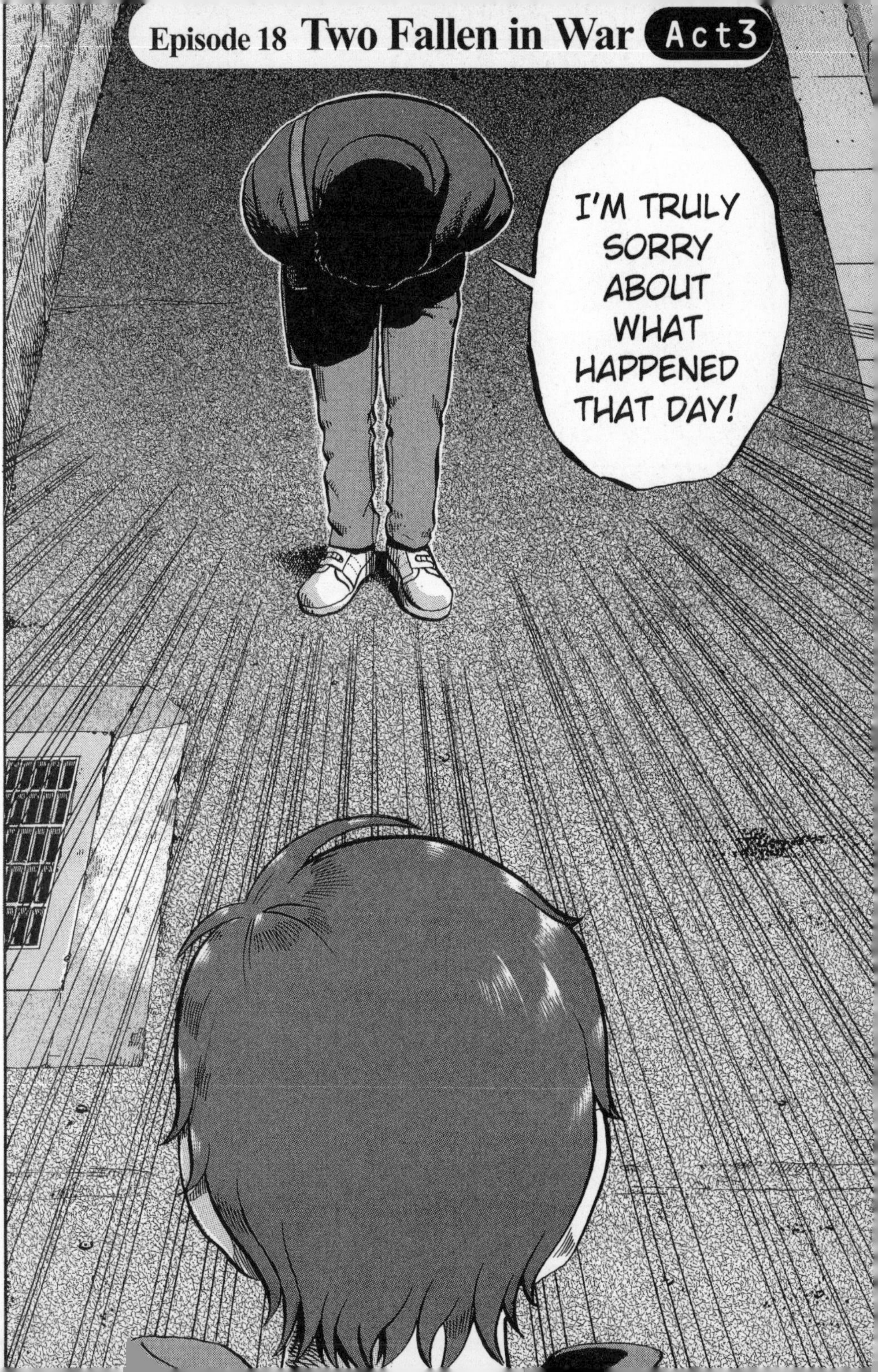
I'M TRULY SORRY ABOUT WHAT HAPPENED THAT DAY!

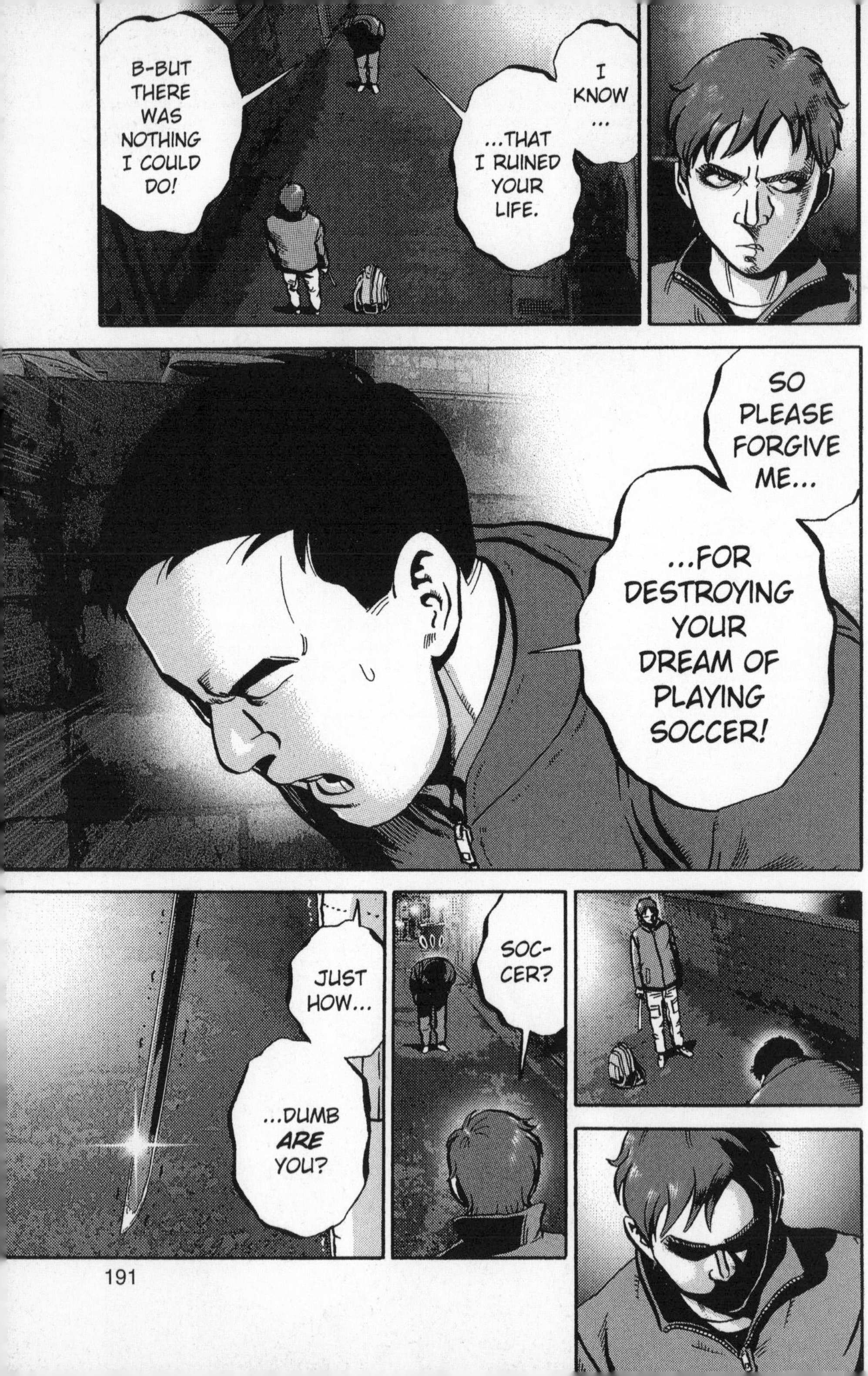
I KNOW...
...THAT I RUINED YOUR LIFE.
B-BUT THERE WAS NOTHING I COULD DO!
SO PLEASE FORGIVE ME...
...FOR DESTROYING YOUR DREAM OF PLAYING SOCCER!
SOC-CER?
JUST HOW...
...DUMB *ARE* YOU?

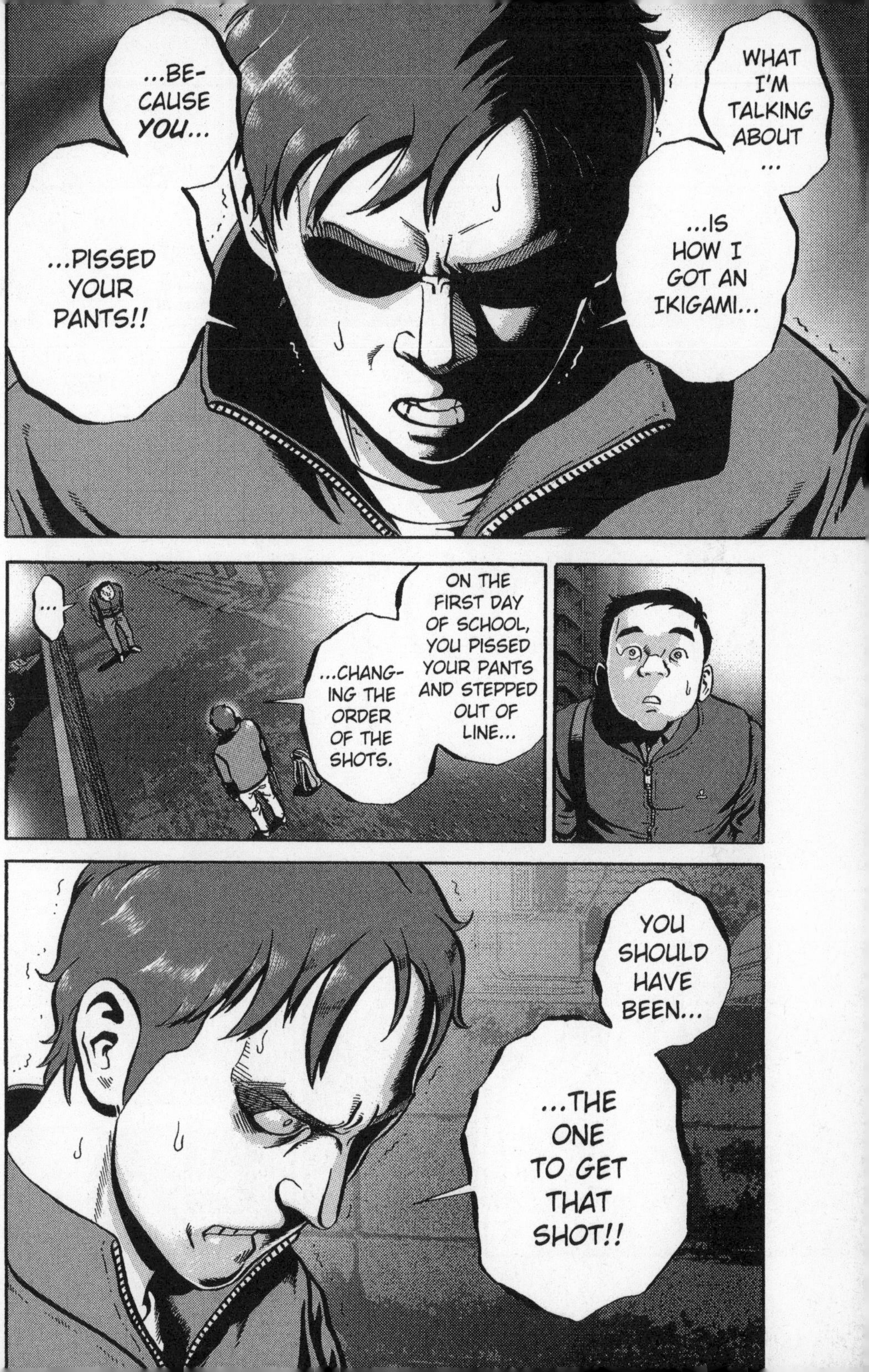
WHAT I'M TALKING ABOUT...
...IS HOW I GOT AN IKIGAMI...
...BE-CAUSE YOU...
...PISSED YOUR PANTS!!
ON THE FIRST DAY OF SCHOOL, YOU PISSED YOUR PANTS AND STEPPED OUT OF LINE...
...CHANG-ING THE ORDER OF THE SHOTS.
...
YOU SHOULD HAVE BEEN...
...THE ONE TO GET THAT SHOT!!

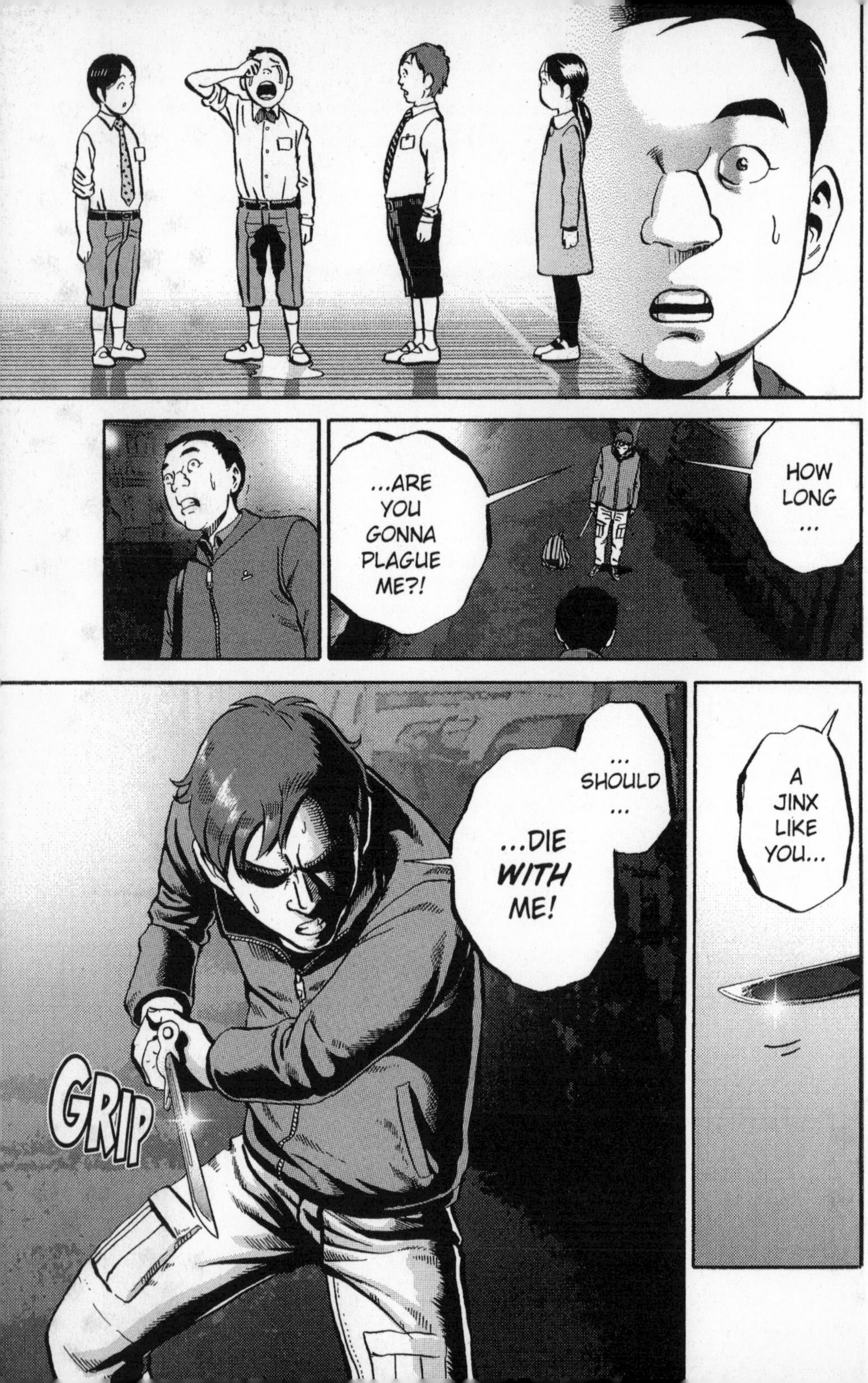
HOW LONG ...
...ARE YOU GONNA PLAGUE ME?!
A JINX LIKE YOU...
... SHOULD ...
...DIE WITH ME!
GRIP

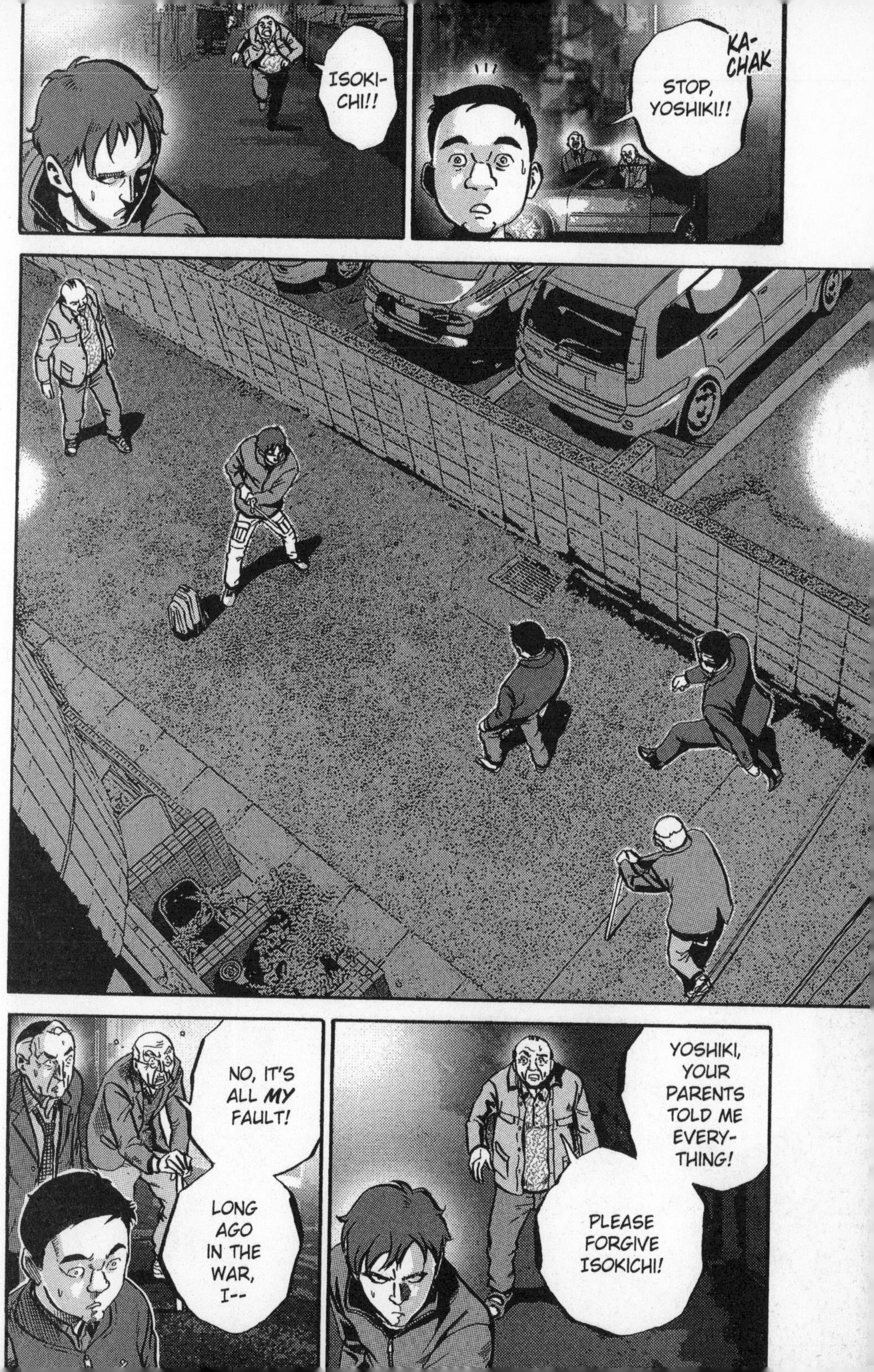
KA-CHAK
STOP, YOSHIKI!!
ISOKI-CHI!!
YOSHIKI, YOUR PARENTS TOLD ME EVERY-THING!
PLEASE FORGIVE ISOKICHI!
NO, IT'S ALL *MY* FAULT!
LONG AGO IN THE WAR, I--

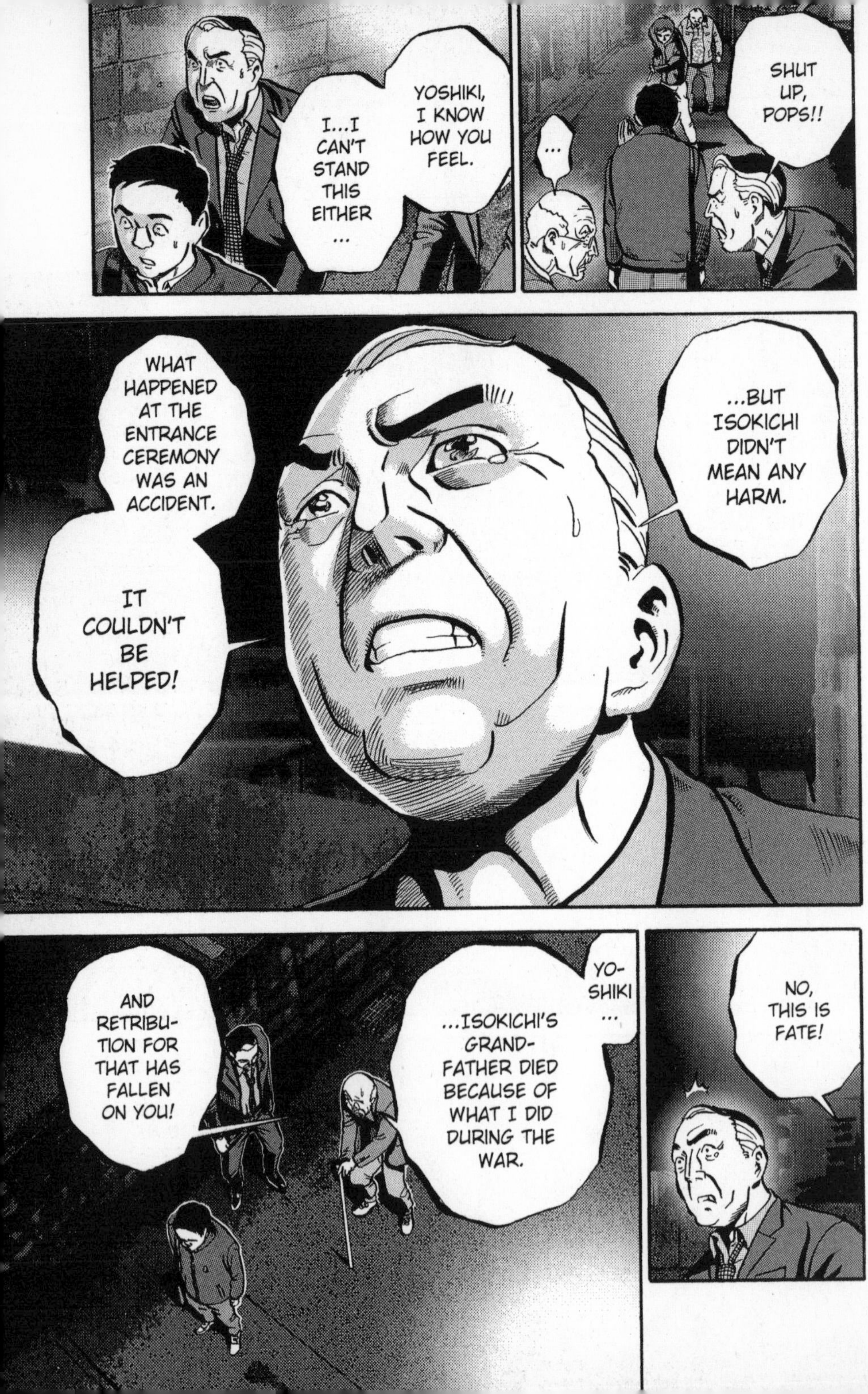
SHUT UP, POPS!!
...
YOSHIKI, I KNOW HOW YOU FEEL.
I...I CAN'T STAND THIS EITHER ...
...BUT ISOKICHI DIDN'T MEAN ANY HARM.
WHAT HAPPENED AT THE ENTRANCE CEREMONY WAS AN ACCIDENT.
IT COULDN'T BE HELPED!
NO, THIS IS FATE!
YO-SHIKI ...
...ISOKICHI'S GRAND-FATHER DIED BECAUSE OF WHAT I DID DURING THE WAR.
AND RETRIBU-TION FOR THAT HAS FALLEN ON YOU!

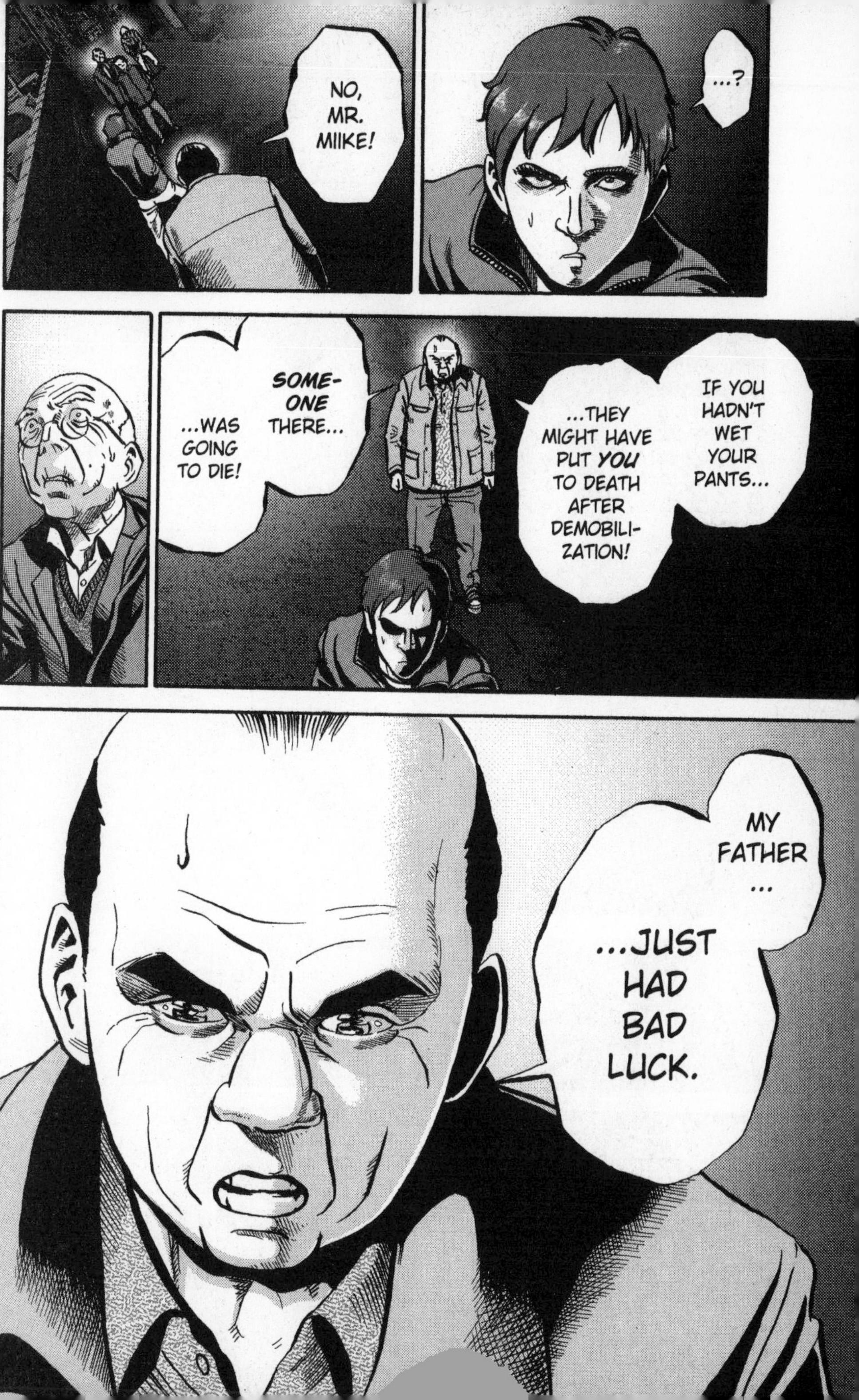
...?
NO, MR. MIIKE!
IF YOU HADN'T WET YOUR PANTS...
...THEY MIGHT HAVE PUT YOU TO DEATH AFTER DEMOBILIZATION!
SOMEONE THERE...
...WAS GOING TO DIE!
MY FATHER ...
...JUST HAD BAD LUCK.

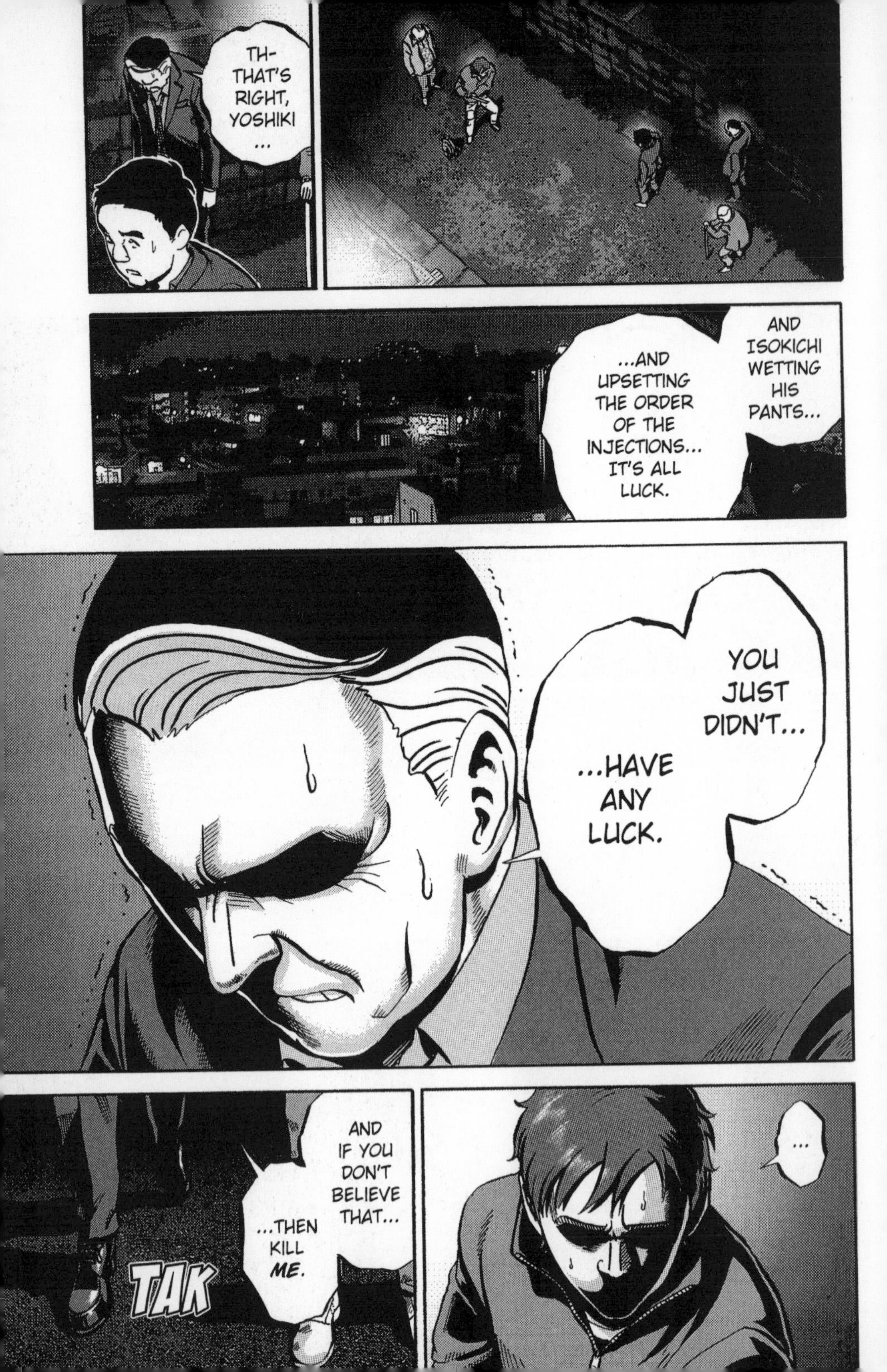
TH- THAT'S RIGHT, YOSHIKI ...
AND ISOKICHI WETTING HIS PANTS...
...AND UPSETTING THE ORDER OF THE INJECTIONS... IT'S ALL LUCK.
YOU JUST DIDN'T...
...HAVE ANY LUCK.
...
AND IF YOU DON'T BELIEVE THAT...
...THEN KILL *ME*.
TAK

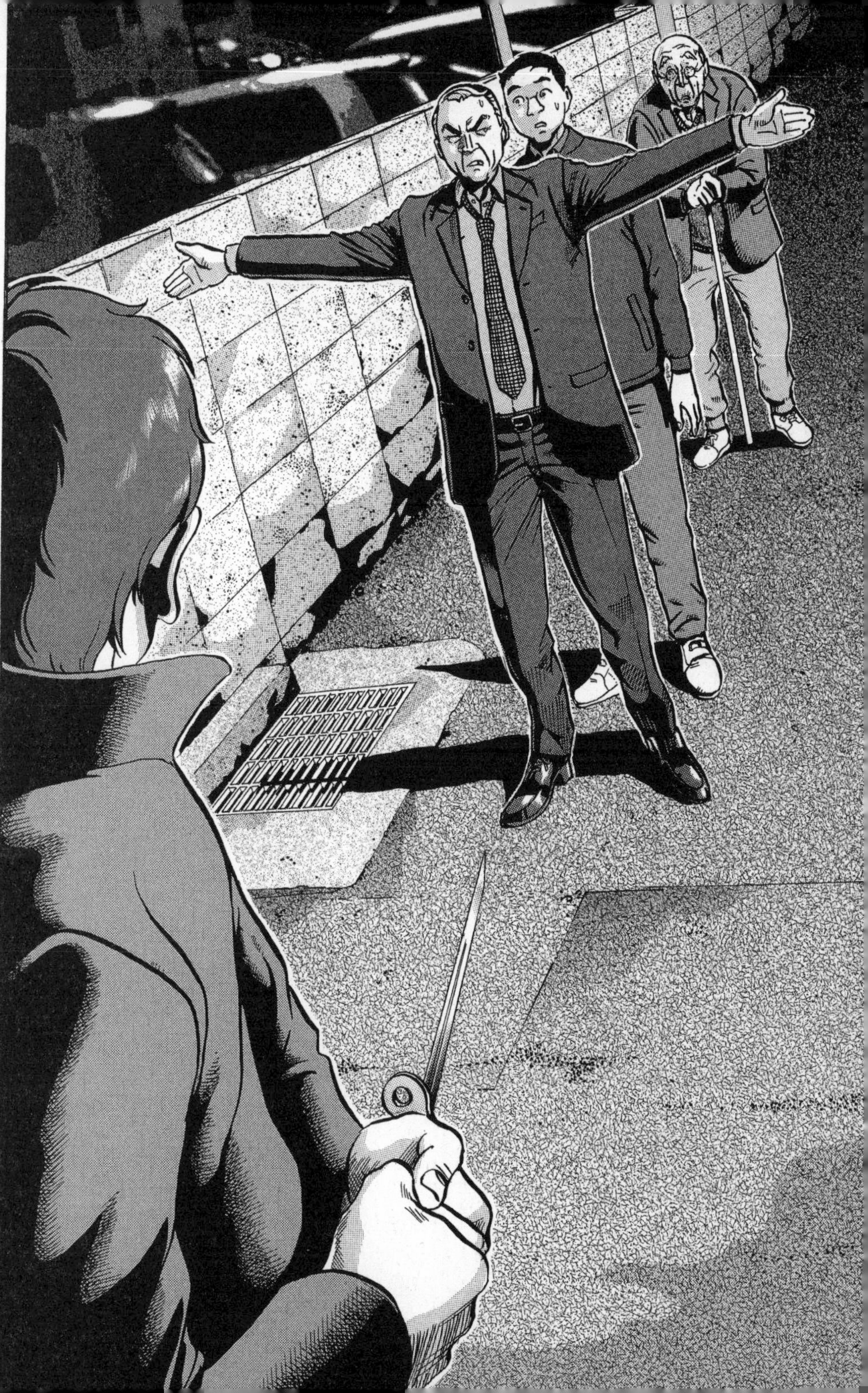

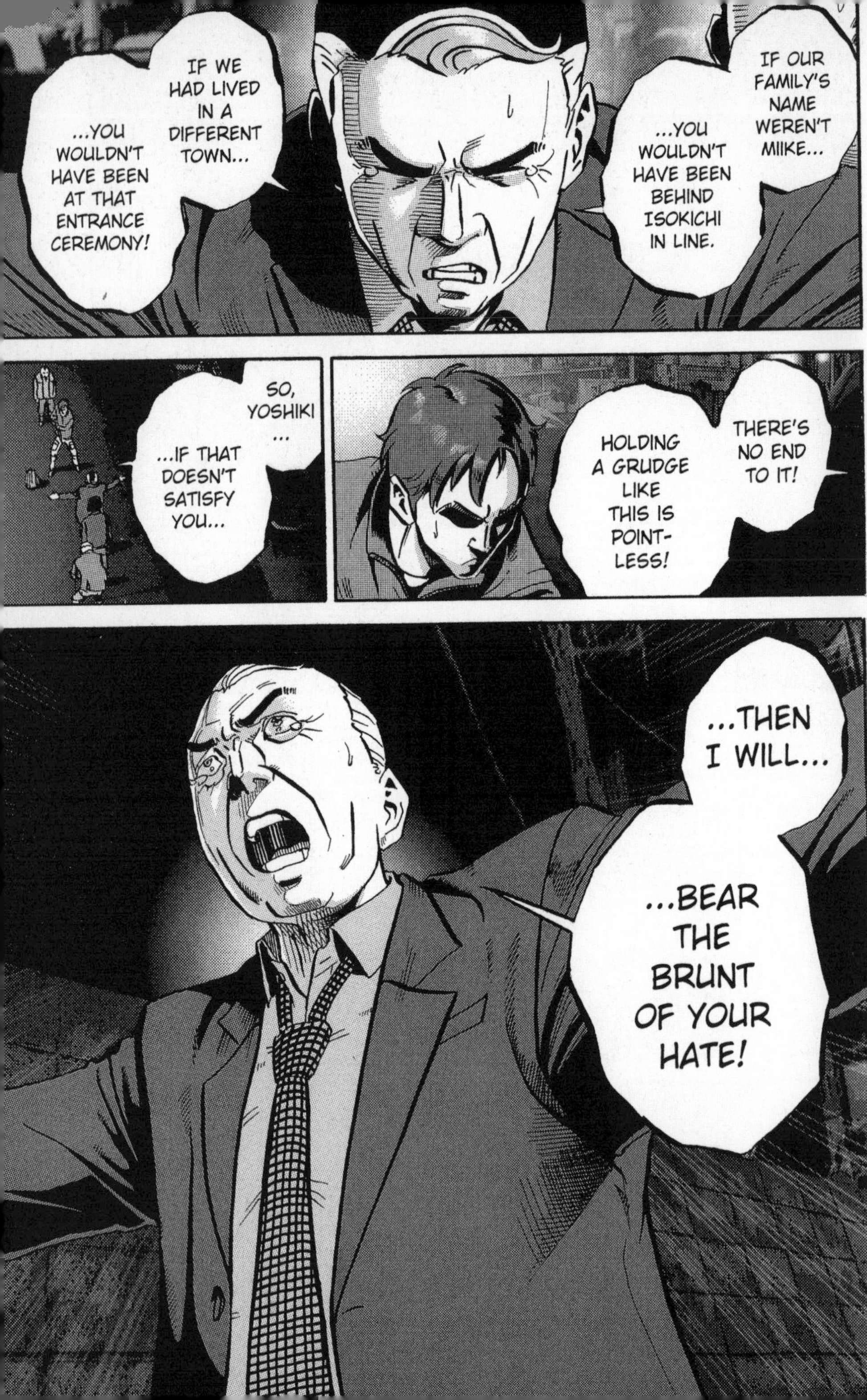
IF OUR FAMILY'S NAME WEREN'T MIIKE...
...YOU WOULDN'T HAVE BEEN BEHIND ISOKICHI IN LINE.
IF WE HAD LIVED IN A DIFFERENT TOWN...
...YOU WOULDN'T HAVE BEEN AT THAT ENTRANCE CEREMONY!
THERE'S NO END TO IT!
HOLDING A GRUDGE LIKE THIS IS POINT-LESS!
SO, YOSHIKI ...
...IF THAT DOESN'T SATISFY YOU...
...THEN I WILL...
...BEAR THE BRUNT OF YOUR HATE!

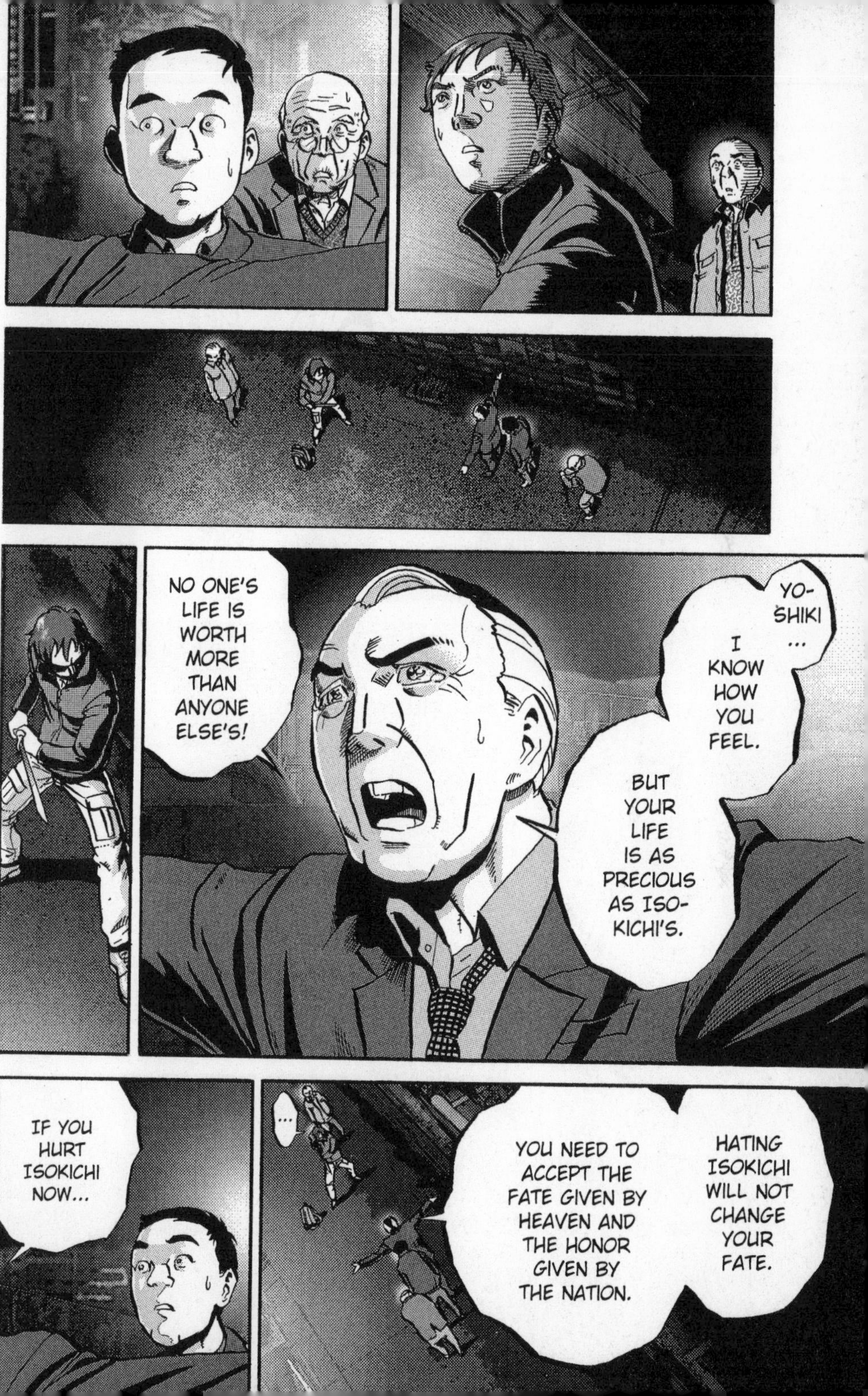
YO-SHIKI...
I KNOW HOW YOU FEEL.
BUT YOUR LIFE IS AS PRECIOUS AS ISO-KICHI'S.
NO ONE'S LIFE IS WORTH MORE THAN ANYONE ELSE'S!
HATING ISOKICHI WILL NOT CHANGE YOUR FATE.
YOU NEED TO ACCEPT THE FATE GIVEN BY HEAVEN AND THE HONOR GIVEN BY THE NATION.
...
IF YOU HURT ISOKICHI NOW...

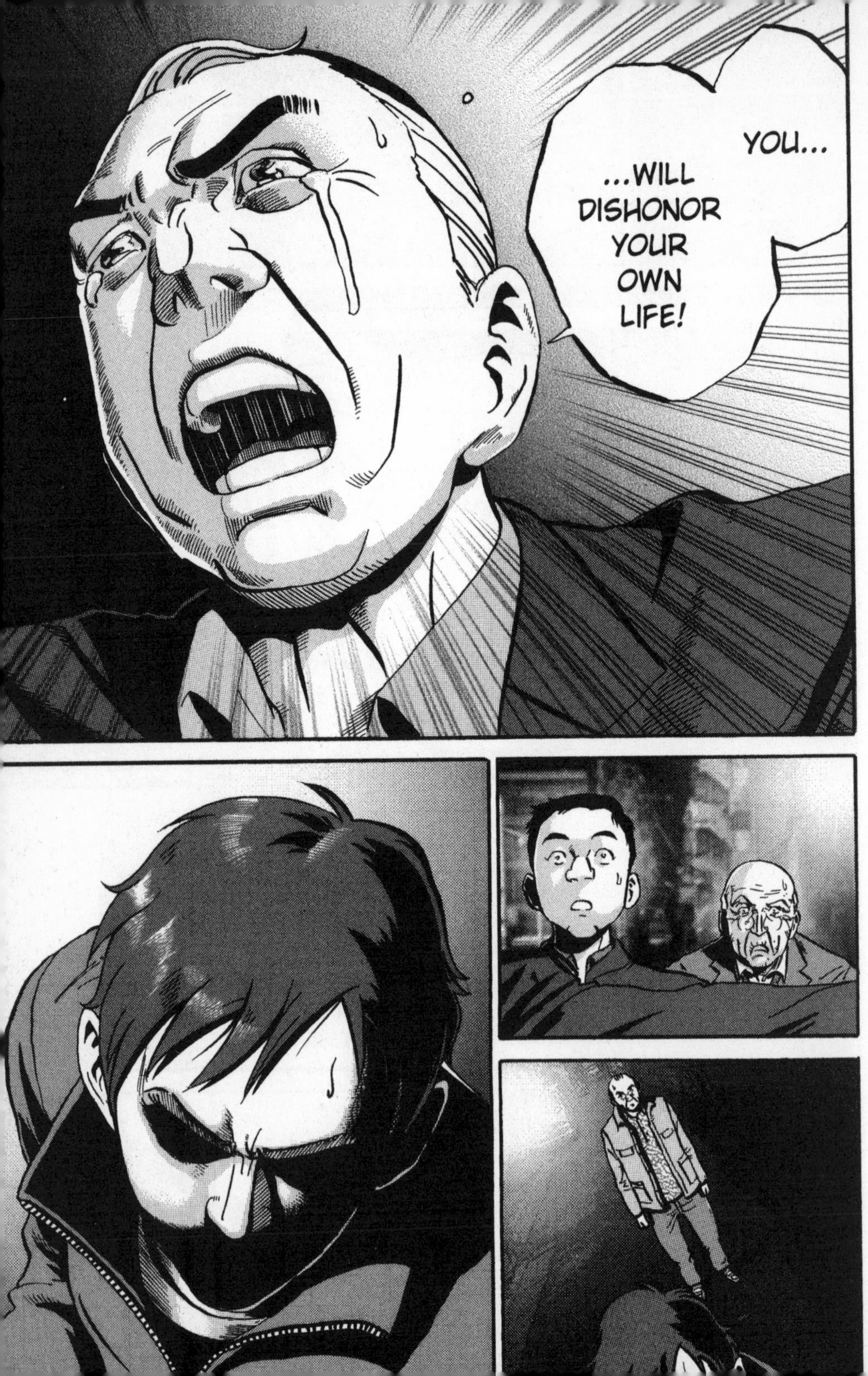
YOU...
...WILL DISHONOR YOUR OWN LIFE!

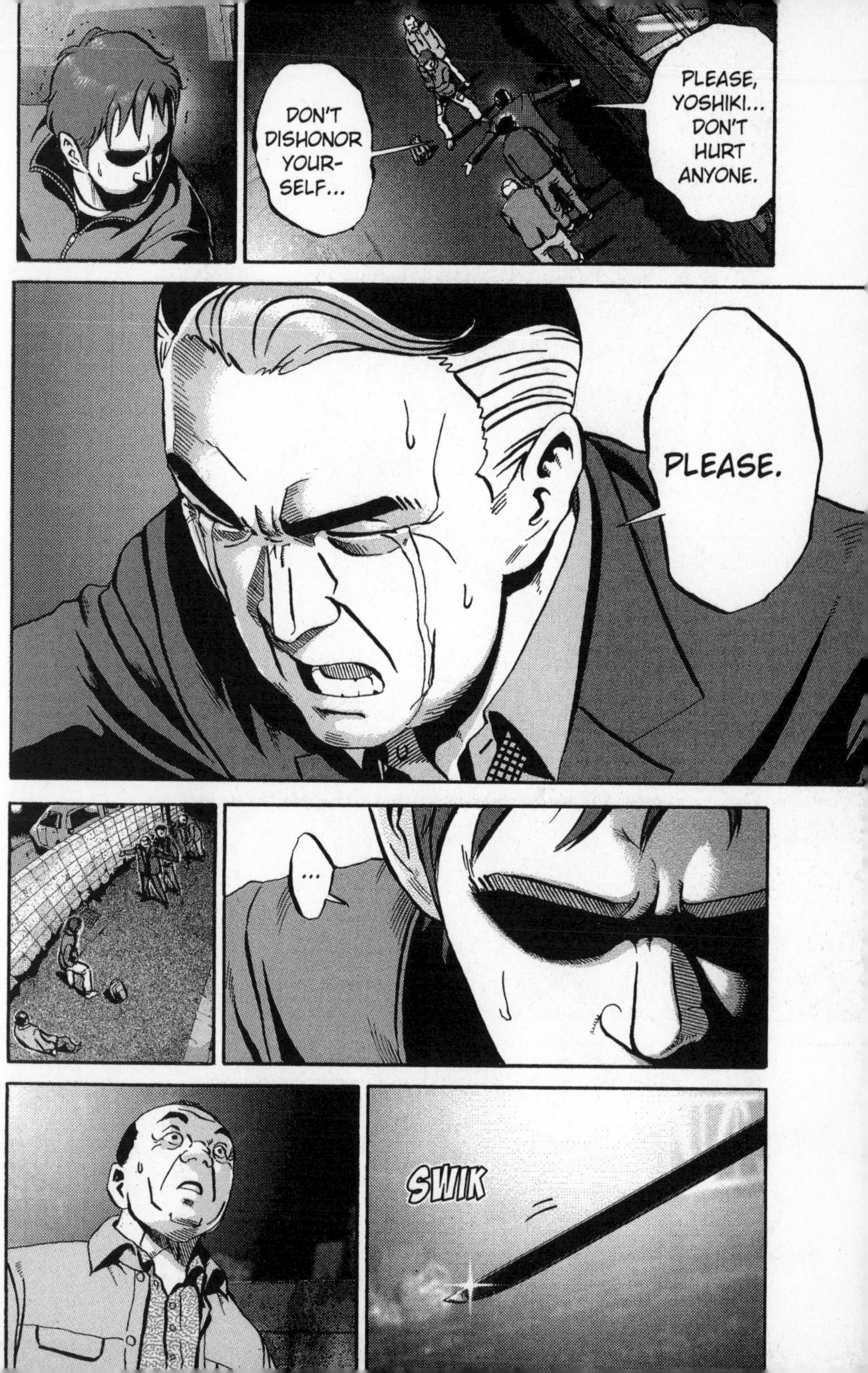
PLEASE, YOSHIKI... DON'T HURT ANYONE.
DON'T DISHONOR YOUR-SELF...
PLEASE.
...
SWIK

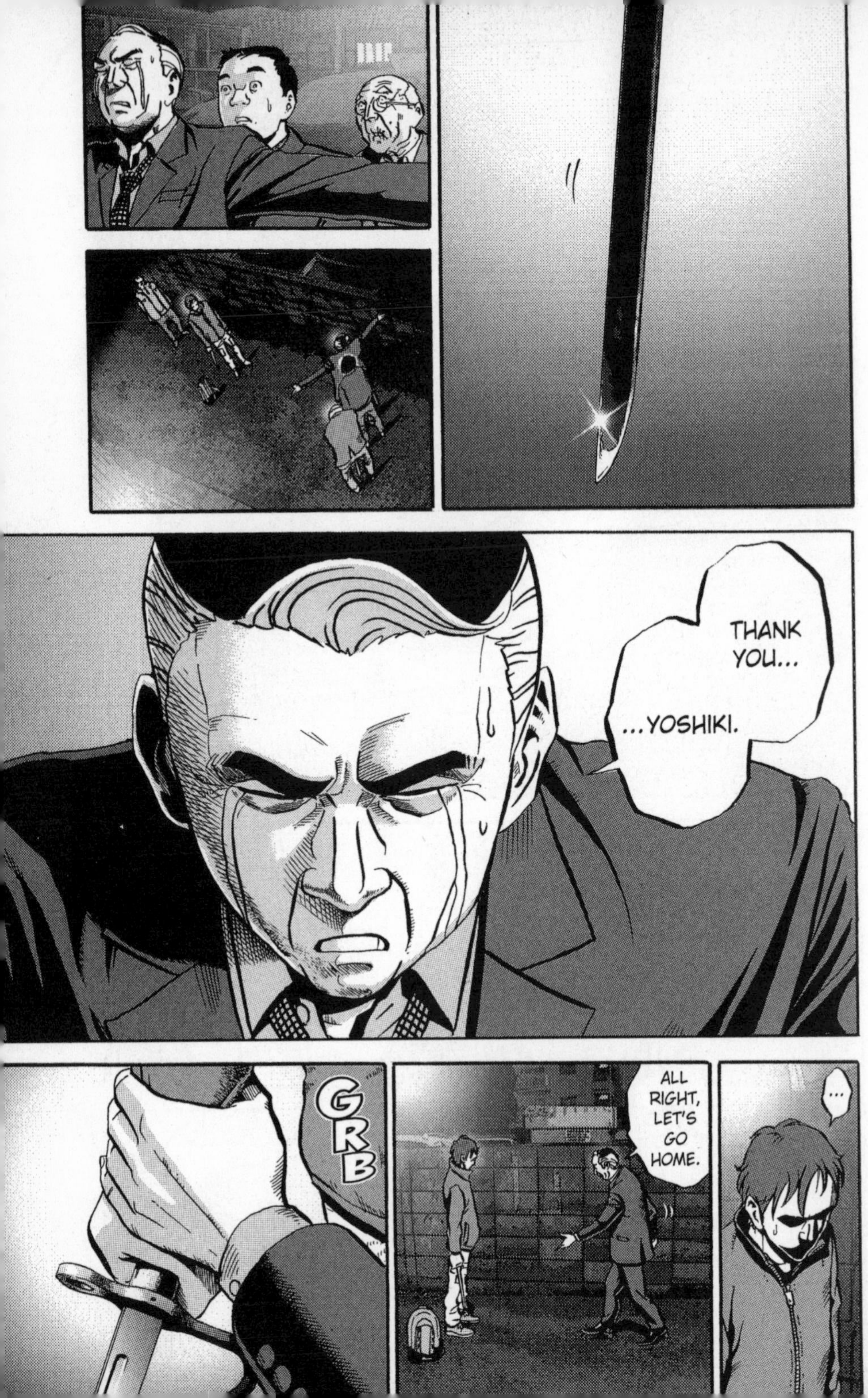
THANK YOU...
...YOSHIKI.
...
ALL RIGHT, LET'S GO HOME.
GRB

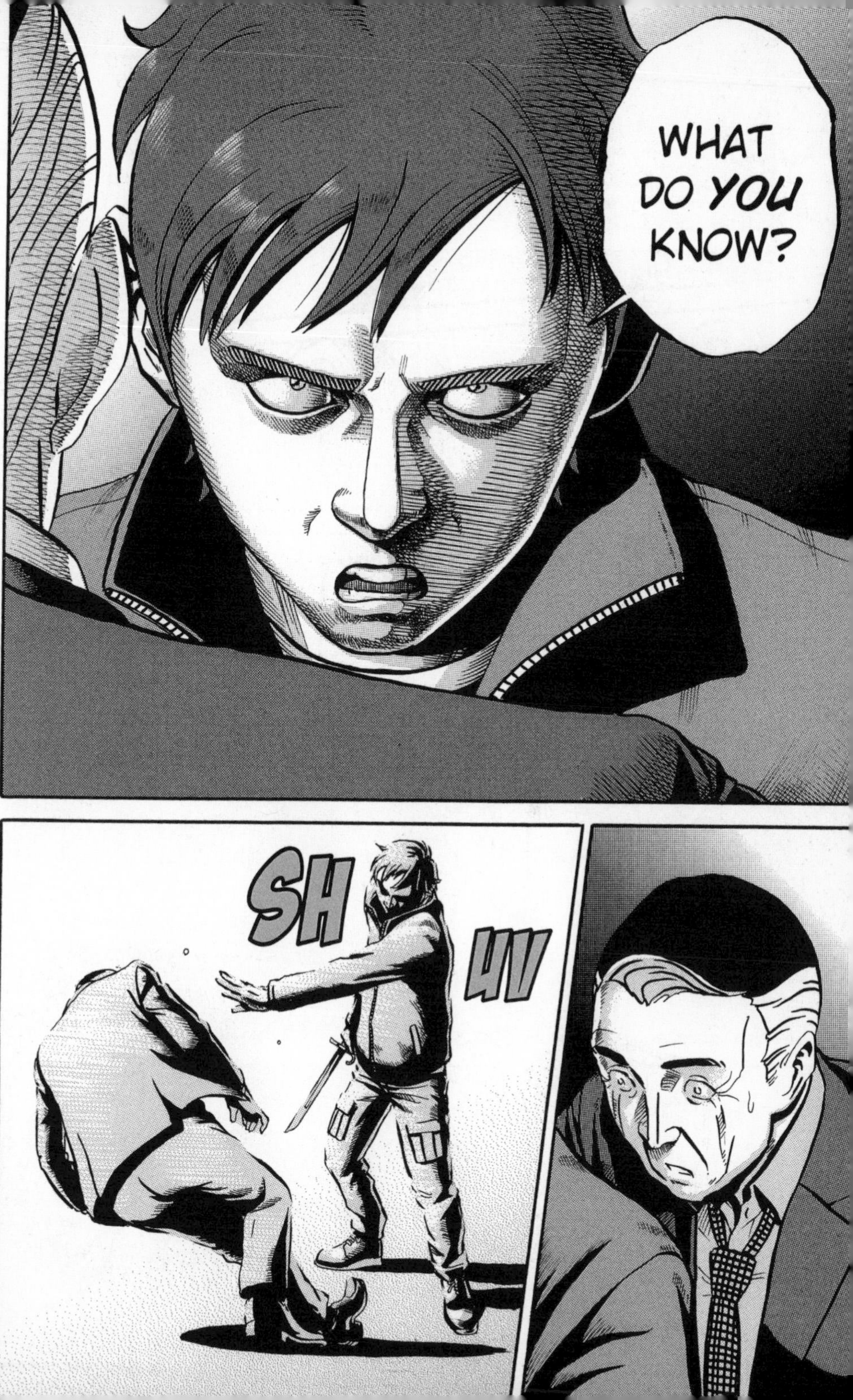
WHAT DO YOU KNOW?
SH
UV

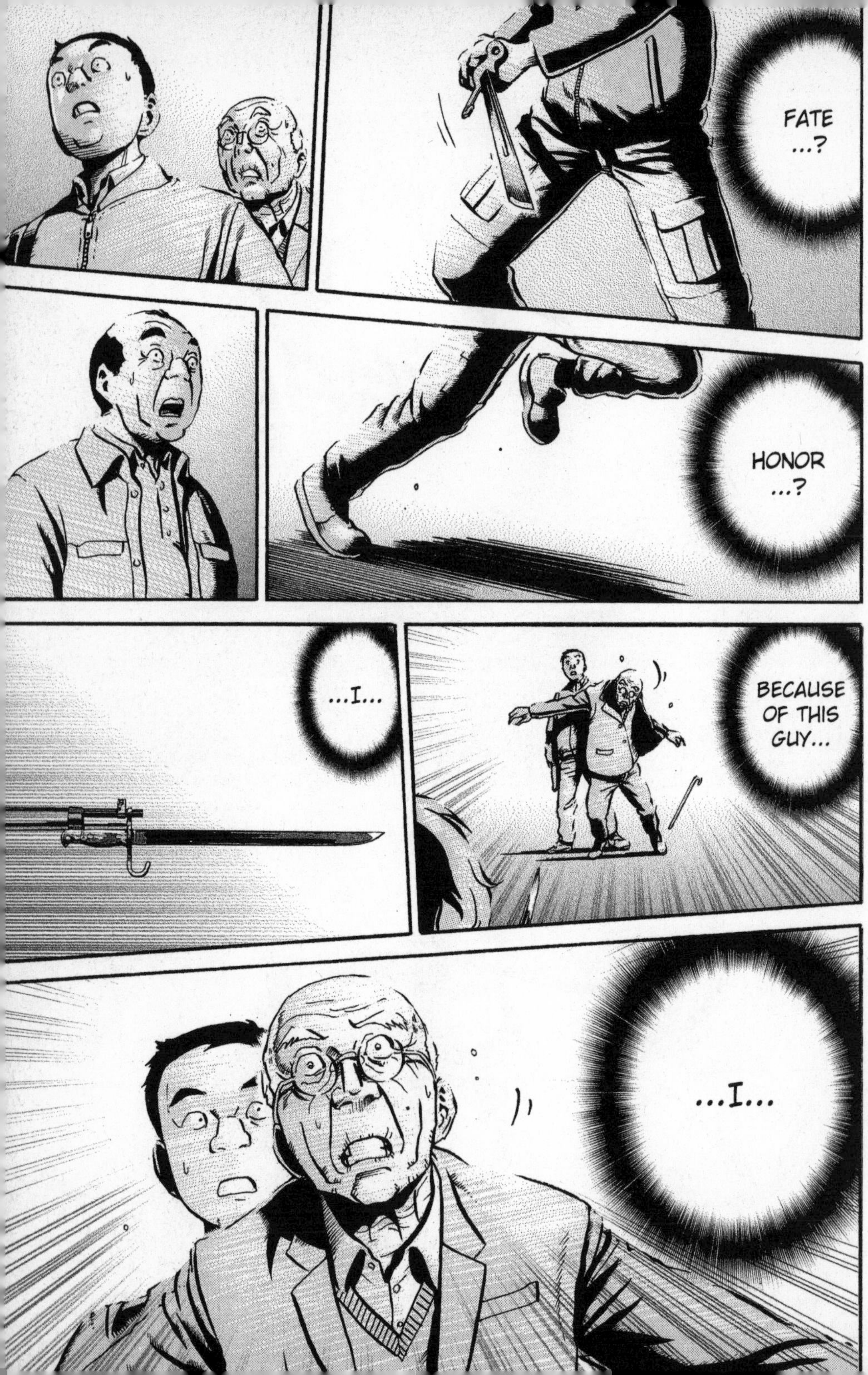
FATE ...?
HONOR ...?
BECAUSE OF THIS GUY...
...I...
...I...

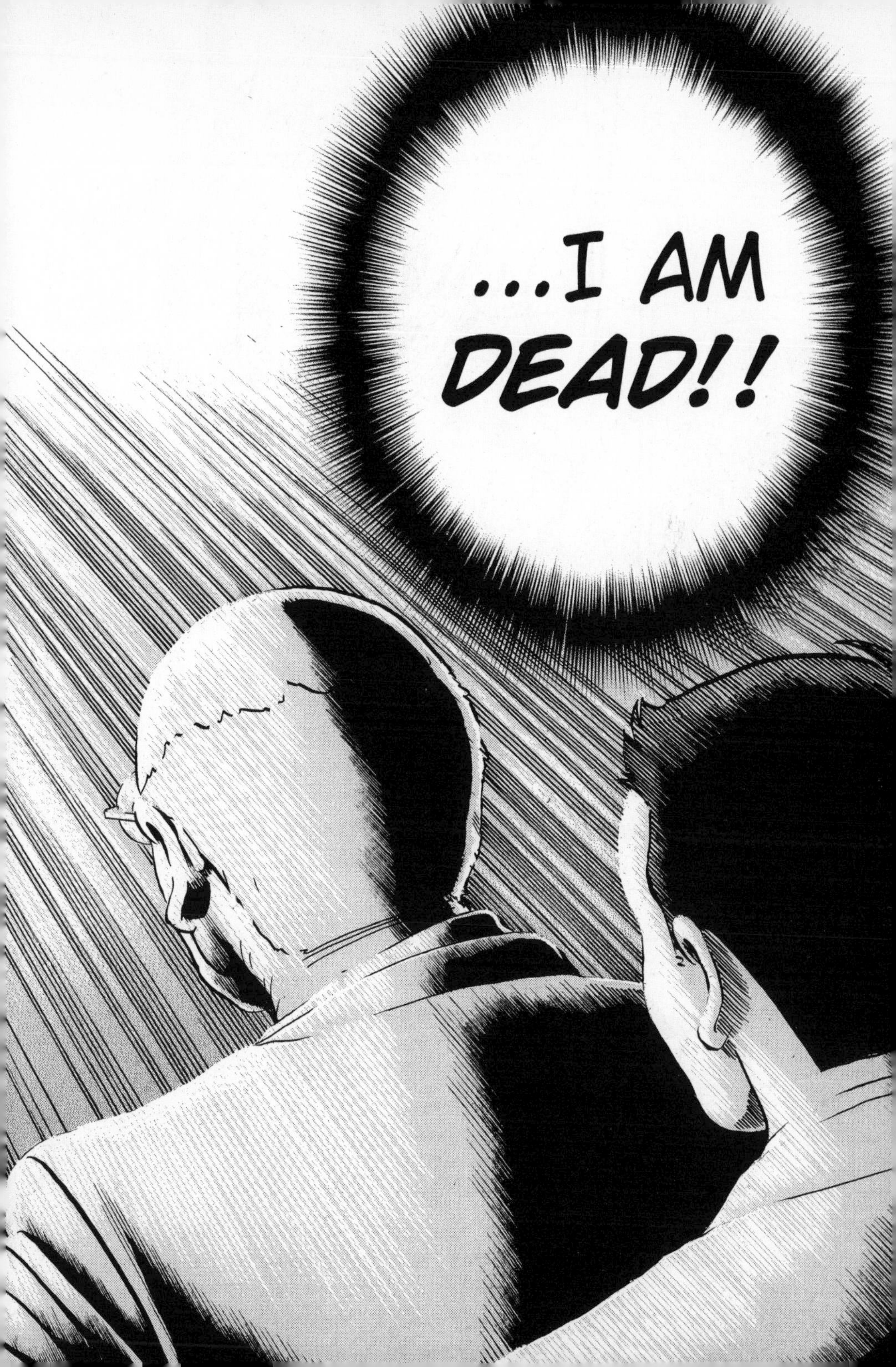
...I AM DEAD!!

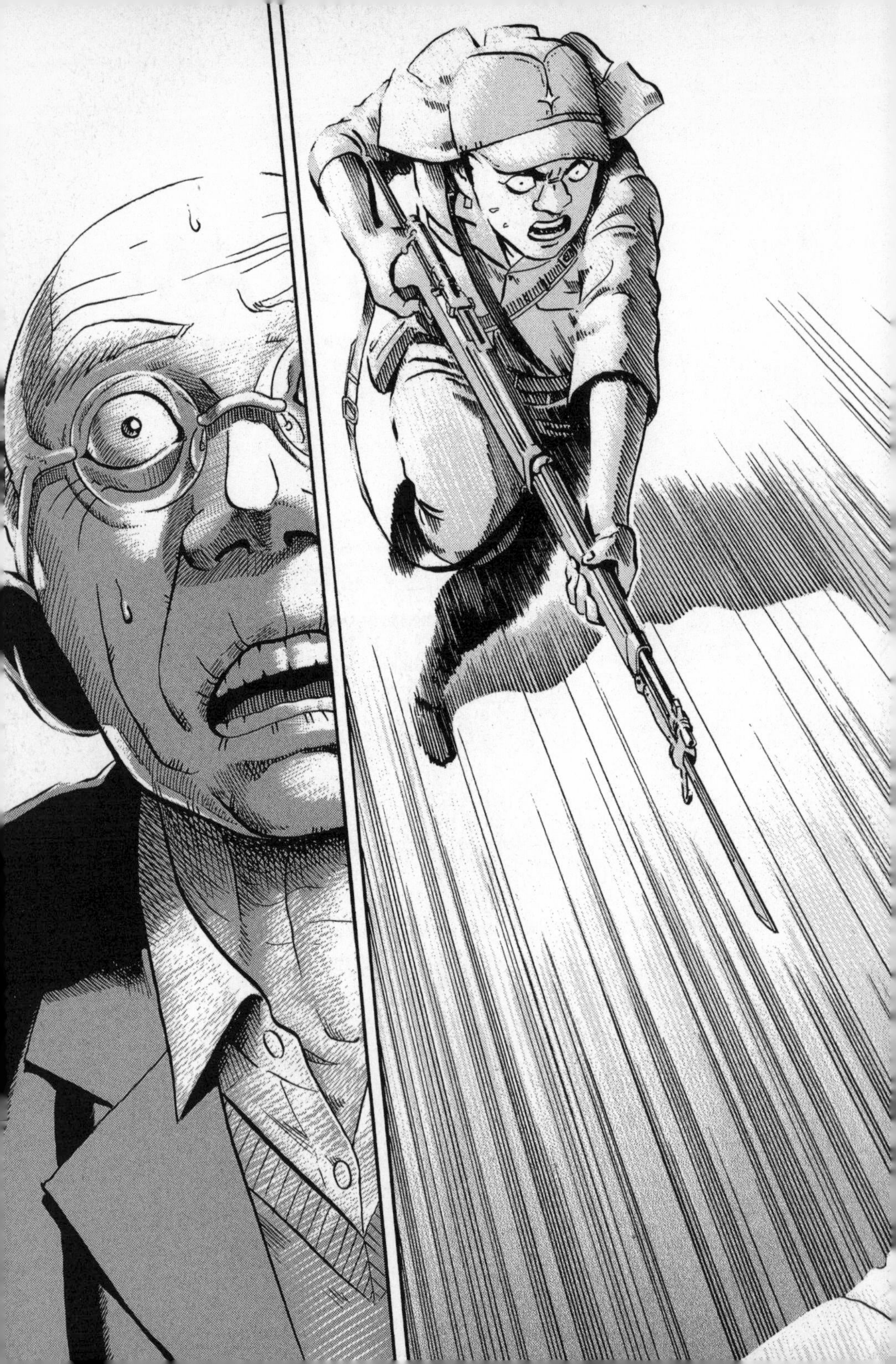

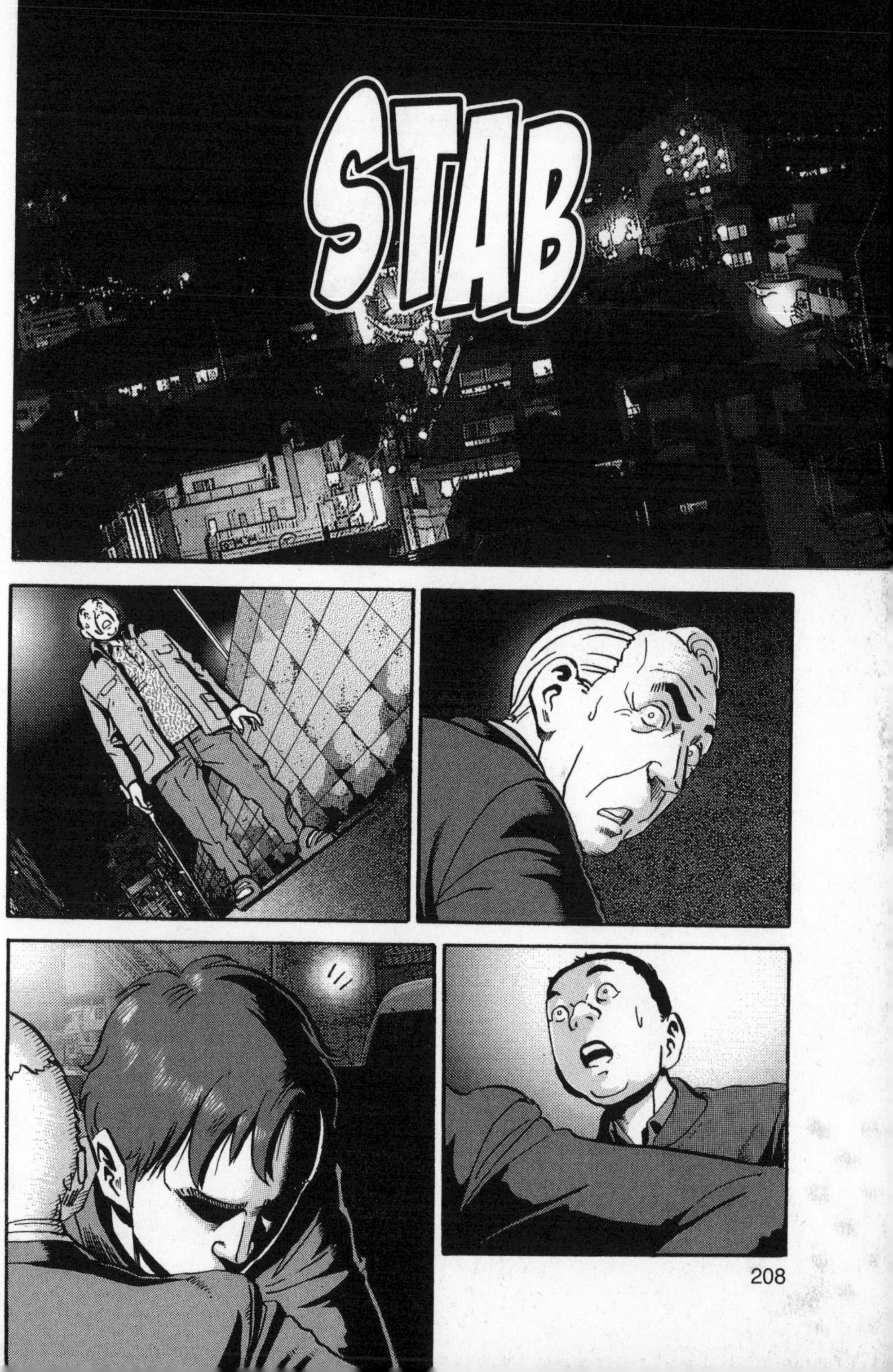
STAB

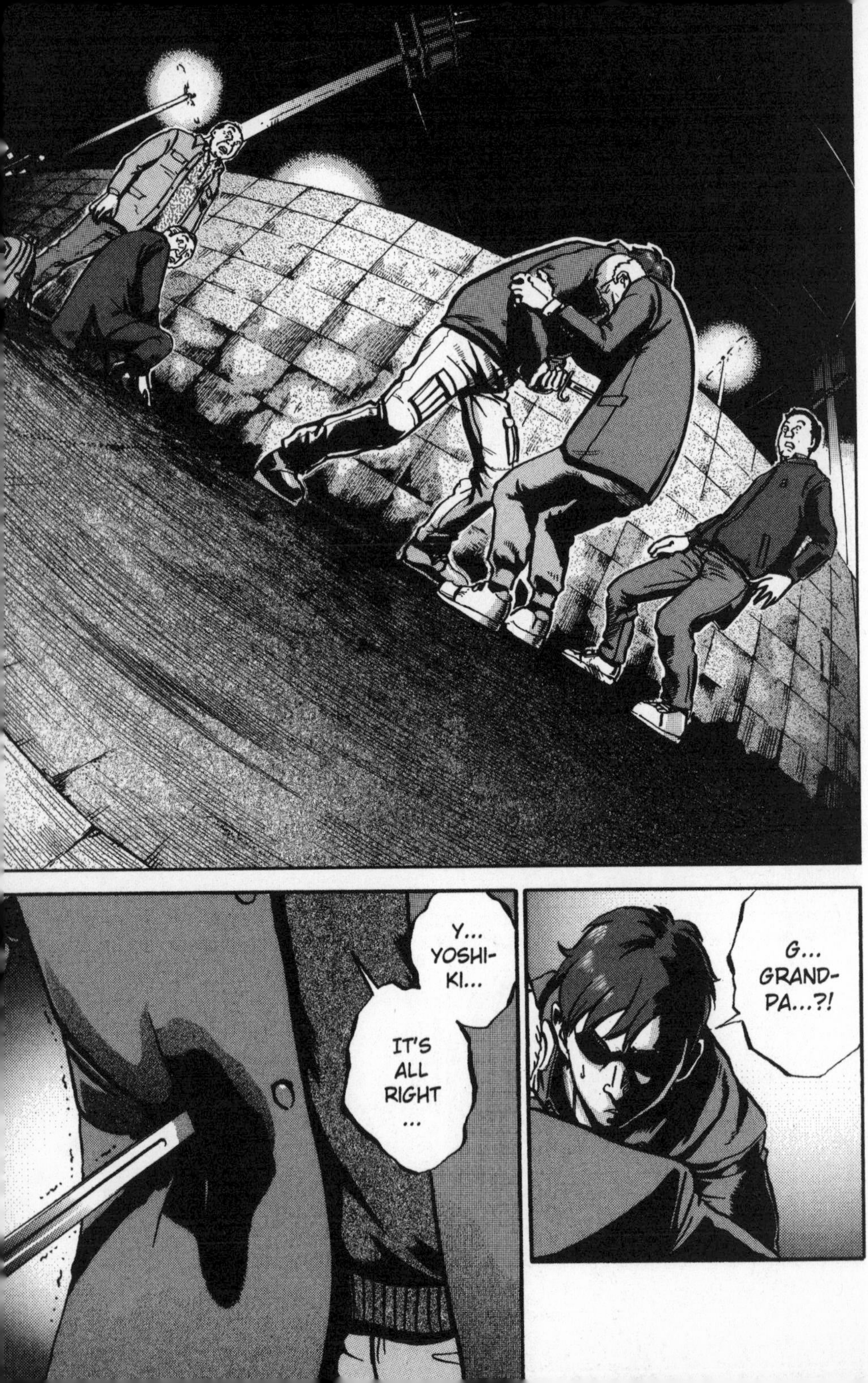
G... GRAND-PA...?!
Y... YOSHI-KI...
IT'S ALL RIGHT ...

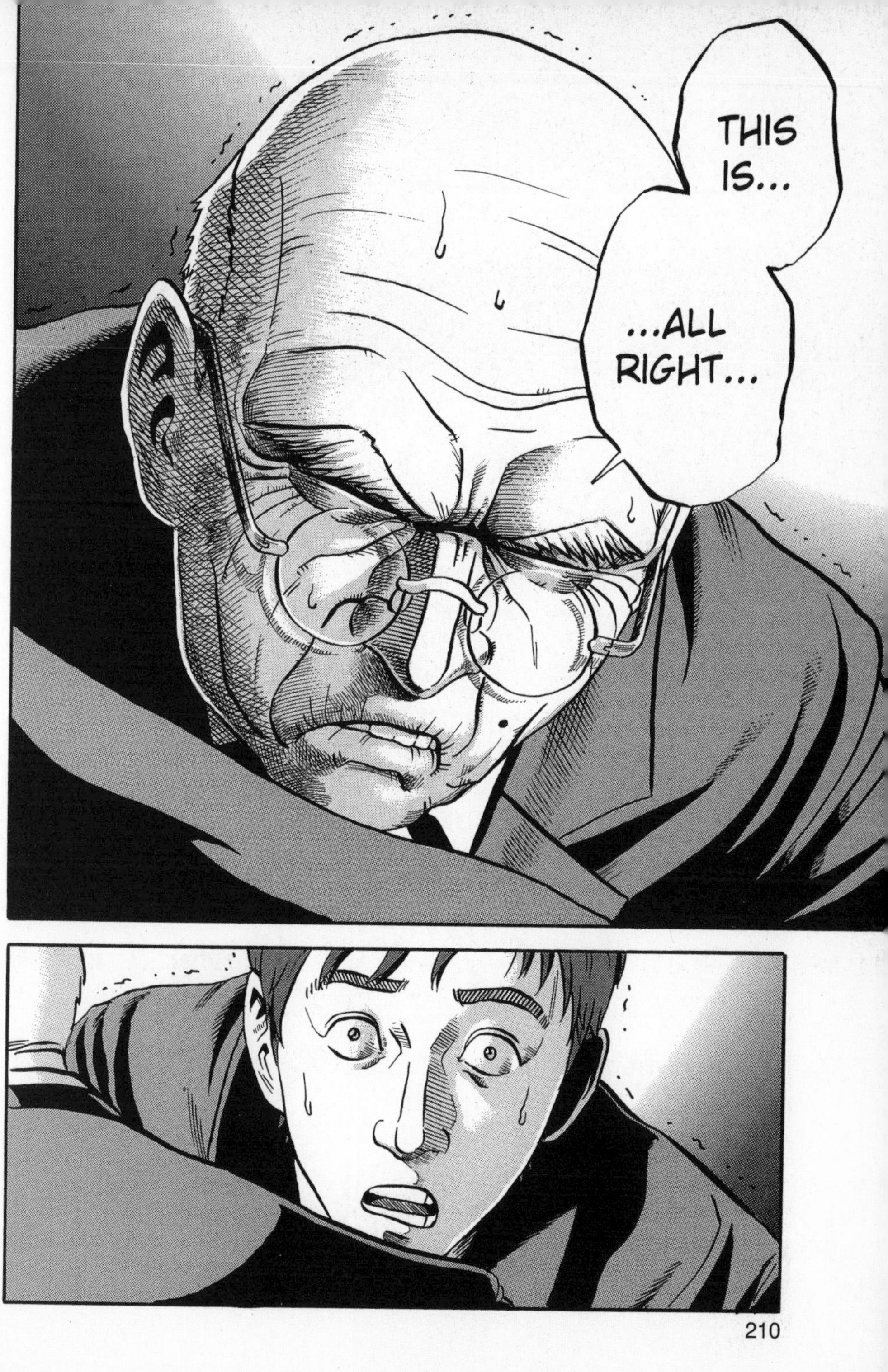
THIS IS...
...ALL RIGHT...

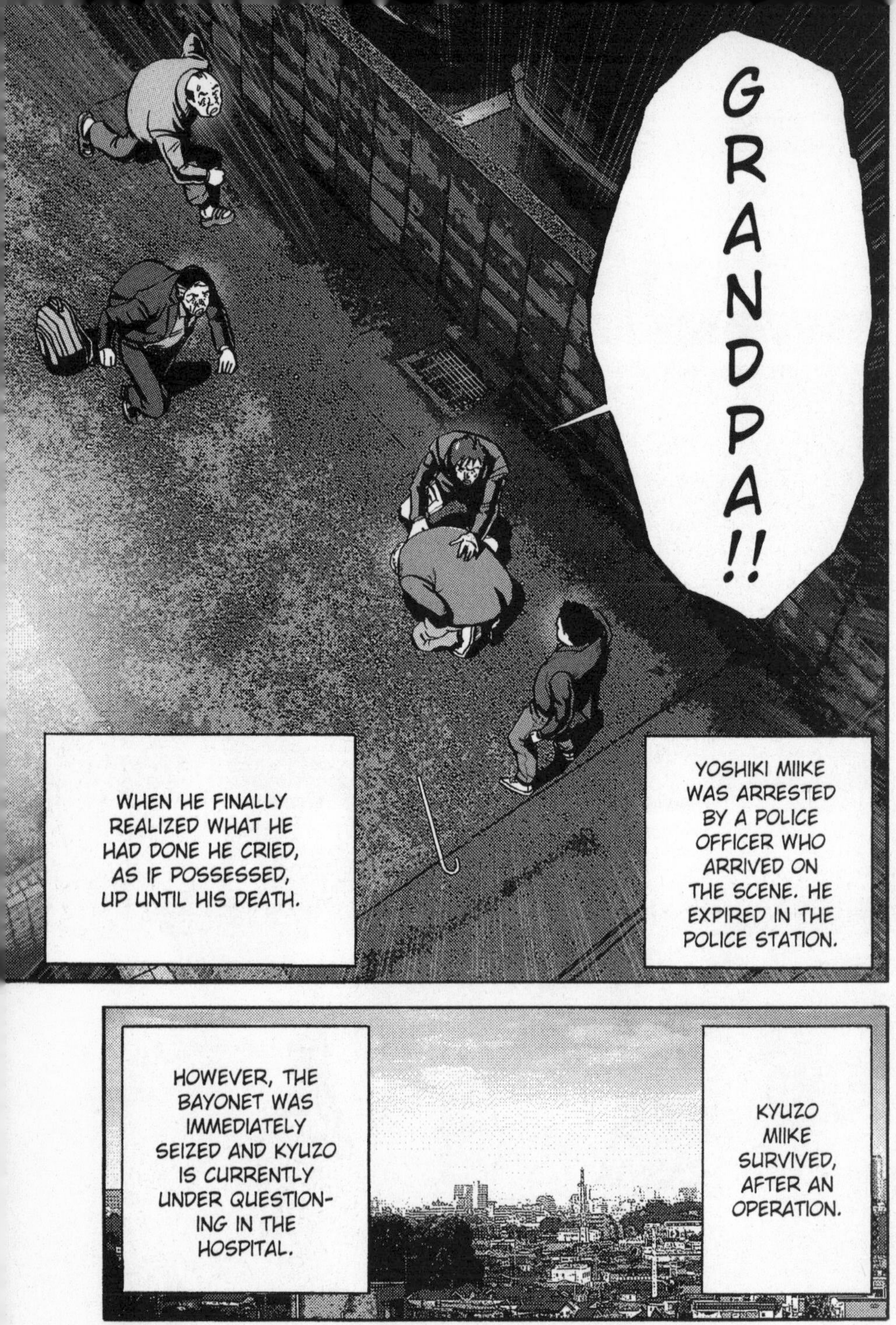
GRANDPA!!
YOSHIKI MIIKE WAS ARRESTED BY A POLICE OFFICER WHO ARRIVED ON THE SCENE. HE EXPIRED IN THE POLICE STATION.
WHEN HE FINALLY REALIZED WHAT HE HAD DONE HE CRIED, AS IF POSSESSED, UP UNTIL HIS DEATH.
KYUZO MIIKE SURVIVED, AFTER AN OPERATION.
HOWEVER, THE BAYONET WAS IMMEDIATELY SEIZED AND KYUZO IS CURRENTLY UNDER QUESTIONING IN THE HOSPITAL.

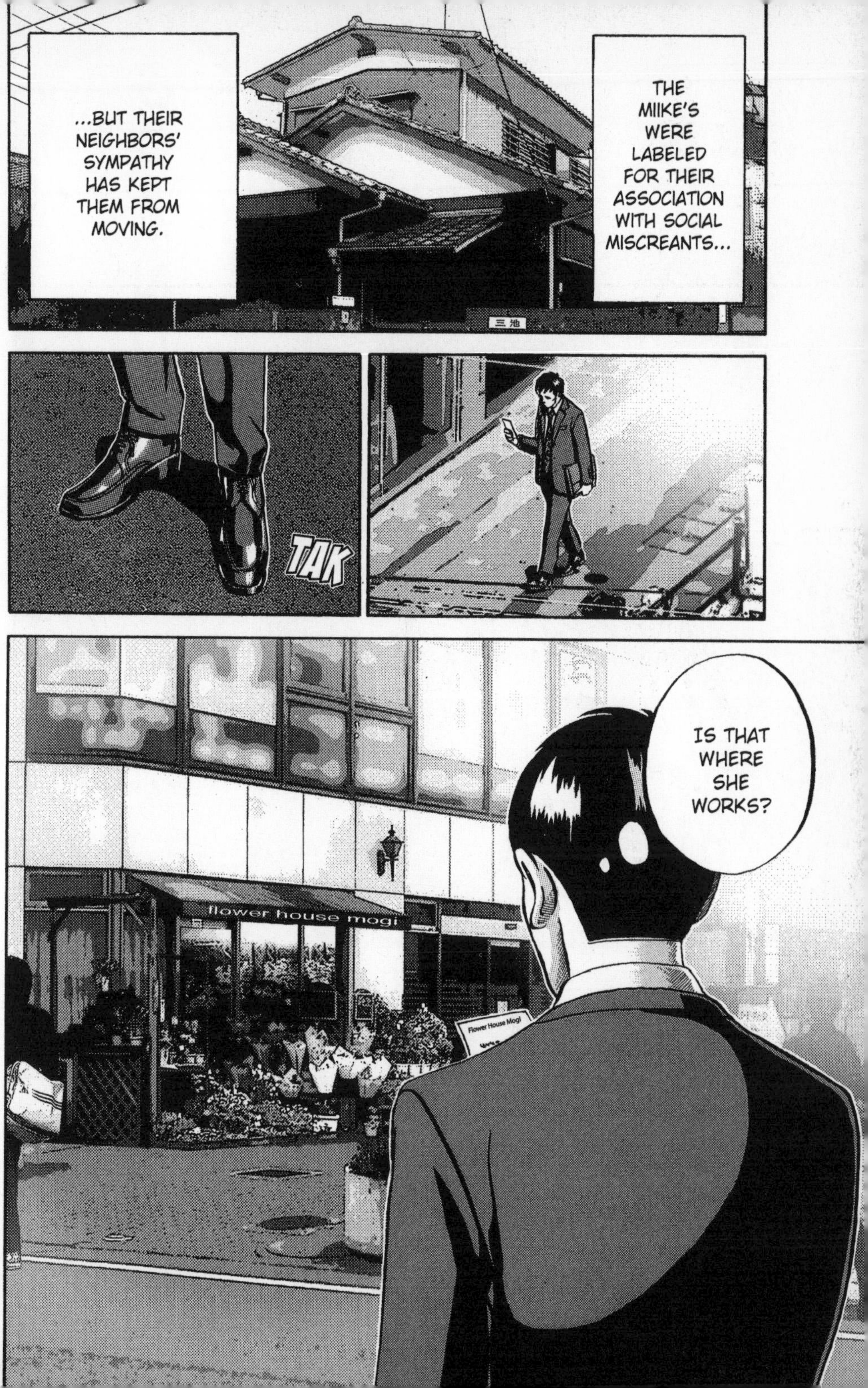
THE MIIKE'S WERE LABELED FOR THEIR ASSOCIATION WITH SOCIAL MISCREANTS...
...BUT THEIR NEIGHBORS' SYMPATHY HAS KEPT THEM FROM MOVING.
三池
TAK
IS THAT WHERE SHE WORKS?
flower house mogi
Flower House Mogi

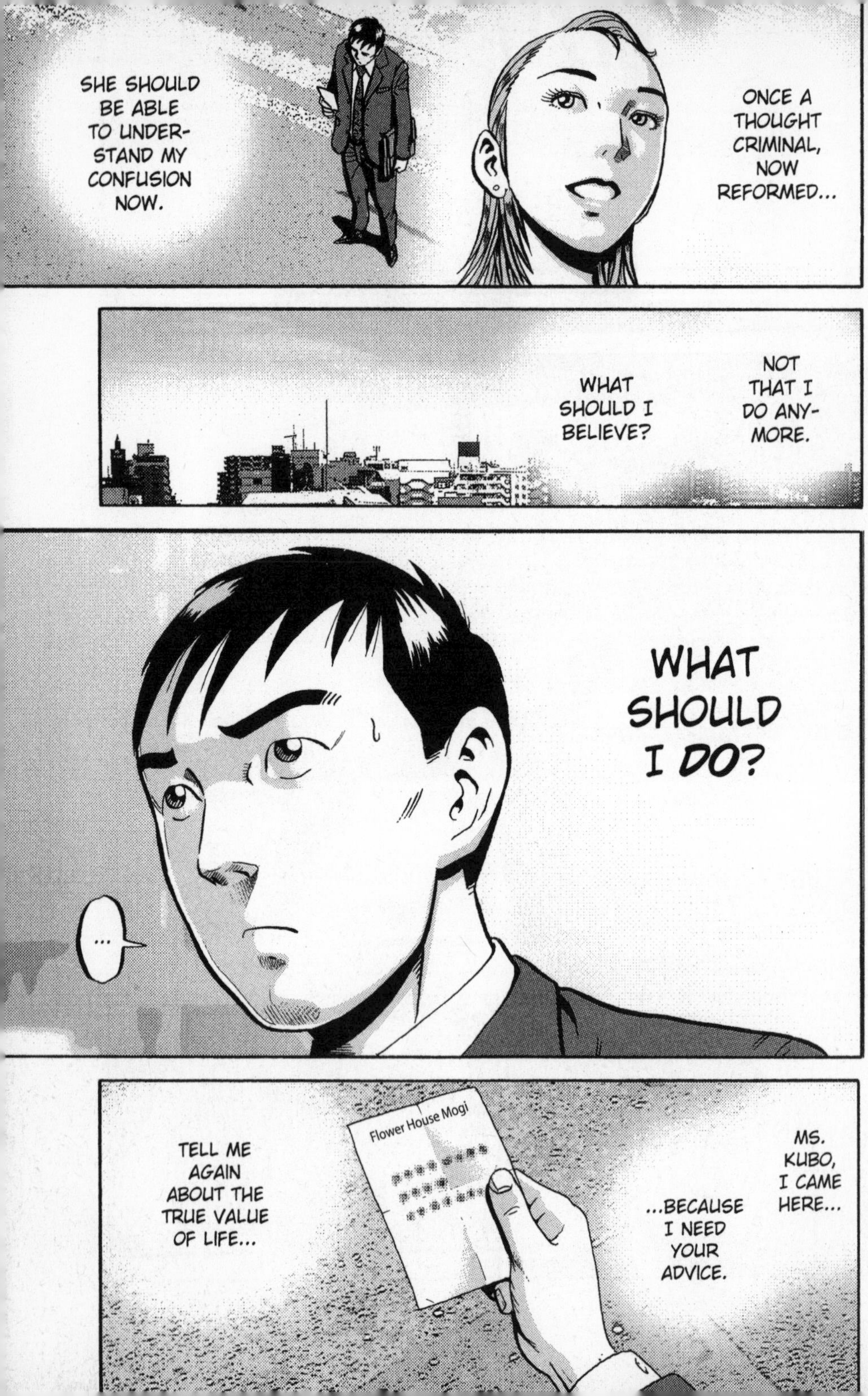
ONCE A THOUGHT CRIMINAL, NOW REFORMED...
SHE SHOULD BE ABLE TO UNDER-STAND MY CONFUSION NOW.
NOT THAT I DO ANY-MORE.
WHAT SHOULD I BELIEVE?
WHAT SHOULD I *DO*?
...
MS. KUBO, I CAME HERE...
...BECAUSE I NEED YOUR ADVICE.
Flower House Mogi
TELL ME AGAIN ABOUT THE TRUE VALUE OF LIFE...

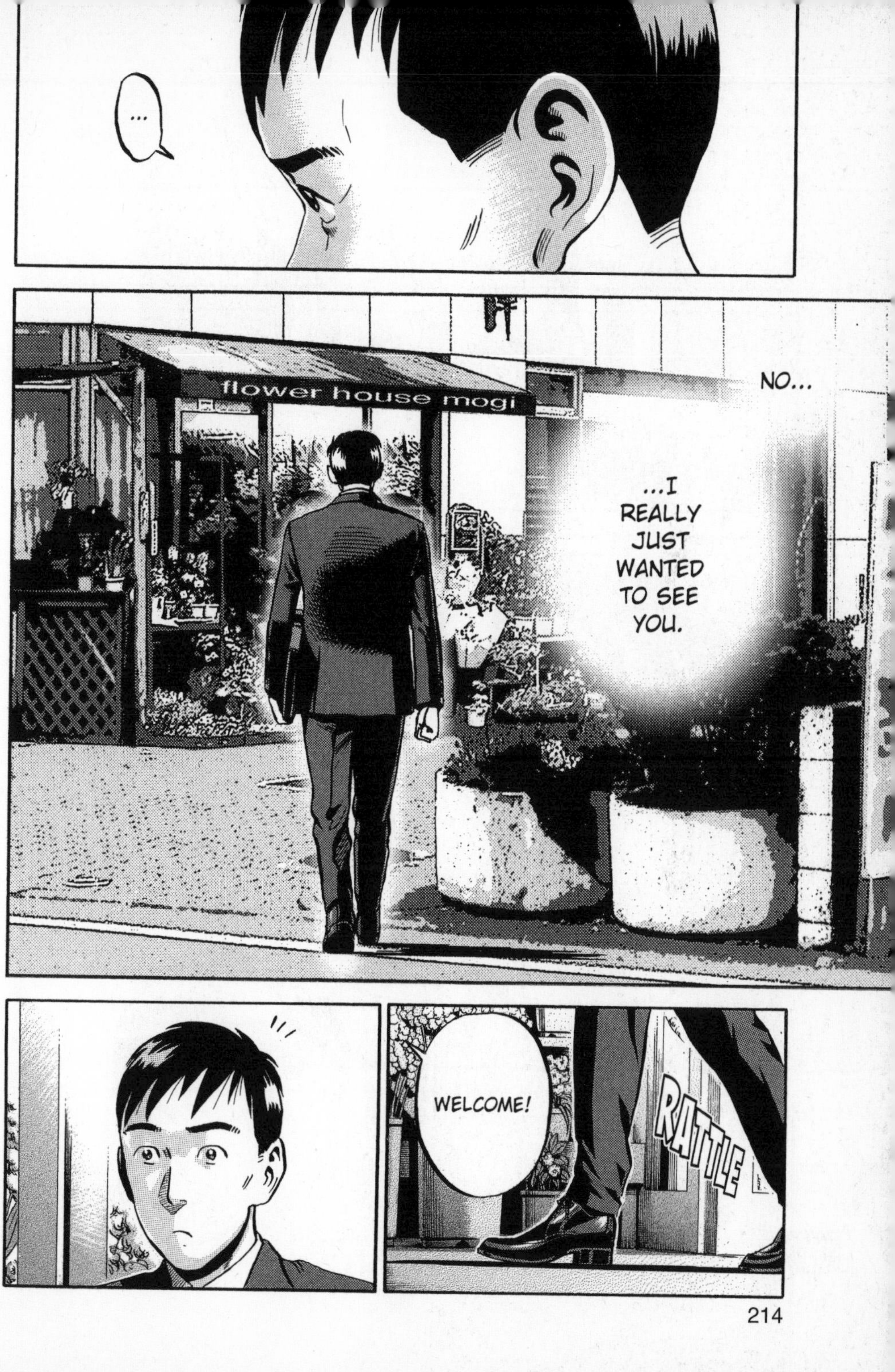
...
flower house mogi
NO...
...I REALLY JUST WANTED TO SEE YOU.
WELCOME!
RATTLE

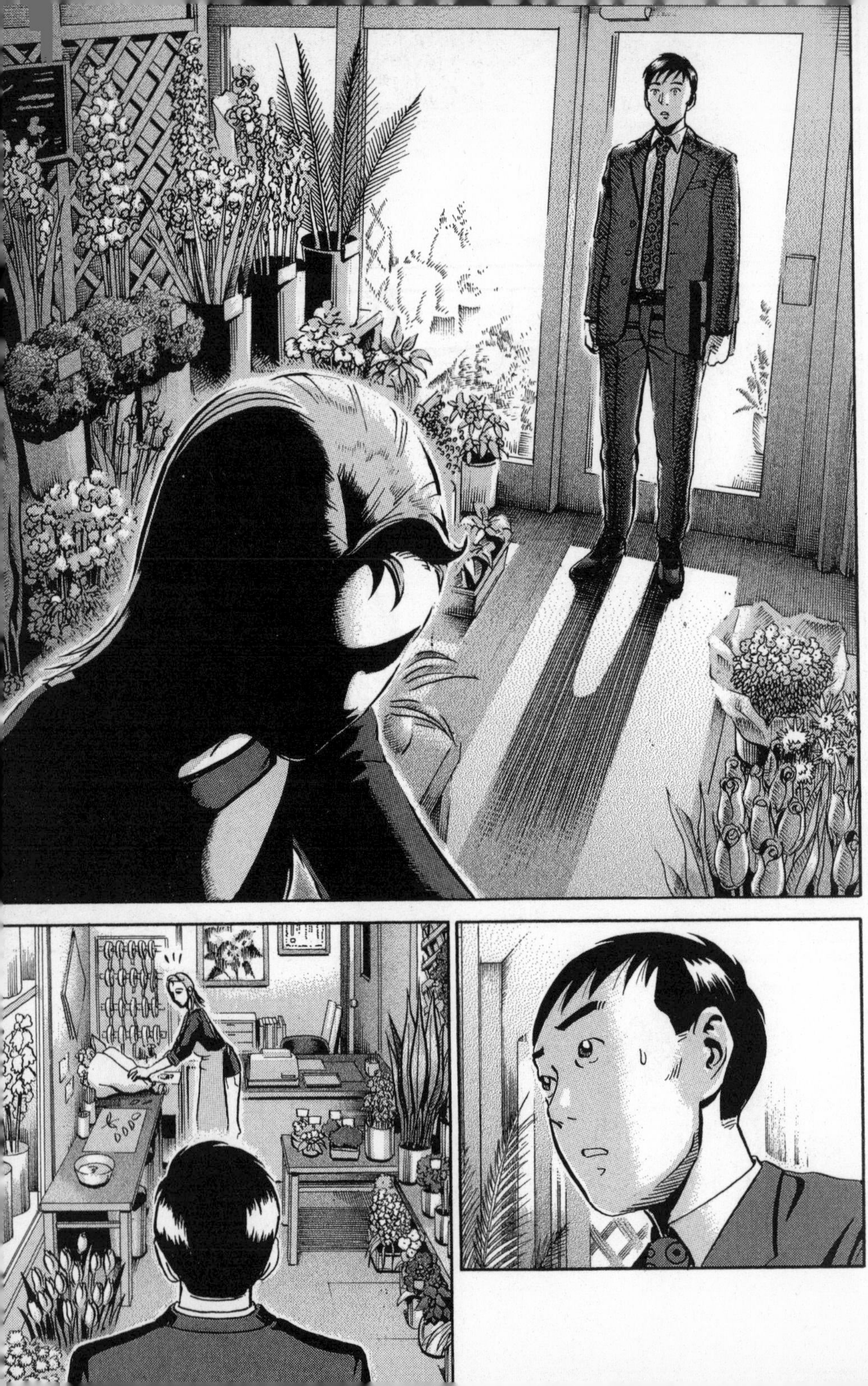

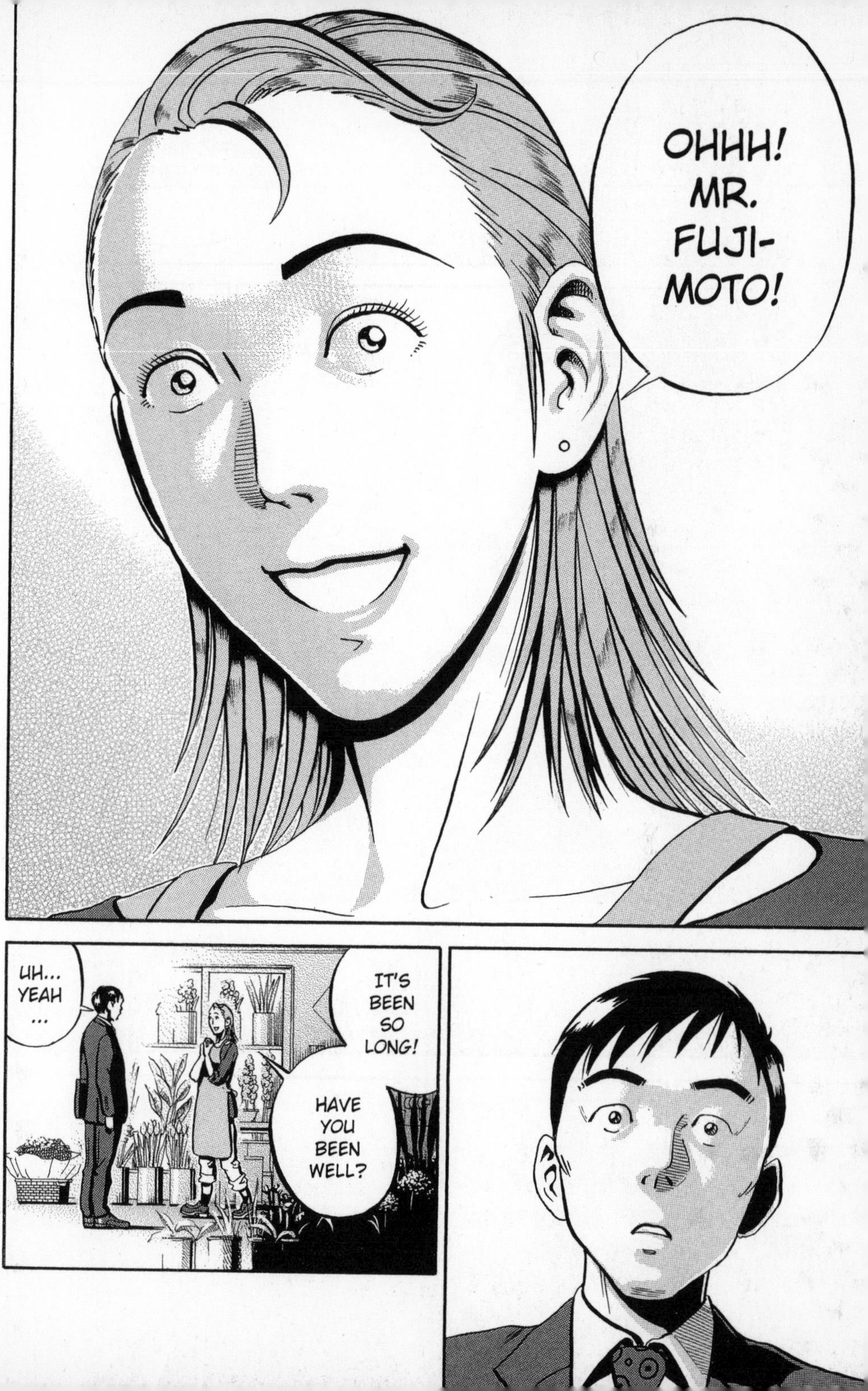
OHHH! MR. FUJI-MOTO!
IT'S BEEN SO LONG!
HAVE YOU BEEN WELL?
UH... YEAH ...

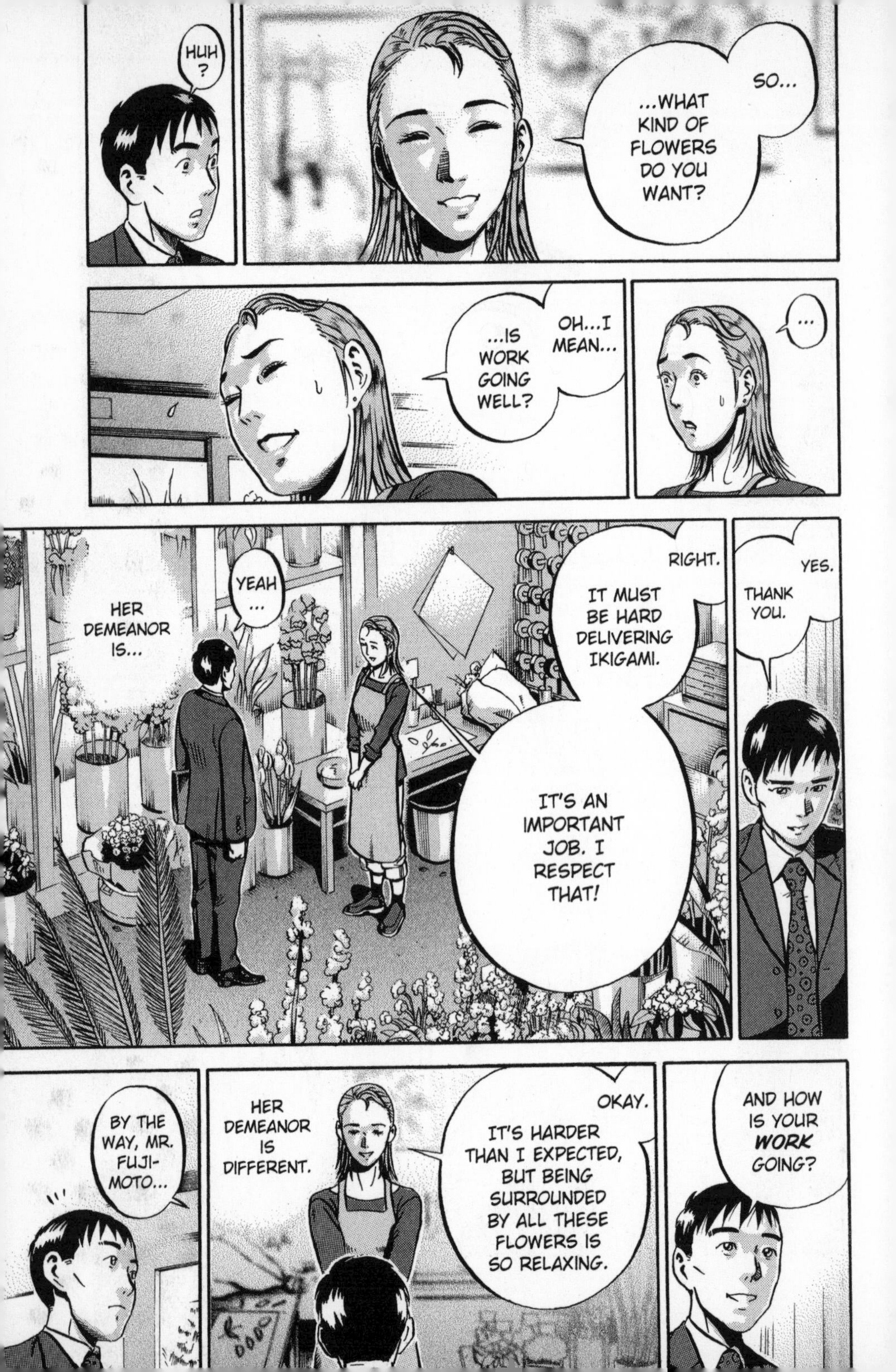
SO...
...WHAT KIND OF FLOWERS DO YOU WANT?
HUH?
...
OH...I MEAN...
...IS WORK GOING WELL?
YES.
THANK YOU.
RIGHT.
IT MUST BE HARD DELIVERING IKIGAMI.
IT'S AN IMPORTANT JOB. I RESPECT THAT!
YEAH...
HER DEMEANOR IS...
AND HOW IS YOUR *WORK* GOING?
OKAY.
IT'S HARDER THAN I EXPECTED, BUT BEING SURROUNDED BY ALL THESE FLOWERS IS SO RELAXING.
HER DEMEANOR IS DIFFERENT.
BY THE WAY, MR. FUJI-MOTO...

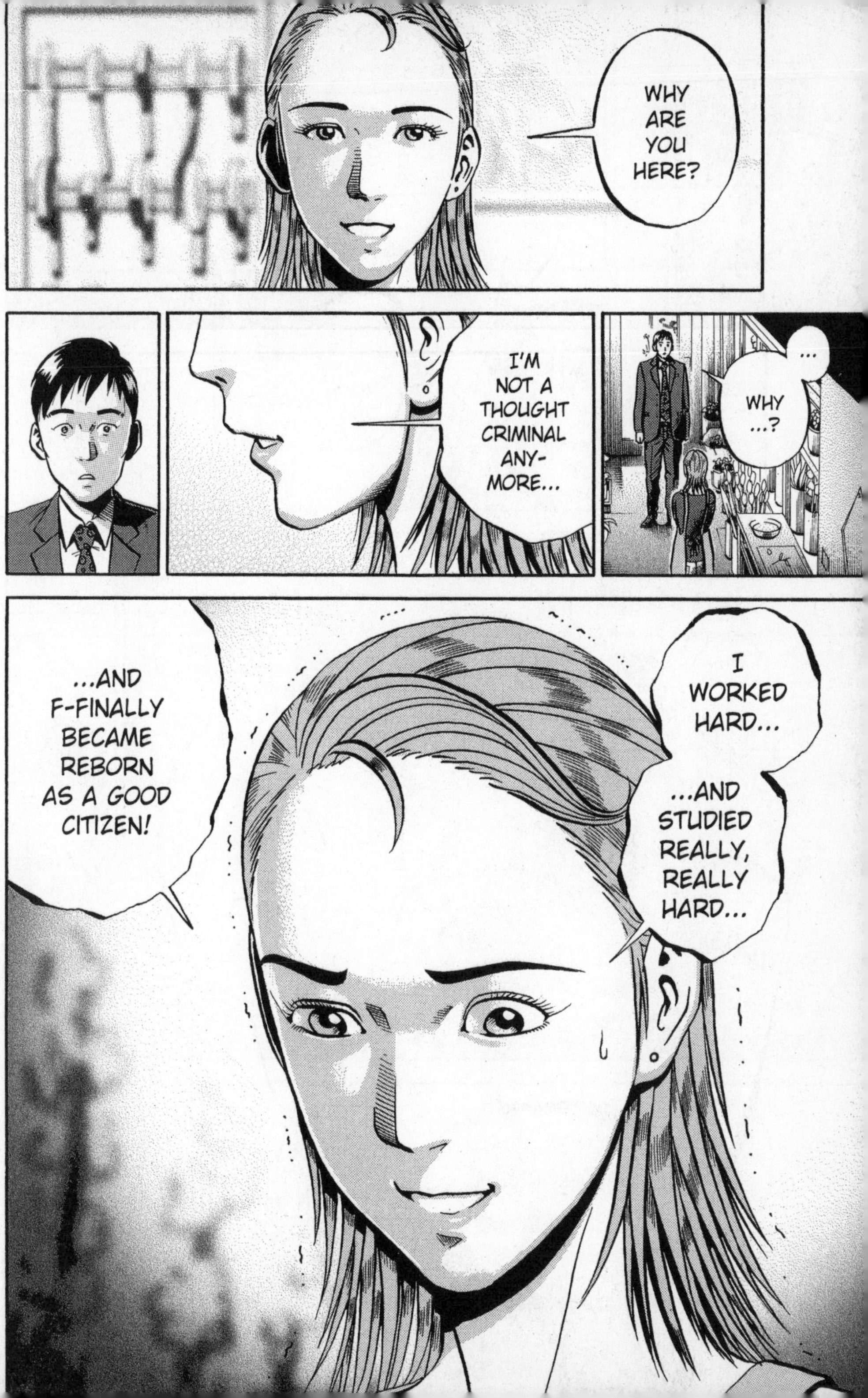
WHY ARE YOU HERE?
...
WHY ...?
I'M NOT A THOUGHT CRIMINAL ANY-MORE...
I WORKED HARD...
...AND STUDIED REALLY, REALLY HARD...
...AND F-FINALLY BECAME REBORN AS A GOOD CITIZEN!

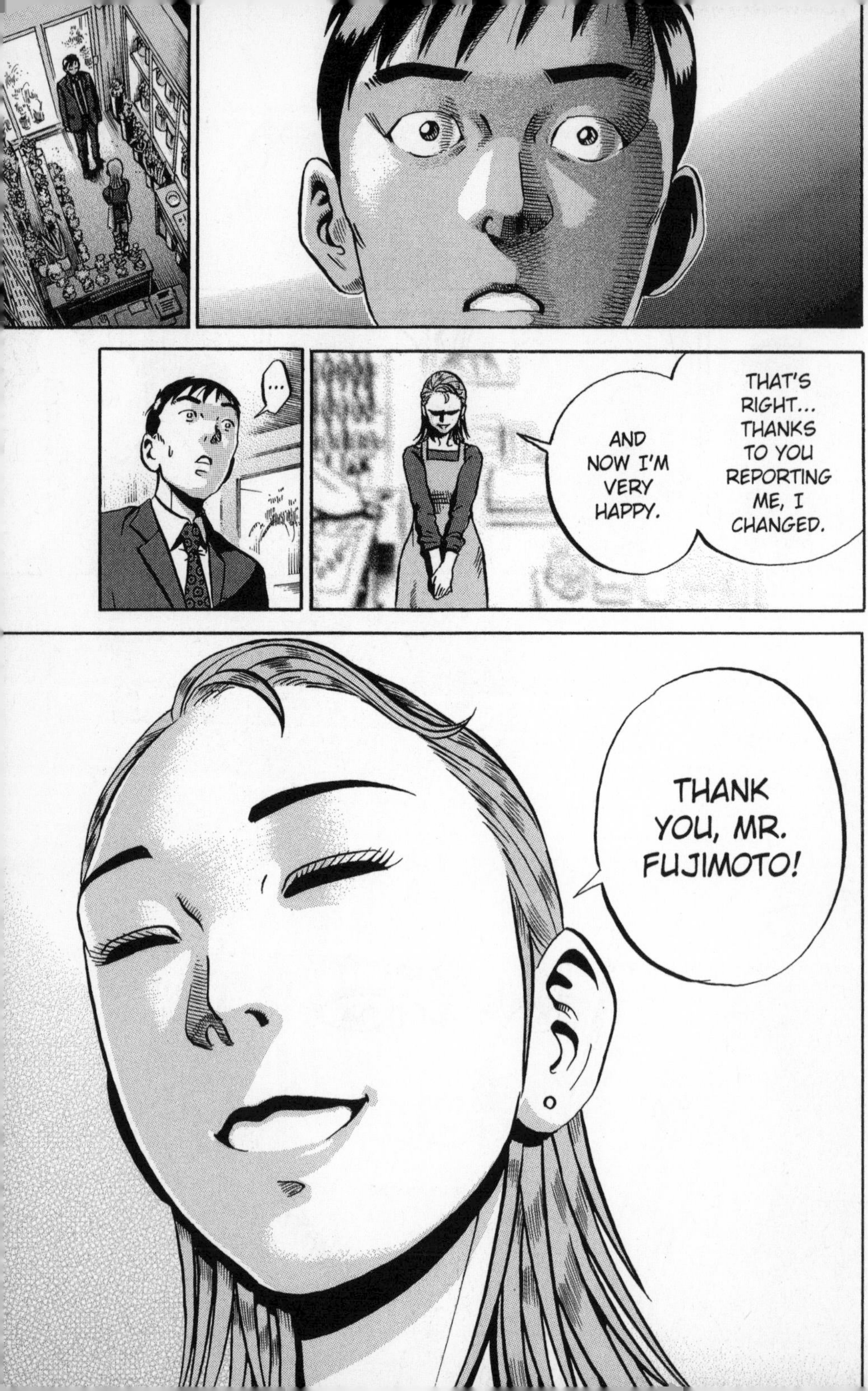
THAT'S RIGHT... THANKS TO YOU REPORTING ME, I CHANGED.
AND NOW I'M VERY HAPPY.
...
THANK YOU, MR. FUJIMOTO!

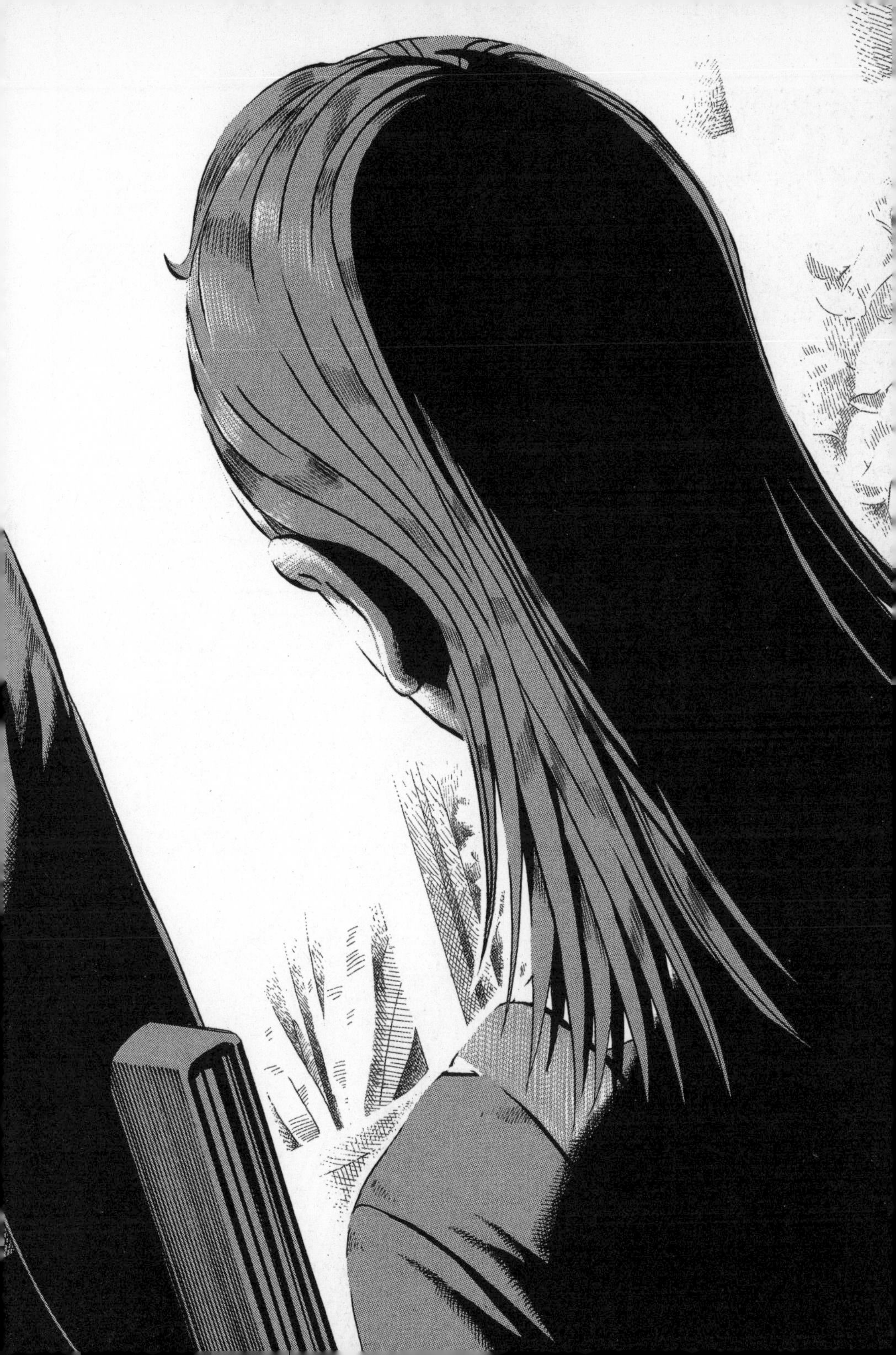

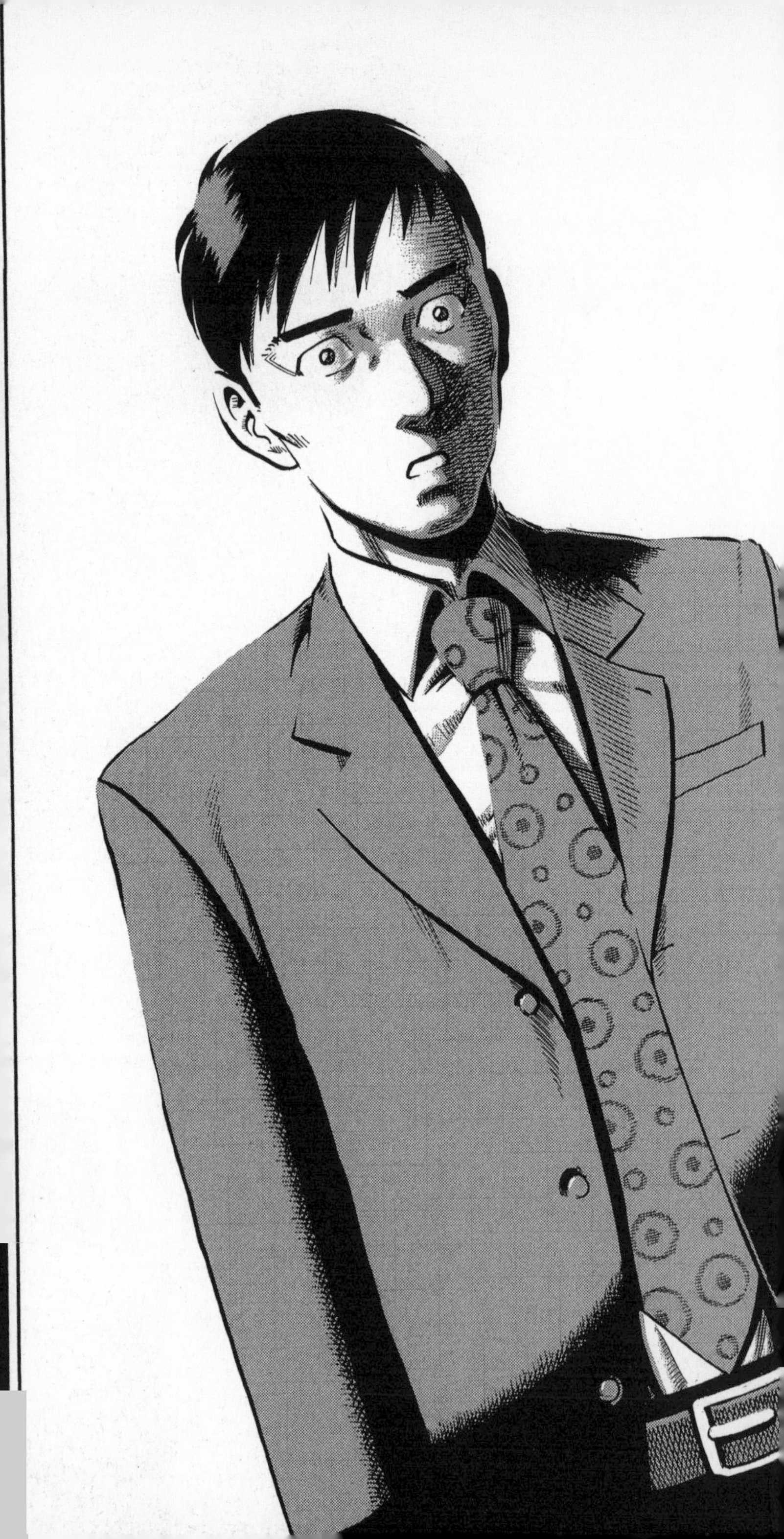
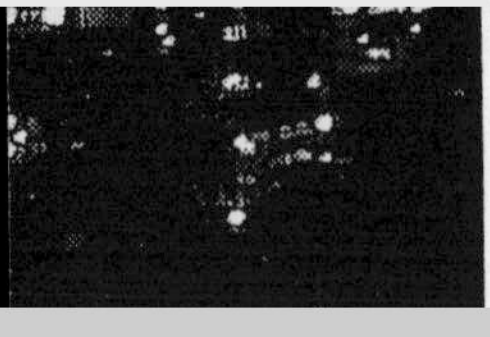

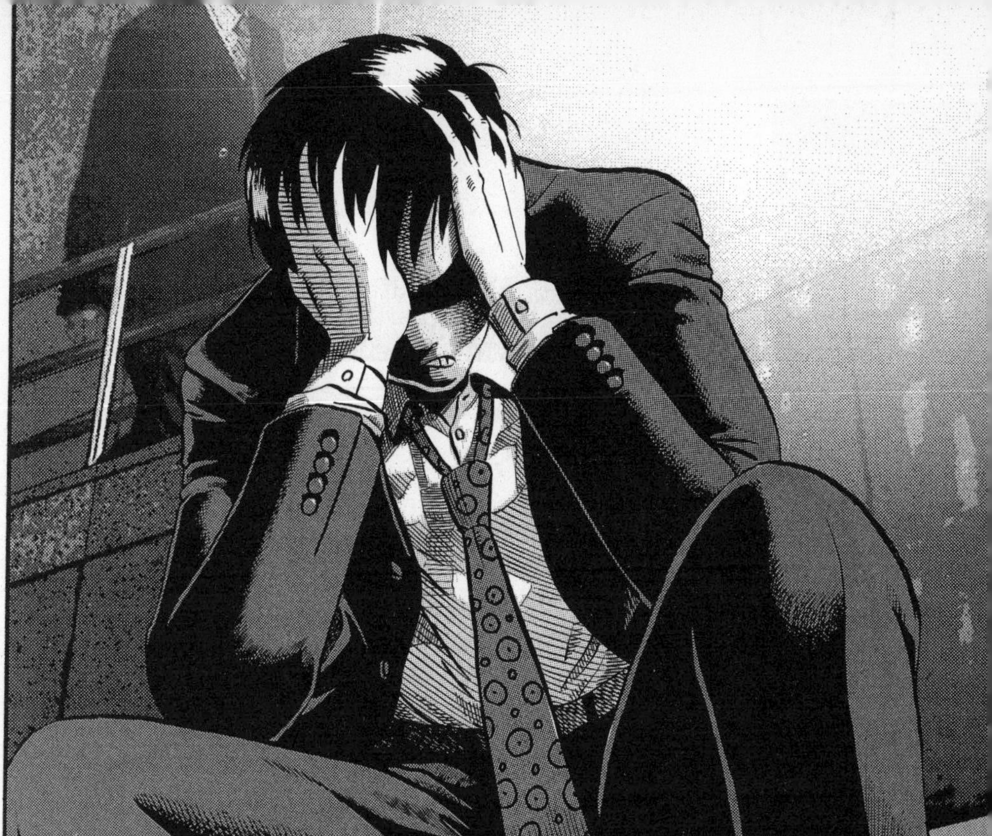

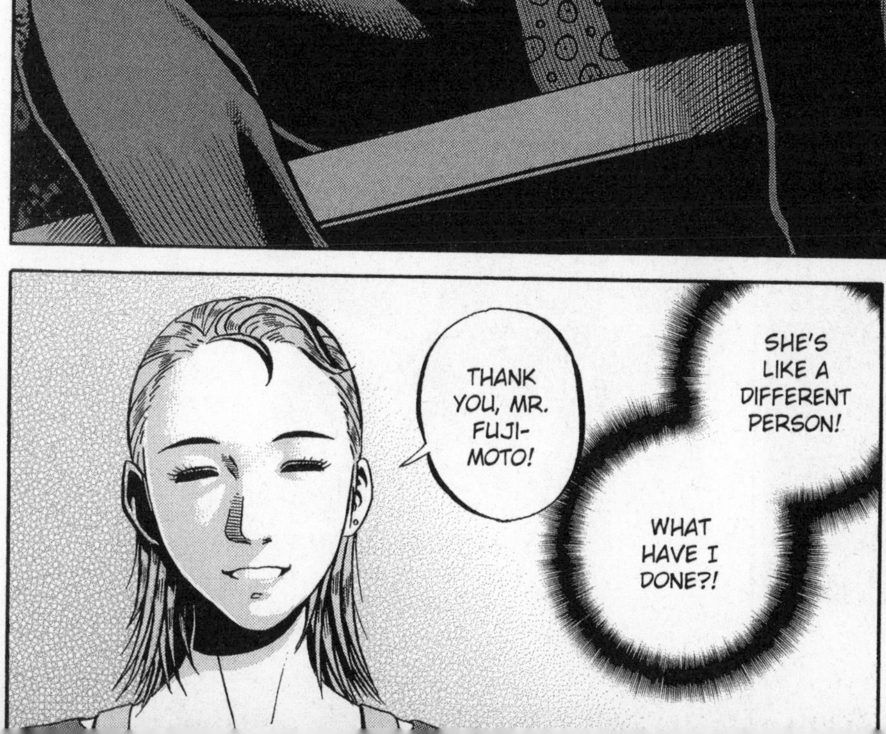
SHE'S LIKE A DIFFERENT PERSON!
THANK YOU, MR. FUJI-MOTO!
WHAT HAVE I DONE?!

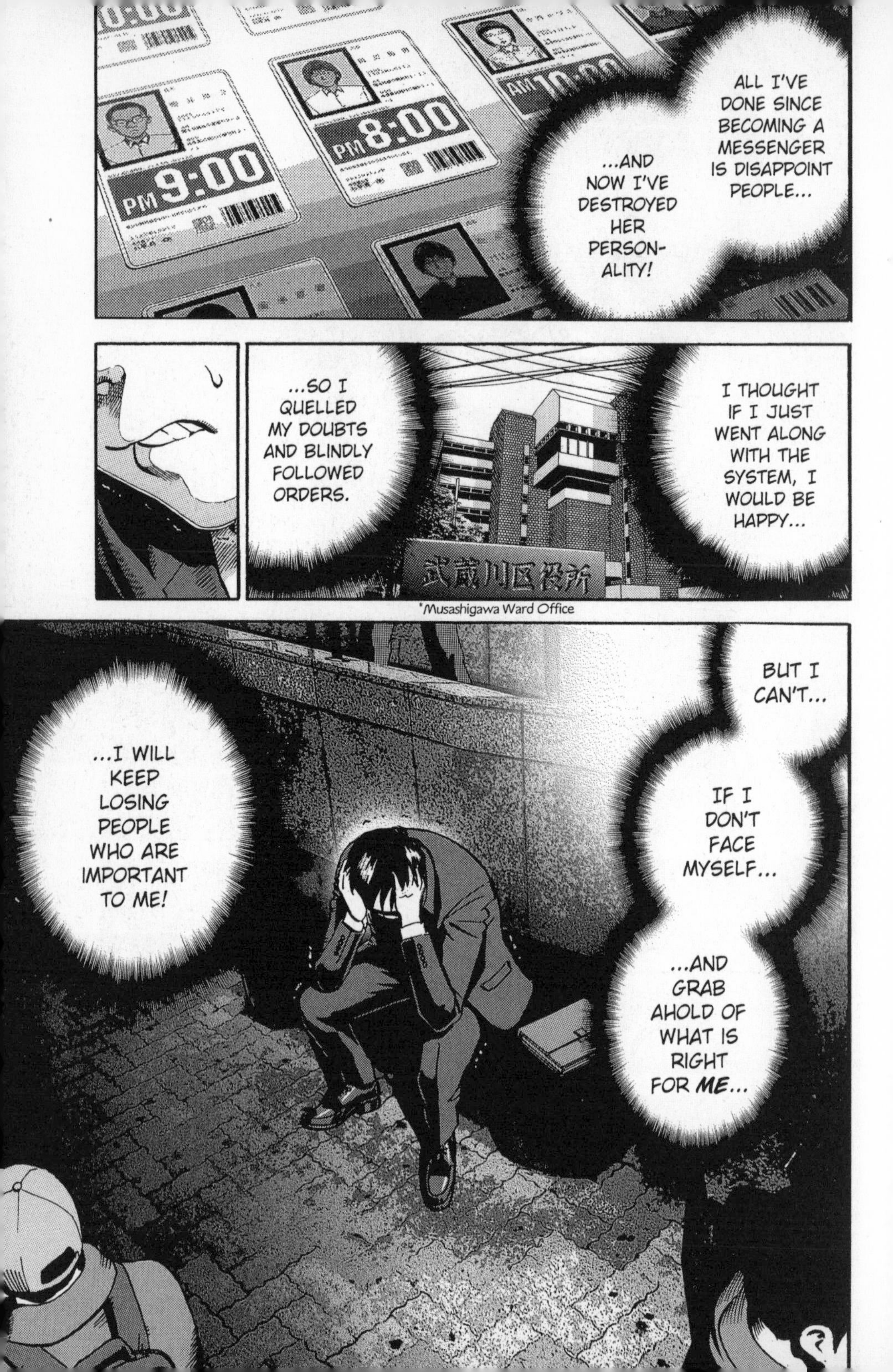
PM 8:00
PM 9:00
ALL I'VE DONE SINCE BECOMING A MESSENGER IS DISAPPOINT PEOPLE...
...AND NOW I'VE DESTROYED HER PERSONALITY!
I THOUGHT IF I JUST WENT ALONG WITH THE SYSTEM, I WOULD BE HAPPY...
...SO I QUELLED MY DOUBTS AND BLINDLY FOLLOWED ORDERS.
武蔵川区役所
*Musashigawa Ward Office
BUT I CAN'T...
IF I DON'T FACE MYSELF...
...AND GRAB AHOLD OF WHAT IS RIGHT FOR *ME*...
...I WILL KEEP LOSING PEOPLE WHO ARE IMPORTANT TO ME!

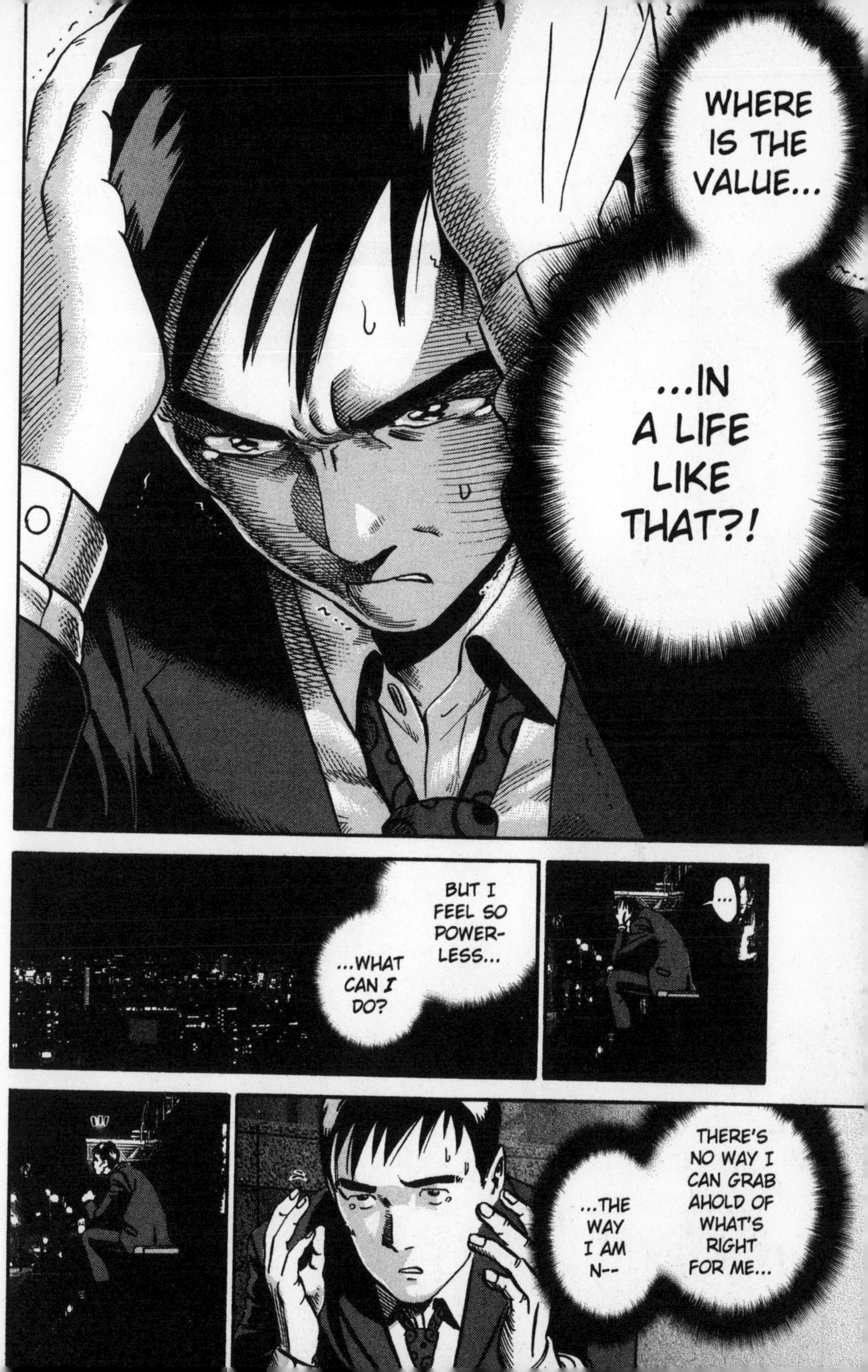
WHERE IS THE VALUE...
...IN A LIFE LIKE THAT?!
...
BUT I FEEL SO POWER-LESS...
...WHAT CAN I DO?
THERE'S NO WAY I CAN GRAB AHOLD OF WHAT'S RIGHT FOR ME...
...THE WAY I AM N--

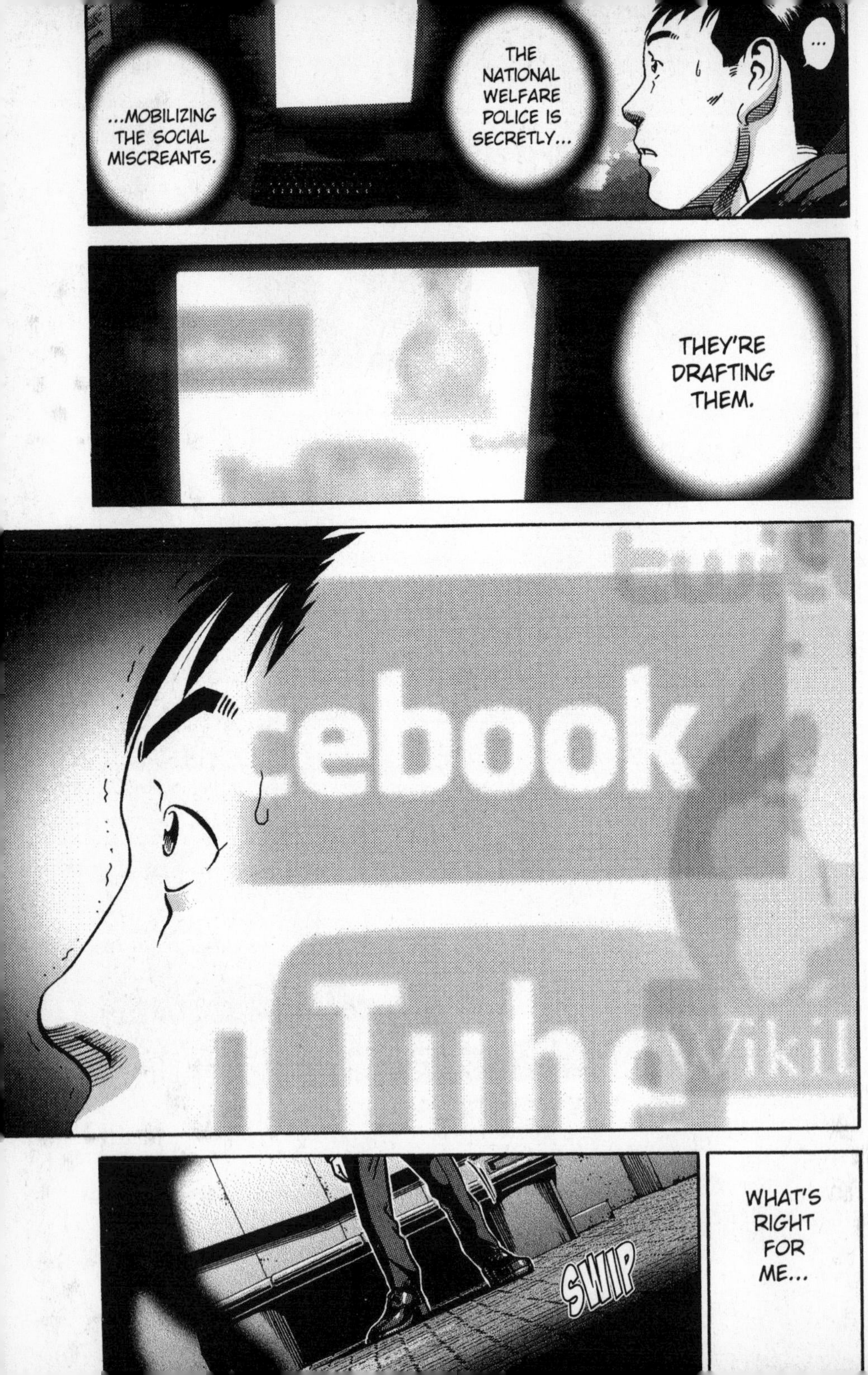
...
THE NATIONAL WELFARE POLICE IS SECRETLY...
...MOBILIZING THE SOCIAL MISCREANTS.
THEY'RE DRAFTING THEM.
cebook
WHAT'S RIGHT FOR ME...
SWIP

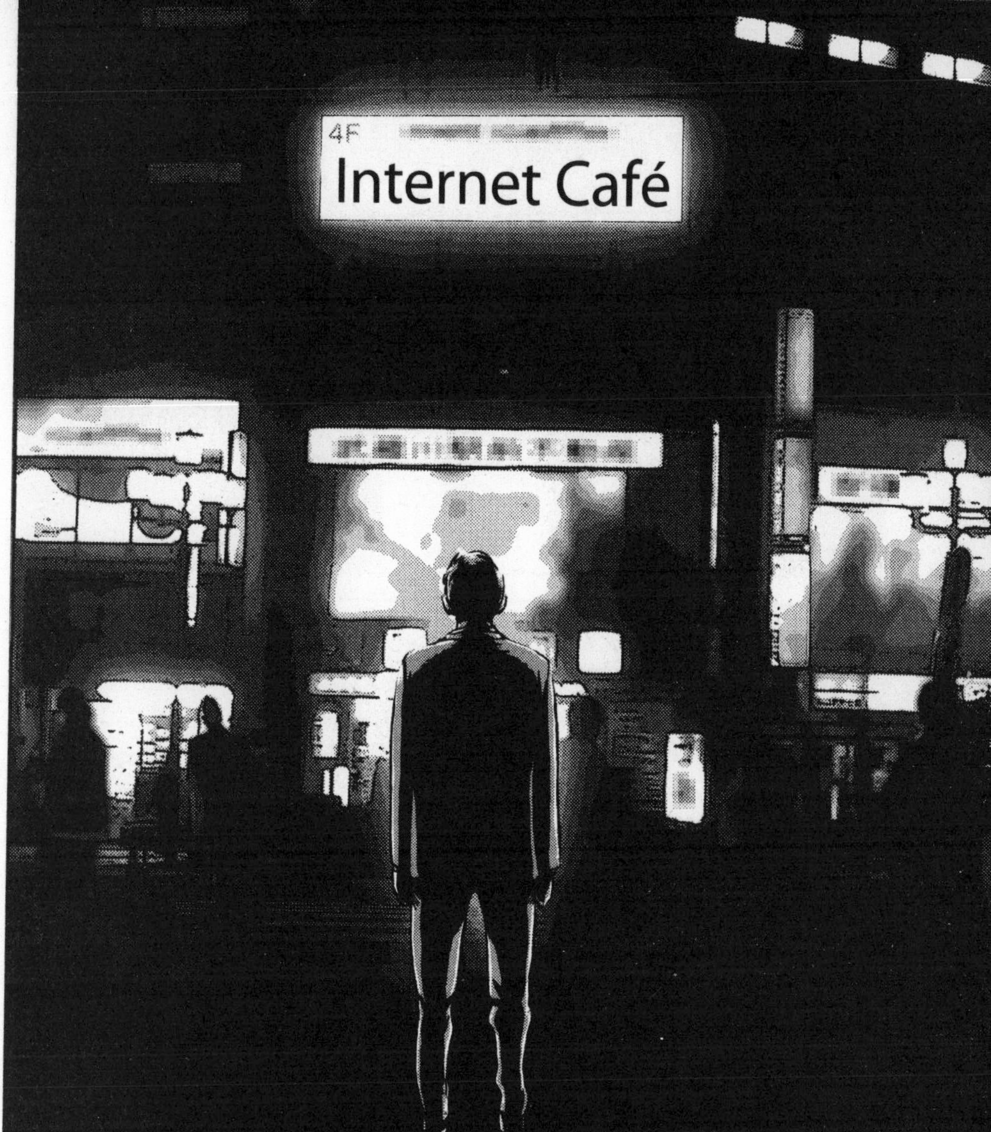
4F
Internet Café

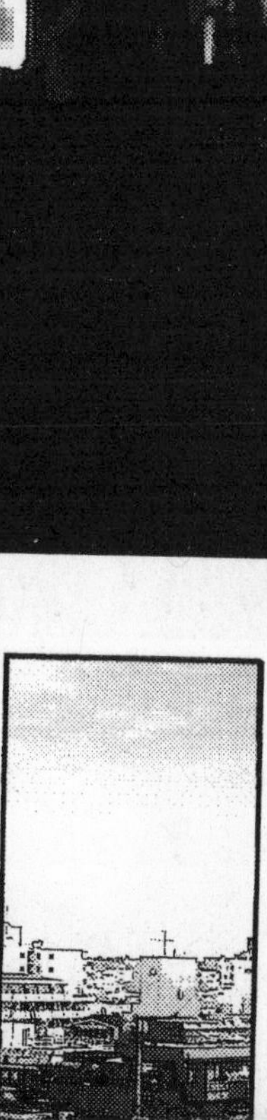

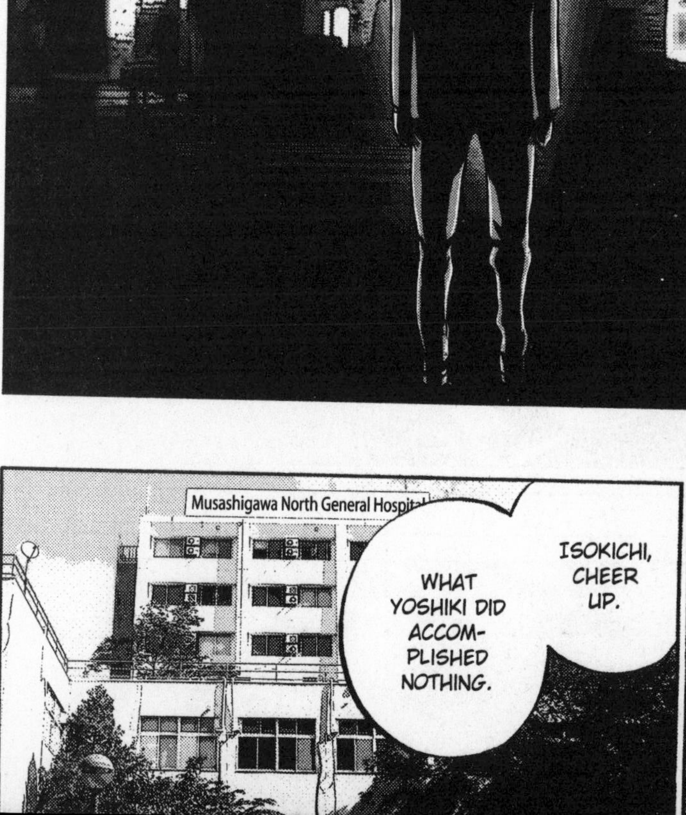
Musashigawa North General Hospital
ISOKICHI, CHEER UP.
WHAT YOSHIKI DID ACCOM-PLISHED NOTHING.

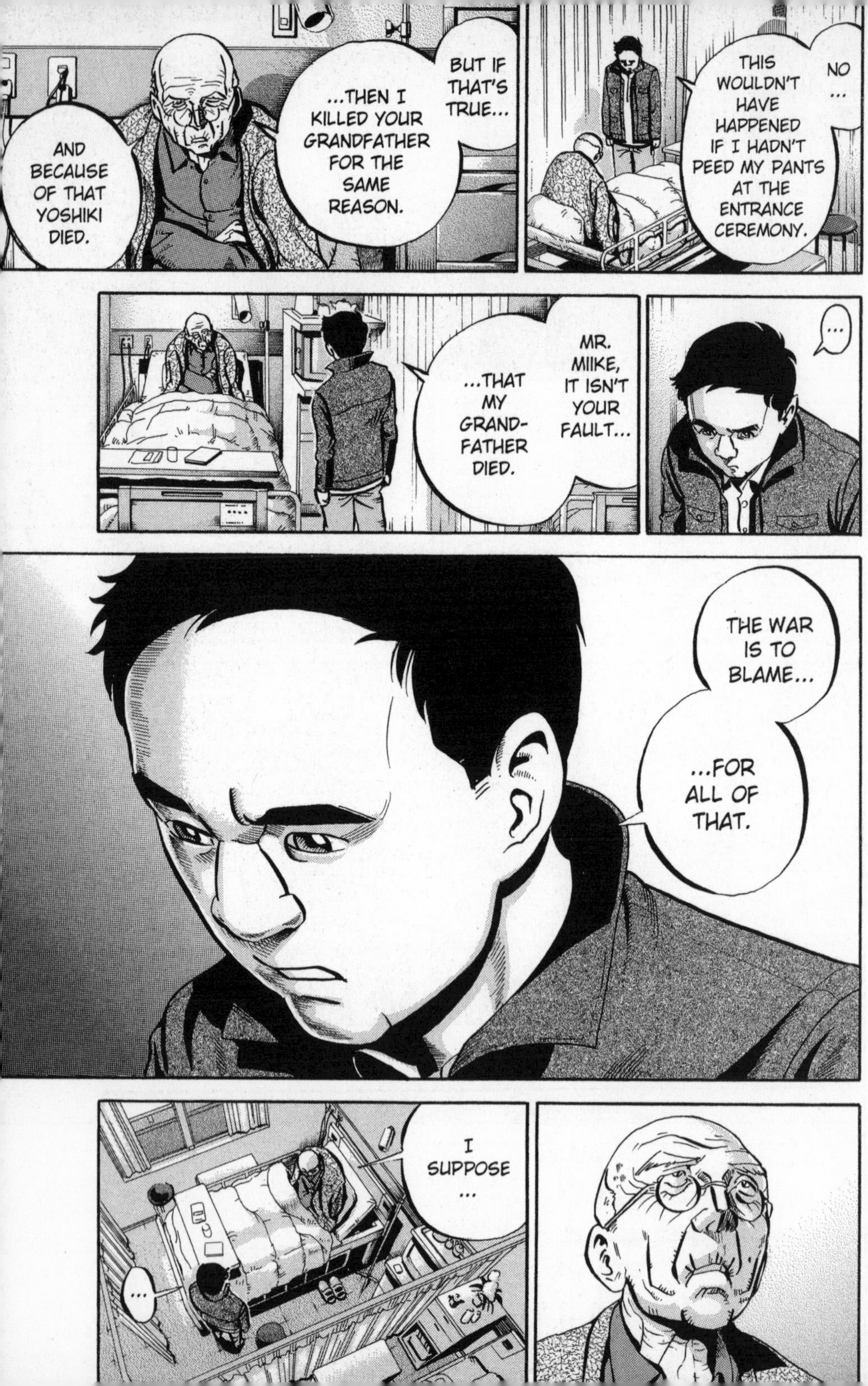
NO ...
THIS WOULDN'T HAVE HAPPENED IF I HADN'T PEED MY PANTS AT THE ENTRANCE CEREMONY.
BUT IF THAT'S TRUE...
...THEN I KILLED YOUR GRANDFATHER FOR THE SAME REASON.
AND BECAUSE OF THAT YOSHIKI DIED.
...
MR. MIIKE, IT ISN'T YOUR FAULT...
...THAT MY GRAND-FATHER DIED.
THE WAR IS TO BLAME...
...FOR ALL OF THAT.
I SUPPOSE ...
...

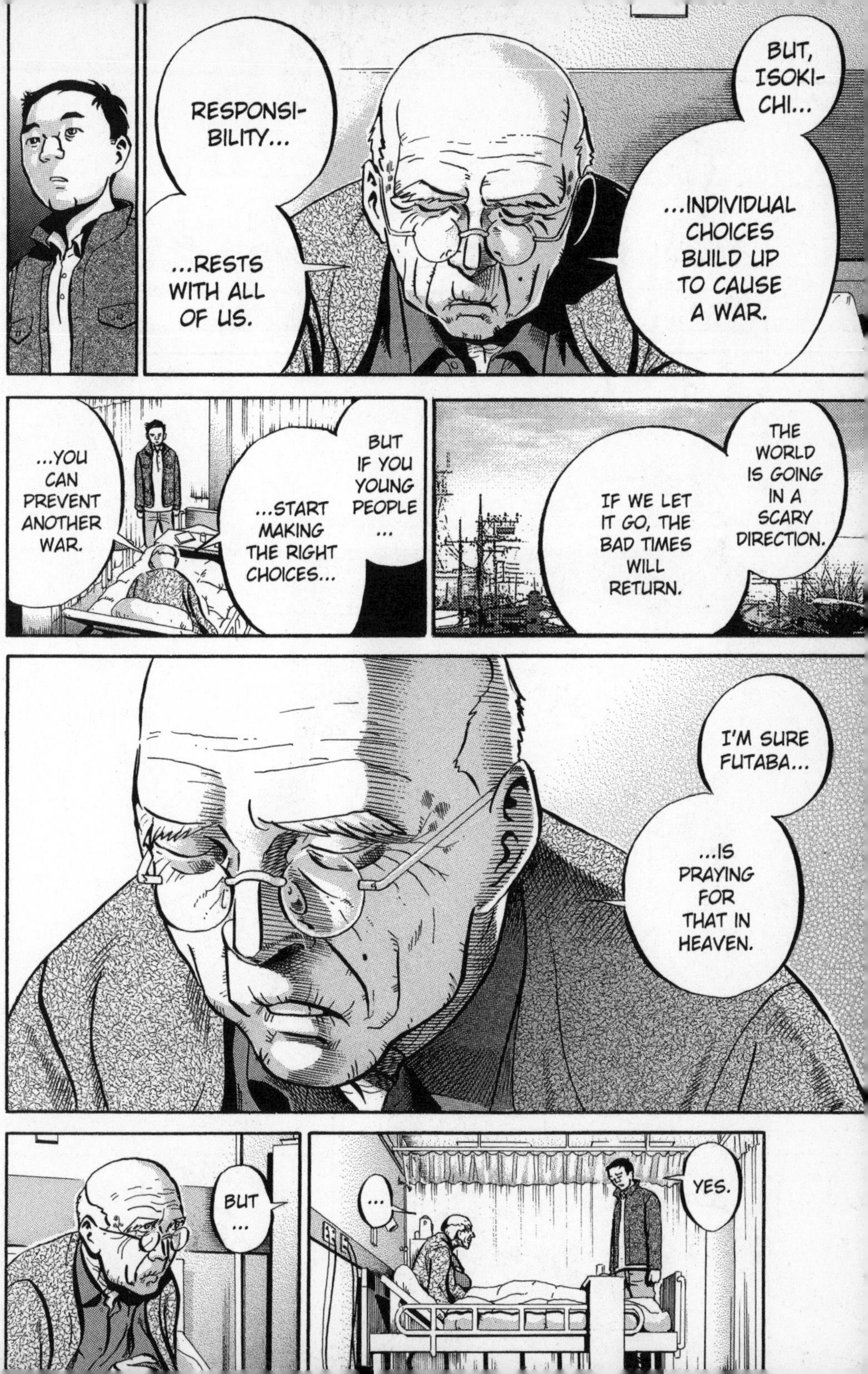
BUT, ISOKI-CHI...
...INDIVIDUAL CHOICES BUILD UP TO CAUSE A WAR.
RESPONSI-BILITY...
...RESTS WITH ALL OF US.
THE WORLD IS GOING IN A SCARY DIRECTION.
IF WE LET IT GO, THE BAD TIMES WILL RETURN.
BUT IF YOU YOUNG PEOPLE ...
...START MAKING THE RIGHT CHOICES...
...YOU CAN PREVENT ANOTHER WAR.
I'M SURE FUTABA...
...IS PRAYING FOR THAT IN HEAVEN.
YES.
...
BUT ...

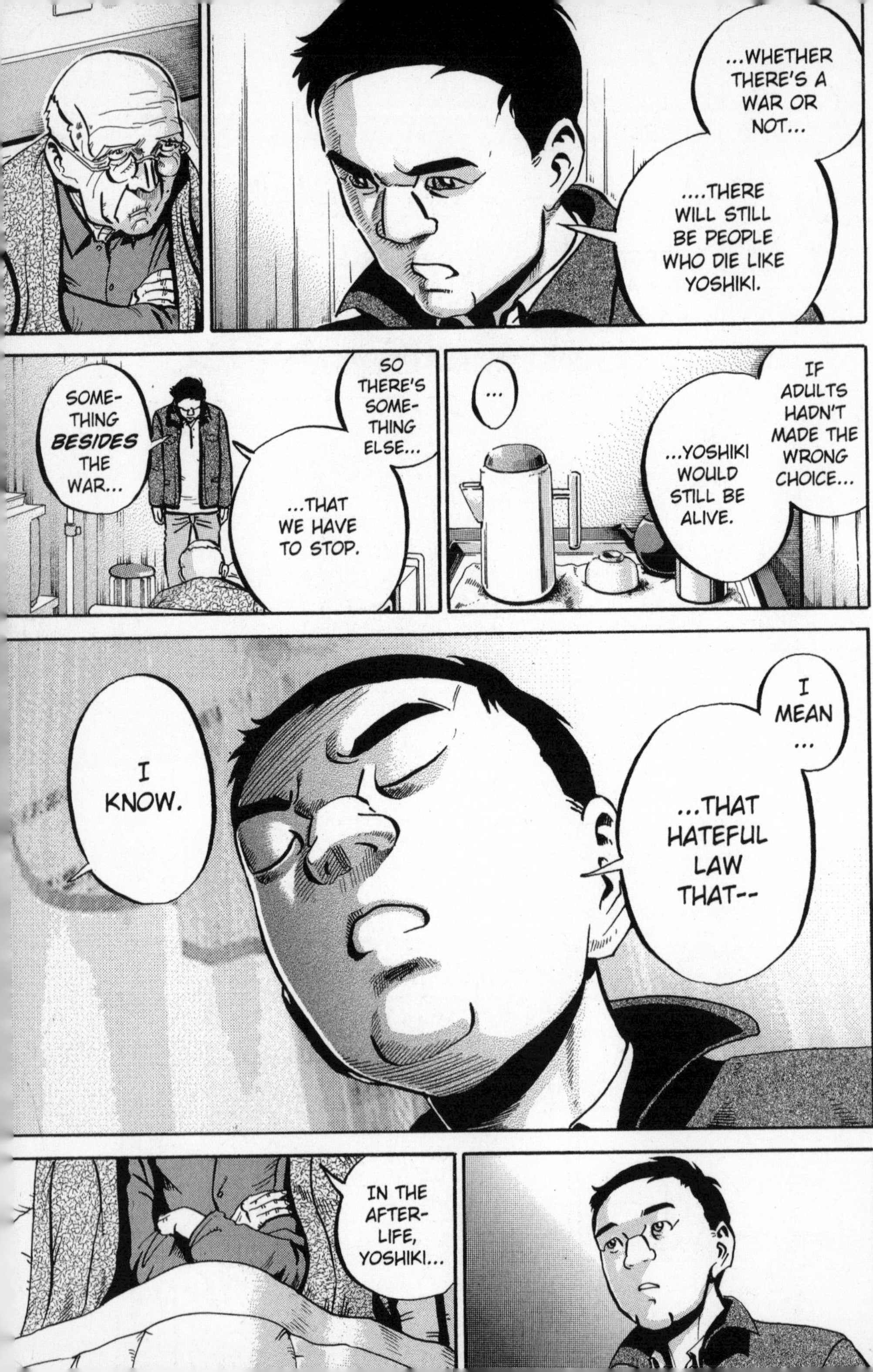
...WHETHER THERE'S A WAR OR NOT...
....THERE WILL STILL BE PEOPLE WHO DIE LIKE YOSHIKI.
IF ADULTS HADN'T MADE THE WRONG CHOICE...
...YOSHIKI WOULD STILL BE ALIVE.
...
SO THERE'S SOME-THING ELSE...
...THAT WE HAVE TO STOP.
SOME-THING *BESIDES* THE WAR...
I MEAN ...
...THAT HATEFUL LAW THAT--
I KNOW.
IN THE AFTER-LIFE, YOSHIKI...

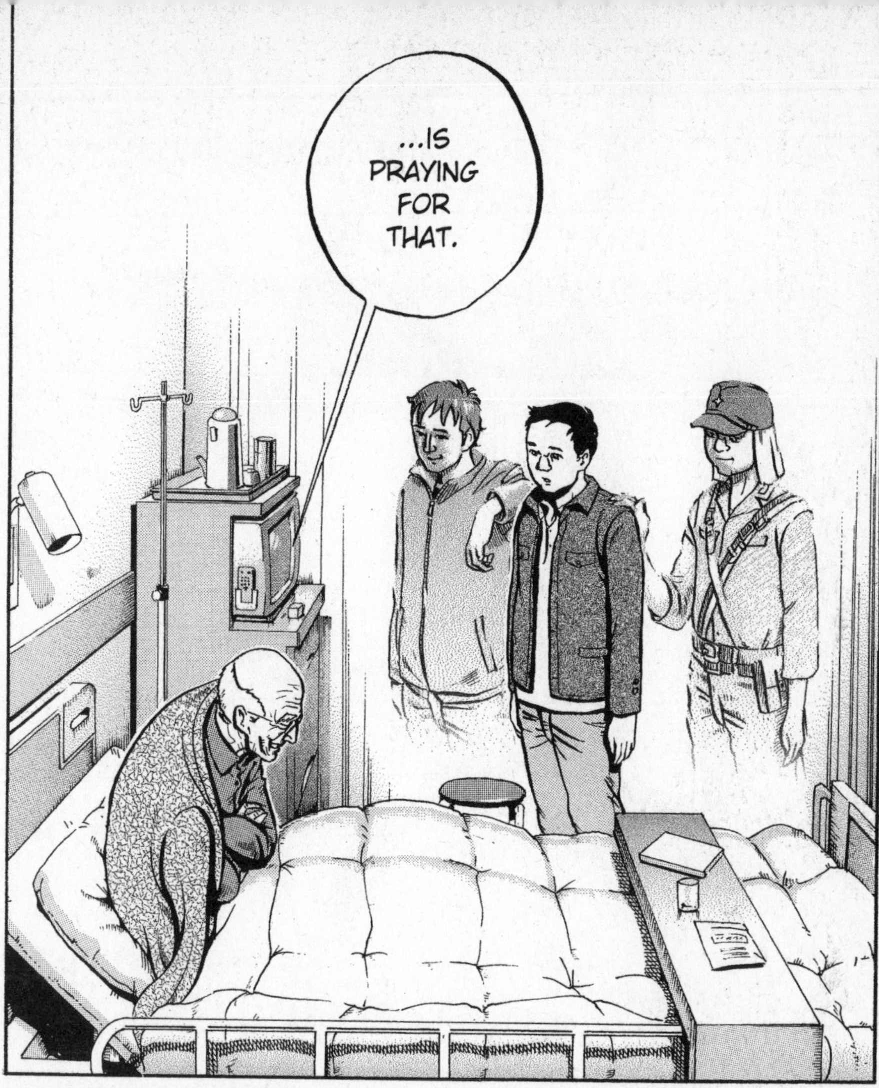
...IS PRAYING FOR THAT.

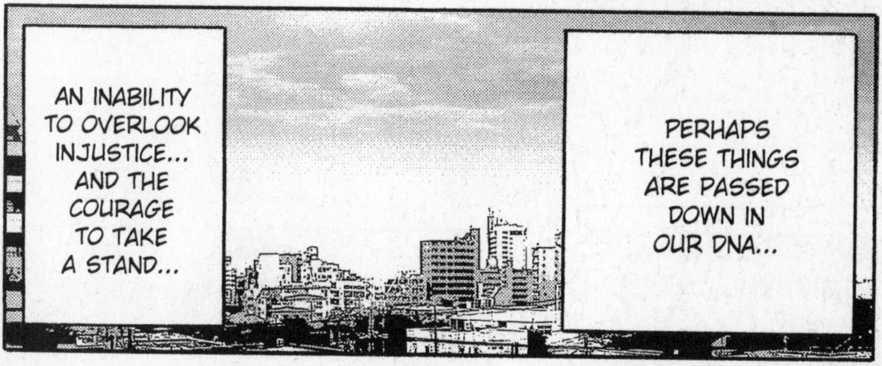
AN INABILITY TO OVERLOOK INJUSTICE... AND THE COURAGE TO TAKE A STAND...
PERHAPS THESE THINGS ARE PASSED DOWN IN OUR DNA...

Ikigami 9 / The End

Motoro Mase was born in Aichi in Japan in 1969 and is also the artist of *Kyoichi* and, with Keigo Higashino, *HEVDS*, which, like *Ikigami*, was serialized in *Young Sunday*. In 1998, Mase's *AREA* was nominated for Shogakukan's 43rd grand prize for a comic by a new artist.

SURPRISE!

 P9-AEW-746

You may be reading the wrong way!

It's true: In keeping with the original Japanese comic format, this book reads from right to left—so action, sound effects, and word balloons are completely reversed. This preserves the orientation of the original artwork—plus, it's fun! Check out the diagram shown here to get the hang of things, and then turn to the other side of the book to get started!

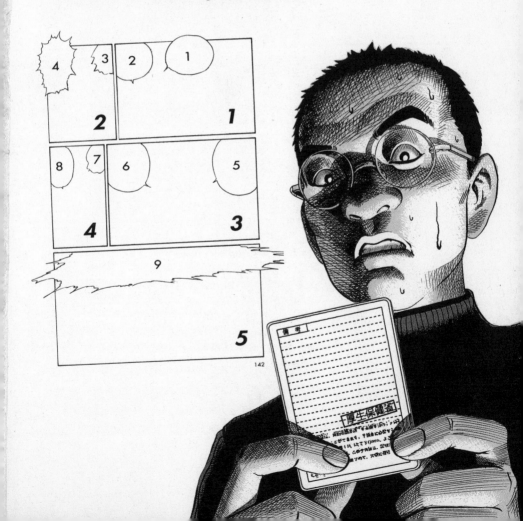